Reforming Punishment

The LAW AND PUBLIC POLICY: PSYCHOLOGY AND THE SOCIAL SCIENCES series includes books in three domains:

Legal Studies—writings by legal scholars about issues of relevance to psychology and the other social sciences, or that employ social science information to advance the legal analysis;

Social Science Studies—writings by scientists from psychology and the other social sciences about issues of relevance to law and public policy; and

Forensic Studies—writings by psychologists and other mental health scientists and professionals about issues relevant to forensic mental health science and practice.

The series is guided by its editor, Bruce D. Sales, PhD, JD, ScD(hc), University of Arizona; and coeditors, Bruce J. Winick, JD, University of Miami; Norman J. Finkel, PhD, Georgetown University; and Valerie P. Hans, PhD, University of Delaware.

* * *

Reforming Punishment

PSYCHOLOGICAL LIMITS
TO THE PAINS OF IMPRISONMENT

Craig Haney

AMERICAN PSYCHOLOGICAL ASSOCIATION

WASHINGTON, DC

Published by
American Psychological Association
750 First Street, NE
Washington, DC 20002
www.apa.org

To order
APA Order Department
P.O. Box 92984
Washington, DC 20090-2984
Tel: (800) 374-2721
Direct: (202) 336-5510
Fax: (202) 336-5502
TDD/TTY: (202) 336-6123
Online: www.apa.org/books/
E-mail: order@apa.org

In the U.K., Europe, Africa, and the Middle East, copies may be ordered from
American Psychological Association
3 Henrietta Street
Covent Garden, London
WC2E 8LU England

Typeset in Goudy by World Composition Services, Inc., Sterling, VA

Printer: Book-mart Press, Inc., North Bergen, NJ
Cover Designer: Berg Design, Albany, NY
Technical/Production Editor: Devon Bourexis

The opinions and statements published are the responsibility of the authors, and such opinions and statements do not necessarily represent the policies of the American Psychological Association.

Library of Congress Cataloging-in-Publication Data

Haney, Craig.
    Reforming punishment : psychological limits to the pains of imprisonment / Craig Haney.
        p. cm.— (Law and public policy)
    Includes bibliographical references and index.
    ISBN 1-59147-317-9
        1. Imprisonment—United States. 2. Imprisonment—Psychological aspects.
    3. Prisons—United States. 4. Punishment—United States. I. Title. II. Series.

HV9471.H33 2006
365'.973—dc22   2005014480

British Library Cataloguing-in-Publication Data
A CIP record is available from the British Library.

Printed in the United States of America
First Edition

To my family

To my family

CONTENTS

PREFACE

This book develops a simple but stark thesis. It is that the amount of prison pain that has been inflicted in the United States over the last 3 decades—the distress, anguish, and hurt that policies of mass incarceration have brought about—has pushed our criminal justice system to the brink of a genuine crisis, one with social, legal, and even moral dimensions. This crisis has been created in part by a political process that seems capable of generating limitless amounts of such pain. The pain is not only excessive in amount but too often dispensed without regard to consequence. Indeed, it is being inflicted with the broad and sometimes enthusiastic support of the public, many of whose members lack real knowledge about the nature and effects of the punishments imposed in their name. The magnitude of the problem has been expanded by the rise of what some have termed a modern *prison industrial complex* that now wields unprecedented political and economic influence in our society.[1] And it has been exacerbated by the actions of the mass media, which have significant interests in "making crime pay" by amplifying and sensationalizing stories that perpetuate misleading myths about crime and criminals.[2]

The result has been that American society over the last several decades has become increasingly committed to—and skilled at—inflicting prison pain on incarcerated persons. The mechanisms by which this pain is delivered

---

[1] The term *prison industrial complex* was first coined in the 1980s to describe a phenomenon that has grown considerably since. Indeed, the cover story of the *Multinational Monitor* described spreading the pains of imprisonment as one of the "new growth industries" in the modern multinational economy. *See* E. Lotke, "The Prison-Industrial Complex. The New Growth Industries," *Multinational Monitor* 17 (November 1996): 18.

[2] Katherine Beckett, *Making Crime Pay: Law and Order in Contemporary American Society* (New York: Oxford University Press, 1997).

have become more sophisticated, far reaching, and expensive. In the final analysis, however, there is little evidence that they have produced significant reductions in crime that are commensurate with the price they have exacted. In the long run, in fact, they may have become distinctly counterproductive. I argue in this book that we are rapidly reaching the upper limit of the social and economic costs that we can afford to incur in the name of this commitment to penal pain. Indeed, many of the prison policies and practices that have evolved over this period appear to have crossed the line from inflicting pain to doing real harm.

These separate trends have coalesced and reached crisis-level proportions in part because so few countervailing forces remain in our society to restrain them. Expressions of humane concern for persons who are perceived as "other" now often seem illegitimate; they are fleeting and fragile in those rare moments when they occur at all. This shift in popular consciousness, combined with the politicizing of the question of prison pain by the courts—many of which seem to have abdicated their regulatory function in deference to explicitly popular and political pressures—means that there are few, if any, limits on what can be done in the name of "corrections," even as our current criminal justice system has abandoned hope of correcting much of anything.

The need to develop alternative policy perspectives is an urgent one. The combination of empirical, legal, and political developments that I describe throughout this book raise the specter of what I have characterized as a "coming crisis in Eighth Amendment law"[3]—an undermining of the primary constitutional safeguard against cruel treatment in prison. The implications of this crisis are troublesome and far reaching. They derive from the fact that, as I noted, harsh punishment not only is widespread but has become the *raison d'être* of American corrections.

The U.S. Supreme Court's methodology for defining unconstitutional cruelty—whether a punishment fails to serve any legitimate penological purpose, on the one hand, and whether there is evidence of its widespread legislative or public repudiation, on the other—breaks down when pain is made the very purpose of imprisonment, when lawmakers' political success is enhanced by their willingness to increase (but never decrease) levels of prison pain, and in an era in which the public has been kept uninformed about what prison is really like and the long-term consequences of its overuse. Many citizens remain ignorant of the pains of imprisonment and the harm that can result when vulnerable persons are subjected to harsh

---

[3]C. Haney, "Psychology and the Limits to Prison Pain: Confronting the Coming Crisis in Eighth Amendment Law," *Psychology, Public Policy, and Law* 3 (1997): 499.

conditions for too long a time.[4] Some have become convinced that cruel treatment is a carefully considered strategy of crime control, and perhaps the only one that will work. In many quarters, extreme forms of correctional harm have become less "unusual," and as a result, they are no longer regarded as "cruel."

However, despite the dire state of our current prison policy, this book is structured around a hopeful irony: At the same time that these disturbing trends were underway, a great deal of sophisticated psychological research was being conducted that laid the groundwork for a wholly different course of action. Thus, I argue that the corrections crisis with which we are confronted can be resolved in large part by relying more directly on insights derived from contemporary psychological theory and research. These insights can provide a deeper understanding of the true pains of imprisonment and underscore the need for more humane and effective prison policies and strategies of crime control.

Specifically, I suggest that that the overuse of imprisonment in the United States over the last several decades has been based on a faulty conception of human behavior, one that is better suited to the 19th century in which it was wholeheartedly embraced than the 21st century, in which it still shapes criminal justice policy. The insights of modern psychological theory offer a principled alternative framework for limiting the excessive amounts of prison pain that our correctional system has come to dispense. In fact, for the first time in its history, the discipline of psychology is in a position to address the causes of crime in a systematic and truly scientific way that has profound implications for the reframing of contemporary prison policy and the redirection of criminal justice resources.

We now understand and can document the powerful "criminogenics" of background and social history: the ways in which the roots of much criminality can be traced to traumatic childhood experiences, exposure to damaging mistreatment, and other destructive life circumstances. Moreover, we have a much greater appreciation of the important role played by the immediate situation or context in which crime occurs. Indeed, many of the psychological forces that influence, encourage, provoke, and enable criminality emerge from broad inequalities of circumstance and the range of interrelated behaviors that they engender.

---

[4]Careful analyses of public opinion concerning crime and punishment indicate that citizens tend to overestimate the amount of violent crime with which society is plagued, view crime as always "on the rise" (even when, as in recent years, rates have consistently fallen), and underestimate the severity of penal sanctions that are routinely imposed by the criminal justice system. For an especially thoughtful synthesis, *see* Julian Roberts and Loretta Stalans, *Public Opinion, Crime, and Criminal Justice* (Boulder, CO: Westview Press, 2000).

The traditional conception of behavior on which prison is premised—an outmoded form of psychological individualism in which crime is viewed as the exclusive product of defective personalities and their faulty choice-making—must be seen as a partial and simplistic view. Thus, we know that crime can be fully understood only by examining past and present *context*. As a result of these insights, more sophisticated and nuanced policies of crime control can be pursued to reach beyond the mere imprisonment of individuals and touch the broad range of criminogenic forces that have helped to shape their lives.

In addition, as I argue at length in this book, the same emphasis on past and present context has clear implications for understanding the effects of prison itself. Prison is one of the most powerful and potentially debilitating contexts to which persons can be exposed. Because it shapes present and future behavior, it can have long-term criminogenic effects of its own that will influence the life course of prisoners once they are released. Our understanding of the psychological costs of incarceration raises serious moral and practical questions about the wisdom of the policies that have placed vast numbers of people in harsh correctional institutions for exceedingly long periods of time.

In fact, perhaps the most powerful argument against this recent over-dependency on prison is that, given what we now know about the roots of criminality and the potentially negative effects of exposure to powerful institutional contexts like prison, these policies simply will not and cannot work in the long run. Norwegian criminologist Nils Christie's observation in this regard bears repeating: "There is no inevitable connection between the levels of crime and punishment," and even today the relationship between them remains "badly understood."[5] Thus, the widespread pains of imprisonment to which we have become accustomed in recent years are too often inflicted unnecessarily, without a clear scientific justification or valid psychological rationale.

To preempt some of the inevitable misunderstanding that critical statements about prison policy may provoke, however, let me also say very clearly, at the outset of this book, that this analysis is not intended as a critique of the use of imprisonment per se or as a suggestion that it should not be retained as an essential component in an intelligent strategy of crime control.[6] I acknowledge that any realistic discussion of prison policy must

---

[5] Nils Christie, *Limits to Pain* (Oxford, England: Martin Robertson, 1982), 33.

[6] I will leave others to debate the important question of whether the toll that the institution of prison per se takes on society is justifiable, or whether there are other, radically different approaches to crime control to pursue that would supplant incarceration entirely. Scholars such as Thomas Mathiesen have put prison "on trial," found it wanting, and argued that it should be abolished. *See, e.g.,* Thomas Mathiesen, *The Politics of Abolition* (London: Martin Robertson, 1974) and Thomas Mathiesen, *Prisons on Trial*, 2d. English ed. (Winchester, England: Waterside Press, 2000). Like

concede the importance of imprisonment in our current criminal justice system and that some degree of pain is a necessary part of the prison experience. The deprivation of liberty—the essence of imprisonment—is inherently painful. But there must be limits.

I also know firsthand that there are better and worse prisons, that there are people who belong in prison and, sadly, even a few who probably now can live nowhere else. And I know that there also are many good people who work in prison, who try hard to be helpful and caring, and a large number who succeed in making a positive difference in the lives of the prisoners with whom they interact.[7] But these facts do not alter the nature of the current crisis we face. They cannot alleviate the problematic nature of prison policy in general or its overall drift toward inflicting too much pain. Nor do they reduce the urgent need to develop alternatives to the harsh approaches we have been pursuing—if for no other reason than that we know they will not succeed in the long run.

In the interests of further clarifying the perspective from which this book is written, I also should acknowledge that in addition to the literature on the effects of imprisonment that I cite extensively in the pages that follow, I rely heavily for context and perspective on my own observations in evaluating conditions of confinement in numerous maximum-security prisons throughout the United States. After my involvement as one of the principal researchers in the much-discussed Stanford Prison Study in 1971,[8] I spent the better part of the last 30 years studying the psychology of imprisonment directly, evaluating particular institutions and their effects on the persons who lived and worked there. These evaluations have included hundreds of interviews conducted with prisoners and correctional staff and administrators, beginning in the early 1970s and continuing to the present. Although I do not quote directly from these interviews and observations, the insights that I have gained from this work inform much of what follows.

---

many others who have studied this institution and become deeply concerned about the direction that prison policy has taken over the last several decades, I am sympathetic to many of the critical points Mathiesen and others make. Indeed, in somewhat different form, some similar criticisms appear in some of the chapters that follow. However, contemplating the abolition of prison at this stage of correctional history seems like more of an intellectual exercise than a practical endeavor.

[7] In fact, many conscientious correctional officials counseled restraint as the nation rushed to expand the reach of its prisons to its current unwieldy proportions. They did so in part because their direct experiences with prisons taught them about the limitations of correctional quick fixes to the problem of crime and also about the potential harms of too much incarceration or incarceration that was too painful.

[8] Discussions of this study can be found in a variety of places, including C. Haney, C. Banks, and P. Zimbardo, "Interpersonal Dynamics in a Simulated Prison," *International Journal of Criminology and Penology* 69, no. 1 (1973): 69; Craig Haney and Philip Zimbardo, "The Socialization Into Criminality: On Becoming a Prisoner and a Guard," in *Law, Justice, and the Individual in Society: Psychological and Legal Issues*, ed. June Tapp and Felice Levine (New York: Holt, Rinehart, & Winston, 1977); and C. Haney and P. Zimbardo, "The Past and Future of U.S. Prison Policy: Twenty-five Years After the Stanford Prison Experiment," *American Psychologist* 53 (1998): 709.

I have learned as much as I could about the psychology of imprisonment from those people who have lived it and worked closest to it and will try to do justice to the many contributions they have made to my understanding of these issues.

Some of my direct experience with prisons was gained in the context of prison litigation, and it undoubtedly colored my views about the need to create limits to prison pain and the strategies by which this might come about. Along with many other experts (including a number of psychologists), I have participated in litigation that addressed the constitutionality of the conditions of confinement and overall treatment to which prisoners were exposed—in essence, whether they were being subjected to cruel and unusual punishment.

In nearly all of these cases, especially when judges were willing to be brought close to the shocking day-to-day realities inside the prisons themselves—to see and feel at least some of the impact of the harsh and even brutal conditions of confinement that were under scrutiny—they made sound decisions designed to bring about badly needed prison change. In virtually every such instance, they identified serious constitutional violations and then entered sweeping judicial orders that directed prison systems to reform conditions of confinement, improve their treatment of inmates, and modify applicable correctional policies.

Yet the issues that I address in this book are somewhat different from the ones that are posed in the course of prison litigation. Although they are related to many of the questions that arise in specific cases, the topics I address here are much broader. Thus, my concern is with *overall* prison policy and whether our correctional system as a whole has shifted the way we think about and impose the pains of imprisonment. These are the kinds of questions that, because of the way that our law is structured, judges do not often get an opportunity to address in the course of case-by-case litigation.

I also allude briefly to my background experience with actual prison conditions and reform-oriented litigation, in part to acknowledge what I hope is seen as a virtue: that, despite my extensive reliance on systematic research and empirical data, published literature, and the framework of modern psychological theory, my views on these issues are very much informed by my own direct experience with prison itself. However, it is also by way of conceding that I know I have not seen many American prisons at their best. Although I have evaluated numerous prisons and conducted interviews over a period of several decades, I do recognize that many of the places I toured in the context of litigation were perhaps at their worst during the times I saw them. Litigation, of course, is precipitated by colorable claims that problematic conditions exist or that some form of abusive treatment is underway.

And yet, in some ways, that is the perfect view to have in light of the theme of this book—to see institutions when too little time and attention have been given to the important issue of limiting prison pain. The test cases are the ones in which those limits have been lacking, not where they thankfully are in place. The fact that the limits have been absent so frequently is telling. So, too, is the fact that state attorneys and prison system officials often defended these troubled institutions by confidently asserting that the conditions inside them were unproblematic and that they did not warrant any additional legal regulation or fundamental change. These views seem to me to underscore the dimensions of the corrections crisis with which we now are threatened.

Indeed, we are at something of a crossroads with respect to prison policy in the United States. Almost without second thought, we have pursued a very expensive and very painful policy of mass incarceration over the last several decades. In the process, we have overlooked many of the psychological costs of this policy—ones that now are beginning to register and mount in significant and unsettling ways in many communities across the country. As hundreds of thousands of ex-convicts return home from the harsh prisons where they have been kept, and the cycle of crime and incarceration too often begins anew, there is a growing sense that it is time to seriously rethink what we have done.

Yet the framework that has taken us this far seems impervious to real change. We are at the point where the damage is threatening to become irreversible, and the social, political, and economic accommodations to these widespread but destructive policies may become so entrenched that we can no longer turn away from them. In fact, among the most significant but unstated sacrifices made in the course of pursuing these policies may have been the loss of imagination—a declining ability to envision a rationale for doing things differently—and perhaps the will and capacity for developing alternative policies that are both effective and humane. Much of the analysis that follows is devoted to developing that rationale and surfacing some of those alternatives.

One final issue warrants brief discussion at the outset of any analysis of contemporary prison policy. As sociologist Erik Wright once reminded, "the punishment of crime is a political act."[9] The pains of imprisonment are imposed by the state and reflect a range of choices—what acts to punish and, by implication, whom to punish, and how. These choices are always made in a political context. This has been particularly evident over the last

---

[9] Erik Wright, *The Politics of Punishment: A Critical Analysis of Prisons in America* (New York: Harper & Row, 1973), 22.

several decades. The dramatic increases in the overall amount of prison pain that occurred during this period were brought about, at least in part, in response to a set of powerful and direct political influences. Indeed, I doubt that there has been another time in our history in which issues of crime and punishment have been so deeply and broadly politicized.

Obviously, no attempt to understand the causes of the increases in prison pain about which I write can ignore entirely this process of politicization. Thus, the analysis that follows is one that proceeds mindful of the political context in which prison policy is set. I know that this context helps to determine whether the psychological consequences brought about by one or another kind of prison setting, practice, or procedure will be acknowledged and by whom. It also greatly influences the practical viability of any of the psychologically informed set of prison reforms that I or anyone might propose.

Yet, I fortunately have the luxury of writing as a psychologist rather than a politician or correctional administrator. Although I make brief, passing mention of some of the political forces at work in shaping certain aspects of prison policy, my concerns are intellectual rather than political. The goal of this book is to present the theoretical basis for a reorientation of prison policy—a paradigm shift of sorts. The political and practical obstacles that might thwart the implementation of the particular policies and practices that are implied by this reorientation are, at this stage, less important than a frank airing of the nature of, and the need for, the shift in perspective itself. If ideas still matter in this arena of public policy, then for perhaps the first time in history, many of the ideas that are coming out of the discipline of psychology are on the side of those who would limit the reach of the criminal justice system and reduce the amount of pain that it inflicts. That story seems important enough to tell on its own terms.

ACKNOWLEDGMENTS

I owe a significant intellectual debt to three scholars, one of whom has been part of my professional career nearly from the moment it began, another of whom I have admired for many years but with whom I have only recently enjoyed personal contact, and a third whom I have never met. Philip Zimbardo and I collaborated closely on literally all aspects of the landmark Stanford Prison Experiment when I was still a graduate student. He encouraged me to pursue my interests in the social psychology of institutions and provided me with support of all sorts when I ventured into the nontraditional real world of prisons. He, especially, and others in the psychology department at Stanford continued to give me an intellectual home and make me feel welcome long after I had strayed into law school and began focusing virtually all of my work on psycholegal issues.

Hans Toch is the dean of American psychologists who study imprisonment, and he has served as an inspiration for several generations of psychologists and others interested in correctional issues. He has provided them—and me—with an unmatched (and probably unmatchable) model of how a psychologist can both rigorously and empirically evaluate the prison system and retain his humane values and human concerns in the process. I was delighted to finally meet him just a few years ago, after many years of learning from his written work.

Nils Christie, whom I never had the pleasure of meeting, wrote many remarkably insightful words about the nature of imprisonment and the human dilemmas that confound society's attempt to resolve the issues of crime and punishment. His unmistakably direct and often profound perspective has taught much to all of us who hope to understand the relationship of prisons to humane society. As will soon become obvious, I have not only used his words as the epigraphs with which to begin each of the chapters of this book, but—as with Hans Toch—his perspective informs much of what follows.

In addition, I owe an enormous debt to numerous attorneys, special masters, judges, and public officials with whom I have worked on the evaluation of the cruel and unusual aspects of the U.S. prison system. I have had the great good fortune to work with a large group of extraordinarily dedicated people over the last 30 years, ones who never hesitated to bring a powerful and righteous sense of indignation to the human rights abuses they saw, a deep commitment to the uniqueness and inherent value of persons who live and work in prison, and a tireless devotion to legal change—in this context, prison reform. They include people from the U.S. Department of Justice, the ACLU Prison Project, the NAACP Legal Defense Fund, the Prison Law Office, Public Advocates, Inc., and many other private law firms and governmental agencies with whom I have worked often and seen much over the years.

I also want to acknowledge the incredible amount of knowledge I gained from literally hundreds of prisoners and prison officials with whom I conducted interviews over the last several decades. I will not quote them directly in the pages that follow, but needless to say, their insights and observations have had an enormous impact on my understanding of the nature of imprisonment.

On a personal note, I want to thank Mary Lynn Skutley and the staff of the Books Department of the American Psychological Association, without whose wise counsel and tireless assistance this book would not have been published. Finally, as always, I am deeply grateful to my family—Lynne, Erin, Matt, Arcelia, Bonnie, Chanel, Pepe, and especially, my wife Aida (who keeps us all well-loved, inspired, and connected). For countless special reasons, this book is dedicated to them.

Reforming Punishment

1

HUMANE VALUES, PSYCHOLOGY, AND THE PAINS OF IMPRISONMENT

A suitable amount of pain is not a question of utility, of crime control, of what works. It is a question of standards based on values. It is a cultural question.

—Nils Christie[1]

Prison policy represents a compromise between competing sets of values—a vital concern for the protection of the social order and a counter-vailing respect for humane justice. On the one hand, legal theorists agree that "the criminal sanction is the paradigm case of the controlled use of power within a society."[2] Nowhere in our society is more forceful and sustained control over persons exercised than in its prisons. This control is applied in the name of achieving and preserving civil order, and the machinery with which it is accomplished is both potent and pervasive. Indeed, some have argued that the inherent violence of prison itself permeates the legal system that regularly resorts to it. For example, legal theorist Robert Cover once wrote that "the experience of the prisoner is, from the outset, an experience of being violently dominated, and it is colored from the beginning by the fear of being violently treated."[3]

On the other hand, diverse commentators have noted that a basic measure of civilization in any society can be found in the way it treats its most unfortunate and disfavored citizens—its prisoners. As Home Secretary in 1910, Winston Churchill observed that the "mood and temper of the public in regard to the treatment of crime and criminals is one of the most unfailing tests of the civilization of any country."[4] Similarly, Dostoevsky

3

wrote that a "society which looks upon such things [as the harsh punishment of its citizens] with an indifferent eye is already infected to the marrow . . . ."[5] And, writing in very different political times from the ones that now prevail, the United States Supreme Court recognized that "the methods we employ in the enforcement of our criminal law have aptly been called the measures by which the quality of our civilization may be judged."[6]

Thus, a society's shared sense of what is "humane" should constrain what the state may do to its citizens in the name of law and order, setting the limits to the pain that is inflicted in the pursuit of domestic tranquility. This tension frames a centuries-old debate over the proper relationship between necessary levels of social control and minimal standards of humane treatment. The balance has proven difficult to strike. Historically, when governments have lost sight of the principles that are supposed to limit punishment, they often have faced collective resistance and even violent citizen protests. Thus, popular movements, professional organizations, religious groups, and political factions have lobbied, argued, risen up, and taken direct action against sanctions that were perceived as too harsh and repressive. The storming of the Bastille and the American Revolution are two such well-known events, precipitated in part by governments that meted out severe punishments that citizens saw as extreme and unjustified.

In recent years in the United States, the terms of the debate over limits to punishment have become lopsided. It could be argued that—for the first time in the 200-year history of imprisonment in this country—the debate itself has been largely suspended. In fact, the political mandate for punishment became so overriding and absolute over the last several decades that few widely shared countervailing values could be interposed to balance or leaven the pain that was permissible to inflict in the pursuit of civil order. What has been called the "rage to punish"[7] was indulged so often by the popular media and political interest groups that it regularly overwhelmed any competing concern for humane justice. We entered the "mean season" of corrections in which what passed for "penal philosophy" amounted to little more than devising "creative strategies to make offenders suffer."[8] Indeed, one commentator suggested that the greatest price to be paid for what has been termed the *imprisonment binge* that occurred over the last several decades may be "the enormous moral toll bulging prisons are having on the social and moral fabric of American society."[9]

Many scholars have lamented the recent passing of humane values from public, political, and legal discussions of punitive social control.[10] I share their concerns, but from a different vantage point. As a psychologist myself, I argue in this book that my profession bears some degree of responsibility for the current crisis in American prison policy. Throughout the history of imprisonment, as I discuss in some detail in the next chapter, the discipline of psychology contributed significantly to the intellectual framework with which much corrections policy was built. Long before the current corrections crisis, psychological justifications were offered for prison policies in general and for particular penal practices in specific. As a matter of historical fact, our ideas helped to justify—if not create—policies of imprisonment. They also served as a restraining edge of sorts to modify, mend, or limit the nature and amount of imprisonment that was used and the adverse consequences of incarceration.

However, several decades ago—as an era of harsh punishment was ushered in—the longstanding connection between the discipline of psychology and the practice of imprisonment was largely severed. The discipline remained on the intellectual sidelines during the period in which the nation's penal system was used in an inhumane, expensive, and, I believe, in the long run, dangerous political tug-of-war over who could lock up the most people for the longest amount time. Notwithstanding very important work that was underway at the outset of these punitive trends, when the harsh policies of overincarceration began to emerge—work by psychologists like Stanley Brodsky, Carl Clements, and Ray Fowler at the University of Alabama's Center for Correctional Psychology,[11] and Hans Toch, throughout his long and distinguished career studying a wide variety of prison-related issues[12]—few psychologists were seriously engaged in the debates and discussions concerning the severity of new prison policies and the excessive use of imprisonment they entailed. Experts in the emerging area of "psychology and law" were largely absent from the policymaking arenas in which modern American corrections became increasingly punitive,[13] and inflicting psychic pain became the very essence of the enterprise.

Ironically, the discipline of psychology was silent at a time when it arguably had more to offer to the debate over prison policy than at any other period in its history. Indeed, the task that Frances Cullen set for criminologists a decade ago is one that psychological theory could have been—and still can be—instrumental in helping to achieve: "to help fashion an alternative plausible narrative that can move us beyond harm as the organizing principle of corrections."[14] I suggest in this book that there is a very direct pathway out of these punitive, harm-oriented times, precisely the kind of "alternative plausible narrative" that Cullen challenged criminologists and others to fashion. That pathway involves the thoughtful application of modern psychological theory to the issues of crime and punishment.

I believe that this new framework for understanding human behavior not only has the capacity to rekindle a debate about humane limits to prison pain but also provides a blueprint for more intelligent prison policies that are highly effective yet fair and compassionate. However, the discipline of psychology must play a more significant role in helping to fashion this new narrative about the importance of limiting prison pain. In this regard, modern psychological theory can be used to make the intellectual and practical connections between what is now understood about the nature of crime and how our society goes about administering punishment. This chapter surfaces some of the ways in which that can be done.

MODERN PSYCHOLOGICAL THEORY AND THE REVAMPED ROLE OF PRISON

Prison is a supremely individualistic response to the social problem of crime. It is a clear reflection of a long-standing belief in our culture that crime should be addressed primarily by identifying and incarcerating those responsible for committing it.[15] As I discuss at some length in the next chapter, it was during the 19th century that the emerging discipline of psychology and the dominant paradigm of individualism on which it was based helped to shape the prevailing cultural ethos and political worldview through which people were seen as the exclusive causal locus of behavior. Psychological individualism reached its pinnacle in the United States at virtually the same time that prisons were proliferating across the country. Indeed, it was a time when what was then regarded as the highly developed "American prison form" was being studied and emulated by nations throughout the world.[16]

However, more than a century later, modern psychological theory offers a fundamentally different perspective with which to understand the causes of social behavior—including criminality. The framework has shifted from the exclusive focus on individuals to a much more contextually oriented approach. This new perspective raises basic questions about the wisdom of continuing to rely on traditional forms of imprisonment as the primary approach to the control of criminality. It has implications for both the control of crime and our understanding of the power of the social context of prison itself.

Indeed, a broad consensus has emerged in the discipline of psychology that underscores the importance of social context. Extensive empirical research documents the various ways in which "the immediate social situation can overwhelm in importance the type of individual differences in personal traits or dispositions that people normally think of as being determinative of social behavior."[17] A wide range of social settings has been shown to exert a powerful influence over behavior, and a wide range of social behaviors has been shown to be influenced by the situations in which they occur. Situations and social contexts have powerful effects on diverse forms of behavior, including clinical syndromes (such as depression),[18] altruism,[19] coping,[20] cheating,[21] and even a police officer's decision to take someone into custody.[22] Psychologists also have demonstrated that the cognitive representations of the settings in which people act exercise an important effect on the nature and consistency of their actions.[23] In fact, there is an emerging area of developmental psychology that examines how social context shapes and affects the developmental process itself.[24] Thus, there is widespread recognition of the causal role of both past and present situations and social contexts in shaping present behavior.

We also know that variations in past and present social setting and context play an important causal role in the incidence of criminality, aggression and violence, and homicide. Indeed, numerous studies have now shown that exposure to various background situations and developmental contexts (such as extreme poverty and forms of parental maltreatment) constitute significant "risk factors" for a broad range of adolescent delinquent behaviors and later adult criminality.[25] As one reviewer aptly summarized, "the contribution of childhood abuse and neglect to later psychopathology, antisocial behavior, and criminality is well established in the psychological and criminological literature."[26]

Immediate context matters, too. For example, as one scholar put it, "Transient criminality is largely the result of stressful events combined with the simultaneous absence or destruction of social bonds. The suggestion is that transient criminality is due more to environmental influences than enduring characteristics of the person."[27] Similarly, situational analyses of misconduct and violent behavior in prisons themselves underscore the importance of social context in influencing behavior in institutional settings.[28]

Although modern psychological analyses of behavior are interactional and continue to take personal characteristics explicitly into account,[29] there is no doubt that situation, context, and social structure have attained newfound empirical and theoretical significance. The problems of crime and violence—formerly viewed in almost exclusively individualistic terms—are now understood through multilevel analyses that grant equal, if not primary, significance to situational, community, and structural variables.[30]

This modern psychological theory—especially the proposition that context matters—has several significant implications for contemporary criminal justice and prison policy. Unfortunately, virtually all of these implications have been overlooked, ignored, or disregarded over the last several decades as politicians and prison policymakers have pressed for the increased use of imprisonment and the delivery of heightened levels of prison pain. Yet, as the chapters that follow are designed to show, they have much relevance for the revamping of prison policy. In summary form, they include the following:

1. Exclusively individual-centered approaches to crime control, such as imprisonment, are self-limiting and likely to fail over

the long run unless they simultaneously address the contexts that help to cause crime. This fact argues in favor of redirecting crime-fighting resources and strategies away from nearly complete reliance on prisons and into ones that emphasize preventative programs and interventions that are designed to reduce many of the social historical and structural causes of criminal behavior.

2. Prison environments are themselves powerful and potentially damaging situations whose negative psychological effects must be taken seriously, carefully evaluated, purposefully regulated and controlled, and, when appropriate, changed or eliminated. This fact argues in favor of creating and enforcing more realistic and effective legal limits to the nature and amount of prison pain that is dispensed inside these institutions.

3. The long-term effects of exposure to powerful and destructive situations, contexts, and structures mean that prisons themselves also can act as criminogenic agents—in both their primary effects on prisoners and secondary effects on the lives of the persons who are connected to them. Thus, at certain very high rates of imprisonment and in certain communities that are most adversely impacted by the cycle of incarceration, prison paradoxically may serve to increase the amount of crime that occurs. This fact argues not only in favor of relying on incarceration more sparingly overall but also of taking very direct steps to limit or reduce its criminogenic effects on the people and communities it touches most.

4. Programs of prisoner change cannot ignore the situations and social conditions that prisoners encounter after they are released if there is to be any real chance of sustaining whatever positive growth or personal gains were achieved during imprisonment. This fact argues in favor of viewing crime control as a continuum of programs that address the structural and contextual causes of crime in community settings before and after imprisonment, as well as during the period in which someone is incarcerated.

These context-based implications underscore the need for a fundamental reformulation of crime control and prison policy. They also can serve as the framework for the development of much more psychologically informed limits to the amount of prison pain that we are willing to inflict in the name of social control.

THE PROBLEMATICS OF PAIN: LIMITING PRISON EXCESS

Nils Christie once observed that the seriousness of the "core phenomena" within penal law—the penalties themselves—is easily forgotten by scholars, legal decision makers, and members of the public. Indeed, compared with the "enormous wealth of detail and subtle distinctions" contained in books about criminal law and legal procedure, there is a "remarkable reservation" among authors against discussing what is at the very heart of the criminal justice system—the true nature of the *punishments* that this system imposes. That is, we are loath to describe "how the punishment hurts, how it feels, the suffering and the sorrow. . . ."[31]

The task of focusing scholars, legal decision makers, and the public on the nature and seriousness of these core phenomena remains formidable. Despite the enormous investment we have made in imprisonment over the last several decades, there has been little open discussion of the psychological consequences of the punishments imposed—not only how they feel, but the long-term effect of having unprecedented numbers of persons in our society feel them. There are political reasons for avoiding this topic. Like any policy, harsh punishment is more easily advocated when it is portrayed as simple and cost free. There are psychological reasons as well. When punishment is justified through the demonization of those against whom it is directed, emphatic responses are thwarted. As a result, it has not been fashionable to discuss the suffering of people whom we have decided to punish harshly.

In addition, literary critic Elaine Scarry provides another dimension to the difficulty of the task of describing how punishment hurts. In her compelling discussion in the *The Body in Pain*, she asserted that "whatever pain achieves, it achieves in part through its unsharability, and it ensures this unsharability through its resistance to language."[32] Indeed, Scarry focused on the fundamental difference between the vivid experience of "having pain," which she characterized as "the most vibrant example of what it is to 'have certainty,'" as opposed to the experience of "hearing about pain," which she suggested was so elusive as to serve as "the primary model of what it is 'to have doubt.'"[33] This distinction underscores an important issue that is present in much of the discussion that follows—talking about pain, whether in prison or elsewhere, takes us into doubt-inspiring territory. Yet, like Scarry, I believe that "verbally expressing pain is a necessary prelude to the collective task of diminishing pain."[34]

Thus, one of the real problems in conveying the urgent need to develop limits to certain kinds of prison pain is that so few people are still able to, using Scarry's word, "share" it. It is especially difficult to appreciate this unusual form of pain at a distance. Worse, the lack of knowledge about prison pain is distributed in a troublesome, problematic way: The relatively small number of people in a position to effectively limit this pain are among the least likely to experience and understand it. For them, like many others in our society, "to hear about [prison] pain is to have doubt."[35] So part of my task involves convincing people who have not thought much about the pains of imprisonment to begin to do so.

I use the term *pain* advisedly throughout the chapters that follow because it is an admittedly elusive concept, one that is easier to bemoan than operationalize. Even largely medically oriented discussions of pain concede that it is "an intensely subjective experience," one that is colored by psychological factors as much as any objective indicators: "Pain's inherently emotional quality is what makes it so difficult to define. Emotions like sadness, fear, anxiety, and anger, as well as childhood memories, all contribute to the landscape of pain."[36]

Of course, prison has always been painful. However, when I talk about limiting prison pain, I am talking primarily about the psychic pain that the overuse of imprisonment inflicts. This pain comes from the physical insult and deprivation that prison entails, and from the psychological distress and deterioration that certain forms of incarceration impose. There has been much of both kinds administered in recent decades. By almost any comparative standard, the amounts have been severe and—at least in terms of the numbers of persons affected—unprecedented.

As I have said, some of the pain of imprisonment is inevitable. At the core of the prison experience is the loss of liberty that—especially in a society that values freedom—is the essence of the punishment that confinement in a prison imposes. In addition, prison necessarily entails a myriad of minor deprivations—things like mediocre food, sparse living conditions, and limited personal property. Together they form an uncomfortable and unpleasant baseline against which other, more serious deprivations are registered. Beyond reductions in the material conditions under which they live, prisoners also lose contact with loved ones. In most prisons, they experience a loss of privacy and find that their behavior is subject to constant regulation, restriction, and monitoring. Some are exposed to very dangerous conditions and live with the possibility that they may themselves be victimized.

Some of the pains of imprisonment may be hurtful as well as painful. That is, they may do damage as well as bring discomfort. Indeed, for some prisoners, incarceration may prove to be a deeply traumatic experience. Thus, as I suggest in a later chapter, there are prisoners who leave prison with what is termed *posttraumatic stress disorder* or *PTSD*—the lingering effects of having been exposed to severely traumatizing experiences. These and other direct reactions to the pains of imprisonment will vary as a function of the nature and duration of the adverse conditions and the resiliency of the prisoners exposed to them, but few escape unscathed.

Although many of the chapters that follow discuss the painfulness of imprisonment in direct, experiential terms—it hurts and, at a psychological level, can have hurtful consequences—there are other dimensions to prison pain. For example, some of the painfulness of our current prison policies derives from their excessive reach. Specifically, hundreds of thousands of people have been locked up in American jails and prisons who would not have been incarcerated in any other modern Western society for the same misdeeds. In fact, many of them would not have been incarcerated in this country if they had committed their crimes at almost any other time in American history. Included among those touched directly by the excessiveness of prison pain over this period are prisoners with mental illness who belong in hospitals or residential care facilities rather than in prison, drug offenders whose violations stem from untreated addictions rather than fully autonomous choices to commit crime, and petty criminals serving staggeringly long prison terms for relatively trivial offenses that triggered newly enacted, draconian sentencing laws.

Similarly, it is possible to think of correctional policies as too painful because they hurt persons who are not the legitimate or deserving targets of pain—not only prisoners with serious mental illness or developmental disabilities who are punished for actions they did not fully understand or could not completely control, but also innocent family members or loved ones who suffer as a result of their relationship to incarcerated persons. Thus, in addition to the intensity of the direct effects on the persons who are the targets of prison pain—the prisoners themselves—the sheer scope of imprisonment in the United States is so unprecedented that it has touched much wider constituencies and affected many other aspects of our society.

In this way, harsh prison policies have broad, secondary effects that add to their excessiveness. The family members who share in some of the pains of imprisonment are the most obvious examples of this kind of hurt. In increasing numbers, blameless spouses, children, relatives, and other loved ones have suffered these losses. The losses are not trivial nor are they easily overcome. Over half of the persons who are incarcerated in our nation's state and federal prisons have children, and unfortunately, having a parent in prison is one of the strongest predictors of a wide range of adjustment problems, including future lawbreaking.[37]

Moreover, because there have been so many people caught in the net of imprisonment in recent years, entire communities have been adversely affected—pained in some ways—by these policies. Certain neighborhoods are plagued by shockingly large numbers of residents—one third or more of the young men who live there—who are either currently incarcerated, recently returned from prison, or on their way back in. The organization and infrastructure of these communities are compromised by and cannot absorb the transience, the disruption and instability that are introduced into family life, and the spread of the special psychological problems that the cycle of incarceration brings about. Social service agencies, personnel, and welfare policies strain and falter under the weight of these burdens.[38] Here, too—in the loss of cohesion, caring, and stability—the pains of imprisonment have grown large.

Especially in a society that now resorts to prisons so quickly and so broadly, recognizing these multiple dimensions to the painfulness of prison policies may not make hearing about the subjective experience of pain any more compelling, but it establishes a broader context for understanding the full range of its consequences. In addition to understanding them, thoughtful ways must be devised to register, address, and alleviate the direct and indirect or secondary forms of prison pain. In Scarry's useful formulation, hearing about these different pains of imprisonment will assist in the important "collective task of diminishing pain."[39]

The issue of cruelty also is important to surface and parcel out early in this discussion. Legally, of course, the cruelty of prison pain is one measure of whether it should be limited (i.e., determining whether, in legal terms, it is "cruel and unusual"). From a psychological perspective, the gratuitous infliction of pain is one hallmark of cruelty.[40] Thus, "part of what is so truly awful about cruelty is its gratuitous nature."[41] By implication, then, the infliction of even extreme pain would not necessarily be cruel if it were an absolutely crucial part of a procedure or policy that was needed to achieve an essential, legitimate end. Viewed in this way, policies that are unnecessarily hurtful are cruel.

As crime comes to be understood as the product of destructive social histories and criminogenic situations and social conditions, rather than simply the morally blameworthy choices of its perpetrators, punishing only individuals and ignoring the contexts from which they come appears increasingly misdirected—indeed, unnecessary. In that sense, the severe pains of imprisonment take on a gratuitous quality that they did not have before these social contextual insights were so widely acknowledged. Similarly, even when it is justified to punish individuals—as it often is—any more punishment than is absolutely necessary takes on an element of cruelty. The needlessly harsh punishment of unprecedented numbers of people to which we have become accustomed in recent years can be seen in this light.

To be sure, cruel policies do not require cruel people (or people with cruel intentions) to implement them. The issue of whether prison policymakers, officials, and staff intend to harm prisoners is in some ways irrelevant (even though, as I point out in a later chapter, the U.S. Supreme Court has made it the touchstone of unconstitutionally cruel punishment). Although I have encountered very few truly cruel or sadistic prison employees, I have encountered many cruel, harmful prison environments—that typically are run by well-intentioned officials.

But whatever the intention or rationale by which pain-oriented policies are applied, their psychological consequences are important to take into account in assessing the overall value and effect of the policies themselves. In both legal and moral terms, recognizing the potential cruelty of a policy is one basis for beginning to develop ways of limiting its use. Gradations in the severity of punishment—and, especially, the point at which punishment moves beyond simply being painful to becoming harmful and cruel—are elusive, especially when the punishment is inflicted over a period of years. These matters require the kind of constant attention that has been lacking in the last several decades.

ADAPTING TO LONG-TERM INCARCERATION: THE DEFERRED PAINS OF IMPRISONMENT

Because pain is aversive, people try to avoid it when they can and adapt to it—to dull its effects—when they cannot. Even brief exposure to traumatic pain can exact a high psychological price, and its consequences often are felt long after the experience itself. But long-term exposure to less extreme forms of pain also can produce negative psychological consequences as people struggle to adapt to and otherwise reduce its effects. For many prisoners, the long-term experience of painful imprisonment inflicts this kind of adaptive damage. Thus, it is important to acknowledge that prisons do more than painfully "contain" or "incapacitate" prisoners, "scare them straight," or provide them with their "just deserts." Prisoners make a variety of long-term adaptations to reduce the amount of pain they experience on a day-to-day basis during their confinement; they are changed—often in problematic, adverse ways—as a result. Years later, at the time of release, many of these "deferred pains of imprisonment" are experienced anew. Some of this damage can be described briefly and preliminarily, with the caveat that later in the book I elaborate on much of it and the dynamics that produce it.

People who enter hostile prison environments often are alienated by them, made to feel even more marginalized and different from other citizens than when they entered. Many end up feeling worthless, believing that no one does or will ever care for them; some are depressed by this realization, some angered. Normal social interaction is impeded and may be precluded entirely by the extraordinary routines of maximum security prisons. In too many places, prisoners are taught few, if any, useful interpersonal skills, and they rarely are encouraged to retain whatever ones they had. Some prisoners are victimized and leave prison humiliated and terrified by the prospect that they could be abused again. Many develop an impenetrable, defensive shell to prevent anyone from ever truly knowing them, because prison is a place where others readily exploit such knowledge to manipulate or harm them (or threaten to do so). These kinds of lessons are psychologically difficult to relinquish once prisoners are released.

Many male prisoners have learned to hide behind an exaggerated image of manhood. They may overreact to the slightest affront, or take offense at things most people do not even notice. For others, this hypervigilance turns into something else—an irritable edginess instilled by years of institutionalization in which passivity or tolerance in the face of even a minor slight can be mistaken for weakness. Still others, having lived too long in environments where they were forced to fight too quickly and too often, are more likely to use force rather than reason to resolve disputes. Many prisoners react another way, by becoming sad, depressed, lethargic, or hopeless. In other contexts this syndrome has been termed *learned helplessness*,[42] the consequence of having lived in an environment where few actions reliably reduce pain or bring pleasure.

Many prisoners become highly dependent on the structure and routine of the prison, sometimes at the expense of many skills and abilities they will need once released. Over time, they may lose the capacity to initiate behavior, make plans, exercise intelligent choices, or anticipate consequences. The impact of this institutional dependency is made worse by the lack of work experience and poor educational skills that many prisoners bring to prison and with which many later leave. The lack of education and job training is compounded by stigma and the prisoners' long-term absence from the rapidly changing labor market. Thus, the pains of imprisonment may include knowing that an already marginal connection to the workplace is getting worse in the course of incarceration and threatens to become permanent.

Finally, of course, prisoners are offered no explicit insights into the prison dynamics that they must confront. That is, they are given no direct help or counseling to make sense of the psychological distress they feel or the nature of the adaptations they are forced to make. Prison is not an environment that encourages much self-reflection of this sort or provides many structured opportunities for real personal growth. Traditional psychotherapy and prison counseling are scarce in punishment-oriented prisons. Moreover, when they are available at all, these services usually are reserved for prisoners or other inmates with mental illness who are experiencing acute psychiatric crises and need immediate stabilization. They are rarely used to address the general pains of imprisonment or the psychological price of prison survival. Thus, whatever knowledge prisoners gain about the direct and potentially harmful effects of imprisonment—how they are being changed by the experience or what they are likely to go through once they are released—they typically must obtain on their own, from each other, if at all.

Most prison systems still do not provide meaningful transitional programs or counseling programs that are effectively designed to help prisoners identify and undo those aspects of their institutionalization that will pose the greatest problems for them once they are released. Of course, ex-convicts are expected—indeed, required—to adjust quickly and unproblematically to a world that is fundamentally different from the one to which they have been forced to adapt, and to which they know they will be returned if their transition falters. Few parole systems or local social service agencies offer forms of genuine support that will ease or assist ex-convicts with their reintegration. Prisoners who have been forced to adapt to a world in which they make few decisions for themselves move abruptly into one in which they are entirely on their own.

I confess that I do not know whether or how, exactly, describing these things will help to bridge Scarry's great divide between actually experiencing and merely hearing about prison pain. But unless people who are not touched directly by the pains of imprisonment become concerned about the consequences of the harsh policies of imprisonment we have pursued over the last several decades, it is likely that the number of persons exposed to painful and potentially damaging forms of imprisonment will continue to increase. That number will include many persons who do not need to be in prison, and many who will be made worse rather than better by the experience.

VICTIMS' RIGHTS AND PRISON PAIN

I know that there are many people reading the words I have written so far who can scarcely contain the very strong objections they already have formulated: Why all this talk about the pains of imprisonment rather than the pain that the victims of crime have suffered? What about *their* deep desire to see perpetrators suffer? Indeed, what about the social and moral value of retribution—inflicting pain in the pursuit of a philosophical principle—in society at large? These are important questions, and, at the very outset of this book, it is critically important to disentangle them from the questions on which I focus.

The increased recognition of the needs of crime victims has been one of the few positive developments in criminal justice policy over the last several decades. Historically, crime victims often were treated with an inexcusable callousness by the legal system, which lacked any direct way to address the trauma they experienced. Because the system was set up primarily to process and punish criminal offenders, the crime victims' significance or value to legal decision makers often was restricted to the role they could play in obtaining desired guilty verdicts and maximizing prison sentences. Victims and witnesses reported feeling used by the system; many left the criminal justice process with the clear sense that their victimization perhaps had served the goals of the legal professionals and no one else. Nils Christie wrote more than 20 years ago that "the victim in a criminal case is a sort of double loser in our society. First, vis-à-vis the offender, secondly vis-à-vis the state. He is excluded from any participation in his own conflict."[43] Until recently, Christie was absolutely right.

In certain respects, the situation has changed. Victim support groups have formed in many parts of the country, many victims' rights organizations are highly visible in political and legal forums, and some have exercised significant influence over criminal justice policies and decisions. Many politicians pay homage to the concept of victims' rights, and some states have passed laws that give victims a voice in the proceedings in which the fate of their perpetrator is adjudicated. In addition, there are a number of jurisdictions in which agencies devoted to providing victims' services of some sort have been established, and legislators have allocated monies to various victims' funds out of which they can recoup some of the economic costs of victimization.

Yet, in many ways, crime victims are still seen as valuable to the criminal justice system primarily to the degree that they serve the ends of harsh punishment. The proposal to enact a constitutional amendment that establishes "victims' rights" is an illustrative example.[44] Although the political rhetoric that has surrounded the proposed amendment is couched in broad terms that speak of helping victims, its provisions focus primarily on hurting defendants. Rather than addressing the economic or psychological needs of victims, the amendment seeks little more than to institute legal procedures that will further increase the amount of pain that is inflicted on criminal defendants (for the most part by giving victims a larger role in deciding punishment) and to hasten the process by which this is accomplished. I agree with Lynne Henderson's thoughtful analysis of this issue, that

> all too often, the compassion for a victim's suffering transforms into attacks on the criminal justice process and "criminals," rather than inquiring into how we can help victims to recover and heal. The current trend toward encouraging victims to be rageful overlooks all but a part of the process of living after trauma.[45]

Victims of crime are certainly entitled to a vengeful perspective, and no one can or should begrudge them it. For some crime victims, the anger and pain that they experience over victimization does seem to be allayed by indulging the impulse to strike back, to discharge one's own suffering in the suffering of those responsible for it. If having a voice in the punishment process is all we can offer them, then they undoubtedly should have it. But I also sense a cruel cynicism at work in which many people with separate agendas of their own have helped to convince victims that the only thing they should want and can expect from the criminal justice system is vengeance or retribution. In instances in which crime victims themselves urge restraint, understanding, or compassion for persons who have committed crimes, they may find that they have lost their newly gained standing in the criminal justice system, quickly are re-relegated to a marginal role, or risk being shut out of the process entirely. If their voices cannot be used to support the punitive equation on which our system has come to depend, in the way they are expected to, then they often are shunted aside.

Indeed, thoughtful, critical analyses of prison policy have been derailed in recent years by the seemingly unshakable assertion that the only way to do something for victims of crime is to take actions against its perpetrators. It is one of the most damaging legacies of the way that questions of crime and punishment have been so deeply politicized over the last several decades. Yet, setting humane limits to prison pain requires a frank debunking of the notions that any voice raised on behalf of moderating punishment is one that somehow dishonors the victims of crime, or that there is an intrinsic connection between pain for perpetrators and justice for victims. There is no such intrinsic connection. In fact, these notions not only have impeded prison reform but also have helped to deny victims the resources with which to heal from their trauma and its aftermath. Encouraging them to seek and be satisfied with little more than vengeance and retribution is another layer to the victimization about which Christie wrote.

One of the most important contributions that a psychologically informed approach to crime and punishment can make to crime victims is to help ensure that there are fewer of them in the future. The development of effective strategies of crime control that are premised on valid psychological theories is, or should be, a victims' rights issue. Among other things, it will allow the goal of helping crime victims to move beyond merely hurting those who have committed crimes. Indeed, in ways that I hope many crime victims will appreciate, I intend the analyses, criticisms, and proposals included in this book—especially in the closing chapter—to contribute not only to more humane prison policies but also to a more effective system of crime control.

CONCLUSION

Understanding the criminogenic potential of excessive prison pain may help to convince crime victims that their needs and concerns are connected in a direct way to discussions about the fairness of the criminal justice system and the development of meaningful limits to the pains of imprisonment. Each of these interrelated issues is part of a larger discourse about ways to advance the collective interests that all citizens share in devising prison policies and crime control strategies that not only are fair and humane but also work.

In the next chapter, I begin to develop this discourse by analyzing its roots—the early historical relationship between psychology and prison policy. I continue to trace some of the ways that that relationship developed into the 20th century and examine the promising direction in which it appeared to be moving at the start of the 1970s, when, quite suddenly, prison policy was decoupled from psychological theory and the two moved in decidedly different directions. The nature and consequences of the new— and, in my opinion, very problematic—direction of the nation's prison policy are examined in some detail in several additional chapters. In particular, in chapter 3, I examine the current state of the prisons, and in chapter 4, the ways our increasingly punitive approach to crime and punishment has affected certain groups of people far more often—and more harshly— than others.

In the remainder of the book, I juxtapose the approach we have been following with a new, more psychologically informed perspective on crime and punishment. Thus, chapter 5 examines the various ways in which the discipline of psychology has confirmed the fact that "context matters" across a whole range of social behaviors that includes criminal behavior. In chapters 6 and 7, I apply that contextual perspective to prison itself, arguing that imprisonment places people in one of the most powerful behavior-distorting environments in our society. Thus, the dimensions of this experience, and the long-term consequences for prisoners, provide an important justification and road map for prison reform. In chapter 8, I examine some of the ways in which the experience of imprisonment is especially painful and problematic for "special-needs" prisoners—those with mental illness or developmental disabilities.

The law's inability to protect special-needs prisoners from the onslaught of the surrounding prison environment, in large part because the courts fail to carefully examine that environment or acknowledge its psychological impact, is part of a larger problem that limits the value of legal regulation and intervention. In fact, chapter 9 is devoted more broadly to the nature, and limits, of the legal reform of prisons. To extend this discussion of the potential for and possibilities of change, chapter 10 examines the implications of a modern social contextual perspective on behavior for future prison policy and reform. I argue that there are a number of fundamental changes that can and should be brought about in our approach to crime control, the nature and quality of the prison experience, and the way our society understands and responds to the challenge of postprison adjustment.

NOTES

1. Nils Christie, *Crime Control as Industry: Towards Gulags, Western Style?* (London: Routledge, 1993), 183.

2. Herbert Packer, *The Limits of the Criminal Sanction* (Palo Alto, CA: Stanford University Press, 1972), 10.

3. R. Cover, "Violence and the Word," *Yale Law Journal* 95 (1986): 1601, 1608 (footnote omitted).

4. Winifred Elkin, *The English Penal System* (London: Penguin, 1957), 277.

5. Fyodor Dostoevsky, *The House of the Dead* (London: Dent, 1962), 194.

6. Coppedge v. United States, 369 U.S. 438, 449 (1962).

7. Lois Forer, *A Rage to Punish: The Unintended Consequences of Mandatory Sentencing* (New York: W. W. Norton, 1994).

8. F. Cullen, "Assessing the Penal Harm Movement," *Journal of Research in Crime and Delinquency* 32 (1995): 338, 340.

9. R. Ayre, "The Prison Crisis: An Essay on the Social and Political Foundations of Criminal Justice Policy," *Public Administration Quarterly* 19 (1995): 42, 42.

10. See, e.g., Todd Clear, *Harm in American Penology: Offenders, Victims, and Their Communities* (Albany, NY: State University of New York Press, 1994); John Irwin and James Austin, *It's About Time: America's Imprisonment Binge* (Belmont, CA: Wadsworth, 1994); Michael Tonry, *Malign Neglect: Race, Crime, and Punishment in America* (New York: Oxford University Press, 1995).

11. Although the Center itself did not survive subsequent changes in funding and political climates, its scholars continued to write about prison issues from a critical and insightful perspective. See, e.g., Stanley L. Brodsky, *Families and Friends of Men in Prison: The Uncertain Relationship* (Lexington, MA: Lexington Books, 1975); S. Brodsky, "Correctional Change and the Social Scientist: A Case Study," *Journal of Community Psychology* 10 (1982): 128; Stanley L. Brodsky and Kent S. Miller, "An Alabama Prison Experience," in *Prevention, Powerlessness, and Politics: Readings on Social Change*, ed. George W. Albee, Justin M. Joffe, and Linda A. Dusenbury (Newbury Park, CA: Sage, 1988); S. Brodsky and F. Scogin, "Inmates in Protective Custody: First Data on Emotional Effects," *Forensic Reports* 1 (1988): 267 (1988); C. Clements, "Crowded Prisons: A Review of Psychological and Environmental Effects," *Law and Human Behavior* 3 (1979): 217; C. Clements, "Towards an Objective Approach to Offender Classification," *Law & Psychology Review* 9 (1985): 45; Carl Clements, "Psychologists in Adult Correctional Institutions: Getting Off the Treadmill," in *Behavioral Approaches to Crime and Delinquency: A Handbook of Application, Research, and Concepts*, ed. Edward K. Morris and Curtis J. Braukmann (New York: Plenum, 1987); C. Clements, "Delinquency Prevention and Treatment: A Community-Centered Perspective," *Criminal Justice & Behavior* 15 (1988): 286; R. D. Fowler and S. Brodsky, "Development of a Correctional–Clinical Psychology Program," *Professional Psychology* 9 (1978): 440; Raymond D. Fowler, "Assessment for Decision in a Correctional Setting," in *Assessment for Decision*. Rutgers Symposia on Applied Psychology, ed. Donald R. Peterson and Daniel Fishman (New Brunswick, NJ: Rutgers University Press, 1987).

12. *See, e.g.*, Hans Toch, *Men in Crisis: Human Breakdowns in Prison* (Chicago: Aldine, 1975); Hans Toch, *Living in Prison: The Ecology of Survival* (New York: Free Press, 1977); Robert Johnson and Hans Toch, ed., *The Pains of Imprisonment* (Beverly Hills, CA: Sage, 1982); Hans Toch and Kenneth Adams, *The Disturbed Violent Offender* (New Haven, CT: Yale University Press, 1989).

13. In our own way, Philip Zimbardo and I also tried to participate in this critical dialogue about prison conditions. For example, *see* C. Haney, W. Banks, and P. Zimbardo, "Interpersonal Dynamics in a Simulated Prison," *International Journal of Criminology and Penology* 1 (1973): 69; Craig Haney and Philip Zimbardo, "The Socialization into Criminality: On Becoming a Prisoner and a Guard," in *Law, Justice, and the Individual in Society: Psychological and Legal Issue*, ed. J. Tapp and F. Levine (New York: Holt, Rinehart, & Winston, 1977); Philip Zimbardo and Craig Haney, "Prison Behavior," in *International Encyclopedia of Psychiatry, Psychology, and Neurology*, vol. 4, ed. Benjamin Wolman (New York: Human Sciences Press, 1978). But I do not pretend that this commentary has been nearly enough or nearly as effective as it might have been.

14. Cullen, "Assessing the Penal Harm Movement," 352.

15. C. Haney, "Criminal Justice and the Nineteenth-Century Paradigm: The Triumph of Psychological Individualism in the 'Formative Era,'" *Law and Human Behavior* 6 (1982): 191.

16. Ibid.

17. *See* Lee Ross and Richard Nisbett, *The Person and the Situation: Perspectives of Social Psychology* (New York: McGraw-Hill, 1991), xiv. *See also* Walter Mischel, *Personality and Assessment* (New York: Wiley, 1968); Roy Baumeister and Dianne Tice, "Toward a Theory of Situational Structure," *Environment & Behavior* 17 (1985): 147; Adrian Furnham and Michael Argyle, eds., *The Psychology of Social Situations: Selected Readings* (Oxford, England: Pergamon, 1981); David Magnusson, ed., *Toward a Psychology of Situations: An Interactional Perspective* (Hillsdale, NJ: Lawrence Erlbaum, 1981).

18. *See, e.g.*, Constance Hammen, "Vulnerability to Depression: Personal, Situational and Family Aspects," in *Contemporary Psychological Approaches to Depression: Theory, Research, and Treatment*, ed. Rick E. Ingram (New York: Plenum Press, 1990).

19. *See, e.g.*, J. Darley and D. Batson, "From Jerusalem to Jericho: A Study of Situational and Dispositional Variables in Helping Behavior," *Journal of Personality and Social Psychology* 27 (1973): 100; C. Holahan, "Effects of Urban Size and Heterogeneity on Judged Appropriateness of Altruistic Responses: Situational vs. Subject Variables," *Social Psychology Quarterly* 40 (1977): 378.

20. *See, e.g.*, Robert McCrae, "Situational Determinants of Coping," in *Personal Coping: Theory, Research, and Application*, ed. Bruce N. Carpenter (Westport, CT: Praeger/Greenwood, 1992).

21. *See, e.g.*, J. Leming, "Cheating Behavior, Situational Influence, and Moral Development," *Journal of Educational Research* 71 (1978): 214.

22. *See, e.g.*, R. Worden, "Situational and Attitudinal Explanations of Police Behavior: A Theoretical Reappraisal and Empirical Assessment," *Law & Society Review* 23 (1969): 667.

23. *See, e.g.,* B. Krahe, "Similar Perceptions, Similar Reactions: An Idiographic Approach to Cross-Situational Coherence," *Journal of Research in Personality* 20 (1986): 349.

24. R. Lerner and M. Kauffman, "The Concept of Development in Contextualism," *Developmental Review,* 5 (1958): 309, 324–325. *See also* Martin Richards and Paul Light, ed., *Children of Different Social Worlds: Development in a Social Context* (Cambridge, MA: Harvard University Press, 1986).

25. *See, e.g.,* D. Denno, "Victim, Offender, and Situational Characteristics of Violent Crime," *Journal of Criminal Law & Criminology* 77 (1986): 1142; David Farrington, "Implications of Criminal Career Research for the Prevention of Offending," *Journal of Adolescence* 13 (1990): 93; R. Gordon, "Issues in the Ecological Study of Delinquency," *American Sociological Review* 32 (1967): 927; M. Straus, "Discipline and Deviance: Physical Punishment of Children and Violence and Other Crime in Adulthood," *Social Problems* 38 (1991): 133. *See also* chapter 7 and references cited therein.

26. M. Sullivan, "Biography of Heinous Criminals: Culture, Family, and Prisonization," *Journal of Research in Crime and Delinquency* 33 (1996): 354, 356.

27. Anthony Mawson, *Situational Criminality: A Model of Stress-Induced Crime* (New York: Praeger, 1987), 20.

28. *See, e.g.,* Anthony Bottoms, William Hay, and Richard Sparks, "Situational and Social Approaches to the Prevention of Disorder in Long-Term Prisons," in *Long-Term Imprisonment: Policy, Science, and Correctional Practice,* ed. Timothy J. Flanagan (Thousand Oaks, CA: Sage Publications, 1995); F. Deroches, "Anomie: Two Theories of Prison Riots,"*Canadian Journal of Criminology* 25 (1983): 173; A. Pfefferbaum and N. Dishotsky, "Racial Intolerance in a Correctional Institution: An Ecological View," *American Journal of Psychiatry* 138 (1981): 1057; P. Steinke, "Using Situational Factors to Predict Types of Prison Violence," *Journal of Offender Rehabilitation* 17 (1991): 119.

29. *See* A. Bandura, "The Self System in Reciprocal Determinism," *American Psychologist* 33 (1978): 344; M. Duke, "The Situational Stream Hypothesis: A Unifying View of Behavior with Special Emphasis on Adaptive and Maladaptive Personality Patterns," *Journal of Research in Personality* 21 (1987): 239; B. Ekehammar, "Interactionism in Personality from a Historical Perspective," *Psychological Bulletin* 81 (1974): 1026; M. Georgoudi and R. Rosnow, "Notes Toward a Contextualist Understanding of Social Psychology," *Personality and Social Psychology Bulletin* (1985): 5; W. Mischel, "On the Interface of Cognition and Personality: Beyond the Person–Situation Debate," *American Psychologist* 34 (1979): 740; Joseph Veroff, "Contextual Determinants of Personality," *Personality and Social Psychology Bulletin* 9 (1983): 331.

30. *See* J. Hepburn, "Violent Behavior in Interpersonal Relationships," *Sociological Quarterly* 14 (1973): 419; A. McEwan and C. Knowles, "Delinquent Personality Types and the Situational Contexts of Their Crimes," *Personality & Individual Differences* 5 (1994): 339; Robert Sampson and Janet Lauritsen, "Violent Victimization and Offending: Individual-, Situational-, and Community-Level Risk Factors," in *Understanding and Preventing Violence, Vol. 3: Social Influences,* ed. Albert J. Reiss Jr., and Jeffrey A. Roth (Washington, DC: National Academy

Press, 1994); H. Toch, "The Catalytic Situation in the Violence Equation," *Journal of Applied Social Psychology* 15 (1985): 105; E. A. Wenk and R. Emrich, "Assaultive Youth: An Exploratory Study of the Assaultive Experience and Assaultive Potential of California Youth Authority Wards," *Journal of Research in Crime & Delinquency* 9 (1972): 171; K. Wright, "The Violent and Victimized in the Male Prison," *Journal of Offender Rehabilitation* 16 (1991): 1.

31. Nils Christie, *Limits to Pain* (Oxford, England: Martin Robertson, 1982), 15.

32. Elaine Scarry, *The Body in Pain: The Making and Unmaking of the World* (New York: Oxford University Press, 1985), 4.

33. Ibid.

34. Ibid., 9.

35. Ibid., paraphrasing Scarry at 13.

36. Scott Fishman, *The War On Pain* (New York: Harper Collins, 2000). Medical historians—also focusing on the largely physical forms of pain—make essentially the same point about its subjective components: "Earlier experiences of similar pains, the influence of memory which either accentuates or amplifies, or the state of mind when the pain actually occurs are all factors that modify the way we perceive and tolerate pain. The painful experience is therefore always coloured by subjective considerations." Roselyne Rey, *The History of Pain* (Cambridge, MA: Harvard University Press, 1995), 5.

37. For data on the overall numbers of children whose parents are incarcerated, *see* Chistopher Mumula, *Incarcerated Parents and Their Children* (Washington, DC: U.S. Department of Justice, 2000). For a series of separate chapters that address different aspects of the problems that families, children, and parents face during and after imprisonment, *see* Jeremy Travis and Michelle Waul, ed., *Prisoners Once Removed: The Impact of Incarceration and Reentry on Children, Families, and Communities* (Washington, DC: Urban Institute Press, 2003), especially "Part Two: The Impact of Incarceration and Reentry on Children and Families."

38. Criminologists Todd Clear, Dina Rose, and their colleagues have written extensively about this issue, arguing that many communities now hover at a dangerous "tipping point"—the juncture at which the negative effects of such high rates of incarcerating and then returning ex-convicts to neighborhoods begin to destroy the social networks used to combat crime, leading to actual increases rather than decreases in the overall amounts of lawbreaking. *See* T. Clear, D. Rose, and J. Ryder, "Incarceration and Community: The Problem of Removing and Returning Offenders," *Crime and Delinquency* 47 (2001): 335; Todd Clear, D. Rose, E. Waring, and K. Scully, "Coercive Mobility and Crime: A Preliminary Examination of Concentrated Incarceration and Social Disorganization," *Justice Quarterly* 20 (2003): 33; and D. Rose and T. Clear, "Incarceration, Social Capital and Crime: Implications for Social Disorganization Theory," *Criminology* 36 (1998): 441.

39. However, there is one issue on which Scarry and I are not in agreement. She makes what is for her a clear and definite distinction between physical and psychological pain. As a psychologist, I must confess, the distinction is lost on me. To me, the body in pain is often indistinguishable from the psyche in pain.

Pain and suffering have come increasingly to be recognized as subjective states that are sensitive to the contexts in which they occur; as such, they fall squarely within the domain of psychology. Indeed, "more and more, we accept pain and suffering as an affectual state having the same reality whether one finds a lesion impinging on a nerve ending or not. In the truest sense, 'pain is pain.'" R. Barnes, "Pain and Suffering: A Psychosomatic Problem," *Dynamische Psychiatrie* 12 (1979): 162, 163–164. A broad framework that includes—even emphasizes—the psychological harm that prison inflicts is important to apply in deciding when and whether the pains of imprisonment are excessive or even cruel.

40. Psychologists, philosophers, and others agree that cruelty occurs when there is "the gratuitous infliction of unnecessary pain/suffering." G. Carlson, "Moral Realism and Wanton Cruelty," *Philosophia* 24 (1994): 49, 51.

41. C. McKinnon, "Ways of Wrong-Doing, the Vices, and Cruelty," *Journal of Value Inquiry* 23 (1989): 319, 329.

42. Research by Martin Seligman is the best known on the issue. *See* Martin Seligman, *Helplessness: On Depression, Development, and Death* (San Francisco: W. H. Freeman, 1975); Judy Garber and Martin Seligman, ed., *Human Helplessness: Theory and Applications* (New York: Academic Press, 1980). For other work on the topic, see L. Rowell Huesmann, guest ed., "Learned Helplessness as a Model of Depression." *Journal of Abnormal Psychology* 87, no. 1 (1978); and Mario Mikulincer, *Human Learned Helplessness: A Coping Perspective* (New York: Plenum Press, 1994).

43. Nils Christie, *Limits to Pain*, 93.

44. *See, e.g.,* Proposals for a Constitutional Amendment to Provide Rights for Victims of Crime, Hearing on H.J. Res. 173 and H.J. Res. 174 before the House Committee on the Judiciary, 104th Cong. 1, 2 (1996). *See also* several articles by Robert Mosteller, including R. Mosteller, "Victims' Rights and the United States Constitution: An Effort to Recast the Battle in Criminal Litigation," *Georgetown Law Journal* 85 (1997): 1691; and R. Mosteller, "Victim's Rights and the Constitution: Moving from Guaranteeing Participatory Rights to Benefiting the Prosecution," *St. Mary's Law Journal* 29 (1998): 1053.

45. L. Henderson, "Co-opting Compassion: The Federal Victim's Rights Amendment," *St. Thomas Law Review* 10 (1998): 579, 590.

I

PSYCHOLOGY AND THE PRISON FORM

2

HUMAN NATURE AND THE
HISTORY OF IMPRISONMENT

In any case: the causes of crime were firmly placed inside the body.
Criminals were different from most people and they had to be met with
scientific methods .... The intellectual foundations for this way of
thinking were established in the nineteenth century.

—Nils Christie[1]

Reformers insisted that an individualized design for the administration
of criminal justice, a design responding to each offender's particular
needs, would cure the offender and promote the good order of society.
Under this banner, the field of penology became as much the territory
for social workers, psychologists, and psychiatrists as lawyers.

—Edgardo Rotman[2]

French social theorist Michel Foucault once characterized prison as
an expression of the "intelligence of discipline in stone."[3] He also argued
that the shape of that intelligence—the pattern of domination that prevailed
in any society—was determined by the conceptual systems with which that
society had become enamored. What is experienced as the "given" in any
society during a particular age or epoch—the unquestioned status quo—is
part of what gives certain people the power to limit the lives of certain
others. But the historical given also helps to establish the boundaries of
that power—how far the apparatus of social control can go before it violates
prevailing notions of humane treatment.

Psychological theory has been implicated at all levels in the process
by which the institution of prison was made part of the natural order of
things. In fact, historians such as Foucault and Michael Ignatieff have
suggested that "human sciences" like psychology were in large part responsible for the very notion that human behavior could and should be controlled
by the state and, hence, were directly implicated in the proliferation of
prisons that took place in the late 18th and early 19th centuries. For example,

In this society, the imperative to control, to dominate, and to subdue is written deep into the structures of those ways of thinking we call the "human sciences." At the genesis of these sciences in the eighteenth century, their premise that men could be scientifically described and understood was immediately translated into institutional strategies of control and reform. The very act of describing human activity as scientifically knowable implied that it could be subdued, modified, and improved.[4]

Although the claim may be somewhat overdrawn—state power certainly had been used to dominate and subdue troublesome citizens long before the human sciences came on the scene—it is difficult to dispute the notion that these disciplines and the perspective on human nature they helped to formalize greatly influenced the nature of the social control that followed.

In the 19th century, the emerging discipline of psychology certainly contributed to the idea that confinement was an appropriate mechanism of social control and, in this sense, helped solidify the prison form. In the nearly 2 centuries that have passed since imprisonment became the predominant response to criminal deviance in the United States, psychological concepts—and sometimes the discipline of psychology itself—contributed significantly to the shape and manner of prison operations.

However, as I noted in the last chapter, as the punitive expansion of the prison system began in the latter part of the 20th century, prison policy was largely decoupled from contemporary psychological theory and data. As I argue throughout this book, the broad social contextual framework that modern psychology came to embody and advance was at odds with the program of harsh punishment to which the nation was in the process of committing.

Nonetheless, if accurately represented and thoughtfully applied, the new social contextual perspective can serve as the basis for fundamental, progressive change in prison policy and practice. It can play an important role in the creation of meaningful limits to the pains of imprisonment, helping to establish humane boundaries that constrain what can be done in the name of social control. However, this perspective must be distinguished clearly from the one that preceded it and on which so much past prison policy is based.

THE EMERGENCE OF THE PRISON FORM

The perceived need for a place of long-term confinement like prison was linked to changes in prevailing, popular conceptions of criminality that took place centuries ago. Civil societies have always dealt harshly with their most threatening and dangerous criminals, resorting even to execution in the name of social protection. But most persons who violate the law do not represent this kind of extreme threat. As long as the vast majority of criminals were viewed as persons who simply had "wandered astray"—as many still were through much of the 16th century—there were implicit community norms that greatly limited the harm that most people believed could and should be done to petty lawbreakers. This view was gradually transformed until, eventually, social deviance itself was perceived as a significant threat to the social and economic order. Once criminals in general were perceived as out-and-out adversaries—as embodying the characteristics of the "dangerous other"—and urban poverty became chronic, creating large groups of people who were displaced, destitute, and desperate—giving rise to the perception of a "criminal class"—then "physical enforcement became a crucial vehicle for the prevention of crime."[5]

The use of imprisonment to punish criminal conduct was not prevalent until the late 18th and early 19th centuries. Ignatieff called the late 1770s the "point of departure" in the history of the penitentiary because it was the time when "the vision of the total institution first began to take shape out of two centuries of accumulated experience with workhouses, houses of correction, and jails."[6] Before then, as numerous historians have documented, jails and prison-like institutions served primarily as holding facilities for pretrial detention, and to coerce debtors into paying their creditors. As Adam Hirsch put it, these first prisons were "at bottom instrument(s) of coercion rather than sanction, intended to pry open the purse rather than to deter or rehabilitate welchers."[7]

The increased use of coercive physical confinement—the essence of imprisonment—was one result of this fundamental change in perspective by which criminals were viewed as dangerous others. Another was the emergence of a professional police force that was charged with the responsibility of maintaining order through the forceful management of the criminal class, whose members now were viewed as difficult to control and potentially dangerous.[8] The threatening otherness of certain criminals also served to justify treating them with the utmost harshness—as in the use of capital punishment for a broad range of crimes.[9] In addition, lawbreakers increasingly were banished from the communities in which they had offended. Thus, instead of long-term confinement, England initially used banishment or the "transportation of convicts," first to the United States and then to Australia, during the 17th and 18th centuries.[10]

There were additional factors at work in the United States that influenced the perceived otherness of criminals and the psychology of punishment that was embodied in its criminal justice system. Compared with urban centers in England and the rest of Europe, the American Colonies of the

17th and 18th centuries were sparsely populated places whose mechanisms of social control at first concentrated more on "biblical" offenses (like adultery and blasphemy) than on property or violent crime. In theory, at least, this meant that punishments (primarily fines and whippings) were distributed more evenly throughout all segments of society. In practice, however, inequalities still plagued the administration of what came to be known as "criminal justice" and the way it distributed punishment or pain. Then, as now, social and economic circumstances mediated the harshness with which legal sanctions were applied. As one historian noted, although the prosecution of "white, non-servant offenders from all levels of society" seemed to confirm the equality of all sinners in the eyes of God, one's station in life continued to play a role. Thus, for sinners with property, the "impetus to reform" was brought about through monetary fines; for those without property, corporal punishment was the means to a more pious end.[11]

As law enforcement focused increasingly on property crimes—deviance of the sort that was more closely associated with some social classes than others—the uneven distribution of punishment became more pronounced, and the justice system relinquished any claim to egalitarianism. The equality of all sinners eventually gave way to a view of crime that emphasized—indeed, exaggerated—the essential differences between "offenders" and everyone else. Thus, somewhat later in the nation's history, De Tocqueville recognized both the severity of the American prison system and the necessity to define prisoners as "other" before subjecting them to it:

> While society in the United States gives the example of the most extended liberty, the prisons of the same country offer the spectacle of the most complete despotism. The citizens subject to the law are protected by it; they only cease to be free when they become wicked.[12]

Why and how citizens "became wicked" was a matter of public as well as professional concern. Social consensus on these topics underwent a number of transformations in the course of the 19th century, several of which had important implications for prison policy and operations. Psychological theories—conceptions of human nature—figured in each transformation.

PSYCHOLOGICAL INDIVIDUALISM, PERFECTIBILITY, AND PRISON POLICY

The general notion that lawbreakers should be rounded up, taken to centralized locations, and forced to submit to some kind of systematic regimen or correctional experience was necessarily based on some particular view of human nature. Beyond the simple *otherness* of criminals—the belief that their wrongdoing stemmed from the fact that they were "different" from others—there were a number of additional psychological components to what would eventually come to be called *corrections*. For one, prison reflected a view of the human psyche as at least in some ways malleable—capable (in the minds of those who undertook the task) of being improved or perfected. This notion, in turn, was part of an emerging perspective known as *materialist psychology*, a departure from the understanding of human nature that had preceded it. John Locke was among the first to challenge the previously accepted belief that ideas and dispositions were innate, contending instead that character was formed by experience. By this view, material conditions had direct effects on persons exposed to them. Borrowing from and building on this perspective, prison advocates eventually argued that penal institutions could be properly structured to effectively change the character of prisoners.

For example, materialist psychology influenced prominent 18th-century English prison reformer John Howard, who relied on it as the basis of his claim that "men's moral behavior could be altered by disciplining their bodies."[13] It is worth noting that Howard's scathing critiques of prison mismanagement and inhumane practices were expressly scientific in nature. That is, he was deeply devoted to data collection, and recorded the precise physical dimensions and nature of the institutional regime of every prison he studied. In fact, his descriptions were so detailed that, as Ignatieff reported, "the Royal Statistical Society in the 1870s . . . laud[ed] him as a father of social science."[14] In any event, the materialist psychology on which he and others relied was the basis of the belief that "through routinization and repetition, the regimens of discipline would be internalized as moral duties."[15]

By the 18th century, the collective doctrines of legal culpability that flourished under feudalism had been largely replaced by ones locating primary responsibility in individuals. Legal models of human behavior had undergone corresponding change as greater significance was attached to individual autonomy and personal dispositions. The very concept of criminal responsibility was intertwined with a model of behavior that both presumed and required a "durable and constant" personal autonomy, as illustrated in David Hume's early 18th-century discussion of legal culpability:

> [Where actions] proceed not from some *cause* in the character and disposition of the person who performed them, they can neither redound to his honour, if good, nor infamy, if evil . . . The person is not answerable for them; and as they proceeded from nothing in him that is durable and constant, and leave nothing of that nature behind them, it is impossible [that] he can, upon their account, become the object of punishment or vengeance.[16]

Historian Herman Franke has observed that psychological individualism was reflected in another aspect of the prison policy that prevailed during this period—the extensive use of solitary confinement that began at the outset of the 19th century. As he noted, the enthusiasm for this form of prison punishment—which occurred in comparatively liberal European nations as well as in the United States—is connected to "the highly individualistic concept of sin and evil avowed by the confessional politicians and members of the societies for moral improvement of prisoners. . . ."[17]

Nineteenth-century American society enthusiastically embraced the concept of psychological individualism, and this enthusiasm eventually facilitated the creation of an elaborate and extensive prison system. Psychological individualism implied—and 19th-century American society largely came to believe—that individuals were the exclusive causal locus of behavior and that social deviance arose largely from some defect inside the person. To be sure, the dominant perspective was never completely one-sided; most people conceded that factors such as poverty, family disorganization, and exposure to the vices and depredations of city life played some role in creating or exacerbating personal defects. Yet, at a pragmatic level, this was an age dominated by individualistic solutions.

Thus, the cure for deviant behavior like crime and insanity invariably was to be found in some significant change or alteration in individual or personal characteristics rather than the conditions that gave rise to them.[18] The use of prison—as the arena in which such change was to be coercively produced in criminals—seemed a logical extension of these prevailing views. As Table 2.1 suggests, the use of prison increased dramatically, and it was during this period that penal confinement would become the American criminal justice system's primary response to crime.

Of course, the rise of imprisonment during the 19th century was entirely consistent with the emphasis on individualism that was enshrined in the entire American legal system during exactly the same period. Like the amateur social scientists of the day who used the paradigm of independent and autonomous human agency in most of their causal attributions, lawyers and judges went about the task of finding and applying the common law

TABLE 2.1
The Growth of the United States Prison Population
in the Late 19th Century

At census year	Prison population	Ratio to total U.S. population
1850	6,737	1 : 3,442
1860	19,086	1 : 1,647
1870	32,901	1 : 1,171
1880	58,609	1 : 855
1890	82,329	1 : 757

Note. Data from "At Hard Labor: Rediscovering the 19th Century Prison," by M. Miller, 1974, *Issues in Criminology,* 9, p. 91, Table 1.

with much the same perspective. Roscoe Pound's sweeping but accurate generalization captured the legal spirit of these times: "The common law knows individuals only. . . . And this compels a narrow and one-sided view."[19]

In addition to individualism, the increased use of imprisonment during this era was also linked to an emerging popular belief in the perfectibility of human nature. The so-called *asylum movement* of the mid-19th century was based in part on what has been termed "the doctrine of the perfectibility of man" and the belief that various maladies, such as insanity, crime, and poverty, were curable through the kind of "moral treatment" that could be provided in institutional settings.[20] These institutions—whether mental hospitals, prisons, or poorhouses—had much in common.[21] Among other things, they shared the same purpose of attempting to improve the character of the individuals whom they involuntarily confined. Here, too, the same psychological assumptions that had inspired such widespread faith in human perfectibility also served as the intellectual underpinning for the extensive use of solitary confinement in the prisons. Such ideas seemed to validate the proposition that "criminals were defective mechanisms whose consciences could be remolded in the sensory quarantine of a total environment."[22]

Similarly, John Bender connected the rise of the penitentiary to changes in the broader cultural meaning attached to perfectibility. In his view, belief in the "power of confinement to reshape personality" led to a restructuring of the penitentiary.[23] Describing a change in perspective that occurred first in England and then in the United States in the second half of the 19th century, Bender argued that although we have come to take the "geometric disposition of individual cells and rigid daily routines" of modern prisons for granted, they actually "sprang suddenly into being." Indeed, they were innovations whose rapid acceptance was made possible in large part by "novelistic ideas of character" that had emerged during that period. These new ideas emphasized the sense in which individual personalities were capable of change and improvement. Penitentiaries, of course, were supposed to be uniquely designed to reshape personalities— that is, "to alter motivation and, ultimately, to reconstruct the fictions of personal identity that underlie consciousness."[24]

During this era, the American prison system went to coercive extremes in order reconstruct individual criminals and render them more "perfect." As Hirsch noted, "the signal feature of incarceration is that it offers an unparalleled measure of control over the deviant, and rehabilitation has been deemed a process which demands such physical control in order to succeed."[25] In the course of the 19th century, this control would include subjecting prisoners to virtually complete isolation—the "Pennsylvania system" of solitary confinement—and forcing them to wear hoods over their heads when they were escorted from their cells. These and other prison practices reflected the view that each prisoner was the causal locus of a potentially "contagious" criminality; as such, they needed to be prevented from contaminating each other. American prisons also eventually shifted to the so-called *Irish system* of grading convicts by their "type"—that is, through a classification system that was "based on character"[26]—and housing them accordingly, in the hope of hastening their reformation.

THE RISE OF PSYCHOLOGICAL AND PRISON "SCIENCE"

The increasingly popular notion that law was in some ways akin to a scientific pursuit during the 19th century was facilitated by its connection to the emerging science of human behavior. The "legal science" of this era was seen, to a large extent, as a science of human behavior. David Hoffman, among the first to advocate a scientific basis for American law, wrote in 1817 that there was such an "intimate relation between mind and matter" that it was impossible to proceed far in jurisprudence "without some acquaintance with the phenomena of mental philosophy."[27] In fact, psychological theories played an important role not only in helping to legitimate the American legal system but in elevating the "scientific" status of prevailing prison policies as well.

The putative ties of the field of corrections to a science of human behavior helped convince the public that penal policy deserved to be regarded less as a manifestation of political expediency (i.e., the mere application of state power to the task of social control) and more as a form of *prison science*. However, the discipline of psychology that emerged as a distinctive academic pursuit in the second half of the 19th century was an amalgam of several distinct intellectual traditions. Although each emphasized the individualism of the enterprise, they sometimes pulled in opposite directions.

For one, early 19th-century American psychology emerged largely as an outgrowth of *moral philosophy*—the loose collection of ideas that served as the precursor of more formal social science disciplines in the United States.[28] As such, psychological "expertise" was heavily influenced by (and at times indistinguishable from) Christianity. In the late 18th and very early part of the 19th century, the noted physician Benjamin Rush, who is often described as not only the "the father of American psychiatry"[29] but also one of the originators of the American prison form,[30] was heavily influenced by Christianity and often relied on religious concepts in his writing.[31] Although he conceived of himself as very much a scientist, Rush was a firm believer in free will. He thought that crimes like murder and theft occurred "when the will becomes the involuntary vehicle of vicious actions, through the instrumentality of the passions. . . ."[32]

In fact, psychologists at the start of the 19th century did little to explicitly challenge or offer alternatives to the many religious concepts that were relied on to formulate public policy. Proponents of the era's "new psychology" needed to reassure a skeptical public that their discipline offered unique perspectives and insights that were nonetheless consistent with prevailing religious norms and values. Scientists like Rush offered views that seemed to supplement, but were careful not to supplant, the dominant religious perspective. Their unflinching support of free-will theory was one important way in which this was accomplished.

Another critically important intellectual strand in the emerging discipline of psychology—and the one that would come to dominate the discipline for much of the next century—was the measurement of individual differences. It preoccupied the emerging human and psychological sciences in both Europe and America. As Edward Sampson has noted, it was during this era that "seeking to understand the individual became a highly cherished cultural project."[33] Psychology was the scientific outgrowth of that cultural project, and it attained great prominence in the late 19th century as the science of measuring individuals.

Many of the psychometricians who perfected these measurement techniques also were eugenicists who believed that humanity could be improved through selective breeding. Most eugenicists, in turn, pressed the notion that human value or worth not only was scientifically measurable but also was genetically transmitted and, hence, largely unmodifiable. Thus, the least capable, most unworthy, and identifiably deviant members of society needed to be genetically isolated from the rest.

For example, one prominent American psychologist of this era, Henry Goddard—sometimes described as the father of intelligence testing in the United States—was director of research at a home for "feeble-minded" children. Goddard also was a eugenicist who believed that intelligence was the basis of the social order and that its precise measurement was the key to ensuring that "the people who are doing the drudgery are, as a rule, in their proper places." [34] He advocated highly restrictive immigration laws, a strict national eugenics policy, and the "colonization of feeble-minded persons" in institutions like his own. Indeed, early in the 20th century, Goddard published a widely read eugenics tract that claimed to have documented the genetic basis of "feeble-mindedness" and its connection to criminality.[35]

Along with its eugenic and moral philosophical or religious origins, American psychology was characterized by its biologism. Indeed, most early psychologists and psychiatrists also believed that the human psyche was very much influenced by biological causes. This was especially true of attempts to analyze and explain persons who exhibited unusual or deviant behavior. There were numerous influential 19th-century treatises suggesting that crime was a form of moral disease or sickness. Often the biological or physical defect that was thought to cause crime was said compromise the exercise of the free will. For example, Benjamin Rush wrote that criminal behavior was a form of "moral derangement" that he believed afflicted the "capacity in the human mind of distinguishing and choosing between good and evil."[36]

Despite its scientific pretensions, however, what passed for "scientific psychology" for much of the 19th century often amounted to little more than a popularized hodgepodge of pseudoscientific fads—from phrenology, to craniometry,[37] to the highly influential eugenics movement[38] that dominated the human sciences near the end of the century. For example, phrenology was a major force in mid-19th-century psychological thought. The *doctrine of the skull* held that aspects of one's personality could be determined by examining the size and pattern of the bumps on the head. Phrenologists regarded the brain as the causal locus of all behavior, and thought that specific brain functions were localized in different parts of the brain. Criminals were thought to be easy to identify because they "were likely to have a 'ruffian head,' with little frontal area but prominence in the posterior regions of the skull."[39] The true nature of an outwardly seemingly kind and gentle person could be belied by a skull that revealed "excessive development of destructiveness and combativeness, and [a] smallness of the organ of justice."[40]

Although these biological theories purported to localize the causes of crime (and all behavior) squarely within the physical makeup of the lawbreaker[41]—and therefore existed in an uneasy tension with free-will doctrines—they did not necessarily ensure lenient treatment when the time came for lawmakers to assign criminal responsibility or decide on punishment. The fact that newly emerging experts in the human sciences believed a criminal offender might suffer from physical defects or moral diseases that ultimately accounted for his deviant behavior typically did little to alter his legal status. Even when a defendant was "insane" enough to be committed to an asylum, typically he was "still held responsible for his willed acts."[42] The legal philosophers of the time generally agreed that "the merciless prosecution of the vicious must not be impeded—no matter how lamentable the circumstances conspiring to form their vicious character."[43]

The biological emphasis in 19th-century American psychology had much in common with the school of so-called scientific criminology that came into prominence in Europe at roughly the same time. This new, ostensibly scientific way of studying criminal behavior was based largely on the work of Italian criminologist Cesare Lombroso, among whose major theoretical innovations was the linking of genetic explanations of criminality with evolutionary doctrine. Thus, Lombroso argued that criminals were evolutionary throwbacks whose atavistic traits were embodied in their physical characteristics.

But Lombroso's ideas—of which American scientists were much enamored—also had harsh implications for the treatment of certain kinds of criminals. Thus, Lombroso's "born criminals" were thought to be beyond redemption. Much as Goddard had argued about the "feeble minded," Lombroso believed that there was little that could be done but to isolate and colonize those who were genetically predisposed to violate the law. Indeed, he advocated an even more extreme sanction for the worst cases: "There exists, it is true, a group of criminals, born for evil, against whom all social cures break as against a rock—a fact which compels us to eliminate them completely, even by death."[44]

PSYCHOLOGICAL SCIENCE AND THE PRAGMATICS OF CONFINEMENT

Whether they premised their approach loosely around a genetic or biological theory like Lombroso's born criminal type, or on one of the numerous "crime-as-sickness" and "moral disease" metaphors that were popular during these years, prison officials and advocates increasingly sought to connect their work to the image of objective science. Eventually, they would borrow directly from the increasing status and respectability of disciplines like psychology and psychiatry in this effort.

Of course, theoretical considerations were not the only factors that helped to determine the precise shape or form of imprisonment during this period of rapid development in the 19th century. Although many of the early penitentiaries were based on a model of individual, isolated confinement in which a "silent system" was imposed—a model that seemed to be supported in some way by all of the prevailing theories of criminality—there were practical issues with which to contend. As one historian put it, "Money was the problem, or one of the problems. Austere, silent prisons were expensive; it was cheaper to let them get noisy and crowded. Even worse, states could not resist the temptation to make money off prisoners, which was difficult in the classic [solitary] penitentiary."[45]

Eventually, the practical demands of managing large groups of involuntarily confined prisoners took precedence over commitments to any particular philosophical or scientific concept. Political and economic pressures required prison officials to economize in whatever ways possible. Yet these concessions to practicality were often merged with some overarching and seemingly legitimizing rationale to make prison practices more palatable to members of the taxpaying public (who, after all, were asked to underwrite the whole enterprise). Science—and, especially the emerging science of human behavior, psychology—was particularly helpful in this regard. Ideally, a way needed to be found to make prisons less expensive, and yet still publicly justify their existence on arguably scientific grounds. Eventually, theoretical justification was joined with practical purpose: "Prisoners were supposed to work; *work was a tool of reformation*. It was also a way to make prisons pay for themselves. The trick was to put prisoners to work on something the state could profitably sell."[46]

At the same time, the possibility that psychologists could bring their own brand of scientific expertise to real-world contexts like prisons added to the credibility of a fledgling discipline seeking professional legitimacy and an intellectual niche. As I noted earlier, the notion that an emerging system of knowledge could be applied to the task of changing people to conform to a preferred ideal had been germinating for most of the century. For example, Benjamin Rush, whose ideas were influential in the late 1700s and early 1800s, was devoted to this cause: "What Rush was interested in was the production of a disciplined individual, and the prison was simply the most attractive of several laboratories in which this new social science could be practiced."[47]

As the 19th century drew to a close, the status of the discipline of psychology inside the new universities was becoming increasingly dependent on its newfound practical utility. By the 1880s, John Dewey wrote glowingly about what he called "the new psychology" and noted, "The cradle and the asylum are becoming the laboratory of the psychologist in the latter half of the nineteenth century."[48] More than the other emerging social sciences, its scientific success was predicated on "delivering the goods to the industrial, governmental, and social audiences." Thus, "the primary goal of psychology became the prediction and control of the 'other'. . . ."[49] Prison seemed an ideal place in which to master this task.

FORMALIZING THE REHABILITATIVE IDEAL

Near the end of the century, the discipline of psychology and the field of prison science were increasingly allied in solidifying the commitment of the American corrections establishment to the individualistic beliefs on which prisons had been founded. For the most part, these beliefs reduced to the core notion that prisoners could and should be remade and reformed through the treatment they received in prison. Thus, Zebulon Brockway— one of the major figures in the development of American penology—wrote confidently at the end of the 19th century that "prison science is working out . . . a methodical system of penology which is in accord with the true science of our common human nature."[50] It is not surprising that the "methodical system" that Brockway touted was largely devoted to the task of rehabilitation or individual prisoner changing.

Indeed, throughout the 19th century, rehabilitation had been practiced in a variety of different ways, most of them bearing only a tangential relation to anything that resembled science. In early penitentiaries, inmates were isolated and encouraged to "do penance" for their lives of crime, and occasionally were visited by "moral instructors" whose goal was to "strengthen [the prisoner's] mind in the direction of virtue."[51] This was how phrenologist Marmaduke Sampson had described the regime at the Eastern State Penitentiary in Pennsylvania in the early 1840s. Eastern State generally was regarded as the nation's model prison at the time, even though it was one of the facilities that Charles Dickens had famously criticized when he toured it. At around the time both Sampson and Dickens visited Eastern State, it had one "moral instructor" who supposedly was "aided by ministers of the Gospel of various denominations" in addressing the rehabilitative and religious needs of approximately 400 prisoners.[52] By the 1870s, this approach had reached all the way to California, where San Quentin prison had its own moral instructor to induce "moral cures" in prisoners whose release depended on showing "satisfactory proof of reformation."[53]

In other penal institutions, prisoners were forced to learn the "habits of labor" by engaging in what was often arduous (and sometimes meaningless) work.[54] Although, as Nichole Rafter noted, wardens in midcentury American prisons fancied themselves "specialists in the treatment of offenders,"[55] they really had no organized body of knowledge on which to draw in providing rehabilitative services of any kind. There were occasional wardens whose devotion to one or another theory of crime led to temporary changes in the institutional regimes they administered, and even some notable improvements in the treatment of prisoners and conditions under which they were housed. But they were hardly systematic programs of rehabilitation implemented on a widespread basis.

In the late 1870s, however, Brockway's Elmira Reformatory was the first to claim to operate explicitly on the principle that inmates were "sick and in need of treatment."[56] Brockway was eclectic in his approach to treatment, using "ethical, industrial, and scholastic training," as well as an elaborate physical fitness program that he hoped would "nullify [the] defective heredity" of his most difficult prisoners.[57] In numerous public pronouncements, he regularly touted what appeared to be remarkable success stories of having produced dramatic changes in unprecedented numbers of prisoners who returned to lives that were free of crime.

Despite his extravagant claims, however, what passed for rehabilitation—even under Brockway's regime—was loosely premised on an ill-conceived and poorly implemented set of ideas about the causes of crime. Brockway's prison science lacked any real empirical support, and there were no systematic demonstrations of success by the prisons that undertook to implement it. Moreover, it is notable that when Brockway's programs began to fail, and he was under pressure to move prisoners rapidly through his increasingly overcrowded institution and release them, he resorted to abusive forms of physical mistreatment. The lengths to which he went were truly extreme. A state investigation into cruelty at Elmira concluded that the "brutality practiced at the reformatory has no parallel in any modern penal institution in this country." In fact, a new group of prison overseers who were installed into Brockway's practices in the midst of the investigations wondered whether such mistreatment actually had helped to create "incorrigible" prisoners rather than cure them.[58]

Indeed, Brockway's unfailing optimism and misrepresentations of his own accomplishments notwithstanding, there was little real evidence that the wide array of programs he described actually had succeeded in producing positive changes in very many of the countless prisoners on whom his techniques were imposed. More generally, in historian Lawrence Friedman's judgment,

> The prison story, in general, was a story of failure; at any rate, it was seen as a failure. Yet there was no going back. Imprisonment was and remained the basic way to punish men and women convicted of serious crimes. The great penitentiaries were not pulled down. There they stood—corrupt and brutal; warehouses for convicts. Prisons did not seem to end crime, or cure criminals.[59]

This history of failure notwithstanding, prison advocates and reformers continued to believe in the efficacy of imprisonment. In the later part of the 19th century they remained devoted to the notion that prisons could cure the varied individual ills from which they assumed prisoners suffered.[60]

PSYCHOLOGY IN THE "PROGRESSIVE ERA" CRIMINAL JUSTICE SYSTEM

The first few decades of the American 20th century—what historians have termed the start of the Progressive Era—were characterized by a heightened moral fervor and a renewed faith in the malleability of human nature. Both notions resonated with the major strands of prison science that were becoming firmly established in the United States. The final decade of the 19th century and the early years of the 20th saw a resurgence in what was termed *moral treatment* in psychiatry—an approach that was described as "a formal recognition of the medical value of a constructive intellectual and emotional environment."[61]

In this context, prison scientists in the Progressive Era alternated between two somewhat inconsistent approaches. On the one hand, many acted on their belief in the malleability of prisoners and the wisdom of trying to create the kind of prison environment in which they could be "morally treated." On the other hand, many still resonated with the legacies of the eugenics movement by advocating "the sterilization of insane, defective and criminal persons in order to improve the race."[62] This latter tendency, as one historian observed, "represented the Progressive attempt to deal with that part of man which was not malleable."[63]

As the first half of the 20th century unfolded, the individualistic focus of penology and prison policy persisted and became even more explicitly psychological in nature. To be sure, belief in eugenics remained influential and widespread—for example, between 1907 and 1931, some 30 state legislatures passed compulsory sterilization laws based loosely on the notion that certain types of people, including habitual criminals, should not be allowed to procreate (lest they pass their defective traits to their offspring).[64] However, there was also a decided shift toward the creation of specialized institutions designed to provide psychological treatment for persons who had committed crimes. The goal of these newly created institutions was to modify criminal behavior on an explicitly individualized level and a case-by-case basis.

For example, the emergence of juvenile courts during this era shifted attention away from the nature of the offense and focused it instead on the character of the child. This legal innovation was premised on the notion that the approach to each case should be determined by the psychological makeup of the individual juvenile lawbreaker. As historian David Rothman put it, the juvenile court was less concerned with what a young person had done than with "his character and life style, his psychological strengths and weaknesses, the advantages and disadvantages of his home environment."[65]

The same focus on individual character was reflected in the increased use of indeterminate prison sentences that premised release on outward signs of a prisoner's personal transformation. Like prison policies in general during this period, these laws were based on the principle that prisoners were incarcerated to be "cured" of whatever had led them into criminal behavior in the first place. If anything, the belief that these personal flaws and deficits could be effectively treated in prison was even more widespread in this era than in the past. The new indeterminate sentencing laws that were passed incorporated a basic psychological insight: that the necessary changes might well take varying (indeed, indeterminate) amounts of time to produce in different people. Similarly, various *good-time laws* were enacted that reflected the belief that prisoners should be released early if their good prison behavior gave evidence of their having been cured sooner rather than later.

As an anonymous prisoner wrote in the pages of the *Atlantic Monthly* in 1911, criminal offenders should remain in prison "until cured, just as a

TABLE 2.2
Individualizing Criminal Justice Reforms in the 19th Century

By year	Good-time laws (no. of states)	Parole laws (no. of states)	Indeterminate sentencing (no. of states)
1850	4	1	0
1860	9	1	0
1870	21	3	0
1880	31	4	0
1890	38	12	1
1900	41	25	4
1915	46	41	26

Note. Data from "At Hard Labor: Rediscovering the 19th Century Prison," by M. Miller, 1974, *Issues in Criminology*, 9, p. 91, Table 1.

person suffering from physical disease or infection is sent to a hospital or asylum, to remain for such period as may be necessary for his restoration to health."[66] Like medical doctors, prison officials also believed that their science could and would soon provide the tools that would enable them to know precisely when their treatments had taken effect; prisoners, just as hospital patients, should be pronounced "healthy" enough to be released. By the early 1920s, approximately half of state prisoners were serving indeterminate sentences that, at least in theory, allowed prison officials to make that determination.[67]

During roughly the same period, the closely related practice of granting *discretionary parole* to prisoners was implemented on a widespread basis. Indeed, parole "came into its own in the twentieth century," and one historian reported that by 1925 all but 2 of 48 states had parole laws.[68] The psychological assumptions reflected in the parole system were similar to those that shaped indeterminate sentencing—that is, that individual prisoners would vary in the amount of time it would take them to be cured of their criminal tendencies, and that a prisoner's behavior in prison gave officials all the information they would need to determine whether and when he was cured sufficiently to return to the freeworld. As Lawrence Friedman noted, "parole, like the indeterminate sentence, was part of the process of making criminal justice better suited to the individual case."[69] As Table 2.2 illustrates, all three sentencing reforms—good-time credit, parole, and indeterminate sentencing—became widespread by the early decades of the 20th century.

Under parole, of course, the ex-prisoner's behavior was carefully monitored by the state after his release, extending the criminal justice system's heightened scrutiny of individual behavior to life outside the prison walls. Indeed, it meant that "prison discipline, in a sense, went with the man onto the streets."[70] Moreover, if the ex-prisoner gave signs of having "relapsed" into a criminal lifestyle, he could be returned to prison by use of an expedited legal process that sidestepped many of the essential constitutional protections and guarantees to which criminal defendants were otherwise entitled.[71] Then, as now, it was much easier to return a parolee to prison than to convict and punish someone who was not on parole; parolees could "violate" the terms of their parole without ever having committed another criminal offense.

This, too, reflected an essentialist, individualistic view of criminality consistent with the psychology of the times. As ex-convicts, parolees were persons who already had revealed their supposed criminal character traits. The fact that they possessed these traits heightened the probability that they would engage in crime in the future. If crime was a sickness, then—as law enforcement and parole officials saw it—parolees had demonstrated that they were predisposed to catch it. The presumption of innocence and associated due-process protections did not need to be afforded to persons prone to be guilty. Thus, the requirement that wrongdoing had to be proven "beyond a reasonable doubt" and based on reliable evidence that was admitted and tested in court was unnecessary in the case of those people whose character was presumed to be less than innocent. Much as with a patient whose illness was merely in remission, criminal justice officials felt justified in lowering the diagnostic threshold for concluding that a parolee had suffered a relapse.

The first few decades of the 20th century also saw the introduction of *probation officers* into the criminal justice system. On the basis of the belief that "diagnosis is as necessary in the treatment of badness as it is in the treatment of illness,"[72] they were charged with the responsibility of gathering a complete record of the offender's life, one that provided "a clear picture of the offender, his traits, habits, abilities, and tendencies."[73] As Sheldon Glueck noted in the 1930s, the first step in any "intensive" probation investigation was to ensure that "the offender [is] examined psychiatrically, psychologically, and physically, and a report of his condition from these points of view" be made.[74]

To facilitate these kinds of intensive investigations, "probation officers were to complete an undergraduate course in sociology and psychology, go on to graduate study in social work. . . . In this way the staff would grasp 'the modern conceptions of human behavior' that had to underlie the program."[75] Obviously, this made sense only in the context of an increasingly individual-centered and psychologically oriented criminal justice system.

All four of these early 20th-century innovations—juvenile courts, indeterminate sentencing laws, the parole system, and the advent of probation officers—were designed to make more extensive use of psychological information in criminal justice decision making. They also represented examples of the way in which the science of behavior and the psychological individualism it embodied were closely joined with an emerging technology of social control. One historian has noted that the crucial changes in the public mood and style of life that occurred in American society during the 1920s were reflected in what once again came to be known as the *new psychology* of the times. This time, however, it was a psychology that "provided information about the instincts, drives, and wants of men" and, therefore, was thought to provide insights into "new ways in which they might be controlled."[76] Criminal justice reforms during this period reflected an appreciation of its potential applications.

Here, too, there was some diversity to the approach that experts brought to bear on these issues. Although some psychologists and psychiatrists clearly recognized the significant role that environmental forces could play in the origins of mental disorder and deviance in general, most were united in their belief in the importance of the "physical and mental, or more accurately, 'biological,' [adaptation] of the individual."[77] Eventually this perspective gave rise to what was termed the "mental hygiene movement" and the "cult of the self," both of which emphasized the "controllability of man."[78] It was an era in which interest in introspective accounts of personal experiences and autobiographical narratives flourished, along with the essentialist notion that there was a "real," inner, or hidden self within each person wherein true character resided.

Even many social workers—whose profession traditionally emphasized the link between environmental conditions and behavioral problems—were converted by the rampant individualism that characterized the behavioral sciences at the end of the 1920s: "By the late twenties casework, under the influence of psychiatry, tended to abstract the client from his 'environmental and cultural milieu' and to emphasize his internal attitudes and even his emotional life. The inner man, not the outer environment, was to be adjusted."[79] Indeed, sociologist Thorsten Sellin characterized the "struggle for the individualization of penal treatment" that focused on the makeup of the offender rather than the nature of his offense" as "one of the most dramatic in the history of thought."[80]

THE PRACTICE OF PRISON PSYCHOLOGY

The professional roles of psychologists and psychiatrists underwent significant changes in the early 20th century. These changes, in turn, affected the way mental health experts functioned in various criminal justice agencies and institutions, including prisons. The increased respectability of the behavioral sciences and the various criminal justice reforms that relied explicitly on psychological expertise in the early decades of the 20th century had an effect on public opinion and trial practice. It is not surprising that psychologists and psychiatrists began to play larger and more explicit roles in different parts of the criminal justice process.

Prison operations also were being structured in such a way that psychological expertise was increasingly relevant. For example, many institutions now used specialized practices like *quarantines* and other forms of classification whereby prisoners were isolated, evaluated, graded, and then assigned to housing units according to their personal characteristics. As Rothman observed, "it was within the framework of these procedures"—procedures that required prisons to focus on and in some ways assess the psychological makeup of individual prisoners—"that psychiatrists and psychologists took up posts inside the prisons for the first time."[81] Indeed, he reported that "the change can be dated precisely. By 1926, sixty-seven institutions employed psychiatrists: thirty-five of them made their appointments between 1920 and 1926. Of forty-five institutions having psychologists, twenty-seven hired them between 1920 and 1926."[82]

There were other correctional innovations that emphasized the increasing importance of the discipline of psychology to prison policy. For example, prison historian Elmer Barnes noted what he termed the "extremely significant step" of creating a psychological clinic inside Sing Sing prison in the early 1900s. In fact, he included this innovation as one of the four most notable "advances in penology" made by the New York prison system during the preceding century.[83] Barnes described the creation of this clinic as "the first thorough application of medical psychology to a study of the causes and treatment of crime,"[84] and praised it highly on this basis.

To be sure, any significant practical impact that mental health professionals like psychologists had on prison treatment per se or on the institutional routines that prevailed during this period was limited by their narrowly defined role and their very limited power within the correctional system. The scientific credentials of mental health specialists lent a certain kind of legitimacy to the prison endeavor without having much impact on day-to-day life within the institution. Thus, Rothman noted that although the Progressive Era saw increased numbers of psychiatrists and psychologists on the prison payrolls, their presence had "more symbolic than real importance."[85]

In addition, although their numbers were increasing, in absolute terms there were still few mental health staff actually employed within prison settings. For example, even in the most treatment-oriented correctional facilities, no more than one psychologist or psychiatrist typically was on hand to administer to the needs of hundreds of prisoners.[86] Moreover, there were very real structural limits imposed on what could be accomplished within the institutions themselves. Thus, even in cases in which mental health staff members compiled detailed social histories and made recommendations for treatment, "the institution . . . had no way to respond."[87]

Of course, if these early 20th-century prisons had been structured in such a way as to take prisoner case histories into account, and to implement recommendations for those prisoners who needed treatment or other kinds of prison programming, then it is possible that the presence of greater numbers of mental health experts and other program-oriented staff might have made a real difference. In enough numbers and with sufficient resources, prison clinicians and others might have significantly influenced the nature and quality of correctional care. But most prisons approached the task of trying to address the needs of prisoners halfheartedly, at best. With respect to prison education, for example, early 20th-century experts declared the undertaking "a tragic failure" throughout the country, and noted that prisons "fared even worse" when it came to providing inmates with badly needed vocational training. Yet, the system's "greatest failure" was said to be its inability to provide prisoners with work to do; the most reliable estimates indicated that approximately half of all prisoners were idle.[88]

Note also that, in addition to the limitations of the institutional roles in which they functioned and the lack of adequate resources with which to implement programming recommendations, the individualistic bent that dominated the behavioral sciences during this period blunted any impulse that psychiatrists and psychologists might have had to attempt to change prison conditions per se. At most, prisons asked mental health staff members to focus on changing what were often assumed to be intractable traits of individual prisoners. The clinicians had neither the correctional mandate nor the professional orientation to critically examine the conditions of confinement under which prisoners were kept. Because most of them were neither trained nor inclined to proceed with an assessment of prisoners' problems that focused on the way they were being treated or the circumstances under which they were confined, typically they did not.

At the same time, it is important to acknowledge that, despite everything I have said about the limitations on what they could accomplish, the presence of mental health staff had one potentially important benefit for prisoners. Although "historically the prison doctor's concern with mental health was for the purpose of diagnosis rather than treatment," it was also the case that "in both the physical and mental sphere" they were "charged with the task of refereeing the punitive excesses of those who administered the penal system."[89] In fact, this foreshadowed the mixed blessing that mental health staff would come to represent in conventional prison settings. On the one hand, despite their relatively modest impact on actual programs and policies, the presence of psychologically trained personnel seemed to legitimize correctional programming as "science" or render harsh forms of treatment as benign "therapy" when those prison practices were anything but scientific or therapeutic. On the other hand, therapists and counselors could act as modest restraining forces against the harshest aspects of the penal system—at times not only refereeing, but also mitigating, punitive excesses and deterring mistreatment at the hands of custodial staff.

PRISON TRENDS AT MIDCENTURY: SCIENCE BEGINS TO PAY MODEST DIVIDENDS

By the middle of the 20th century, many prison officials and policy-makers still endorsed the notion that correctional practice should be better connected to psychological science. In fact, as prison historian Edgardo Rotman noted, there was "an intensification of the therapeutic thrust in prisons after the early 1950s" that served to "increase the input of behavioral scientists in the correctional system." Among other things, this meant that "psychologists and caseworkers gave a more technical orientation to the therapeutic model of rehabilitation."[90]

To be sure, some prison administrators solicited and abided this kind of input and technical orientation much more than others. Moreover, for many of the reasons mentioned previously, psychologists still were unable to transcend the institutional barriers and hierarchies that they confronted in most of the facilities where they worked. Even worse, in some notorious cases, their presence did little more than provide a scientific and therapeutic cover for some otherwise questionable practices (including, in some egregious instances, ones in which they participated).[91]

However, there were several nonobvious aspects to this renewed connection between psychological science and prison policy that offered the possibility of real correctional reform. For one, the discipline of psychology had become far more empirically oriented than in the past. Newly developed approaches to "evaluation research" meant that the effectiveness of various prison practices and programs—including those that involved psychologists directly—could be systematically measured and more objectively judged.[92] Claims about the success of one or another approach to rehabilitation could be, and were, subjected to careful study. In a broader sense, the failure of exclusively individualistic approaches to prisoner treatment and rehabilitative programming to produce lasting change led to questions about the need to modify the nature of correctional intervention, perhaps to directly address more of the social contextual causes of crime and to implement more community-based solutions.

In a related way, the potentially destructive effects of penal institutions themselves began to receive systematic attention from the social and behavioral sciences. Indeed, several empirical analyses suggested that the harsh environment of the prison might be part of the problem rather than the solution. Social scientists like Erving Goffman, Harold Garfinkel, and others were writing persuasively about the negative effects of total institutions.[93] Eventually, their critiques became so widely acknowledged that criminal justice experts—and even prison policymakers—had to address them.

Thus, when the President's Commission on Law Enforcement and Administration of Justice—chaired by former Republican U.S. Attorney General Nicholas Katzenbach—wrote its final report, the opening pages of the section on corrections contained this description:

> Life in many institutions is at best barren and futile, at worst unspeakably brutal and degrading. To be sure, the offenders in such institutions are incapacitated from committing further crimes while serving their sentences, but the conditions in which they live are the poorest possible preparation for their successful reentry into society, and often merely reinforce in them a pattern of manipulation or destructiveness.[94]

By the early 1970s, the nation seemed poised for a fundamental reorientation in its crime control policies. As one knowledgeable criminologist put it at the start of the decade, "In shifting from revenge to a reformation emphasis, corrections still focused on individual offenders. Their behavior, however, was increasingly ascribed to their community relationships, commitments, and rewards rather than to their personal traits alone."[95] Correspondingly, efforts were underway to address poverty, segregation, the deteriorated state of many inner-city neighborhoods, and other structural inequalities whose role in creating racial unrest and increased levels of crime had been clearly identified.[96] In addition, community-based alternatives to prison—recognized as less intrusive and debilitating—were being pursued on a more widespread basis than at any time in recent American history.

CONCLUSION

In the course of the 19th century, the prison form came to dominate the criminal justice landscape in the United States and elsewhere. Although initially reflecting the core premise of materialist psychology that persons were shaped and influenced by their surroundings, it came increasingly to embody the staunchly individualist view that the causes of behavior were internal. Albeit roughly and imprecisely, prison policy reflected a popular and increasingly professionalized consensus about the causes of crime, woven together with strands of religiously based free-will doctrine as well as, at times, seemingly inconsistent beliefs in biological determinism. Nonetheless, prison continued to be thought of as the place where putatively damaged persons were taken to have their defects addressed.

As the century progressed, prison science drew increasingly from the loose set of ideas that were being formalized under the rubric of psychology and the science of human behavior. But the science was metaphor at best. Although the prison advocates had scientific aspirations and pretensions, they relied for most of the century on primitive and unsupported theories and engaged in crude forms of correctional treatment. Even in the case of esteemed penologists like Brockway, their ostensibly noble intentions and supposedly enlightened scientific techniques could quickly degenerate into outright mistreatment.

Yet the early decades of the 20th century brought what seemed to be a more humane vision to bear on prison treatment. The commitment to science—however vague and pro forma—offered the promise that someday prisons might be made more accountable—even if they rarely had been in the past. The human sciences had matured into genuine professions with a host of techniques and approaches to treatment that could be subjected to empirical study and retained or discarded as appropriate. That did not mean that there was a harmonious melding of the prison form and the helping professions. Far from it. But it did add to a growing sense that, to the extent that prison systems genuinely committed to the idea of rehabilitation and invested in its logic, there was a body of scientific knowledge on which to draw.

To be sure, the mental health and program-oriented staff rarely if ever attained sufficient power to significantly transform the standard operating procedures of the penal institutions in which they worked. Yet the professional orientation of persons trained to see themselves as helpers or caregivers was seemingly incompatible with the norms of an institution premised on pain. At times this tension served to introduce a measure of restraint and establish humane limits to behavior in environments where they had been lacking.

The modern, mid-20th-century prison still was primarily about punishment. However, to the extent that prison policymakers entertained the noble purpose of providing opportunities for positive change, there were now formal disciplines and trained personnel from organized professions that could provide them with some amount of assistance. Among other things, it meant that there was a body of developing knowledge that addressed some of the harmful effects of imprisonment. It also meant that, as scientific thinking about the causes of crime evolved to encompass a more social contextual framework, the logic of rehabilitation would be broadened as well. Prisons, it seemed, eventually would be pressed to modify and transform their approaches to the treatment of prisoners and their relationship to crime control policies.

NOTES

1. Nils Christie, *Limits to Pain* (Oxford, England: Martin Robertson, 1982), 23.
2. Edgardo Rotman, "The Failure of Reform: United States, 1865–1965," in *The Oxford History of the Prison: The Practice of Punishment in Western Society*, ed. Norval Morris and David Rothman (New York: Oxford University Press, 1981), 158.
3. Michel Foucault, *Discipline and Punish: The Birth of the Prison* (New York: Random House, 1977), 249.
4. Michael Ignatieff, *A Just Measure of Pain: The Penitentiary in the Industrial Revolution, 1750–1850* (New York: Pantheon, 1978), 218.
5. A. Hirsch, "From Pillory to Penitentiary: The Rise of Criminal Incarceration in Early Massachusetts," *Michigan Law Review* 80 (1982): 1179, 1240. *See also* Louis Chevalier, *Laboring Classes and Dangerous Classes in Paris During the First Half of the Nineteenth Century* (Princeton, NJ: Princeton University Press, 1973), quoting mid-19th-century French commentator M.A. Fregier to the effect that poverty was "the most productive breeding ground of evildoers of all sorts," 141.
6. Ignatieff, *A Just Measure*, 11. Others have noted that the Dutch employed the penitentiary form much earlier. *See* P. Spierenburg, "From Amsterdam to Auburn: An Explanation for the Rise of the Prison in Seventeenth-Century Holland and Nineteenth-Century America," *Journal of Social History* 20 (1987): 439.
7. Hirsch, "From Pillory to Penitentiary," 1182.
8. Although the creation of a professional police force was part of the expansion of the criminal justice system that contributed to the proliferation of prisons, a number of prisons already were in operation by the time this occurred. Most historians agree that the first professional police force was established in London in 1829, with Sir Robert Peel's London Metropolitan Police Act. A number of large cities in the United States developed police departments in the 1840s and 1850s. *See, e.g.*, D. Greenberg, "The Effectiveness of Law Enforcement in Eighteenth-Century New York," *American Journal of Legal History* 19 (1975): 173; M. Haller, "Historical Roots of Police Behavior: Chicago, 1890–1925," *Law & Society Review* 10 (1976): 303; J. Richardson, "The Struggle to Establish a London-Style Police Force for New York City," *New York Historical Society Quarterly* 49 (1965): 175.
9. At times there was a fair amount of controversy and public outcry about the overuse of capital punishment in these societies. Indeed, as popular sentiment changed, the range of crimes for which the death penalty could be applied was restricted and public executions were ended. For example, compare Thomas Laqueur, "Crowds, Carnival and the State in English Executions, 1604–1868,"

in *The First Modern Society: Essays in English History in Honour of Lawrence Stone*, ed. A. L. Beier, David Cannadine, and James Rosenheim (Cambridge, England: Cambridge University Press, 1989); Peter Linebaugh, "The Tyburn Riot Against the Surgeons," in *Albion's Fatal Tree: Crime and Society in Eighteenth-Century England*, ed. Douglas Hay et al. (New York: Pantheon Books, 1975); Louis Masur, *Rites of Execution: Capital Punishment and the Transformation of American Culture, 1776–1865* (New York: Oxford University Press, 1989).

10. Robert Hughes, *The Fatal Shore: A History of the Transportation of Convicts to Australia, 1787–1868* (New York: Knopf, 1987).

11. K. Preyer, "Penal Measures in the American Colonies: An Overview," *American Journal of Legal History* 26 (1982): 326, 335–336.

12. Alexis de Tocqueville, *Democracy in America* (New York: Harper & Row, 1833; 1966), 79.

13. Ignatieff, *A Just Measure*, 67.

14. Ibid., 52.

15. Ibid.

16. David Hume, *An Enquiry Concerning Human Understanding and Concerning the Principles of Morals* (Oxford, England: Oxford University Press, 1975; first published 1739), 98.

17. H. Franke, "The Rise and Decline of Solitary Confinement: Socio-Historical Explanations of Long-Term Penal Changes," *British Journal of Criminology* 32 (1992): 125, 137.

18. These issues are discussed more fully in C. Haney, "Criminal Justice and the Nineteenth-Century Paradigm: The Triumph of Psychological Individualism in the 'Formative Era,'" *Law and Human Behavior* 6 (1982): 191.

19. R. Pound, "Do We Need a Philosophy of Law?" *Columbia Law Review* 5 (1905): 339, 346.

20. A. Luchins, "The Cult of Curability and the Doctrine of Perfectibility: Social Context of the Nineteenth-Century American Asylum Movement," *History of Psychiatry* 3 (1992): 203.

21. David Rothman, *The Discovery of the Asylum: Social Order and Disorder in the New Republic* (Boston: Little, Brown, 1971).

22. Ignatieff, *A Just Meaure*, 213.

23. John Bender, *Imagining the Penitentiary: Fiction and the Architecture of Mind in Eighteenth-Century England* (Chicago: University of Chicago Press, 1987), 1.

24. Ibid., 1–2.

25. Ignatieff, *A Just Measure*, 1203, n. 122.

26. "Transactions of the National Congress on Penitentiary and Reformatory Discipline," reprinted in *Twenty-Sixth Annual Report* (Albany: New York Prison Associations, 1871), 541.

27. David Hoffman (1817), quoted in P. Miller, *The Life of the Mind in America from the Revolution to the Civil War* (New York: Harcourt, Brace & World, 1965), 160.

28. *See, e.g.,* G. Bryson, "The Comparable Interests of the Old Moral Philosophy and the Modern Social Sciences," *Social Forces* 11 (1932): 19; G. Bryson, "The

Emergence of the Social Sciences from Moral Philosophy, *International Journal of Ethics* 42 (1932): 304; and, more recently, A. Fuchs, "Contributions of American Mental Philosophers to Psychology in the United States," *History of Psychology* 3 (2000): 3.

29. *See, e.g.*, C. Farr, "Benjamin Rush and American Psychiatry," *American Journal of Psychiatry* 100 (1944): 3; B. Mackler and K. Hamilton, "Contributions to the History of Psychology: VII. Benjamin Rush: A Political and Historical Study of the 'Father of American Psychiatry,'" *Psychological Reports* 20 (1967): 1287.

30. R. Sullivan, "The Birth of the Prison: The Case of Benjamin Rush," *Eighteenth-Century Studies* 31 (1998): 333.

31. S. Thielman and D. Larson, "Christianity and Early American Care for the Insane: The Work of Doctor Benjamin Rush," *Journal of Psychology & Christianity* 3 (1984): 27.

32. Benjamin Rush, *Medical Inquires and Observations Upon the Diseases of the Mind*, 2d ed. (Philadelphia: John Richardson, 1818), 183.

33. E. Sampson, "The Challenge of Social Change for Psychology: Globalization and Psychology's Theory of the Person," *American Psychologist*, 44 (1989): 914, 920.

34. Henry Goddard, *Psychology of the Normal and Subnormal* (New York: Dodd, Mead, & Co., 1919): 246.

35. *See* Henry Goddard, *The Kallikak Family: A Study of the Heredity of Feeble-Mindedness* (New York: Macmillan, 1912).

36. Rush, *Medical Inquiries*, 357–367.

37. Craniometrists believed that intellectual ability was a direct function of brain size—the bigger the head or the larger the "cranial index," the smarter the person was. They aggregated data from different racial groups, supposedly showing systematic differences in average head sizes between them. Craniometrists used the comparisons as "scientific proof" of racial inferiority. *See, e.g.*, chapters 2–3 of Stephen Gould, *The Mismeasure of Man* (New York: Norton, 1981). Alfred Binet, the creator of the "IQ" test, was an early proponent of craniometry who became disaffected with the theory when his own research failed to demonstrate any relationship between head size and intellectual function.

38. A number of excellent historical studies have examined the interplay between 19th-century science, eugenics, and biologically based explanations (and remedies) for crime and other socially problematic behavior. *See, e.g.*, Troy Duster, *Backdoor to Eugenics* (New York: Routledge, 1990); Mark Haller, *Eugenics: Hereditarian Attitudes in American Thought* (New Brunswick, NJ: Rutgers University Press, 1963); Marouf Hasian, *The Rhetoric of Eugenics in Anglo-American Thought* (Athens, GA: University of Georgia Press, 1996); Edward Larson, *Sex, Race, and Science: Eugenics in the Deep South* (Baltimore: Johns Hopkins University Press, 1995); and Nichole Rafter, *Creating Born Criminals* (Urbana, IL: University of Illinois Press, 1997).

39. W. David Lewis and Eliza Farnham, "Phrenological Contributions to American Penology," in *Rationale of Crime and Its Appropriate Treatment (Treatise on Criminal Jurisprudence Considered in Relation to Cerebral Organization)*, ed.

Marmaduke Sampson and Eliza Farnham (Montclair, NJ: Patterson Smith, 1846; 1973), xii, xv.

40. Ibid., 35.

41. *See, e.g.,* Arthur Fink, *Causes of Crime: Biological Theories in the U.S., 1800–1915* (Philadelphia: University of Pennsylvania Press, 1938).

42. Charles Rosenberg, *The Trial of the Assassin Guiteau: Psychiatry and Law in the Gilded Age* (Chicago: University of Chicago Press, 1968), 66.

43. Ibid.

44. Cesare Lombroso, *Crime; Its Causes and Remedies* (Boston: Little, Brown, 1911), 447.

45. Lawrence Friedman, *Crime and Punishment in American History* (New York: Basic Books, 1993), 156.

46. Ibid., 158 (emphasis added).

47. Sullivan, *The Birth of the Prison*, 342.

48. J. Dewey, "The New Psychology," *Andover Review* 2 (1884): 278, 286.

49. R. Tweney and C. Budzynski, "The Scientific Status of American Psychology in 1900," *American Psychologist* 55 (2000): 1014, 1015.

50. Zebulon Brockway, "President's Annual Address," *Proceedings of the Annual Conference of the National Prison Association of the United States* (Pittsburgh: Shaw Brothers, 1898), 29.

51. Sampson, *Rationale of Crime*, xv.

52. Goddard, *Psychology of the Normal and Subnormal*, 130. *See also* Charles Dickens, *American Notes for General Circulation* (London: Chapman and Hall, 1842).

53. *See* Kenneth Lamott, *Chronicles of San Quentin* (New York: Ballantine, 1972) and Jessica Mitford, *Kind and Usual Punishment* (New York: Knopf, 1973).

54. For example, Rothman reported that a number of early 19th-century prison advocates thought that "the routine of labor" could rehabilitate prisoners by making them into "hardworking citizens," a notion the Quaker reformers in Pennsylvania "especially held out." New York prison officials even tried putting prisoners on a treadmill to force them to "discipline themselves," but this met with little success. *See* D. Rothman, "The Invention of the Penitentiary," *Criminal Law Bulletin* 8 (1972): 555, 569–570.

55. Rafter, *Creating Born Criminals*, 94.

56. Ibid., 95.

57. Ibid., 99–100.

58. Ibid., 103. For another sobering account of the "new penology" carried out at Brockway's Elmira Penitentiary, describing the "extremely severe corporal punishment . . . administered to force conformity and maintain order," see A. Pisciotta, "Scientific Reform: The New Penology at Elmira, 1876–1900," *Crime & Delinquency* 29 (1983): 613, 626.

59. Friedman, *Crime and Punishment*, 159.

60. Thus, Rothman noted that the post-Civil War prison proponents "expressed a very positive and enthusiastic commitment to the idea that prisons and asylums could accomplish rehabilitation and cure." David Rothman, *Conscience*

and Convenience: The Asylum and Its Alternatives in Progressive America (Boston: Little, Brown, 1980), 31.

61. J. Burnham, "Psychiatry, Psychology, and the Progressive Movement," *American Quarterly* 12 (1960): 457, 459–460.

62. Ibid., 460.

63. Ibid.

64. Kenneth Ludmerer, *Genetics and American Society: A Historical Appraisal* (Baltimore: Johns Hopkins, 1972).

65. Rothman, *Conscience and Convenience*, 215.

66. A Prisoner, "The Indeterminate Sentence," *Atlantic Monthly* 108 (1911): 330, 330. Of course, it would be a mistake to assume that all prisoners shared this benign view of indeterminate sentences. They did not. Prisoners understandably complained about the uncertainty of their sentences—never knowing exactly when they would be released—and they resented the significant amount of power the indeterminate sentence vested in the hands of correctional authorities to decide whether and when their sentence would end.

67. U.S. Bureau of the Census, *Prisoners, 1923* (Washington, DC: U.S. Government Printing Office, 1923), 123.

68. Friedman, *Crime and Punishment*, 304.

69. Ibid., 305.

70. Ibid.

71. That continues to be the case. *See, e.g.,* Morrissey v. Brewer, 408 U.S. 471 (1972) (parole revocation hearings required but need not be as elaborate as criminal trials); and Pennsylvania Board of Probation & Parole v. Scott, 118 S.Ct. 2014 (1998) (federal law does not require application of exclusionary rule to improperly obtained evidence introduced into parole revocation proceeding).

72. Warren Spaulding, "Possibilities of a Probation System," speech delivered at the 1907 Massachusetts Conference on Charities (Cambridge, 1908). Quoted in Rothman, *Conscience and Convenience*, 57.

73. Ralph Ferris, "The Case History in Probation Service," in *Probation and Criminal Justice*, ed. Sheldon Glueck (New York: Macmillan, 1933), 137. This typically included arranging "for the physical and mental testing of the offender and incorporat[ing] the examiner's findings into his recommendation" to the court. Rothman, *Conscience and Convenience*, 62. Indeed, the probation officer was supposed to "be certain that each probationer received the full battery of psychological tests and the full benefits of psychological counseling" (ibid., 67).

74. Sheldon Glueck, "The Significance and Promise of Probation," in *Probation and Criminal Justice*, ed. Sheldon Glueck (New York: Macmillan, 1933), 16.

75. Rothman, *Conscience and Convenience*, 84, quoting Edwin Cooley, *Probation and Delinquency* (New York: Nelson, 1927), 319. Like many criminal justice innovations, this one was poorly implemented. Probation officers were undertrained, their agencies were understaffed and underfunded, and they were rarely if ever held accountable for the recommendations that they made. Rothman pronounced the results of the early probation programs "pitiful" and "dismal," *Conscience and Convenience*, 84, 96. However, the probation system was ex-

panded despite this record of failure, in part because judges favored the way it allowed them "ample room for distinctions among offenders, not on the basis of the crime, but on the basis of the person." Ibid., 101.

76. John Burnham, "The New Psychology: From Narcissism to Social Control," in *Change and Continuity in Twentieth Century America: The 1920s*, ed. John Braeman, Robert Bremmer, and David Brody (Columbus: Ohio State University Press, 1968), 353.

77. Ibid., 366.

78. Ibid., 367.

79. Ibid., 397. Rothman argued much the same thing: "Throughout the 1920s and 1930s, psychological explanations for all types of human behavior gained popularity. . . . [Criminal justice] reformers were not about to abandon a psychological orientation just when that perspective was capturing the national imagination." Rothman, *Conscience and Convenience*, 113–114.

80. Thorsten Sellin, "The Trial Judge's Dilemma: A Criminologist's View," in *Probation and Criminal Justice*, ed. Sheldon Glueck (New York: Macmillan, 1933), 101. Sellin emphasized that "new ends of justice" required "the study of the criminal himself," to allow judges to decide whether he could be reclaimed or needed to be confined indefinitely to prevent "further depredations" (ibid., 102).

81. Rothman, *Conscience and Convenience*, 132.

82. Ibid., 132–133.

83. Ibid., 58–59.

84. H. E. Barnes, "The Historical Origin of the Prison System in America," *Journal of Criminal Law and Criminology* 12 (1921): 35, 60.

85. Rothman, *Conscience and Convenience*, 134.

86. For example, Rothman reported that "even the most advanced states" employed no more than a psychiatrist and psychologist or two per institution. Ibid.

87. Ibid., 275.

88. Ibid., 134–138.

89. John Gunn et al., *Psychiatric Aspects of Imprisonment* (London: Academic Press, 1978), 5. Admittedly, the book's first chapter also provides a chronicle of how poorly many prison doctors have managed to discharge this refereeing or moderating function.

90. Rotman, *The Failure of Reform*, 169. *See also* Edgardo Rotman, *Beyond Punishment: A New View on the Rehabilitation of Criminal Offenders* (Westport, CT: Greenwood Press, 1990).

91. As Rotman noted, the "abuse of intrusive therapies" that included behavior modification programs that were little more than "disguised versions of highly punitive practices" occurred in the name of "treatment," discrediting rehabilitation in general and the participation of psychologists in particular. Rotman, *The Failure of Reform*, 171. For some extreme examples, *see* Mitford, *Kind and Usual Punishment*.

92. For examples of the writing on evaluation research during this period, *see* Francis Caro, ed., *Readings in Evaluation Research* (New York: Russell Sage

Foundation, 1971); and Elmer Stuening and Marcia Guttentag, *Handbook of Evaluation Research* (Oxford, England: Sage, 1975).

93. Both Goffman and Garfinkel wrote about the negative psychological effects of institutions early in this modern period. *See* Erving Goffman, *Asylums: Essays on the Social Situation of Mental Patients and Other Inmates* (Garden City, NY: Doubleday, 1961). For a more contemporary discussion of some of the issues Goffman confronted, *see* H. Becker, "The Politics of Presentation: Goffman and Total Institutions," *Symbolic Interaction* 26 (2003): 659. Garfinkel's work was less well known, but nonetheless contributed to the growing sense that institutions like prisons could force inmates to experience events and procedures that negatively transformed them. *See* H. Garfinkel, "Conditions of Successful Degradation Ceremonies," *American Journal of Sociology* 61 (1956): 420.

94. Nicholas Katzenbach et al., *The Challenge of Crime in a Free Society. A Report by the President's Commission on Law Enforcement and Administration of Justice* (New York: Avon Books, 1968), 385.

95. D.Glaser, "From Revenge to Resocialization: Changing Perspectives in Combating Crime," *The American Scholar* 40 (1971): 654, 660.

96. United States, Kerner Commission. *The Kerner Report: The 1968 Report of the National Advisory Commission on Civil Disorders* (Washington, DC: Government Printing Office, 1968).

3

SPREADING PAIN: THE PUNITIVE STATE AND THE STATE OF THE PRISONS

The penal system is [now] there to hurt people, not to help or cure. And the pain is inflicted to further the interests of persons other than those brought to suffer.

—Nils Christie[1]

The last chapter ended on a guarded but optimistic note. Despite the mixed history of the intellectual and practical collaboration between the discipline of psychology and the practice of imprisonment, by the middle of the 20th century the correctional mandate to produce positive change had been opened up to some degree of scientific analysis and evaluation. Prisons were beginning to be subjected to a higher degree of scrutiny and accountability, and, in part as a result, American corrections by that time appeared to be on the verge of significant reform. The decade of the 1960s brought widespread concern about the fairness and efficacy of the criminal justice system in general and the prison system in particular. Scholars, politicians, and members of the public wondered aloud whether our prisons were too harsh, whether they adequately rehabilitated prisoners, and whether there were alternatives to incarceration that would better serve correctional needs and national interests.[2] By the early 1970s, many states already were becoming alarmed over increased levels of prison overcrowding. It was widely understood by legislators as well as penologists that programming resources could be stretched too thin even in prisons that were only *nearly* filled to capacity. Overcrowded prisons also meant that prison administrators had too few degrees of freedom with which to respond to interpersonal conflicts

57

and a range of other inmate problems. And, if anything, the situation in the nation's jails was even more problematic. Here is how one criminologist writing in the early 1970s described it:

> The less affluent accused in America are stored for months in local jails awaiting trial. They are crowded into large cages, kept in complete idleness, with a single guard supervising several cages. Therefore, brutalization of all inmates by the most aggressive inmate cliques in each jail cage is architecturally and administratively assured.[3]

In addition, there was genuine skepticism—even at high levels of the government—about whether prison was an effective solution to the nation's crime problem. For example, in 1973 the National Advisory Commission on Criminal Justice Standards and Goals concluded that prisons, juvenile reformatories, and jails had achieved what it characterized as a "shocking record of failure."[4] Its authors suggested that these institutions may have been responsible for creating more crime than they prevented, and they recommended continuing a moratorium on prison construction for at least another 10 years.

To be sure, there was a fiscal undercurrent to otherwise humanitarian attempts to avoid the overuse of imprisonment during these years. Even then, everyone understood that prisons were extremely expensive to construct and operate. Without clear evidence that they worked very well, it was difficult to justify building and running more of them. Thus, as sociologist Andrew Scull argued, there was little question that economic motives were at the bottom of some of the critique and provided much of the impetus for discussions of noninstitutional alternatives.[5] But there also was a fair amount of genuine concern by members of the public about what was being done to persons behind prison walls, and what the long-term effects on them would be.

In addition, a prisoners' rights movement was growing in size and importance. It eventually raised the political consciousness of large numbers of prisoners, some of whom became effective spokesmen for the cause of prison reform.[6] The public's attention also was drawn to several highly publicized, tragic events that took place in several prisons in different parts of the country.[7] To many observers, these events vividly illustrated the extremes of prisoner mistreatment at the hands of prison authorities and gave credence to the critics' concerns.[8] All these things combined to call into question the wisdom of continuing to rely on prisons as the centerpiece of a national strategy of crime control.[9]

Moreover, changes in the day-to-day operation of many prisons were being propelled by a major transformation that was taking place in American law. Constitutional rights were being extended to previously marginalized groups, and, eventually, these reforms reached the nation's prisons. Prisoners began to assert their newfound identity as rights-bearing persons, and a number of lawless penal institutions—especially in the South—were brought under a higher degree of legal regulation and control.

In fact, the discipline of psychology was beginning to play an important role in some of the efforts to use law—particularly constitutional law—to reform the nation's prisons. For example, psychologists Stanley Brodsky, Carl Clements, and Raymond Fowler were engaged in an important joint effort with a team of lawyers hoping to reform the Alabama prison system in the early 1970s.[10] The optimism with which Fowler wrote about the results of that litigation was characteristic of the times: "The practice of psychology in the nation's correctional systems, long a neglected byway, could gain new significance and visibility as a result [of the court's ruling]."[11] The same sentiments prevailed in a number of similar efforts in different parts of the country, where psychologists were participating in litigation designed to improve living conditions in a number of state prisons.[12]

And then, almost without warning, all of this critical reappraisal and constructive optimism about humane standards and alternatives to incarceration was replaced with something else. A profound counterrevolution in crime and punishment began—slowly and imperceptibly at first, and then with a consistency of direction and effect that could not be overlooked. It eventually moved with such force and seeming inexorability during the 1980s that, as Philip Zimbardo and I characterized it much later, "it resembled nothing so much as a runaway punishment train, driven by political steam and fueled by media-induced fears of crime."[13] The concept that had served as the intellectual cornerstone of corrections policy for nearly a century—rehabilitation—was publicly and politically discredited. It was rapidly and decisively replaced with an explicitly punitive approach. Prison punishment soon came to be thought of as its own reward, serving only the goal of inflicting pain. Indeed, the nation came to embrace a crime control agenda and an approach to imprisonment that fully reversed the trends that had been underway in the 1960s and early 1970s.

Although the exact nature of the underlying political interests and influences that helped to bring these changes about are beyond the scope of this book,[14] it is important to note that the formal discipline of psychology played a relatively insignificant role in the policymaking process that accomplished them. Thus, the decisions by which this new and increasingly harsh perspective on crime and punishment was initiated and implemented were not driven by social scientific analyses indicating that this course of action was necessary or even advisable. In addition, the important developments in the discipline of psychology that I noted earlier and discuss in some detail in chapter 5 were ignored entirely in the policymaking process by which these changes were brought about. In fact, the various decision makers who collectively fashion the nation's correctional policies have continued to disregard most of the lessons that emerged from numerous empirical studies and theoretical pieces published in psychology over the past several decades that underscored the critical importance of situation and context in influencing social behavior, especially in psychologically powerful environments like prisons.

In any event, the country moved abruptly in the mid-1970s—from a society that justified putting people in prison on the basis of the belief that their incarceration would somehow facilitate their productive reentry into the freeworld to one that used imprisonment merely to further something called "just deserts" (i.e., locking people up for no other reason than because they deserved it and for no other purpose than to punish them).[15] At a more practical and less philosophical level, imprisonment was used to disable criminal offenders (i.e., *incapacitation*) or to keep them far away from the rest of society (i.e., *containment*). Unfortunately, the long-term impact of the prison experience on the prisoners who were being punished, incapacitated, and contained was left out of the new corrections equation.

The effect of these new policies on the American prison system was swift and profound. In fact, the several decades of change and transformation in prison policy have brought about what has been described as a *corrections crisis* of unprecedented proportions in the United States. As I have noted, with remarkable speed, prison policy in the United States became extremely punitive—so punitive that the prison system itself was unprepared for the changes that followed. Among other things, the rapid influx of prisoners—one that continued for several decades—produced a severe overcrowding crisis. As historian Lawrence Friedman would later put it, "We [now] throw people into prison at an astonishing rate. There has never been anything like it in American history. Penology is overwhelmed by the sheer pressure of bodies."[16] Numerous commentators acknowledged what has been referred to as a "national scandal of living conditions in American prisons. . . ."[17]

Moreover, the implications of these changes in prison policy extended far beyond the prisons themselves. The crisis that they helped to create threatened the integrity of state and local budgets. The increased pains of imprisonment and their disabling social, economic, and psychological effects consigned many citizens to the legal and economic margins of our society, and the sheer scale of incarceration began to spread disorganization and disadvantage in many communities where people most directly affected by these policies were heavily concentrated. In addition, the single-minded devotion to harsh punishment fostered an unprecedented callousness in the discourse that surrounds crime and punishment. In the remainder of this chapter and the one that follows, I try to describe the full magnitude of these unprecedented changes.

THE CORRECTIONS CRISIS BY THE NUMBERS

As one reviewer in the mid-1990s observed, "for over a decade, virtually every contemporary commentary on corrections in the United States has reminded us that the system is in crisis."[18] Whatever else it has entailed, the corrections crisis has been characterized by dramatic increases in the rates of incarceration and the sheer number of people imprisoned. Concerns about the "unprecedented" levels of prison crowding began to surface in the 1970s and were voiced continuously throughout the period of rapid growth in the prison population that followed. For example, in 1976, a national newsmagazine told readers, "Prisons all across this country are dangerously overcrowded because of a recent, unexpected influx of inmates."[19] Less than a decade later, a well-known corrections expert wrote accurately that "No one has to tell criminal justice practitioners and criminologists that the nation's prisons are seriously overcrowded. Prison populations experienced their largest one-year increase in the nation's history in 1982. . . ."[20] At around the same time, another noted, "It is widely acknowledged that our prisons are now in crisis. . . . Crowding in American prisons and jails is a national problem of epidemic proportions."[21]

Just a few years later—in 1987—the *National Law Journal* described prisons in the United States as "on the precipice," noting that the 600,000 persons then incarcerated in state and federal prisons represented a population larger than Alaska, Vermont, or Wyoming.[22] It also noted that one in five Black men would spend time in prison at some point in their lives.[23] That same year, 46 states and the federal prison system were reporting serious overcrowding problems.[24] Scholars continued to warn about the effects of runaway incarceration rates on the nation's prison system, again describing them as having reached crisis-level proportions. For example, in a representative observation made in the mid-1980s, one commentator wrote that "the doubling of prison populations from approximately 230,000 in 1974 to over 500,000 in 1986 created an unprecedented crisis in American corrections."[25] Several years later, the Bureau of Justice Statistics reported that, in the first 6 months of 1989, the state and federal prison population had soared to nearly 700,000, the highest increase since such records began to be kept 64 years earlier.

The incarceration rate in the United States (calculated as the number of sentenced prisoners in state and federal institutions per 100,000 residents) increased more than 137% in the period between 1971 and 1987.[26] Thus, what began in the mid-1970s continued on a steady course throughout the 1980s. Between 1980 and 1987 alone, the incarceration rate rose 64% over its already record levels.[27] As the decade of the 1980s came to a close, the United States was imprisoning more people for longer periods of time than any other industrialized democracy. As one scholar concluded at the time,

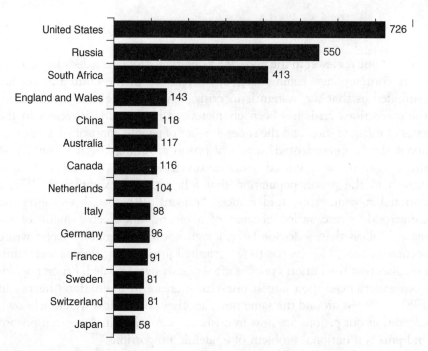

Country	Rate
United States	726
Russia	550
South Africa	413
England and Wales	143
China	118
Australia	117
Canada	116
Netherlands	104
Italy	98
Germany	96
France	91
Sweden	81
Switzerland	81
Japan	58

Figure 3.1. Incarceration rate by country (number of people in prison per 100,000 population). Data from the International Centre for Prison Studies. Retrieved July 1, 2005, from www.prisonstudies.org (calculated from country-specified data obtained for years 2003–2004).

"it is easily demonstrable that America's use of prison is excessive to the point of barbarity, with a prison rate several times higher than that of other similarly developed Western countries."[28]

Just when it seemed clear that we had reached or exceeded any rational upper limit to the use of punitive incarceration, and criminologists agreed that they had never seen anything quite like the imprisonment epidemic of the 1980s, things got much worse. An incarceration rate of 426 persons per 100,000 was reached in 1989—a level virtually unheard of in Western democracies. This rate was several times higher than that of neighboring Canada, which itself had one of the highest rates of incarceration in all the British Commonwealth countries.[29] Even though the U.S. penchant for imprisonment already far outstripped that of all other modern democracies, the rate continued to climb during the 1990s: It reached 504 by 1991 and 519 for the year 1993.[30] This represented roughly 5 times a rate of incarceration that had remained virtually stable in the United States between 1925 and 1975. By 1995, the nation was incarcerating 600 persons per 100,000, a 113% increase over the already record level a decade earlier.[31]

Indeed, just after the turn of the 20th century, the incarceration rate in the United States stood at over 715 per 100,000.[32] As Figure 3.1 illustrates,

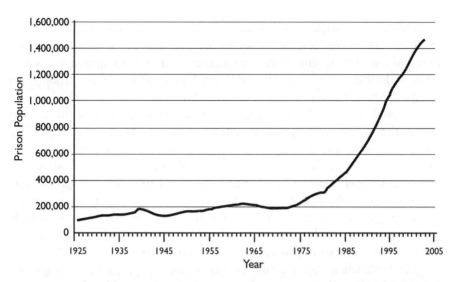

Figure 3.2. State and federal prisoners (1925–2004). Data from *Historical Corrections Statistics in the United States, 1850–1984* [NCJ-102529], by M. Cahalan, December 1986, Rockville, MD: U.S. Department of Justice; and *Sourcebook of Criminal Justice Statistics, 2002* (Table 6.1), by K. Maguire and A. Pastore (Eds.), 2004, Washington, DC: U.S. Government Printing Office; and *Prison and Jail Inmates at Midyear, 2004* [NCJ-208801], by P. Harrison and A. Beck, April 2005, Washington, DC: U.S. Department of Justice. In the public domain.

it is a figure that is unmatched by any other nation.[33] Moreover, the only two countries with even remotely comparable incarceration rates—Russia and South Africa—have both undergone significant political change in the previous several decades and currently are in the throes of serious economic turmoil. The United States has had neither external force at work to explain the extraordinary rate at which it imprisons its citizens.

A historical perspective also underscores the magnitude of the change in policy that was brought about. As Figure 3.2 shows, the dramatic rise in the numbers of persons incarcerated in the United States occurred in the mid-1970s, and continued unabated to the present time. Before then, the numbers of prisoners remained remarkably stable, despite many significant events that might have been expected to impact the extent or amount of incarceration—including the Great Depression, World War II and the Korean War and their aftermaths, and the turbulent 1960s. Thus, it seems clear that what occurred in the mid-1970s reflected a policy choice, rather than an accommodation to historical change or economic pressures.

In a futile attempt to keep pace with this influx of new prisoners, prison construction also proceeded at an unprecedented rate. Building new prisons always has been a costly proposition. This was especially true as the rapid expansion of the system began in earnest in the 1980s, when the average cost of a single new maximum-security prison bed was estimated at $67,000.[34] However, despite an unprecedented amount of prison construction and the historic shift in state expenditures that was required to accomplish it during this period, the additional bed space was not enough to ensure minimally livable conditions of confinement in many of the nation's correctional systems. As one commenator noted at the end of the decade of the 1980s, the correctional system continued to be "overwhelmed" by the increases in the numbers of prisoners: "Despite the addition of more than eighty new prison facilities between 1986 and 1988 and almost 30,000 new beds through renovations or additions to existing facilities, population increases still easily outdistanced capacity."[35] Indeed, many state and federal prisons began or continued operating well above the capacities for which they had been built. For example, by 1992 the federal prison system held 165% of the number of prisoners it had been designed to house.[36]

Overcrowded, deteriorating prison conditions precipitated litigation. In turn, the federal courts became actively involved in legal attempts to mitigate increasingly widespread problems inside the nation's prisons. Indeed, by the early 1990s at least 40 states (plus the District of Columbia, Puerto Rico, and the Virgin Islands) were under court orders or consent decrees to improve conditions either throughout the entire system or in their major institutions.[37]

THE RACIALIZATION OF PRISON PAIN

These aggregate statistics masked an important fact about the nation's prison system: Dramatic increases in incarceration rates over the last several decades have had a highly disproportionate effect on minorities, especially Black men. Although they represent less than one tenth of the general population, African American men constitute nearly half of all persons confined to state prison. On the basis of the 1991 statistics, Blacks were 6.5 times more likely to be imprisoned than their White counterparts.[38] By 1995, that disproportion had grown to 7.5 times.[39] Indeed, by one account there are more young Black men (between the ages of 20 and 29) under the control of our nation's criminal justice system—including those in prison, on probation, and under parole supervision—than the total number of them in college.[40] These racial disparities in incarceration rates, and their corresponding impact on the neighborhoods and communities from which young Black men are taken, and to which they ultimately return, have continued to increase.

Note also that although most of the existing data on racial disparities in the criminal justice system focus on differences between Black and White prisoners, recent increases in the numbers of Latino prisoners now complicate these comparisons. For example, Timothy Flanagan and his colleagues found that the percentage of White prisoners in the New York state prison system actually declined 66% between the years 1956 and 1989, whereas the percentage of Black prisoners increased 25%. During this period, Whites also went from being a clear majority among what he termed "very long term" prisoners (those who had served more than 10 years) to a small plurality compared with increasing proportions of Black and Latino inmates. However, Flanagan found that growth in the number of Latino prisoners in New York was the most dramatic, increasing 284% over the same period. Moreover, among very long term inmates, Latino representation increased a remarkable 1263%.[41]

In California, the racial and ethnic composition of the prisoner population underwent similar although less dramatic changes. Whites were the largest single racial group in the California prison population through the decade of the 1970s. They made up approximately 40% or more of the total until the start of the 1980s, when incarceration rates began to rise dramatically in the state. At the outset of this period of rapid prison growth, African Americans represented approximately one third of the prison population, and Latinos only one fifth of all inmates. However, the unprecedented expansion of the California prison system—one during which the state prisoner population grew from 19,000 in 1977 to over 160,000 in the year 2000—resulted in the incarceration of a much greater proportion of Latino prisoners than at any time in the past. By 1983, Whites had moved behind African Americans as the single largest racial or ethnic group in the California prison system, and by 1993 Latinos had overtaken both groups. In 2005, Latinos were 37% of the total male prisoner population, compared with 29% who were White and 29% African American.[42]

These trends are not restricted to a few states. Differential rates of incarceration are beginning to affect Latino communities in much the same way they have impacted African Americans.[43] Increasingly, the population of prisoners in the United States is composed of persons of color—African American and Latino. In chapter 4, I discuss the interrelated issues of race and prison policy in greater depth.

THE CRISIS EXPANDS:
ACCOMMODATING THE PRESS OF NUMBERS

As the prison population continued to grow in the 1990s, correctional norms and governmental spending priorities shifted to accommodate the new prison realities. Among other things, officials began to subtly shift their definitions of prison overcrowding. As I noted earlier, until this period of unprecedented population growth, correctional facilities that were nearly filled to capacity were regarded as overcrowded because of the high levels of idleness that often followed and because officials lacked the flexibility to move or separate prisoners in response to conflict or other unanticipated problems. However, in the face of this massive influx of new prisoners in the 1980s and 1990s, prison administrators were forced to adjust to overcrowding in facilities that were filled to well above their design limits. In 1979, for example, California prison officials worried about a 96% overall occupancy rate in their correctional system and struggled to manage a total inmate population of just over 18,000.[44] Twenty years later, the system was operating at about 180% of capacity and housed nearly 10 times the number of inmates it had in 1980.

As recently as the late 1970s, there also was a widespread correctional consensus about the evils of *double-celling*—the practice of housing two prisoners in a single cell (a cell that had been designed to hold one person). Even in jurisdictions that were forced to double-cell from time to time, prison administrators understood that it was problematic. For example, as one 1979 correctional task force that included a number of high-ranking prison officials explained,

> According to legislative and departmental policy, the Department of Corrections does not sanction double-celling inmates. This task force agrees with the basic premise that *double-celling violates basic standards of decent housing, health, and institutional security;* however, at present, there is no viable alternative to double-celling inmates as population projections are realized. Thus, while concurring that *double-celling is totally undesirable,* the task force must recommend this, and has attempted to propose gradual population increments and associated staffing to lessen the impact of overpopulation.[45]

Twenty-five years later, these observations now seem woefully anachronistic. Indeed, beginning in the early 1980s, correctional officials and politicians began to take the "totally undesirable" practice of double-celling for granted, even though it was one that they had acknowledged violated "basic standards of decent housing, health, and decent security." To be sure, nothing had changed to alter the undesirability of the practice—except that the overwhelming press of numbers forced correctional administrators, line staff, and, of course, prisoners, to routinely accept it. In fact, many administrators considered themselves fortunate if they were able to maintain a limit of "only" two prisoners to a cell during their worst periods of overcrowding.

The influx of new prisoners, the significant cost of new prison construction, and a greatly expanded scale of prison operations meant that correctional expenditures began to consume major portions of overall state budgets. For example, the corrections budget in California surpassed the state's latest

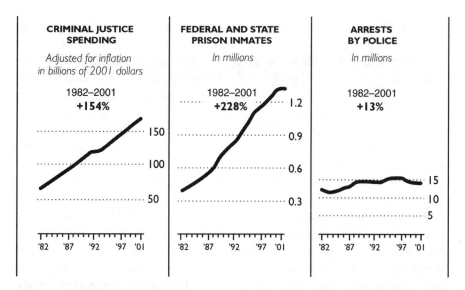

CRIMINAL JUSTICE SPENDING	FEDERAL AND STATE PRISON INMATES	ARRESTS BY POLICE
Adjusted for inflation in billions of 2001 dollars	In millions	In millions
1982–2001 +154%	1982–2001 +228%	1982–2001 +13%

Figure 3.3. Spending on criminal justice (number of persons in prison and arrests in the 1980s and 1990s). Data from *Justice Expenditure and Employment in the United States, 2001* [Bureau of Justice Statistics Special Report NCJ 202792], by L. Bauer and S. Owens, May 2004, Washington, DC: U.S. Department of Justice and from *Sourcebook of Criminal Justice Statistics, 2002* (Tables 4.2 and 6.1), by K. Maguire and A. Pastore (Eds.), 2004, Washington, DC: U.S. Government Printing Office. In the public domain.

fiscal outlays for higher education.[46] In fact, appropriations for the construction and maintenance of prisons grew faster than any other major state budget item during the 1980s, making corrections the state's top budget priority for the sixth straight year in 1989.[47] The same disturbing shifts in governmental priorities were occurring elsewhere in the nation. As William Chambliss summarized, "For the first time in history, state and municipal governments are spending more money on criminal justice than education."[48]

Moreover, as Figure 3.3 illustrates, these dramatic increases in expenditures on criminal justice functions that occurred throughout the 1980s and 1990s, that were matched by even more dramatic increases in the numbers of persons who were incarcerated in the nation's federal and state prisons, were not driven by corresponding increases in the numbers of arrests that occurred over the same period. In fact, in terms of sheer percentage increases, growth in expenditures (154%) and numbers of prisoners (228%) increased over 10 times more than the added number of arrests (13%). Clearly, the rapid rise in the monies allocated to criminal justice and the skyrocketing numbers of people placed in prison reflected a shift in governmental priorities and a choice about how to respond to crime, rather than an accommodation or response to changes in the numbers of persons who were being apprehended.

The high fiscal priority given to correctional interests and needs reflected a significant level of governmental influence. Indeed, the "crime control industry" had grown so large and powerful during these years that it became "virtually immune from the budgetary cuts experienced by other public services." Moreover, the representatives of this industry had become highly skilled at "propaganda, politicking and arm twisting," and law enforcement, corrections officers groups, and crime industry lobbyists were able to preserve and expand government expenditures even as budgets were shrinking during difficult economic times.[49]

Nowhere was the effectiveness of this kind of political influence clearer than in California, where the correctional officers' union funded one of the state's largest political action committees.[50] In addition to influencing individual political campaigns, the correctional officers' union was responsible for almost single-handedly funding and promoting a statewide *victims' movement* that, since its inception, pressured the legislature to enact longer prison sentences for a wide range of crimes. In addition, the union became directly involved in campaigning and providing economic support for the successful effort to pass California's expansive "three strikes" initiative, enacting a law that would add tens of thousands of prisoners to the state's already overcrowded prison system.[51]

Thus, powerful and sophisticated interest groups emerged during this period with the desire and ability to promote punitive correctional policies. Moreover, they often functioned independently of the dimensions of the crime problem that the policies they proposed supposedly were designed to solve. That is, these groups advocated tougher criminal laws and prison sentences even during periods when crime rates decreased, leading one commentator to observe that "the desire for punishment seems to have taken on a life of its own."[52] But the decoupling of the demand for imprisonment from the actual rising or falling of crime rates was just one feature of this newfound enthusiasm for imprisonment that continued through the 1990s to the present.

THE CLIMATE OF HARSH PUNISHMENT

The unprecedented growth in the prison population during the last quarter of the 20th century was both a cause and an effect of the general atmosphere of punitiveness that arose during these same years. The rapid expansion of the prison system and the skyrocketing incarceration rates of the 1980s and 1990s changed correctional norms and modified what many citizens regarded as tolerable—even necessary—levels of prison pain. The growth of the prison system also reflected a growing public and political enthusiasm for punitive crime control policies. Prison policies and criminal justice decision making were significantly affected by this new emphasis on harsh punishment at the expense of most other considerations.

For example, when a national crime bill (variously termed the *Violent Crime Control and Law Enforcement Act* or the *Omnibus Crime Bill*) was introduced in early 1994, thoughtful critics worried that it focused far too much on punishment and too little on prevention. As one of them put it, "The worst feature of the bill is . . . the stunning imbalance between punishment and prevention. [It is] as if the bill's framers had learned nothing from the prison explosion of the past twenty years. . . ."[53] As the bill neared passage, some newspapers editorialized that the proposed law was "being shorn of its more humane measures while its most draconian provisions remain intact."[54] The editorial writers worried that "if the efforts to strip justice and prevention from the legislation succeed, this bill could become downright hazardous to the criminal justice system while doing relatively little to improve public safety."[55] Yet, even though the bill passed the House with its most punitive provisions intact, its sponsors returned just a few months later, calling for the repeal of the few "progressive" provisions that had remained in the bill and seeking to substitute even harsher measures in their place.[56]

The pattern of ratcheting up the punitiveness of crime-related legislation became routine during this era. With each passing year, from the mid-1970s on, the political climate became increasingly punishment oriented, and lawmakers focused more on delivering prison pain than on addressing the social and economic causes of crime that had been the focus of national policy a mere decade earlier.[57] At one level, these changes in criminal justice policy brought about the increased incarceration rates and growing amount of prison overcrowding that I described earlier in this chapter. However, at a deeper level, values and judgments about the severity of state-sanctioned prison pain also were being transformed. The sense of measured proportionality that had once been brought to bear on punishment-related questions in our society began to be transformed. The balance between the need for public safety and standards of humane treatment was placed in serious jeopardy.

For example, versions of three-strikes laws that resulted in a lifetime of incarceration—sometimes even for a minor or trivial offense, so long as it had been preceded by at least two other felony convictions—were hastily enacted in many states without any meaningful public debate about their expected benefits or potential long-term negative consequences.[58] Like the citizen panics that preceded the passage of "habitual criminal" legislation in the 1920s and some of the "career criminal" statutes in the late 1960s,[59] three-strikes laws tended to be politically expedient and anecdote driven rather than carefully crafted responses to increasing crime rates among certain kinds of repeat offenders.

As I noted earlier, the infliction of pain appeared to become an end in itself. There were numerous examples of this phenomenon. The sheriff of one major city in the United States won widespread acclaim for publicly boasting that he ran "a very bad jail," proudly declaring himself "the meanest sheriff in America,"[60] and becoming a leading exponent of "the 'make 'em miserable' school of incarceration. . . ."[61] Punishments previously abandoned as inhumane were reintroduced, sometimes proposed as innovative "reforms." In this vein, several states announced the return of "chain gangs" in which prisoners were chained together and set to work on roadsides. The state of Alabama, which only a few years before had supposedly reformed its antiquated and brutal correctional system in response to protracted federal litigation,[62] initiated the practice in the mid-1990s.[63] Several other states quickly followed suit.[64]

Other outmoded practices returned in modernized form. For example, the once-condemned practice of long-term solitary confinement was merged with more sophisticated corrections technology to create so-called *supermax* prison units. Prison systems around the country began to subject prisoners to extreme levels of isolation and "stark sterility and unremitting monotony" that one federal judge in California characterized as pressing "the outer bounds of what most humans can psychologically tolerate."[65] Even after another federal judge in Texas concluded that these kinds of units deprived prisoners "of even the most basic psychological needs," and created "a frenzied and frantic state of human despair and desperation,"[66] states continued to build them. This approach to managing prisoners became broadly popular with corrections officials, even though humanitarian concerns had prompted the nation to abandon it a century earlier.[67] As Michael Tonry accurately put it as the 1990s came to a close, "we live in a repressive era when punishment policies that would be unthinkable in other times and places are not only commonplace but also are enthusiastically supported by public officials, policy intellectuals, and much of the general public."[68]

PRISON FAILURE BEGETS PRISON GROWTH

The unprecedented reliance on imprisonment and the greatly increased expenditures for the delivery of prison pain during this period were not based on an impressive record of success. There was little to which politicians or correctional policymakers could point that inspired new confidence in the effectiveness of imprisonment as a strategy of crime control. Indeed, one of the unfortunate ironies of this period was that the boundless enthusiasm for policies of imprisonment followed immediately on the heels of a highly publicized and widely accepted declaration that prison rehabilitation programs simply "did not work."[69] It was as if the nation had reached the somewhat surprising conclusion that penal institutions could not possibly accomplish the task to which they had been devoted for nearly a century, and then promptly set about building many more and quickly filling them with unprecedented numbers of prisoners. Although I argue later that the "nothing works" critique of prison was seriously overdrawn, it was a curious premise on which to launch a national program of prison construction and mass incarceration.

Moreover, this was hardly the first time that the effectiveness of prison had been questioned. *Recidivism*—the rate at which prisoners reoffend after their release—typically has been used as a key indicator of prison success or failure. Historically, recidivism rates have *never* generated much optimism about the effectiveness of prison to reduce future crime.[70] The latter part of the 20th century—when the dramatic increases in the rate of incarceration began and continued to accelerate—was no exception. In fact, recidivism rates not only continued to be very high but also—perhaps because of the simultaneous heightened overcrowding and de-emphasis on rehabilitation— appeared to be getting higher. Yet this was precisely the period during which unprecedented increases in the amount and duration of imprisonment were being advocated and implemented.

For example, in several studies that were based on data collected in the early 1960s—well before the heightened levels of incarceration that would become the norm over the next several decades had come about— recidivism rates ranged between 35% and 46%.[71] In a study done at the start of the 1970s, researchers reported that 51% of their original sample of close to a thousand medium-security prisoners were reincarcerated within 36 months after their release.[72] Although approximately the same figure was reported in the 1980s, when the Bureau of Justice Statistics indicated that "over a 20 year period, an estimated *half* of all releases will return to prison, most in the first 3 years after release,"[73] this figure seemed to be a bit of an underestimate (unless the report meant to average the recidivism estimates collected over the preceding 20-year period). In fact, a large-scale U.S. Justice Department–sponsored study that tracked postprison outcomes for approximately one hundred thousand prisoners who had been released in 1983 found that 62.5% were rearrested within a 3-year period.[74]

During an even more recent period in which incarceration rates already had reached historically high levels, recidivism rates appeared to worsen. One large-scale study focused on the fates of over three hundred thousand persons after they had been discharged in 1994 from prisons in some 15 different states where they had been housed.[75] The study found that 67.5% were rearrested during the 3-year period following their release. Comparing this figure unfavorably with the 1983 study cited previously, the authors of the more recent study concluded that "the overall rearrest rate rose significantly" for the 1994 group—persons who were imprisoned when incarceration rates were much higher.[76]

Of course, trends like these are open to multiple interpretations. Although they do not prove conclusively that prisons were doing a progressively worse job over the last several decades, policymakers could not reasonably use them to reach the opposite conclusion either. That is, there was no reason to believe that prisons were becoming more capable of preventing future crimes in a way that had eluded them for the previous 2 centuries. Clearly, then, the urge to imprison was not driven by any convincing evidence that prison would or could effectively reduce future crime by suppressing criminal behavior among persons already punished for having engaged in it. If nothing else, consistently dismal recidivism rates underscored the futility of this approach.

In fact, ironically, if rates of recidivism actually were increasing over the last several decades, then extremely high rates of incarceration might have been a contributing factor. For one, lowering the threshold for incarceration undoubtedly meant that more people were being put in prison for less serious offenses—offenses that in other times would not have resulted in prison sentences. As some researchers have found, when low-risk prisoners are placed in high security prison settings, they are significantly more likely to reoffend than those placed instead in halfway houses.[77] The authors of this study explained the finding by suggesting that low-risk prisoners in particular were likely to manifest a "shift in pro-criminal attitudes and behavior upon exposure to higher-risk [prisoners]" in traditional prison settings.[78] Thus, the failure to properly divert low-risk persons from the prison system "may actually increase the risk of future recidivism."[79]

In addition, the rapid growth in the prison population in the post-1975 era meant that large numbers of persons were exposed to severely overcrowded, often deteriorated living conditions. Although I discuss this issue in more depth in chapters 6 and 7, several issues are worth briefly noting. Many prisoners during this period entered tense, dangerous environments where interpersonal conflicts and violence were commonplace. Prison systems that were overwhelmed with the influx of new inmates were unable to deliver even minimally adequate services. They afforded prisoners few opportunities to participate in basic programming or meaningful daily activities. As a result, many of them served long sentences under conditions of chronic idleness, enduring years of empty, painful imprisonment. For some prisoners, in addition to the way their lack of prison programming compromised employment opportunities once they were released, poor treatment at the hands of prison authorities created frustration and resentment that they found difficult to relinquish, even after they entered free society.

The unprecedented rates of incarceration and high levels of overcrowding helped to establish what Malcolm Feeley and Jonathan Simon described as a "new penology," one that shifted the focus away from individual prisoners and onto "actuarial consideration of aggregates."[80] Feeley and Simon suggested that prison officials and policymakers had ceased considering the individual needs of criminal offenders and instead began to think much like insurance actuaries—predicting risks, probabilities, and likely outcomes for the huge populations of prisoners that they now managed. Under the new scheme, concerns that had dominated the "old penology"—ways that the prison might go about furthering the social and personal transformation of inmates—were replaced by correctional programs aimed at "managing costs and controlling dangerous populations. . . ."[81] As one New York correctional officer described it, the new penology had practical, day-to-day consequences for officers and inmates alike:

> Rehabilitation is somebody else's business. Or, more correctly, nobody's. Federal grants to inmates for post-secondary education were banned in 1995, and other programs at Sing Sing have been pared so drastically that "there isn't much left to cut," a prison administrator said. In practical terms, this leaves inmates with nothing much to do all day, and guards with no mission except to enforce the rules. . . .[82]

Policies that placed unprecedented numbers of persons in prison, of course, eventually placed unprecedented numbers of them on parole. Parole agencies that once sought to facilitate the reintegration of ex-convicts back into free society and monitor their postprison adjustment underwent a dramatic transformation as well. For example, in California in the 1970s—before a policy of mass imprisonment was implemented in the state—parole agents were expected to supervise an average caseload of approximately 45 parolees. By the late 1990s that figure had increased to an average of 80 parolees per agent.[83] It is not surprising that the state's parole authority concluded that this increased caseload had "significantly diminished the quality of parole supervision, as evidenced by the reduced number of monthly contacts between agents and parolees."[84]

But reduced monthly contacts were just a small part of the overall deterioration in parole supervision. In fact, the mission of parole itself was modified, in part in response to an overwhelming number of parolees who simply could not be adequately supervised given the scarcity of available resources. Thus, Jonathan Simon also argued that a new model of parole— what he termed *managerial parole*—arose in the mid-1970s that was consistent with his broader vision of the emerging new penology. No longer focused on "reintegrating the offender into the 'normal' modes of social life,"[85] it became instead "a system that has shifted from supervision to the mechanics of adjudication and punishment."[86]

The transformation came at an especially inopportune time. The failure of the prison system itself to prepare prisoners for release increased the importance of meaningful parole supervision for persons attempting to reintegrate into free society. As Simon and others have observed, it was a challenge that the parole system was unable to meet. Thus, one legislative study in California concluded that "tens of thousands of parolees each year are being released unprepared for a return to society, then committing violations of their conditions of parole that soon lead to their return to prison. . . ."[87] In fact, nowadays in California, more persons are returned to prison through the process of parole revocation than are sent by the criminal courts—approximately 90,000 parole violators per year.[88]

As I argue later in this book, the criminogenic effects of long-term incarceration in the typical American prison now may make parole failure a virtual inevitability for many ex-convicts. In addition, it appears that an increasingly high percentage of persons are returned to prison for technical "violations" that are noncriminal in nature. Thus, what amount to very long—indeed, in some cases, lifelong—prison sentences are "being served on the installment plan," as sociologist Sheldon Messinger put it.[89] In Nils Christie's estimation, "Now it is not necessarily the original crime which brings them back to prison. It is something in their life-style. . . ."[90] Here, too, there is much evidence that the criminal justice system has simply been overwhelmed by the increased workload and now lacks both the resources and the mandate to provide much help. Thus, the "lifestyle" problems for which persons are being returned to prison are ones for which, in earlier times, they might have received assistance, counseling, or tolerance rather than punishment. The consequences of these changes have been significant. For example, 60% of all California parolees are now returned to prison for parole violations before they can complete the terms of their parole.[91]

THE BENEFITS AND BURDENS OF MASS IMPRISONMENT

Whatever the origins of increasingly harsh prison policies and the unprecedented rates of incarceration to which they led—origins that seem more political than psychological in nature—there has been much debate over whether mass imprisonment has "worked." As one commentator put it, the most optimistic spin that could be given on the so-called *penal harm movement* that spurred the massive increase in incarceration levels is that it "promises that the infliction of suffering works to make us safer."[92] To be sure, there are some analysts who have suggested that this very promise—that increased prison pain would reduce crime—has been kept. That is, "recent history provides a prima facie case for the effectiveness of prisons,"[93] and the policy of increasing prison pain, essentially, is a success.

To understand why some observers might have arrived at this conclusion requires a discussion of the causes of the "crime problem" to which mass imprisonment supposedly was a solution. Some conservative scholars blamed the high levels of crime in the 1960s on allegedly "liberal" or lenient sentencing policies, sometimes attributed to Warren Court-era judges whom they characterized as "soft on crime." Arguing that the failure to punish harshly enough had created a lawless atmosphere in which criminals had ceased to fear the criminal justice system, these analysts praised the increased punitiveness of the new approach. Correspondingly, then, they attributed decreases in crime rates that occurred in the 1990s to the success of the "get tough" movement and the long prison sentences it brought about. In fact, some have gone so far as to characterize this alleged cause-and-effect relationship not only as a claim made by "many conservative policy analysts" as might be expected but as a manifestation of "psychological science."[94]

Yet, these conclusions are contradicted by a number of critical facts. For example, whatever other forces may have contributed to the sharp rise in crime rates in the 1960s, simple demographics—rather than social policy— appear to have played the most significant role. The first cohort of the "Baby Boom" generation began reaching its crime-prone years (ages 15–25) in 1963, when crime rates began to spike, and the last cohort matured out of these vulnerable years in approximately 1980.[95] Thus, this demographic trend, rather than the operation of any allegedly liberal social or judicial policies, likely accounted for a significant portion of the 1960s and 1970s crime wave. A downturn in crime at some point over the subsequent decades would have been expected as a simple function of the shift in age distributions.

In addition, there is no evidence that the much tougher treatment of criminals that followed the supposed permissiveness of the 1960s had any direct, immediate impact on crime rates. Thus, during at least the first part of the period in which tougher sentencing laws were enacted and the incarceration rate in the United States increased so dramatically—1970 to 1987—FBI Index crimes actually rose by 143%.[96] In California—one of the states that led the nation in prison construction and the expansion of its prisoner population—the benefits of such massive increases in prison pain were anything but clear. As one analyst concluded,

> California's experience after this feverish decade of prison construction has profound implications for the rest of the United States. California is a trend-setter. And the trend discovered in California? The biggest prison-building program in the history of the world had very little to do with the crime rate. It had a lot to do with politics. . . .[97]

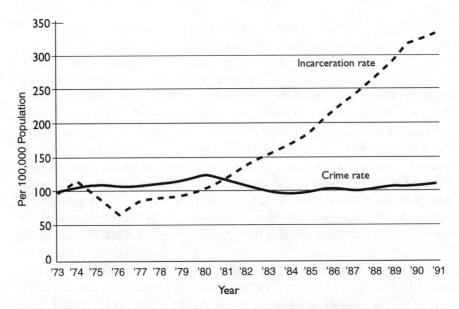

Figure 3.4. California's crime rate versus imprisonment rate (indexed to 1973). From *Urban America: Policy Choices for Los Angeles and the Nation* (p. 191, Figure 10), by J. Steinberg, D. Lyon, and M. Vaiana (Eds.), in "Crime and Punishment in California: Full Cells, Empty Pockets, and Questionable Benefits," by J. Petersilia, 1992, Santa Monica, CA: Rand. Adapted with permission of the Rand Corporation and Joan Petersilia.

This observation appears to be borne out by the trends that are graphed in Figure 3.4. Two things are clear from this comparison of crime rates and separate rates of imprisonment. The first is that the increase in the rate at which Californians sent convicted felons to prison was not driven by any dramatic increase in the amount of crime with which the state had to contend. The state's crime rate over this period was stable, even as its imprisonment rate soared. Moreover, it is equally clear that dramatic increases in rates of imprisonment—part of the "biggest prison-building program in the history of the world"—had little impact on crime rates, which also remained relatively flat, even after so many additional people were sent into the California prison system.

Of course, there was a consistent decrease in the overall crime rate in the United States that began early in the 1990s and continued for most of the decade. As one commentator put it, "the period from 1990 to 1997 represents the closest thing to a sustained decline in crime, or a 'crime bust' that the United States has experienced in more than fifty years."[98] Although some portion of the modest reductions in the overall crime rates that occurred in the 1990s no doubt resulted from the extraordinary increase in incarceration rates and the sheer number of persons placed in prison over a relatively short period, several factors caution against concluding that this policy of inflicting prison pain was a clear success.

For one, there was little evidence that violent crime—what most members of the public believed they were paying dearly to prevent or reduce—was very significantly affected by the extraordinary increases in the rate or amount of imprisonment. For example, several researchers who studied the effect of California's skyrocketing increase in the prison population during the 1980s—one they characterized as "without precedent in the statistical record of imprisonment in the Western world"—concluded that although this unprecedented growth had a modest impact on California's overall crime rate, 94% of the estimated reduction was accounted for by decreases in burglary and larceny rather than in violent crime.[99] Nationally, the results appeared to be similar, with no clear evidence that violent crime rates were significantly affected by the higher rates of incarceration and longer prison sentences that began to be implemented at the start of the 1970s.[100] Moreover, through most of the decade of the 1980s, the period in which increases in the incarceration rate were among their largest, there were very significant increases in crime rates. For example, between 1985 and 1990, the rate of violent crime increased approximately 32% at the same time that the incarceration rate increased another 46% above already record levels.[101]

In a recent analysis of these issues, William Spelman used statistical modeling techniques to estimate how much of the reduction in violent crime rates could be attributed to increased incarceration.[102] He concluded that although much of the decrease likely would have occurred anyway, the massive overall increase in incarceration *was* a significant factor that accounted for about 27% of the drop in crime. But note that the scale of reduction in crime was modest compared with the amount of increased incarceration. In comparative terms, an approximate 500% increase in the overall incarceration rate was responsible for no more than about one quarter of the overall decrease in the amount of violent crime (a decrease that, as I show below, was modest in absolute terms as well).

In addition, the decrease in crime that occurred during the 1990s still did not quite return the nation to the levels that had prevailed before the massive increase in incarceration began. For example, the homicide rate began its steady decline in 1991, reaching a level in 1998 that was "lower than any annual rate *since* 1967." Robbery declined in a similar way and reached a level "lower than any experienced *since* 1969."[103] But these late-1960s points of comparison focused on some of the very years during which crime rates supposedly were spiraling out of control, the ones that had precipitated the policies of mass incarceration that were now being declared a success.

Put somewhat differently, by the turn of the 21st century, nearly 2 million persons were incarcerated in the new prisons and jails that had cost tens of billions of dollars to construct over the preceding several decades. Yet, the crime rate reductions of the 1990s about which law enforcement officials were justifiably proud had simply returned the nation to the earlier point from which it began—the "low" crime rates we enjoyed at the end of the 1990s were almost identical to those that had prevailed in the supposedly turbulent, permissive, and liberal 1960s, before the costly and painful policies of mass imprisonment were implemented. Similarly, the nation's homicide rate in the late 1990s finally returned to its late 1960s level, a time when there had been a virtual moratorium on executions and, according to some commentators, "excessive judicial leniency" supposedly was in full swing.[104]

In fact, Spelman noted, "most of the responsibility for the crime drop rests with improvements in the economy, changes in the age structure [of the population], or other social factors."[105] Thus, no consistent, stable reduction in overall crime rates occurred in the United States until the nation's overall economic outlook began to steadily improve in the early 1990s. Among other things, as several economists have observed, the economic boom of the 1990s was deep enough to positively impact young African American men who had little previous job history. These analysts concluded that it was the decrease in unemployment during this period that appeared to be significantly related to the decrease in crime rates.[106]

Indeed, if the 8-year period during which there was unprecedented economic growth and corresponding decreases in unemployment were removed from the crime rate calculations, the unprecedented expansion of the nation's prison system over the last several decades of the 20th century would not have had any obvious effect on overall crime rates. From this perspective, the possibility that the economy may someday return to its pre-1990s condition is reason for concern. Some reports indicate that poverty and unemployment—especially among already economically vulnerable minority groups—have begun to increase, along with a rise in what has been termed deep poverty among African Americans.[107] It is not surprising that the downward trends in the crime rate already have begun to level off. In some areas, for some crimes categories, they may have begun to reverse direction. Yet, the incarceration rate remains at an all-time high.

One final issue is worth considering as I conclude this assessment of the state of the prisons. Economists are practiced at estimating what they term opportunity costs—potential gains that were lost or forfeited from options that were not pursued in lieu of courses of action that were. The opportunity costs of mass incarceration are difficult to calculate with any real precision. However, note that expenditures for state prisons in 1996 reached approxi-

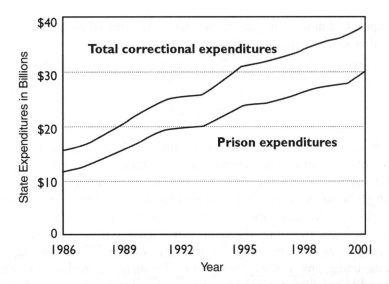

Figure 3.5. Expenditures on corrections and prisons over time. Data from *State Prison Expenditures, 2001* (Bureau of Justice Statistics Special Report NCJ 202949; p. 1), by J. Stephan, June 2004, Washington, DC: U.S. Department of Justice. In the public domain.

mately $24.5 billion, roughly four times the expenditure (in constant dollars) of just a little more than a decade earlier.[108] As Figure 3.5 illustrates, these costs have continued to rise steadily, even through the decade of the 1990s in which, as noted previously, there was a consistent decrease in crime rates. By 2001—at the end of nearly a full decade of declining crime rates—it was costing taxpayers $29.5 billion to maintain the nation's adult state prisons.[109] In theory, at least, some significant portion of these funds could have been used to develop and implement other kinds of crime-reduction programs.

For example, the large sums spent on prison construction and maintaining high rates of incarceration over the last several decades likely came at the expense of alternatives that could have focused instead on things like early childhood intervention, child abuse prevention programs, drug counseling and treatment, community-based counseling programs for at-risk adolescents, enhanced educational and literacy programs to combat delinquency, job training and placement programs, and the like. Or, as Spelman calculated it, the billions of dollars spent on increased levels of incarceration "could provide child care for every family that cannot afford it, or a college education to every high school graduate, or a living-wage to every unemployed youth."[110] Instead, we invested in a vast network of penal institutions that remain significantly overcrowded and continue to be organized around the principle of administering pain rather than delivering rehabilitative services and other kinds of needed assistance.

CONCLUSION

In the modern political economy of prisons, there is now an inelasticity to the relationship between crime and the demand for prisons that is quite unlike anything that exists in the economic world. When the crime rate is stable, the public is told that more prisons are needed to reduce it further; when the rate decreases, more prisons are advocated to ensure that it does not go back up; and when the crime rate begins to rise, so does the claim that prisons are urgently needed to reestablish control. There is simply no scenario under which more prisons is not the answer. Somehow a way must be found to intelligently question this irrational devotion to a policy that has delivered marginal benefits at very substantial cost.

Over the last several decades in which these drastic changes in prison policy were implemented, the public was often misled about the nature and magnitude of the crime problem and misinformed about what could be expected from exclusively pain-based solutions. In fact, as psychologist Carl Clements has pointed out, elected officials continue to exploit crime- and punishment-related issues, citing the very fears that they helped to create.[111] Even those lawmakers who know that these policies are not likely to have any real impact on the crime problem continue to support them because of their powerful electoral cache. Many members of the public, lacking accurate information and without the benefit of serious debates over the human and economic costs of our current policies, in fact have clamored for the draconian laws that politicians still compete with one another to pass. Psychologically informed perspectives—ones based on empirical data and sound theory rather than anecdotes or ideology—are needed to break this counterproductive cycle.

In the next chapter I address several interrelated, problematic policies that have been followed over the last several decades—particularly the way in which reforms in sentencing practices and the intense focus on drug-related crimes have resulted in the disproportionate incarceration of minorities, especially African Americans. It is a powerful cautionary tale about the costs of ignoring insights from modern psychological theory. The consequences of the unquestioning pursuit of these policies for the nation's prison system have been profound. The policies have had a destructive impact not only on the minority prisoners against whom they have been directed but also on their families and on the communities to which they are returned following incarceration.

NOTES

1. Nils Christie, *Limits to Pain* (Oxford, England: Martin Robertson, 1982), 36.
2. In several other articles, I have tried to provide more detail about some of the social and policy-related changes that took place during this period. *See, e.g.,* C. Haney, "Psychology and Prison Pain: Confronting the Coming Crisis in Eighth Amendment Law," *Psychology, Public Policy, and Law* 3 (1997): 499; C. Haney and P. Zimbardo, "The Past and Future of U.S. Prison Policy: Twenty-Five Years After the Stanford Prison Experiment," *American Psychologist* 53 (1998): 709. Some of the flavor of the public and scholarly concern is captured in American Friends Service Committee, *Struggle for Justice: A Report on Crime and Punishment* (New York: Hill & Wang, 1971); George Jackson, *Soledad Brother: The Prison Letters of George Jackson* (New York: Coward-McCann, 1970); Jessica Mitford, *Kind and Usual Punishment: The Prison Business* (New York: Knopf, 1973); and Min Yee, *The Melancholy History of Soledad Prison* (New York: Harper's Magazine Press, 1973)
3. D. Glaser, "From Revenge to Resocialization: Changing Perspectives in Combating Crime," *The American Scholar* 40 (1971): 654, 658. On the state of the jails in this era, *see also* Bruce Danto, *Jail House Blues: Studies of Suicidal Behavior in Jail and Prison* (Orchard Lake, MI: Epic, 1973).
4. National Commission on Criminal Justice Standards and Goals, *Task Force Report on Corrections* (Washington, DC: Government Printing Office, 1973), 597.
5. *See, e.g.,* Andrew Scull, *Decarceration: Community Treatment and the Deviant: A Radical View* (Englewood Cliffs, NJ: Prentice-Hall, 1977).
6. *See, e.g.,* Jackson, *Soledad Brother*; Ronald Berkman, *Opening the Gates: The Rise of the Prisoners' Movement* (Lexington, MA: Lexington Books, 1972); Samuel Melville, *Letters from Attica* (New York: Morrow, 1972); Derrick Morrison and Mary-Alice Waters, *Attica: Why Prisoners are Rebelling* (New York: Pathfinder Press, 1972); Eve Pell et al., eds., *Maximum Security: Letters From California's Prisons* (New York: E. P. Dutton, 1972).
7. For example, by the time George Jackson and several other prisoners and guards were killed in a failed escape attempt inside San Quentin Prison, Jackson already was a public figure and published author (*see* Jackson, *Soledad Brother*). The tragic events at San Quentin were covered extensively by the national and international news media. See e.g., "Death in San Quentin," *Time Magazine*, September 6, 1971, p. 17. Just 2 weeks later, *Time's* coverage of the bloody riot that occurred in New York's Attica Prison ended with this observation: "The troubles at Attica dramatize again the fact that much of the U.S. prison system is still inhumane and brutalizes rather than rehabilitates. The ills are not remedied by riots. The public has every reason to be outraged by the beatings, or as in last month's smaller but more violent uprising at San Quentin, the killing of guards. Yet, given the persistence of dehumanizing conditions in so many prisons, it is perhaps lucky that there have not been more Attica-scale rebellions." "Uprising in Attica," *Time Magazine*, September 20, 1971, p. 12, 14. *Time's* cover story the next week, "The Bitter Lessons of Attica," contained

graphic photos as well as several articles about the events that had shocked the nation, including "War at Attica: Was There No Other Way?" *Time Magazine*, September 27, 1971, p. 18. In fact, the Attica riot was so widely publicized that the report of the governmental committee investigating its causes appeared the next year as a book: New York State Special Commission on Attica, *Attica: The Official Report of the New York State Special Commission on Attica* (New York: Praeger, 1972).

8. *See, e.g.*, Herman Badillo and Milton Haynes, *A Bill of No Rights: Attica and the American Prison System* (New York: Dutton, 1972); Tom Wicker, *A Time to Die* (New York: New York Times Books, 1975).

9. Before the advent of prisoners' rights litigation, many Southern prisons subjected their charges to "unspeakable cruelty and inadequate" resources amidst an entrenched plantation-like culture. M. Feeley and V. Swearingen, "The Prison Conditions Cases and the Bureaucratization of American Corrections: Influences, Impacts and Implications," *Pace Law Review* 24 (2004): 433, 437. Feeley and Swearingen were right to suggest that judicial reform of these institutions required "not just improvement but a reconceptualization of the [Southern prison] enterprise" and also were right to suggest that many federal judges took appropriate steps to accomplish exactly that. Ibid.

10. Among the landmark cases on which they worked, the most important and best known is Pugh v. Locke, 406 F. Supp. 318 (1976). For a description of the litigation and the changes in the Alabama prisons it brought about, *see* Larry Yackle, *Reform and Regret: The Story of Federal Judicial Involvement in the Alabama Prison System* (New York: Oxford University Press, 1989).

11. R. Fowler, "Sweeping Reforms Ordered in Alabama Prisons," *APA Monitor* 7 (April 1976): 1, 15, 15.

12. For discussions of some of the thinking that went into this work, *see* Craig Haney and Philip Zimbardo, "The Socialization into Criminality: On Becoming a Prisoner and a Guard," in *Law, Justice, and the Individual in Society: Psychological and Legal Issues*, ed. June Louin Tapp and Felice J. Levine (New York: Holt, Rinehart, & Winston, 1977); T. Hilliard, "The Black Psychologist in Action: A Psychological Evaluation of the Adjustment Center Environment at San Quentin Prison," *Journal of Black Psychology* 2 (1976): 75–82. For several cases outside of Alabama in which psychologists collaborated with lawyers in litigation focusing on prison conditions in these early years, *see* Spain v. Procunier, 408 F. Supp. 534 (1976), *aff'd* in part, *rev'd* in part, 600 F.2d 189 (9th Cir. 1979); Hotowit v. Ray (E.D. Wash. 1980), 682 F.2d 1237 (9th Cir. 1982); Toussaint v. McCarthy, 553 F. Supp. 1365 (N.D. Cal. 1983); 722 F.2d 1490 (9th Cir. 1984); Dohner v. McCarthy, 635 F. Supp. 408 (C.D. Cal. 1986).

13. Haney and Zimbardo, *The Past and Future*, 712.

14. Katherine Beckett does an excellent job of analyzing them. *See* Katherine Beckett, *Making Crime Pay: Law and Order in Contemporary American Society* (New York: Oxford University Press, 1997). *See also* C. Haney, "Riding the Punishment Wave: On the Origins of Our Devolving Standards of Decency," *Hastings Women's Law Journal* 9 (1998): 27.

15. Andrew von Hirsch, *Doing Justice: The Choice of Punishment* (New York: Hill & Wang, 1976).

16. Lawrence Friedman, *Crime and Punishment in American History* (New York: Basic Books, 1993), 316.

17. Melvin Gutterman, "The Contours of Eighth Amendment Prison Jurisprudence: Conditions of Confinement," *Southern Methodist University Law Review* 48 (1995): 373, 374, citing several books, films, and speeches that made similar characterizations over the last several decades.

18. Francis Cullen, "Assessing the Penal Harm Movement," *Journal of Research in Crime and Delinquency* 32 (1995): 338, 338.

19. "Yesterday's 'Baby Boom' is Overcrowding Today's Prisons," *US News & World Report*, March 1, 1976, p. 65, 65.

20. P. Finn, "Prison Crowding: The Response of Probation and Parole," *Crime & Delinquency* 30 (1984): 141.

21. S. Gottfredson, "Institutional Responses to Prison Crowding," *New York University Review of Law and Social Change* 12 (1983–1984): 259, 259, 260.

22. *National Law Journal*, 10 August 1987, p. 50.

23. Ibid., 50.

24. Bureau of Justice Statistics, *Prisoners in 1987* (Washington, DC: U.S. Department of Justice, April 1988), 5, table 8.

25. M. Zalman, "Sentencing in a Free Society: The Failure of the President's Crime Commission to Influence Sentencing Policy," *Justice Quarterly* 4 (1987): 545, 553 (reference omitted).

26. Based on data cited in Diana Gordon, *The Justice Juggernaut: Fighting Street Crime, Controlling Citizens* (New Brunswick, NJ: Rutgers, 1990), 16.

27. Ibid.

28. G. Newman, "Punishment and Social Practice: On Hughes's *The Fatal Shore*," *Law and Social Inquiry* 13 (1988): 337, 346 (footnote omitted).

29. See J. Brodeur, "Truth in Sentencing," *Behavioral Sciences & the Law* 7 (1989): 25, 35; Nils Christie, *Crime Control as Industry: Towards Gulags, Western Style?* (London: Routledge, 1993), 28.

30. See, e.g., "Incarceration in U.S. Reaches Record Level," *San Francisco Chronicle*, 13 September 1994, p. A6, cols. 5–6.

31. "Prison, Jail Rolls Increase 113% in 10 Years," *San Francisco Chronicle*, August 19, 1996, p. A6, cols. 3–6.

32. The rate has continued to rise through the early years of the 21st century. For example, between June 30, 2003, and June 30, 2004 (the last date for which figures are available), the incarceration rate rose from 716 to 726 persons per 100,000. See Paige Harrison and Alan Beck, *Prison and Jail Inmates at Midyear 2004* [NCJ-208801], (Washington, DC: Bureau of Justice Statistics, 2005).

33. Internationally, during the 1990s, the United States and Russia were the world's leaders in incarceration rates. From time to time, especially during periods of economic and political unrest in Russia, the United States was a close second.

But in the closing years of the decade, the United States established itself as the clear leader in this dubious category.

34. George Camp and Camille Camp, *The Corrections Yearbook—1988* (South Salem, NY: Criminal Justice Institute, 1988).

35. Alexis Durham, "Managing the Costs of Modern Corrections: Implications of Nineteenth-Century Privatized Prison-Labor Programs," *Journal of Criminal Justice* 17 (1989): 441, 442. *See also* George Camp and Camille Camp, *The Corrections Yearbook—1987* (South Salem, NY: Criminal Justice Institute, 1987); Camp and Camp, *The Corrections Yearbook—1988.*

36. D. Freed, "Federal Sentencing in the Wake of Guidelines: Unacceptable Limits on the Discretion of Sentences," *Yale Law Journal* 101 (1992): 1681, 1700, n. 2.

37. E. Koren, "Status Report: State Prisons and the Courts—January 1, 1992," *The National Prison Project Journal* 7(1) (1992): 13.

38. *See, e.g.*, A. King, "The Impact of Incarceration on African American Families: Implications for Practice," *Families in Society: The Journal of Contemporary Human Services* 74 (1993): 145.

39. Bureau of Justice Statistics, *Sourcebook of Criminal Justice Statistics, 1996* (Washington, DC: U.S. Department of Justice, 1996).

40. Marc Mauer, *More Young Black Males Under Correctional Control in U.S. Than in College* (Washington, DC: The Sentencing Project, 1990).

41. See T. Flanagan, D. Clark, D. Aziz, and B. Szelest, "Compositional Changes in a Long-Term Prisoner Population: 1956–89," *The Prison Journal* 80 (1990): 15.

42. These data are contained in a number of statistical reports compiled by the Data Analysis Unit of the California Department of Corrections entitled "Historical Trends, California Department of Corrections," summarizing trends over 20-year periods, beginning with 1976 forward. They may be accessed electronically at http://www.cdc.state.ca.us/pdf/hist00.pdf.

43. Many of these issues are discussed at length in Nancy Walker, Michael Senger, Francisco Villarruel, and Angela Arboleda, *Lost Opportunities: The Reality of Latinos in the U.S. Criminal Justice System* (Washington, DC: National Council of La Raza, 2004).

44. Housing Inventory and Population Impact Task Force, *Prison Overcrowding: A Plan for Housing Felons Through FY 1986/87* (Sacramento, CA: California Department of Corrections, 1979), iv.

45. Ibid., iv (emphasis added).

46. *See, e.g.*, F. Butterfield, "New Prisons Cast Shadow over Higher Education," *New York Times*, April 12, 1995, p. A21; Hallye Jordan, "'96 Budget Favors Prison Over College; '3 Strikes' to Eat Into Education Funds," *San Jose Mercury News*, July 8, 1995, p. 1A.

47. *San Jose Mercury News*, August 8, 1989, p. 6A, col. 1.

48. William Chambliss, "Policing the Ghetto Underclass: The Politics of Law and Law Enforcement," *Social Problems* 41 (1994): 177, 183.

49. Ibid., 191.

50. It contributed twice as much money to political campaigns in the early 1990s as the state's teachers' association (which had 10 times as many members). It

also provided the single largest financial contribution in several consecutive gubernatorial election campaigns, prompting the union president to boast in 1992, "we think we put [the governor] over the top." V. Schiraldi, "The Undue Influence of California's Prison Guards' Union: California's Correctional–Industrial Complex," *In Brief* (Center on Juvenile and Criminal Justice, October 1994), 2.

51. Ibid.
52. S. McConville, "Prisons Held Captive," *Contemporary Psychology* 34 (1989): 928, 928.
53. E. Currie, "What's Wrong With the Crime Bill?" *The Nation*, January 31, 1994, p. 118.
54. Editorial, "Is There Room for Justice in the Crime Bill?" *San Francisco Chronicle*, July 22, 1994, p. A22, cols. 1–2.
55. Ibid.
56. This, even though "Clinton and his aides argue that Republicans, who now denounce the crime bill as social spending pork, voted for it in April, when the House passed its version of the legislation. . . ." See Ann Devroy and Kenneth Cooper, "White House Works to Revive Crime Bill," *San Francisco Chronicle*, August 13, 1994, p. A3.
57. There were three separate presidential commissions assembled in the late 1960s to address a wide range of crime-related issues. They each concluded that crime needed to be addressed through a sustained effort to improve the social and economic plight of the nation's disadvantaged. Thus, the President's Commission on Law Enforcement and Administration of Justice filed a lengthy report in 1968 on the "challenge of crime in a free society" and recommended "eliminating social conditions closely associated with crime." President's Commission on Law Enforcement and Administration of Justice, *The Challenge of Crime in a Free Society* (New York: Avon Books, 1968), 40. A second commission focused on the causes of civil unrest—primarily, race riots—that had plagued the nation. It emphasized the role of persistent race-based disadvantage and discrimination, the decay of the inner cities, and the racially insensitive and at times provocative policies followed in parts of the criminal justice system (especially by the police). *See* Otto Kerner, *Report of the National Advisory Committee on Civil Disorders* (New York: Bantam Books, 1968). The third and final commission, the National Commission on the Causes and Prevention of Violence, began its report by noting, "the way in which we can make the greatest progress toward reducing violence in America is by taking the actions necessary to improve the conditions of family and community life for all who live in our cities, and especially for the poor who are concentrated in the ghetto slums." National Commission on the Causes and Prevention of Violence. *To Establish Justice, to Insure Domestic Tranquility, Final Report* (Washington, DC: Government Printing Office, 1969), xxi.
58. For example, see V. Sze, "A Tale of Three Strikes: Slogan Triumphs Over Substance as Our Bumper-Sticker Mentality Comes Home to Roost," *Loyola of Los Angeles Law Review* 28 (1995): 1047. Moreover the laws were retained despite evidence that they contained a host of flaws. For example, one legal

commentator summarized the status of three strikes by concluding that it "may not be living up to its expectations." He noted the "glaring problems and severe inequalities in sentencing" that resulted in violent and nonviolent offenders being treated in much the same way. In addition, he observed that "African Americans, in particular, appear to be hard hit by such disproportionate sentencing." Finally, he characterized the way three-strikes laws treated juvenile offenses as the equivalent of adult convictions as "inherently unfair because juvenile cases do not carry the protection of a trial by jury." H. Gee, "New Paradigms of Criminal Justice for the Twenty-First Century: A Review Essay," *Ohio Northern University Law Review* 27 (2000): 29, 32–33 (footnotes omitted).

59. R. Kramer, "From 'Habitual Criminals' to 'Career Criminals': The Historical Construction and Development of Criminal Categories," *Law and Human Behavior* 6 (1982): 273.

60. Joe Arpaio, the sheriff of Phoenix, Arizona, also took the unusual step of "deputizing" thousands of citizens (including the state's governor)—many of whom were armed—to serve as his "standing posse." He confined many of his prisoners in a facility that intentionally inflicted substandard—by some accounts, barely tolerable—conditions of confinement. S. Mydans, "Hard Time: What We Have Here Is a Failure to Tolerate," *San Jose Mercury News*, March 7, 1995, p. 9A, cols. 1–5.

61. *See, e.g.*, "Tough Arizona Sheriff Stirs Inmates' Enmity," *San Francisco Chronicle*, May 27, 1996, p. D1, cols. 1–2. "Forget the Bastille. With jails in dozens of communities around the country facing unprecedented shortages of beds, [the sheriff's] 'Tent City' solution has become a modern-day symbol of the 'make 'em miserable' school of incarceration. . . ."

62. *See, e.g.*, J. Conrad, "From Barbarism Toward Decency: Alabama's Long Road to Prison Reform," *Journal of Research in Crime and Delinquency* 26 (1989): 307; Larry Yackle, *Reform and Regret: The Story of Federal Judicial Involvement in the Alabama Prison System* (New York: Oxford University Press, 1989).

63. R. Bragg, "Chain Gangs to Return to Roads of Alabama," *New York Times*, March 26, 1995, p. 9, cols. 1–6.

64. For example, "Like Alabama and Arizona earlier this year, Florida is resurrecting the practice of putting prison inmates in leg irons to work under armed guard along roadsides." Although Florida and Arizona declined to follow Alabama's practice of also chaining their prisoners together on the work crews, they were quick to point out that the decision was not reached on the basis of humanitarian concerns. Rather, as one department of corrections official explained, "You can get more work done if people are not chained together." M. Navarro, "Florida Prisons to Revive Using Chain Gangs—But With Limits," *San Francisco Chronicle*, November 21, 1995, p. A7.

65. Madrid v. Gomez, 889 F. Supp. 1146 (N. D. Cal. 1995), at 1267. *See also* C. Haney, "Infamous Punishment: The Psychological Effects of Isolation," *National Prison Project Journal* 8 (1993): 3, 3; C. Haney and M. Lynch, "Regulating Prisons of the Future: A Psychological Analysis of Supermax and Solitary Confinement," *New York Review of Law & Social Change* 23 (1997): 477; M. Isikoff, "Hard Time: The Mission at Marion; Federal Prison Revives Debate

on How to Handle Incorrigible Felons," *Washington Post*, May 28, 1991, p. A1, col. 1.

66. Ruiz v. Johnson, 37 F. Supp.2d 855 (S.D. Texas 1999), 913.

67. A number of states experimented with long-term solitary confinement in the 19th century, but abandoned its use because of its harmful psychological effects. By the end of the century, U.S. Supreme Court Justice Miller could summarize a hundred years of experience with solitary since the first cells were constructed at the Walnut Street Jail in Philadelphia this way: "There were serious objections to it . . . and solitary confinement was found to be too severe." In re Medley, 134 U.S. 160, 168 (1890). Specifically, as Miller recounted,

> A considerable number of the prisoners fell, after even a short confinement, into a semi-fatuous condition, from which it was next to impossible to arouse them, and others became violently insane; others still, committed suicide; while those who stood the ordeal better were not generally reformed, and in most cases did not recover sufficient mental activity to be of any subsequent service to the community.

Id. See also Haney and Lynch, *Regulating Prisons*, 481.

68. M. Tonry, "Rethinking Unthinkable Punishment Policies in America," *UCLA Law Review* 46 (1999): 1751, 1751. In fairness, early in the 21st century the United States Supreme Court did establish one clear limit to the punitive practices that were being used in at least some of the nation's prisons: In Hope v. Pelzer, 536 U.S. 730 (2002), Alabama corrections officers had disciplined a prisoner by painfully handcuffing him to a hitching post, leaving him there in the hot sun for 7 hours, taunting him, denying him water, and refusing to allow him the opportunity to use a toilet. The Court concluded that they had gone too far, and declared this practice unconstitutionally cruel. Chief Justice Rehnquist and Justices Thomas and Scalia dissented.

69. *See, e.g.*, R. Martinson, "What Works? Questions and Answers About Prison Reform," *The Public Interest* 22 (Spring 1974): 22.

70. Recidivism rates vary as a function of the amount of time since release and how, exactly, *reoffending* is defined (i.e., whether a person has simply been re-arrested, returned to prison for reasons that may include parole violations, or actually convicted of a subsequent criminal offense). *See, e.g.*, D. J. van Alstyne and M. A. Gottfredson, "Multidimensional Contingency Analysis of Parole Outcome," *Journal of Research on Crime* 15 (1978): 172; B. Benda, "Predicting Return to Prison Among Adolescent Males: A Comparison of Three Statistics," *Journal of Criminal Justice* 17 (1989): 487. Also, because some prison systems do a better job than others in preparing prisoners for life on the outside and providing them with transitional and support services once released, recidivism rates vary somewhat by jurisdiction. *See, e.g.*, E. Cullen, "The Grendon Reconviction Study," *Issues in Criminological & Legal Psychology* 21 (1994): 103 (citing recidivism rates in England and Wales of 42% and 47%, respectively); S. Turner and J. Petersilia, "Focusing on High-Risk Parolees: An Experiment to Reduce Commitments to the Texas Department of Corrections," *Journal of Research in Crime & Delinquency* [Special Issue: Experimentation in Criminal Justice] 29

(1992): 34. (Recidivism rates for parolees in Texas varied between 18 and 30% over a 1-year period.)

71. *See* Daniel Glaser, *The Effectiveness of a Prison and Parole System* (Indianapolis: Bobbs-Merrill, 1964). Another study based on data from 1962-to-1964 prison releases found an identical rate—35%—of reconviction or "binding over for trial" during a subsequent 5-year period. *See* A. Hopkins, "Imprisonment and Recidivism: A Quasi-Experimental Study," *Journal of Research in Crime and Delinquency* 13 (1976): 13. A third study found that ex-convicts were returned to prison at a higher rate—46%—but over a longer time frame of 8 years. *See* Don Gottfredson and Kelley Ballard, *The Validity of Two Parole Prediction Scales: An Eight Year Follow Up Study* (Vacaville, CA: Institute for the Study of Crime and Delinquency, 1965). A fourth study reported an overall recidivism rate of 39.4%. *See* D. Babst and J. Mannery, "Probation Versus Imprisonment for Similar Types of Offenders: A Comparison by Subsequent Violations," *Journal of Research in Crime and Delinquency* 2 (1965): 60.

72. Gene Kassenbaum, David Ward, and Daniel Wilner, *Prison Treatment and Parole Survival—An Empirical Assessment* (New York: John Wiley, 1971).

73. Bureau of Justice Statistics, *Report to the Nation on Crime and Justice*, 2d ed. (Washington, DC: U.S. Department of Justice, 1988), 111 (emphasis added).

74. Allen Beck and Bernard Shipley, *Recidivism of Prisoners Released in 1983* [special report NCJ 116261] (Washington, DC: Bureau of Justice Statistics, April 1989).

75. Patrick Langan and David Levin, *Recidivism of Prisoners Released in 1994* [special report NCJ 193427] (Washington, DC: Bureau of Justice Statistics, June 2002).

76. Ibid., 11. Again, the rates vary by jurisdiction. In some other studies published in the 1990s, recidivism rates were estimated at considerably higher levels. For example, one Florida study found that upwards of 80% of prisoners recidivated over a 5-year period. L. Smith and R. Akers, "A Comparison of Recidivism of Florida's Community Control and Prison: A Five-Year Survival Analysis," *Journal of Research in Crime & Delinquency* 30 (1993): 267.

77. J. Bonta and L. Motiuk, "The Diversion of Incarcerated Offenders to Correctional Halfway Houses," *Journal of Research in Crime & Delinquency* 24 (1987): 302.

78. Ibid., 312.

79. Ibid.

80. M. M. Feeley and J. Simon, "The New Penology: Notes on the Emerging Strategy of Corrections and Its Implications," *Criminology* 30 (1992): 449, 449.

81. Ibid., 465.

82. T. Conover, "Guarding Sing Sing," *The New Yorker*, April 3, 2000, 54, 59–60.

83. Legislative Analyst's Office, *Reforming California's Adult Parole System*, Sacramento, CA: Author, March 30, 1999), 6.

84. Ibid.

85. Jonathan Simon, *Poor Discipline: Parole and the Social Control of the Underclass, 1890–1990* (Chicago: University of Chicago Press, 1993), 13.

86. Ibid., 201.

87. Legislative Analyst's Office, *Reforming California's Adult Parole System*, 1.

88. This also represented a major shift in the proportion of parolees in the population of persons going to prison in California. For example, in 1978, parole violators represented approximately 8% of the total number of persons who were entering the state's prison system. By 1998, that figure had risen to 71%. J. Petersilia, "Challenges of Prisoner Reentry and Parole in California," *CPRC Brief 12* (June 2000): 1, 2.

89. Christie, *Crime Control as Industry*, 112.

90. Ibid., 114.

91. Legislative Analyst's Office, *Reforming California's Adult Parole System*, 6.

92. Cullen, "Assessing the Penal Harm Movement," 343.

93. William Spelman, "The Limited Importance of Prison Expansion," in *The Crime Drop in America*, ed. Alfred Blumstein and Joel Wallman (New York: Cambridge University Press, 2002), 97. As I emphasize later in this chapter, although Spelman repeated this contention, he did not necessarily endorse it.

94. *See, e.g.*, T. O'Brien and D. Jones, "A Balanced Approach for Corrections Policy Needed," *American Psychologist* 54 (1999): 784, 785. *See also* in direct response, C. Haney, "Ideology and Crime Control," *American Psychologist* 54 (1999): 786.

95. *See, e.g.*, the discussion in Neil Weiner and Marvin Wolfgang, "The Extent and Character of Violent Crime in America, 1969–1982," in *American Violence & Public Policy: An Update on the National Commission on the Causes and Prevention of Violence*, ed. Lynn Curtis (New Haven, CT: Yale University Press, 1985). *See also* the thoughtful analysis of Ted Gurr, who attributed the short-term increase in violent crime in the 1960s and 1970s to a variety of social and economic factors (including the way in which war legitimized violence, rapid urbanization, economic downturns, and demographic shifts), but not to the leniency of the criminal justice system. Ted Robert Gurr, "Historical Trends in Violent Crime: A Critical Review of the Evidence," in *Crime and Justice: An Annual Review of Research*, ed. Michael Tonry and Norval Morris (Chicago: University of Chicago Press, 1981), 295.

96. *See* tables 3 and 4 of Gordon, "The Justice Juggernaut," 207 (based on a comparison of Uniform Crime Reports 1970 and Uniform Crime Reports 1987) *See also* Neil Weiner and Marvin Wolfgang, "The Extent and Character," 230, showing a 69% increase in total violent index crimes, and a 49% increase in total property index crimes, between 1969 and 1982.

97. J. Berthelsen, "Room at the Inn: Prison Population Growth Slows," *California Journal* (June 1992): 291.

98. G. La Free, "Social Institutions and the Crime 'Bust' of the 1990s," *Journal of Criminal Law and Criminology* 88 (1998): 1325, 1325.

99. F. Zimring, G. Hawkins, and H. Isber, "Estimating the Effect of Increased Incarceration on Crime in California," *CPS Brief* 7 (July 1995): 1, 2. Cf. Lori Montgomery, "Prison Population Rises at Record Pace," *San Jose Mercury News*, December 4, 1995, p. 13A.

100. "Violent Crime Rates Remain Unchanged," *San Francisco Chronicle*, April 18, 1995, p. A4.

101. *See, e.g.*, Alfred Blumstein, "Disaggregating the Violence Trends," in *The Crime Drop in America*, ed. Alfred Blumstein and Joel Wallman (New York:

Cambridge University Press, 2002). He noted that the homicide rate peaked in 1980, decreased until 1985, and peaked again in 1991, and that robbery followed a similar oscillating pattern—all the while the rate of incarceration continued to soar.

102. Spelman, "The Limited Importance," 82. Spelman attempted to estimate what he termed the "elasticity of crime due to incarceration"—the percentage drop in crime that was the result of a 1% increase in incarceration.

103. See Blumstein, "Disaggregating the Violence," 13 (emphasis added).

104. *See also* James Fox and Marianne Zawitz, *Homicide Trends in the United States* (Washington, DC: U.S. Department of Justice, December, 1998).

105. Spelman, "The Limited Importance," 125.

106. Richard Freedman and William Rodgers, *Area Economic Conditions and the Labor Market: Outcomes of Young Men in the 1990s Expansion* [Working Paper 7073]. (Cambridge, MA: National Bureau of Economic Research, April 1999). *See also* Richard Freeman, "The Economics of Crime," in *Handbook of Labor Economics*, vol. 3, ed. Orley Ashenfelter and David Card (Amsterdam, Netherlands: Elsevier Science, 1999); J. Doyle, E. Ahmed, and R. Horn, "The Effects of Labor Markets and Income Inequality on Crime: Evidence From Panel Data," *Southern Economic Journal* 65 (1999): 717.

107. *See, e.g.,* S. Dillon, "Report Finds Number of Black Children in Deep Poverty Rising," *New York Times*, March 22, 2005, p. 10.

108. James Stephan, *State Prison Expenditures, 1996* [Bureau of Justice Statistics Special Report NCJ 172211] (Washington, DC: U.S. Department of Justice, August, 1999).

109. James Stephan, *State Prison Expenditures, 2001* [Bureau of Justice Statistics Special Report NCJ 202949] (Washington, DC: U.S. Department of Justice, June 2004).

110. Spelman, "The Limited Importance," 97.

111. C. Clements, "Psychology, Attitude Shifts, and Prison Growth," *American Psychologist* 54 (1999): 785.

4

ATTRIBUTION ERROR
AS CRIME CONTROL
AND PRISON POLICY

Crime is not a "thing." Crime is a concept applicable in certain social situations where it is possible and in the interests of one or several parties to apply it. We can create crime by creating systems that ask for the word. We can extinguish crime by creating the opposite types of systems.

—Nils Christie[1]

Anyone with knowledge of drug-trafficking patterns and of police arrest policies and incentives could have foreseen that the enemy troops in the War on Drugs would consist largely of young, inner-city minority males.

—Michael Tonry[2]

Imposing criminal sanctions is the harshest—and most violent—thing that governments are permitted to do to their citizens. However, the willingness to use such violence—as well as the public's general support for doing so—varies widely from society to society and from one historical period to another. Because crime is a socially constructed concept rather than a category of nature, social and political forces influence how it is defined. They shape the decisions we make about what kinds of behaviors are declared criminal and deemed deserving of state-sanctioned pain. For reasons that I discuss later in this chapter, these same forces render the criminal law especially susceptible to various forms of race-based discrimination.

Throughout the history of the American criminal justice system, race has played a major role in the distribution of prison pain. Simply put, minority suspects, defendants, and prisoners have been treated more harshly than others. Indeed, the forces that create and maintain racial discrimination in the larger society appear to be amplified when people are empowered to make moral judgments designed to deliver pain to others. Moreover, despite the apparent progress that has been made in reducing the pernicious influence of racial discrimination in other areas of American society, race-based disparities continue to plague our system of justice.

In fact, even after controlling for a host of other variables that might account for differential treatment, the data that I review later in this chapter show that patterns of invidious racial discrimination not only persist but, in some ways, also appear to have gotten worse over the last several decades. Combined with the special emphasis that has been placed on prosecuting and imprisoning drug offenders during those decades, these discriminatory patterns mean that the pains of imprisonment have been concentrated in minority communities much more than in others. No serious discussion of whether and how to create more humane prison policies can ignore the implications of these persistent differentials.

THE PUNITIVE LEGACY OF SLAVERY

In American society, racial disparities in the distribution of prison pain have been directed primarily against African Americans.[3] Of course, there is a historical legacy at work here. The disproportionate punishment of African Americans in the United States dates back to the institution of slavery. Before the Civil War, the overwhelming number of Blacks in the American South were slaves who, when they committed crimes, typically were "whipped and sent back to work (or hanged in more serious cases)."[4] Thus, even in the South, the very first prisons housed predominately White prisoners. However, once the Civil War ended and the official system of slavery was dismantled, the subjugation of African Americans took other forms. Indeed, "racial facts powerfully influenced southern penal policy,"[5] and the pattern of racialized imprisonment in the American criminal justice system began in earnest.

The continuing economic marginalization of Blacks and their repeated social dislocation in the United States led to elevated crime rates in many areas of the country. Moreover, Black crime was often met with an exaggerated response on the part of the White-run criminal justice system.[6] The law was used as a weapon to control African Americans in some of the same ways that slavery once had. Southern prisons were soon "fill[ed] with blacks—to be precise, young black men."[7] Eventually, as African American citizens migrated from the South, the pattern of disproportionate imprisonment followed them, spreading first to the East, then to the Midwest, and finally to the Western United States.

Although racial disparities in treatment at the hands of the criminal justice system may have been rooted in the evils of slavery,[8] they did not diminish significantly with the passage of time. For example, in the post–Civil War 1880s, when African Americans constituted approximately 13.1% of the population, Black men made up 28.6% of all state prisoners; more than a century later, that percentage had nearly doubled.[9] Thus, by the start of the 21st century, African Americans made up 46% of all prison inmates. In fact, nearly two thirds of prisoners are persons of color (i.e., Blacks, Latinos, and Native Americans), whereas Whites make up just a little more than one third of the prisoner population in the United States.[10]

African American men were especially adversely affected by the policies of mass imprisonment that began in the mid-1970s.[11] As recently as the early 1990s, the rate of incarceration of White males in the United States still compared favorably with the low rates in most Western European nations, including those in countries regarded as the most progressive and least punitive in the world. When the punitiveness of the American criminal justice system increased in the late 1970s and throughout the 1980s, African American citizens felt its pains most acutely. Although the rate of incarceration for Whites in the United States began to rise in the late 1980s, and eventually surpassed rates in Western European nations, it never came close to the incarceration rate for African Americans. Indeed, by the early 1990s the United States imprisoned African American men at a rate approximately 4 times that of Black men in South Africa.[12]

Some analysts have suggested that the disproportionate number of Black Americans in prison can be explained by their higher arrest rates.[13] However, arrest rates do not fully account for the size of these race-based disparities. For example, according to the Bureau of Justice Statistics, by the end of the 1980s—a decade of truly expansive prison growth—Blacks made up approximately 12% of the U.S. population, accounted for 27% of all arrests, and represented 46% of state prison inmates.[14] Similarly, data collected on prisoners released in the mid-1990s showed that, compared with their White counterparts, Black parolees were more likely to be rearrested (72.9% vs. 62.7%), reconvicted (51.1% vs. 43.3%), returned to prison (54.2% vs. 49.9%), and given a new prison sentence (28.5% vs. 22.6%).[15] In fact, no aspect of criminal justice decision making appears to be exempt from the influence of racial factors, and it is difficult to know what baseline statistic to select as a neutral point from which to calculate race effects.[16]

Of course, *explicitly* race-based decision making has been formally eliminated from the criminal justice system. Yet, even the use of seemingly race-neutral criteria results in these disparate outcomes. For example, although presentence reports rarely contain any information about the race of the offender, as William Sabol noted, "due to the correlation between race and those characteristics deemed to be significant predictors of probation failure, blacks will systematically be incarcerated at higher levels than whites because they will receive probation at lower rates than whites."[17] Similarly, judicial guidelines that were designed to reduce bias by narrowing the discretion that judges may exercise still rely on factors that often are correlated with race.

Thus, completely disentangling the role that racial bias plays in the various subjective judgments that are made within the criminal justice system is difficult, if not impossible, to do. Factors that affect numerous decisions—including perceived social dangerousness, the characteristics that police have come to associate with what have been called *symbolic assailants*,[18] the kind of behavior and evidence that they believe constitute probable cause, the public's view of the relative heinousness of particular kinds of crimes, lawyers' estimates of the likelihood that a defendant will be convicted, jurors' prior beliefs about a defendant's probable legal guilt and level of moral blameworthiness, a judge or prison administrator's estimate of a convicted person's fitness for rehabilitation, a classification officer's assessment of institutional adjustment, and a parole board member's prediction about someone's likely postprison adjustment—are all subject to the subtle influence of racial discrimination. The cumulative effects of these decisions, in turn, directly affect things like arrest rates, the likelihood of being prosecuted, conviction rates, average sentence length, prison classification level, the likelihood of being housed in disciplinary segregation, rates of release from prison, and the probability of being returned to custody.[19]

There are several psychological reasons why racial animosity appears to operate with greater force and effect inside institutions that have been constructed explicitly to deliver pain or punishment. For one, it is easier to punish persons more harshly if they already have been demonized, are perceived as somehow less than fully human, or are regarded as fundamentally "other."[20] The despised status of the criminal class certainly lowers inhibitions against subjecting its members to harsh punishment. Indeed, in a general sense, the increased levels of punishment that our legal system has routinely administered since the mid-1970s seems related to the intense derogation of criminal offenders in media and political discourse over the same period.

In fact, the kind of otherness that attaches to criminal offenders is in some ways analogous to the perception of difference that racial prejudice engenders. Of course, the harsh and painful treatment that the targets of racial prejudice experience in our society comes about as a result of who they are, rather than anything that they have done. But it is easier to believe that people from already disfavored—here, racially stigmatized—groups have done bad things if belief in their inherent "badness" is part of their stigma.[21] Belief in this badness also makes it easier to ignore the possible flaws in the legal processes by which they are blamed and punished for their transgressions. Similarly—because they are more feared and despised to begin with—it may be easier to exaggerate the seriousness of the things that members of already disfavored groups have been found guilty of doing (i.e., to believe that whatever crimes they have committed are per se more heinous whereas, if they were committed by members of one's own group, they would be less so). Finally, because it is more difficult to identify or empathize with persons perceived as "other," dominant group members can more easily distance themselves from the pains of whatever punishment the others receive, even in cases in which such punishment is unjustly administered or excessive in amount.

These psychological mechanisms help to explain how racism in the society at large is intensified in a system designed to deliver punishment and inflict pain. But even these powerful dynamics cannot explain what has happened in the American criminal justice system in recent years. Rapid increases in the rates of incarceration for racial minorities cannot easily be attributed to preexisting (and presumably constant, if not decreasing) levels of racism within the society at large. Thus, the widening of racial disparities in rates of imprisonment suggests that something other than simple racism is at work.

In the remainder of this chapter, I argue that two factors—the de-contextualizing of crime and punishment in general and the heightened focus on particular kinds of drug-related criminal behavior in specific—help to account for these increasing race-based disparities. More specifically, the advent of an offense-based sentencing model that requires context to be ignored in sentencing has intensified the racialization of prison pain. It mandates that whatever racialized differences in life circumstances may contribute to differences in crime rates must be systematically excluded from decisions about who goes to prison and for how long. This practice appears to have worsened racially disparate criminal justice outcomes and disparities in the rates at which African Americans are sent to prison. In a related way, the intense focus on apprehending, prosecuting, and punishing persons for certain kinds of drug offenses also has had a differential effect on minority group members. Here, too, dispositionalizing drug addiction—regarding it as reflecting little more than the free choice of drug users—rather than a predictable and sometimes uncontrollable adaptation to a painful set of social and psychological conditions—has had more drastic consequences for African Americans than others.

CONTEXT AND CRIMINAL LAW: "FUNDAMENTAL ATTRIBUTION ERROR" AS CRIME POLICY

In this section I explore some of the ways in which the *increased* racialization of prison pain over the last several decades has been brought about by the legal codification of a narrow and decontextualized view of crime that—although it is politically endorsed and publicly embraced—

nonetheless is based on an increasingly outmoded model of behavior. The trend toward offense-based sentencing has required courts and other criminal justice decision makers to ignore the life circumstances and contextual causes of the crimes for which long prison sentences are being meted out. Among other things, as I suggest, this has led to the overpunishing of minority defendants by placing disproportionate numbers of them in prison.

In a sense, African American and other minority defendants have been subjected to the worst of two legal worlds. For the most part, the race-based inequities that they suffer in the society at large are barred from being considered at the time of sentencing. That is, they can play no overt role in determining the appropriate magnitude or comparative fairness of the prison terms that African American (or other minority) defendants receive. Yet, the individualistic sentencing processes through which they must pass still permit the influence of racial bias (as evidenced by race-based differentials that plague virtually every criminal justice decision point). In this way, the legal requirement that sentencing calculations be purged of all contextual considerations further institutionalizes what social psychologists have termed the *fundamental attribution error*—systematically discounting the important social, historical and situational determinants of behavior (in this case, criminal behavior) and correspondingly exaggerating the causal role of dispositional or individual characteristics.[22]

There are a number of factors that can cause fundamental attribution error to be increased or intensified. For example, social psychologists know that this error is exacerbated by the tendency to focus on a selective and biased sample of information about the targets of negative attributions. By looking primarily at negative aspects of the behavior of persons we already regard negatively, our bad (and faulty) attributions about them appear to be confirmed and may increasingly harden. Rarely do people voluntarily expose themselves to inconsistent or contradictory data. As observers, we also tend to interact with the targets of our invidious attributions under the same limited set of circumstances. This means that often the apparent consistency in their behavior—which we erroneously attribute to their stable traits—actually is produced by the common situations in which *we* observe them.

All of these processes are exaggerated in the criminal justice system, in which legal decision makers as well as members of the public tend to focus narrowly on a defendant's criminal behavior, with little or no knowledge about the criminogenic circumstances under which it occurred, or the range of noncriminal behavior in which the person has engaged across a wide range of other, different circumstances. The stereotypic, one-dimensional way in which the media depict criminal offenders reinforces this tendency to understand criminality exclusively in terms of the internal pathological characteristics of criminals.

As I discussed in chapter 2, a dominant psychological individualism has influenced criminal justice decision making throughout our nation's history.[23] Until recently, however, it functioned largely as an implicit premise—the causes of crime were presumed to reside inside those who committed them. But the presumption that crime resided only in the character of criminals was subject to at least a partial rebuttal. By providing an opportunity for observers—in this case, legal decision makers—to examine the circumstances and situations that might have played a role in causing the criminal behavior, it was possible to challenge this individualistic assumption.

Thus, in cases in which powerful social forces seemed to have influenced what the defendant did and why, attorneys were permitted to highlight these social contextual factors and argue that they affected the defendant's culpability. Although this was by no means routinely done or often successfully accomplished, those arguments at least had some chance of being taken into account. Judges could (and, on occasion, did) exercise judicial discretion at the time of sentencing to modify levels of punishment accordingly, sometimes avoiding unintended, undeserved, or needlessly harsh or destructive outcomes. Even though so-called extenuating circumstances or social factors in mitigation were irrelevant to guilt determinations or basic assessments of criminal responsibility, they could be brought to bear in reducing the amount of prison pain that was imposed.

However, the sentencing reforms that began in the mid-1970s greatly constricted judicial discretion and eliminated the opportunity for social context to be considered at all in these kinds of legal proceedings. Whatever else was accomplished by excluding what Nils Christie termed "the whole question of social justice"[24] from the sentencing calculus, this change essentially institutionalized fundamental attributional error in the criminal justice system. Thus, one of the very few opportunities to explicitly assess the situational factors and social forces that might have influenced a criminal defendant's behavior was eliminated—formally deemed irrelevant to the legal decisions that were being made about blameworthiness and punishment.

At another level, the fact that the criminal justice system and larger society intensified their focus on punishing individuals, but did little to address the social contextual causes of crime, further disadvantaged minority defendants. Despite the enormous economic investment in crime-fighting made since the mid-1970s—including the costly expansion of an already sizable prison system—criminogenic social conditions remained largely untouched. The indisputable fact that was acknowledged in the War on Poverty and by the various presidential commissions that addressed these issues in the late 1960s—that minorities were disproportionately exposed to impoverished and deplorable economic and social disadvantage and therefore were placed at much greater risk to commit criminal offenses than others—continued to be ignored.[25]

The operation of fundamental attribution error added significantly to the problem by ensuring that the repetitive nature of much structurally based crime was explained primarily in terms of intractable criminal predispositions of the perpetrators (rather than the persistence of the structural inequalities to which they were exposed). Whenever minority group members engage in repeated acts of criminality—because of the tendency for stable structures to produce repetitive patterns of behavior—fundamental attribution error leads observers to blame deep-seated, intractable criminal traits instead of persistent criminogenic conditions. In this way, the invidious joining of race and crime—in policy and in the popular consciousness—is solidified.

In fact, these supposed, unmodifiable criminal dispositions—ones whose existence is demonstrated by the "habitual" nature of the behavior to which they are thought to give rise—now serve as the basis for special enhancements in the amount of punishment that is imposed. The racially disproportionate impact of three-strikes laws is an illustration of an extreme form of the fundamental attribution error at work in contemporary criminal justice policy. The differentials are large: In some states—like California and Washington—African Americans represent around 5% of the population but constitute between 37% and 44% of the three strikes commitments to prison.[26]

In the next section of this chapter, I describe in greater detail some of the social contextual facts of life that minorities in the United States continue to confront but which the movement toward the decontextualizing of crime and punishment has required legal decision makers to systematically exclude from consideration. Because these are important determinants of high crime rates in minority communities, ignoring them in assessments of blameworthiness and in calculations of the amount of punishment that particular persons are thought to deserve places legal decision makers and prison policymakers very much at the mercy of fundamental attribution error.

MANDATED IGNORANCE: DISPOSITIONALIZING RACE-BASED DISPARITY

During the period in which the American prison system underwent its rapid expansion and the spreading of prison pain was increasingly racialized, minorities continued to suffer from a wide range of social and economic disadvantages. Despite the perception among many White Americans during the 1970s and 1980s that the major barriers to racial equality had been largely eradicated, there was much evidence to indicate otherwise. In many areas of the country, far too little had been done to "actively strive to dismantle . . . the segregated structure"[27] that racism had created or the deep-seated psychological tendencies that it had generated and maintained.

In the midst of the prison-based crime control policies that had emerged over the last several decades, scholars addressed what they termed the "myth of Black progress," a myth belied by reports of continuing racial disparities in unemployment and income.[28] Otto Kerner's *Report of the National Advisory Committee on Civil Disorders*—written by a group of experts impaneled in the late 1960s to address issues of minority unrest, lawlessness, and violence—had placed primary responsibility on the continued drift toward separate but unequal societies for Blacks and Whites, and the widespread race-based disadvantage and discrimination that existed in the United States.[29] Although there certainly was some initial—if short-lived—progress made on these issues in the late 1960s,[30] the economic situation of African Americans once again deteriorated as the social welfare and neighborhood empowerment programs set up to address the problem of race-based poverty soon were terminated.

Thus, a follow-up to the Kerner Commission study conducted some 20 years later observed that "In the 1980s, even in the metropolitan areas with the greatest economic growth and tightest overall labor markets, both the color line and racial inequalities persist."[31] Another study concluded that, between the early 1970s and late 1980s, "the quality of life for poor African Americans" had declined "on nearly every indicator." The declining indicators included a dramatic decrease in labor force participation among Black high school dropouts and a near tripling of the joblessness rate among Black men.[32]

Numerous studies indicated that throughout the 1980s—the same period during which the United States used increasingly higher rates of imprisonment to address the social problem of crime—a sizable gap between White and Black family income remained virtually unchanged from the 1960s. Thus, in 1966, Black family income was 58% that of Whites, whereas in 1983 the percentage actually had dropped slightly to 57%.[33] In the mid-1980s, researchers characterized the economic experience of Black and Hispanic men as still "rather bleak" after decades of civil rights litigation. Although some progress had been made, "the gap between them and majority men [remained] substantial."[34] Kimberle Crenshaw ended her review of this literature by concluding that "continuing disparities exist between Afro-Americans and whites in virtually every measurable [socioeconomic] category."[35] Another author poignantly described the continuing oppression of African Americans in the United States during this period as "slavery unwilling to die."[36]

Other analysts discussed what they termed the "quiet riots"[37] that were occurring during these years. In this case, the interpersonal and social unrest took the form of unemployment, chronic poverty, disintegration of families, disorganization of social ties, and high rates of crime that were caused in part by continuing racism and persistent inequality. These riots were "quiet" only in the sense that they were disorganized and dispersed, and appeared to reflect individual rather than collective dissatisfaction. If these wide-ranging social maladies had been measured and assessed in aggregate terms, they would have been recognized as collective symptoms of a much broader set of structural problems that required large-scale political action and social change to solve.

However, because they were characterized as acts of individual deviance, dissatisfaction, or pathology—rather than collective unrest—their real causes were easily ignored. Instead, as the actions of problematic individuals, they were relegated to the criminal justice system, where they could be handled on a case-by-case rather than collective basis. What should have precipitated careful analysis of structural inequalities and serious consideration of broad socioeconomic reform was translated into a mandate for enhanced social and crime control.

The ease and expedience with which these structural problems could be conceptualized as individual-level phenomena did not alter the underlying inequalities in the society at large or reduce their powerful effects. Continuing to reinterpret socioeconomic problems in criminal justice terms may have made them more politically palatable, but it did little to solve them. Thus, as one statistical analysis of employment data through 1982—when the "race to incarcerate" already had begun to gain momentum—concluded, "the social and legal changes that reduced occupational segregation might be expected to reduce the gap in employment and joblessness, but they have not done so."[38]

Indeed, well into the decade of the 1990s—when an unprecedented period of economic prosperity finally began to filter down to those at the lowest rungs of the American labor market—the proportion of Black men who were actively participating in the workforce remained steady or was declining.[39] Other statistical analyses suggested that the nature or character of joblessness among Black men became more chronic during the several decades in which there was massive prison growth. That is, in the mid-1960s, approximately 5% of Black men between ages 25 and 54 were out of work for an entire calendar year. By the mid-1980s that number had grown to 14%. However, over the same period, this kind of chronic unemployment increased only from 3% to 5% for White men.[40]

Moreover, even when African Americans gained increased access to educational opportunity—the goal toward which many legal efforts to end discrimination had been directed—the desired effects often failed to materialize. Thus, research showed that Blacks were not as highly rewarded as Whites for educational attainment or for labor market experience. As one reviewer put it, "Without exception, these studies show that the actual earnings of black men are smaller than those of white men, even after blacks and whites are statistically matched with regard to factors [like education] that influence earnings."[41] Other indicators also showed that basic economic disparities were widening in the mid-1980s, when trends toward high levels of incarceration were in full swing: "In terms of purchasing power, blacks not only are failing to catch up with whites, they are falling further behind."[42] Similarly, a report written later in the same decade focused on minority participation in higher education and concluded that a growing segment of Black, Latino, and other minority groups was likely to be "effectively removed from contributing productively to the life of the nation"[43] by the start of the 21st century.[44]

The increased emphasis on incarceration as a strategy of social control in state and federal government coincided with a de-emphasis on equal opportunity enforcement efforts during the 1980s. Federal agencies took pressure off private-sector employers, many of whom drastically reduced or eliminated related positions in their personnel departments that had been held by minority employees. By the late 1980s, African American leaders began to complain that "the ranks of blacks in corporations [have been] . . . decimated."[45] The research director of a prominent management institute explained why: "For years, blacks and women were steered into jobs that were not central to the organization. Now those jobs are precisely the jobs that are being eliminated."[46]

Other researchers focused on the effects of the racially segregated housing that had become an enduring feature of urban life in the United States. Noting that the most commonly used measure of race-based residential segregation showed virtually no decline in 30 key metropolitan areas in the country between the years 1970 and 1990, one analyst summarized the long-term consequences this way:

> Segregation systematically builds deprivation into the residential structure of black communities and increases the susceptibility of the neighborhood to spirals of decline. A harsh and extremely disadvantaged environment also creates an oppositional culture that further separates ghetto residents from the majority of society. In isolating African Americans geographically, segregation undermines political support for jobs and services in the ghetto.[47]

Although perhaps more complicated and less well understood during these years, the economic status of Latinos in the United States was equally problematic.[48] Latinos continued to experience poverty rates that were more than twice as high as those in the White population.[49] Their levels of poverty grew significantly during the years in which incarceration growth in the United States was greatest: 21.8% of Latinos lived in poverty in 1979; by

1987 the number had grown to 28.2%.[50] The Children's Defense Fund reported that poverty rates among Latino children also increased significantly during the 1980s, reaching 36.2% by the end of that decade. The same report noted that the proportion of Latino hourly workers who were paid below-poverty wages had more than doubled over the decade of the 1980s, making Latinos more likely than white or Black workers to be paid inadequate wages.[51]

Indeed, although unemployment rates among Latinos were not as high as for Black Americans, sociologist Joan Moore speculated that this was likely the result of the relatively high percentage of Latinos who were employed in poorly paid jobs.[52] More recent data seem to confirm this. Latinos tend to be much less residentially segregated than African Americans, and their poverty is less the result of chronic joblessness. Although Latinos still have unemployment rates significantly higher than those of Whites, they "are the working poor—high employment rates but generally working below official poverty levels."[53]

Moreover, the system of public education in the United States has not served Latinos especially well or dramatically improved their economic status. Latino immigrants typically enter the United States with comparatively less education than other ethnic groups, and Latinos in general suffer the very highest school dropout rates.[54] In fact, although the rate at which Latinos complete high school has improved steadily since the 1970s,[55] it is still the case that 41% of Latino men between the ages of 25 and 54 have not completed a high school degree (compared with 14% of African Americans and only 7% of Whites).[56] And Latinos lag far behind Whites and African Americans in terms of the percentage who have completed 4 years of college, with less than 10% having done so.[57]

The journal *Social Problems* devoted a special issue to the topic of poverty in the United States at the outset of the 1990s, when prison growth had reached its highest level to date. The data cited showed "virtually no change in the extraordinarily high rates of Black (31.9%) and Hispanic (28.1%) poverty" over the preceding several decades, leading the issue editor to conclude simply that "racism remains at the core of much poverty in the United States."[58] As I discuss at length in the next chapter, we know that these persistent race-based economic disparities are criminogenic—they play a significant role in generating higher rates of crime within minority communities. Yet this fact has had little impact on crime control efforts. Nor has it had any ameliorating effects on the harsh prison policies that continue to disproportionately and negatively affect minority communities.

Moreover, the new decontextualizing legal doctrines that emerged over the last several decades required decision makers to ignore these realities—in both the crime control policies that they implemented and the sentencing models on which they relied. These policies of procedurally enforced indifference to social context have consigned minority citizens to chronically disadvantaged life circumstances in which they are simultaneously at greater risk of both committing and being victimized by crime. But they also have ensured that these same groups of people are far more likely to suffer harsh treatment at the hands of a criminal justice system that incarcerates them in lieu of addressing the persistent structural and social contextual barriers to equality that they still confront.

DRUG LAWS: WAGING WAR WITH PRISON PAIN

In addition to new legal policies that codified a decontextualized view of crime and narrowed the scope of factors that could be considered at the time that punishment was meted out, racial disparities in rates of imprisonment were influenced by another important factor: the panoply of harsh new laws and aggressive law enforcement practices that were implemented as part of the so-called War on Drugs.[59] Disproportionately punishing the kinds of drug offenses that African Americans, in particular, were more likely to commit and differentially enforcing the drug laws themselves ensured that the war on drugs would take its greatest casualties inside minority communities. This war literally has transformed the composition of the nation's prison population and had an enormous impact on both the amount and distribution of prison pain in American society. It is difficult to overstate the severity of the consequences produced by these policies.

A brief historical perspective is in order.[60] For most of the 20th century, despite various changes in the way certain crimes were categorized, there was a high degree of consistency in the types and proportions of offenses for which people were incarcerated in the United States.[61] Specifically, for the 75-year period from 1910 to 1984, approximately 60% to 70% of the nation's prison population was made up of persons convicted of committing property offenses. Among the remaining groups, between 13% and 24% were persons convicted of crimes against persons (now called *violent crime*), and about 20% were those who had committed public order and morals violations (which included drug offenses). Finally, an average of about 10% of those persons incarcerated over this period had been convicted of committing "other" kinds of offenses (such as juvenile offenses and unspecified felonies).

But these distributions have changed dramatically over the past several decades. For one, the federal government now incarcerates people for a wider range of criminal violations, and both state and federal prisoners remain incarcerated for longer periods. In addition, as Figure 4.1 illustrates, the percentage of prisoners incarcerated for violent offenses has risen somewhat over the last several decades. But this change is dwarfed by the increase

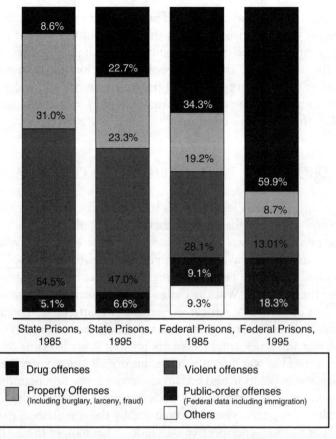

8.6%	22.7%	34.3%	59.9%
31.0%	23.3%	19.2%	8.7%
54.5%	47.0%	28.1%	13.01%
		9.1%	18.3%
5.1%	6.6%	9.3%	

State Prisons, 1985   State Prisons, 1995   Federal Prisons, 1985   Federal Prisons, 1995

■ Drug offenses   ■ Violent offenses

■ Property Offenses   ■ Public-order offenses
(Including burglary, larceny, fraud)   (Federal data including immigration)

□ Others

Figure 4.1. Changes in estimated distribution offenses: Persons in state and federal prisons, 1985 and 1995. Data from *Correctional Populations in the United States, 1995* [Bureau of Justice Statistics Bulletin NCJ-163916; Tables 1.12 and 1.14], by A. Beck et al., June 1997, Washington, DC: U.S. Department of Justice. In the public domain.

in the percentage of persons being sent to prison for drug offenses. In 1985 less than 9% of state prisoners were incarcerated for drug crimes, in contrast to nearly 23% by 1995. The proportion of federal prisoners held for drug violations nearly doubled during roughly the same period. Thus, in 1985, a little more than 34% of federal prisoners were incarcerated for drug violations, but by 1995, the proportion had risen to almost 60%.[62]

In addition to increases in the sheer number of persons incarcerated for drug offenses, racial disproportions were greatly intensified by new drug enforcement policies implemented over this period. Thus, although Blacks and Whites use drugs to approximately the same extent,[63] African Americans have been arrested for drug offenses at a much higher rate than Whites.[64] For example, criminologist Michael Tonry has cited data showing that as

TABLE 4.1
Change in Estimated Number of Sentenced Prisoners by Most Serious Offense and Race at the Height of the War on Drugs

Most serious offense	Total % change 1985–1995	White % change 1985–1995	Black % change 1985–1995
Total	119	109	132
Violent offenses	86	92	83
Property offenses	69	74	65
Drug offenses	478	306	707
Public-order offenses[a]	187	162	229
Other/unspecified[b]	–6	–72	64

Note. Adapted from *Prisoners in 1996* [NCJ-164619] (p. 10), by C. J. Mumoloa and A. J. Beck, 1997, Rockville, MD: Bureau of Justice Statistics. In the public domain.
[a]Includes weapons, drunk driving, escape, court offenses, obstruction, commercialized vice, morals and decency charges, liquor law violations, and other public-order offenses.
[b]Includes juvenile offenses and unspecified felonies.

the drug war intensified in the United States between 1985 and 1989, Black drug arrests doubled whereas White arrests increased only by 27%.[65] However, arrest rates were only a small part of the story. In 1984 the average prison sentence for African Americans was 28% higher than for Whites. By 1990, as the War on Drugs was being waged more vigorously, the disparity had grown to 49%.[66] In some areas of the country, the application of these drug-related sentencing policies produced even more dramatic effects. Thus, commitments to prison for drug offenses among White men rose almost 500% between 1980 and 1990 in one state (Pennsylvania), but increased a staggering 1600% among nonwhite men.[67]

As the drug war continued, the racial disproportions intensified. As Table 4.1 illustrates, between 1985 and 1995, the number of African Americans incarcerated in state prisons in the United States because of drug violations (defined as their only offense or their most serious offense) rose 707%. In contrast, the number of Whites incarcerated in state prisons for similar drug offenses underwent a 306% change.

Looked at somewhat differently, in 1986 only 7% of Black prison inmates in the United States were imprisoned for drug crimes, compared with 8% of Whites. By 1991, however, the Black percentage had more than tripled to 25%, whereas the percentage of White inmates incarcerated for drug crimes had increased by only half, to 12%.[68] By the mid-1990s, the numbers of African Americans incarcerated for drug violations in the *federal* prison system were much higher: Fully 64% of male and 71% of female Black prisoners incarcerated in federal institutions in 1995 had been sent there for drug offenses.[69]

There are a number of explanations for these stark differentials. One involves differences in the way "crack" versus powdered cocaine users and dealers are sentenced. Federal guidelines treat possession of one ounce of crack cocaine as the equivalent of possession of 100 ounces of powdered cocaine, a policy that clearly has contributed to significant race-based sentencing disparities.[70] As one commentator noted, despite the fact that the two drugs are "pharmacologically identical," statistics show that "the overwhelming majority of those arrested for crack cocaine are black. Thus, blacks convicted under such laws are virtually certain to receive a greater punishment for a seemingly racially neutral drug offense than will white offenders."[71] In the mid-1990s, in fact, there were a number of federal judges who agreed that the disparities in the operation of the sentencing guidelines were discriminatory and wrote opinions to that effect.[72] However, all of them had been overruled by the end of the decade,[73] and the widespread disparities persisted.[74]

It is important to acknowledge the real effects of the so-called crack cocaine "epidemic" and concede that it did appear to have destructive effects in many urban areas, perhaps especially in a number of African American communities. Drug researchers generally concede that, although the epidemic was overreported in the media beginning in the mid-1980s, widespread crack addiction nonetheless had very serious consequences for many people and for the communities where it was most concentrated:

> There were the highs, binges, and crashes that induced addicts to sell their belongings and their bodies in pursuit of more crack; the high addiction liability of the drug that instigated users to commit any manner and variety of crimes to support their habits; the rivalries in crack distribution networks that turned some inner-city communities into urban "dead zones," where homicide rates were so high that police had written them off as anarchic badlands. . . .[75]

However, the lack of any empirical support for the notion that crack cocaine had special potency or addictive properties undermined the justification for the sentencing disparities that were imposed.[76]

Moreover, the crack epidemic of the 1980s did not emerge in a vacuum. That is, it occurred in precisely those African American communities that suffered from widespread poverty, chronic unemployment, and other socio-economic problems that had become deeply entrenched during this period. In turn, heightened levels of depression, hopelessness, and despair were generated among many people facing these bleak conditions and pessimistic futures. Indeed, one analysis of the crack epidemic noted that thousands of young men in the inner city, poorly educated and plagued with limited or no job skills, faced a steady decline in wages and increased unemployment rates throughout much of the 1980s. The economic lure of the emerging crack trade was difficult to resist in such an environment.[77]

More generally, the higher rates of incarceration suffered by African Americans in the war on drugs did nothing to address either the psychological or the economic aspects of the problem, and may have worsened them. Some communities have been so deeply affected by these policies that one third or more of their minority male population is under some form of correctional control. As William Chambliss warned, "crime control policies are a major contributor to the disruption of the family, the prevalence of single parent families, and children raised without a father in the ghetto, and the 'inability of people to get the jobs still available.'"[78] Thus, drug-related, race-based differences in the distribution of prison pain appear to have had significant adverse effects of their own on African American communities, and they threaten to have the same impact on Latinos in the decades ahead.[79] Indeed, by the end of the 1990s, nearly half (45%) of the defendants charged with a federal drug offense were Latino.[80]

Despite the critical attention that was devoted to many of these issues in the 1990s—including data showing that very little reduction in drug use had been brought about by the intense law enforcement focus on drug-related crimes,[81] a consensus among scholars that Tonry's characterization of the War on Drugs as reflecting "malign neglect" toward young Black men was largely accurate, and politicized controversies over the way differentials in sentencing policies appeared to disfavor minority defendants convicted of drug offenses—the policies continued relatively unchanged. Thus, in the year 2002, drug offenses still represented about one third (32.4%) of felony convictions in state court and a higher amount (42%) in federal court. Most of the people who are convicted of drug offenses in state court (including those whose conviction is for mere possession) are incarcerated for their offense, and nearly everyone (90%) convicted in federal court is.[82] Moreover, the intense law enforcement focus on minority drug offenders, the high rates at which they are incarcerated for their drug-related convictions and the long sentences that they receive—especially in the federal system— mean that racial disparities in imprisonment are likely to persist.[83]

RACE, DRUGS, AND PRISON POLICY: A NEXUS OF CAUSES AND CONSEQUENCES

These two interrelated trends—the further decontextualizing of sentencing policies and the waging of a targeted, aggressive War on Drugs— have contributed significantly to the racialization of prison pain. Obviously, the unprecedented use of imprisonment per se represents an explicit policy choice to single out (and incarcerate) individual lawbreakers instead of targeting the root causes of their behavior. As I noted earlier in this chapter,

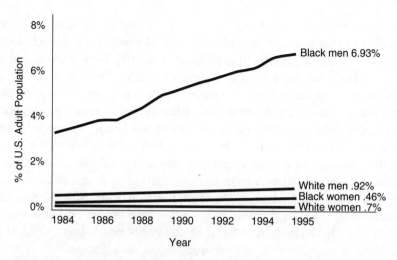

Figure 4.2. Consequences of the War on Drugs: Percentage of U.S. adult population in state or federal prisons or in local jails, by race and gender, 1984 to 1995. Data from *Correctional Populations in the United States, 1995*. [Bureau of Justice Statistics Bulletin NCJ 163916; p. 7, Figure 1], by A. Beck et al., June 1997, Washington, DC: U.S. Department of Justice. In the public domain.

when crime control and prison policies ignore situation and context, they inevitably lead to higher rates of incarceration among those citizens who more often confront social and economic conditions that are systematically related to criminal behavior. In societies like the United States, in which exposure to such criminogenic contexts is so closely tied to race, these policies have significant, predictable racial consequences. As Figure 4.2 illustrates, during the period in which the War on Drugs was most aggressively waged—from the mid-1980s through the mid-1990s—African American men were the group most dramatically affected.

The additional policy choice to vigorously prosecute and harshly punish drug-related crimes also specifically ignores a range of important contextual factors. For example, by disregarding the way in which the lack of employment opportunities helps to lead young minority men into certain kinds of drug-related criminal activities, or the tendency to turn to drugs as a form of "self-medication" in communities characterized by despair and hopelessness, these policies fail to address many of the real causes of drug use. Rather, they reflect a dispositional and invariably discriminatory approach to crime control that does nothing to improve the life chances of the young minority men against whom they are directed.

In addition, the individualism of legal policies like these that locate the causes of behavior exclusively inside the persons who engage in it facilitates the same attitude among prison administrators. Thus, much as the legal system neglects the role of situational factors in understanding and punishing criminal wrongdoing, correctional decision makers discount the effects of the prison context itself and minimize the need to create and maintain appropriate environments that address the special needs of prisoners. For example, despite the extraordinary focus on prosecuting and punishing drug-related crimes, and the acknowledged role of drug use and addiction in a high percentage of other crimes, few prisons operate any effective drug treatment programs, and legislators in many states are loath to fund them.

This is another example of the asymmetries and ironies brought about by a heavily individualistic approach to crime and punishment. Such an approach ignores variations in context in favor of a one-size-fits-all mentality in both the attribution of criminal responsibility and the design of the places to which prisoners are later taken. It contributes to treating people the same way who have special needs or problems that would justify treating them differently. In the case of drug offenders, for example, this includes ignoring the ways in which prison classification, housing, and treatment should take their addiction-related problems and needs into account. It is ironic that ignoring context in the name of individualism has meant failing to provide specialized treatment that the unique needs of individuals would otherwise require.

This irony extends to the way in which ignoring the prison context itself jeopardizes the long-term chances of prisoners whose individual characteristics systematically disadvantage them while they are incarcerated. For example, African American prisoners who are routinely given low status jobs in prison will be compromised in their postrelease adjustment because of low skill levels and what appear to be unimpressive work records in prison. If they leave prison with little or no transferable job skills or experience, at best qualified for minimum-wage jobs in an increasingly demanding freeworld economy, then their incarceration will have solidified their economic marginality. Latinos also confront many of these same issues in prison, where it is "clear that discriminatory policies and the lack of bilingual personnel and programs resulted in differential treatment towards Latino prisoners"[84] that can produce the same long-term consequences.

In addition, as prison pain has become increasingly racialized, its costs continue to be localized in the communities that are given little or no voice in deciding whether it has become excessive or overly harsh. Decision makers entrusted with the responsibility of determining whether our prisons are cruel because they violate evolving community standards, or deciding whether punitive drug policies are too severe in light of the limited benefits they produce, typically lack any connection to the communities in which the effects of these policies are felt. As a consequence, not only do individualistic crime control strategies ignore the causal role of situation and circumstance, but they also discount the adverse effects of these policies on the social

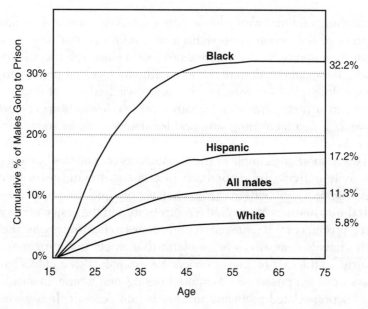

Figure 4.3. Differences in likelihood of imprisonment over a lifetime. Data from *Prevalence of Imprisonment in the U.S. Population* [Bureau of Justice Statistics Special Report NCJ 197976; p. 8, Figure 4], by T. Bonczar, August 2003, Washington, DC: U.S. Department of Justice. In the public domain.

contexts—the families, neighborhoods, and communities—where they tend to be most concentrated.

As Figure 4.3 illustrates, nearly 1 in 3 Black men, and 1 in 6 Latino men in the United States can expect to go to prison at some point during their lifetimes. These statistics underscore the extent to which certain groups in American society are much more at risk of experiencing the potentially life-altering pains of imprisonment. They also highlight the extent to which certain families, neighborhoods, and communities—and not others—must somehow absorb the social and economic consequences of high numbers of imprisoned citizens and, eventually, returning ex-convicts.

As I have noted in this chapter, African Americans in particular have been negatively affected by the policies of mass imprisonment implemented over the last several decades. However, these race-based effects not only touch other minority groups in our society (Latinos in particular) but also extend to juveniles as well as adults. In fact, calculations of the rate at which juveniles are incarcerated in state-run detention facilities reveal even more dramatic race and ethnicity-based disparities. These disparities are especially large for drug offenses. One study found that African American juveniles with no prior admissions to an institution were 48 times more likely to be incarcerated for drug-related offenses than White juveniles, and

Latinos were 13 times more likely to be incarcerated for these kinds of offenses than their White counterparts.[85] In another study, researchers found that approximately 3 out of 4 drug offenses involving African American youth were formally processed compared with about half of those involving Whites.[86]

Indeed, the magnitude and persistence of *disproportionate minority confinement* in the juvenile justice system is so widely understood among researchers and policymakers that it is referred to by its acronym, DMC. The differential effects of such widespread and intrusive criminal justice system intervention include added strain on already burdened families, neighborhoods, and communities. The policies that produce DMC thus contribute to cycles of crime and incarceration. Yet—perhaps in part because of their social and geographical distance from the contexts in which the impact of their policies will be felt—few legal decisionmakers are in a position to accurately perceive the long-term criminogenic effects that reverberate through these communities—higher levels of future crime and continuing overincarceration of minorities.

Moreover, the number of persons who are incarcerated in minority communities has grown so large that a new dimension has been added to the tension between dispositional and social contextual approaches to crime and punishment. Because felony convictions disqualify ex-convicts from voting in a number of jurisdictions,[87] a disproportionate number of minority men have been politically disenfranchised and denied the opportunity to participate in the democratic process through which decisions about their communities are made.[88] Approximately 30 states prohibit parolees from voting, 21 exclude probationers and, in 14 states, ex-convicts are permanently disenfranchised even after their sentence has been discharged. Indeed, the number of persons who are incarcerated in minority communities has grown so large that this has become a large-scale problem for many of them. Recent estimates suggest that there may be nearly 4 million citizens in the United States—including nearly 1.5 million African American men—who have been denied the right to vote as a result of their prior felony convictions.[89]

In certain states, in fact, this has translated into a very high percentage of African American voters who have been shut out of the electoral process. For example, one study estimated that the overall number of African Americans felons who have been excluded from voting is approximately 13% of the total of potential African American male voters. However, in Alabama and Florida, more than 30% of them have been disenfranchised because of their criminal records.[90]

In a certain sense, this aspect of what one commentator has termed the "internal exile"[91] that plagues prisoners even after their release also reflects an essentialist, dispositional view of criminality. That is, it appears to be based on the belief that, among other things, criminal offenders lack the moral capacity to make responsible electoral decisions. As one legal commentator put it,

> Both the social contract and the moral competence arguments for disenfranchisement locate the source of deviance within the individual. . . . By rationalizing and facilitating a tendency to localize the blame for crime in the individual, disenfranchisement helps to obscure the complexity of the roots of crime and their entanglement with contingent social structures.[92]

However, political disenfranchisement operates to distance ex-convicts from the communities in which they are expected to someday become participating members. Here, too, making irrebuttable inferences about the individual traits of persons who have committed crimes has adverse social contextual effects that are left out of the policymaking equation.

Moreover, regarding prisoners as decontextualized entities with no community roots or ties has allowed them to be counted in the Census— for important political and economic purposes—as residents of the prison towns where they are incarcerated rather than the communities from which they come (and to which they will return). Thus, prison towns actually get financial and political "credit" for citizens who are unable to partake of any community services or participate in any of the political or civic life there. However, the prisoners' home districts lose a corresponding amount of economic resources and political representation and voice.[93]

One final, recent legal trend further illustrates the discriminatory implications of the approach taken by courts and other criminal justice decision makers who ignore life circumstances and socioeconomic context in the punishment of drug offenders and then discount the impact of these policies on the social environment where they take their greatest toll. As one critical analysis put it, the so-called *zero tolerance* approach to drug-related offenses has rendered decision makers "blind to the most basic distinctions between types of offenses," requiring severe sanctions for all of them.[94] However, these laws also avoid distinctions between types of lawbreakers by requiring decision makers to punish infractions without any consideration of the role of context and circumstance in crime causation. By holding those persons most accountable for actions that may be most attributable to the situation in which they occur, the laws have institutionalized fundamental attribution error.

The narrowness of the zero tolerance approach is reflected in several laws enacted during the War on Drugs era. For example, a portion of the Anti-Drug Abuse Act[95] authorized federal housing officials to evict low-income tenants from their homes if anyone in their household—including guests—was determined to be engaged in drug-related activity. Moreover, it specified that the sanctions must be imposed regardless of whether the tenant knew or should have known about the activity in question.[96] Combined with a provision of the so-called "welfare reform" bill—the Personal Responsibility and Work Opportunity Reconciliation Act—which imposed a lifetime ban on assistance to needy families (including food stamps) to anyone with a felony drug conviction,[97] drug users and their families and friends are likely to lose publicly assisted housing as well as their welfare benefits.

Thus, rather than attempting to address the criminogenic conditions that help to ensnare minority group members in drug use and drug-related criminal activity, these laws have taken a bad social context and systematically made it worse. Ostensibly to control substance abuse—but doing so through a narrow decontextualized model of purely individual-level blame— zero tolerance has adversely impacted the living conditions of drug users and their families in ways that are likely to contribute to a long-term and largely racialized exacerbation of the drug problem itself.[98]

CONCLUSION

In this chapter I have argued that two interrelated trends—the ill-advised reform of criminal sentencing and the intense law enforcement focus on drug offenses—helped to account for the continued overrepresentation of minorities in prison and, in a variety of ways, placed their communities in real jeopardy. The law's decontextualized view of the social behavior of crime meant that race-based differences in exposure to criminogenic circumstances were largely ignored. The failure to improve the life chances of persons exposed to these poor and problematic conditions—and instead to intensify their criminal prosecution and incarceration—reflected an intrinsically dispositional approach to crime control. It also allowed the racial characteristics of the perpetrators (rather than their circumstances) to be used as the basis of causal inferences that were not only erroneous but racialized in nature.

In fact, criminal justice initiatives like the War on Drugs helped to institutionalize fundamental attribution error, sending a clear, but inaccurate, message that crime could be reduced only by intensifying the incarceration of those persons who engaged in it. At various points in the process, this error—blaming individuals exclusively for behaviors that were caused in part by situational factors—compounded the very problems that the policies were supposed to solve. It certainly contributed to higher levels of public miseducation—"fundamental attribution error as public policy"—and helped siphon resources away from more contextually oriented preventative approaches to crime control that might have been pursued instead. It also worsened the positions of already marginalized groups in our society.

Moreover, as I discuss in several later chapters, imprisonment itself—what has become our major weapon in the War on Crime—can have long-term criminogenic effects. The individual psychological consequences of prison pain and the broader social consequences of incarceration often persist beyond the terms of confinement. Among other things, many people find the stigma of their ex-convict status nearly impossible to overcome, further handicapping already difficult odds against successful reintegration into free society. The disproportionate incarceration of minorities and drug offenders—especially under current prison policies that de-emphasize programming, treatment, and other forms of rehabilitation—virtually ensures a difficult transition back into the freeworld settings from which they were taken.

NOTES

1. Nils Christie, *Limits to Pain* (Oxford, England: Martin Robertson, 1982), 74.
2. Michael Tonry, *Malign Neglect: Race, Crime, and Punishment in America* (New York: Oxford University Press, 1995), 4.
3. *See, e.g.,* G. Heaney, "The Reality of Guidelines Sentencing: No End to Disparity," *American Criminal Law* Review 28 (1991): 161; C. Hebert, "Sentencing Outcomes of Black, Hispanic, and White Males Convicted Under Federal Sentencing Guidelines," *Criminal Justice Review* 22 (1997): 133.
4. Lawrence Friedman, *Crime and Punishment in American History* (New York: HarperCollins, 1993), 156.
5. Ibid. Historian Edgardo Rotman characterized the post-Civil War southern prisons this way: "These institutions, in which blacks made up more than 75 percent of the inmates, took their inspiration from slavery. The result was a ruthless exploitation with a total disregard for prisoners' dignity and lives. The states leased prisoners to entrepreneurs who, having no ownership interest in them, exploited them even worse than slaves." Edgardo Rotman, "The Failure of Reform: United States, 1865–1965," in *The Oxford History of the Prison: The Practice of Punishment in Western Society*, ed. Norval Morris and David Rothman (New York: Oxford University Press, 1998), 157.
6. As Randall Kennedy concluded, "indeed, in terms of procedural fairness, black defendants charged with serious, inter-racial crimes were better off before the abolition of slavery than for a long time afterward." Randall Kennedy, *Race, Crime, and the Law* (New York: Vintage Books, 1997), 80.
7. Ibid.
8. *See, e.g.,* W. Sabol, "Racially Disproportionate Prison Populations in the United States," *Contemporary Crises* 13 (1989): 405; Thorsten Sellin, *Slavery and the Penal System* (New York: Elsevier, 1976). It is also worth noting that the existence of racial disparities in the application of prison pain is not unique to the United States. In Canada, for example, the proportion of native people in the general population is approximately 2%, yet they account for 10% of the nation's federal prison population. J. Brodeur, "Truth in Sentencing,"

Behavioral Sciences & the Law 7 (1989): 25, 32. Similarly, the Maoris are significantly overrepresented in New Zealand's prisons—at a rate approximately 10 times their percentage in the general population. Greg Newbold, *Punishment and Politics: A History of the Maximum Security Prison in New Zealand* (Auckland: Oxford University Press, 1989).

9. M. Cahalan, "Trends in Incarceration in the United States Since 1880: A Summary of Reported Rates and the Distribution of Offenses," *Crime and Delinquency* 23 (1979): 9.

10. *See* James Stephan and Jennifer Karberg, *Census of State and Federal Correctional Facilities, 2000* (Washington, DC: Bureau of Justice Statistics, August, 2003), 3.

11. *See, e.g.,* F. Dunbaugh, "Racially Disproportionate Rates of Incarceration in the United States," *Prison Law Monitor* 1(9) (1979): 205, 219.

12. A. King, "The Impact of Incarceration on African American Families: Implications for Practice," *Journal of Contemporary Human Services* 74 (1993): 145. Thus, the rate at which White men were imprisoned between 1985 and 1995 increased from 528 per 100,000 in 1985 to 919 per 100,000 in 1995. However, in absolute terms, the impact of incarceration on African American men, Hispanics, and women of all racial and ethnic groups was much greater. For example, the number of African American men who were incarcerated rose from 3,544 per 100,000 in 1985 to an astonishing 6,926 per 100,000 in 1995. Also, between 1985 and 1995, the number of Hispanic prisoners rose by an average of 12% annually. Christopher Mumola and Allen Beck, *Prisoners in 1996* [Bureau of Justice Statistics Bulletin NCJ 164619] (Rockville, MD: Bureau of Justice Statistics, June 1997).

13. *See, e.g.,* A. Blumstein, "On the Racial Disproportionality of United States' Prison Populations," *Journal of Criminal Law and Criminology* 73 (1982): 1259.

14. Bureau of Justice Statistics, *Report to the Nation on Crime and Justice,* 2d ed. (Washington, DC: U.S. Department of Justice, 1988), 47.

15. Patrick Lanagan and David Levin, *Recidivism of Prisoners Released in 1994* [Bureau of Justice Statistics Special Report NCJ 193427] (Washington, DC: U.S. Department of Justice, June 2002), 7. Persons who are returned to prison without a new prison sentence are those incarcerated as parole violators.

16. Indeed, it can be argued that the very definition of crime, at least as reported in the FBI's Uniform Crime Reports Index, is structured in such a way that it overrepresents African Americans and underrepresents Whites. That is because "Part I" offenses that are used in the "Crime Index" reports of crime rates include primarily "street" crimes (like murder, rape, robbery, burglary, and car theft) and exclude "white-collar" crimes (like fraud, embezzlement, forgery, and counterfeiting), which are listed as "Part II" offenses that get much less public attention. The fact that "the UCR Crime Index plainly is intrinsically biased away from the arrest of of mostly white collar criminals and toward blacks and blue collar offenders" means that "the public's beliefs about crime, such as what types of people are more likely to commit crime, where crime is more likely to occur, and who is most likely to become a victim" are skewed as a result. *See* Dennis Rome, *Black Demons: The Media's Depiction of the African American Male Criminal Stereotype* (Westport, CT: Praeger, 2004), 45.

17. Sabol, "Racially Disproportionate Prison Populations in the United States," 428.

18. Jerome Skolnick, *Justice Without Trial: Law Enforcement in Democratic Society* (New York: Wiley, 1975).

19. *See, e.g.,* C. Bond, C. DiCandia, and J. MacKinnon, "Responses to Violence in a Psychiatric Setting: The Role of Patient's Race," *Personality and Social Psychology Bulletin* 14 (1988): 448; M. Farnworth and P. Horan, "Separate Justice: An Analysis of Race Differences in Court Processes," *Social Science Research* 9 (1980): 381; A. Lizotte, "Extra-Legal Factors in Chicago's Criminal Courts: Testing the Conflict Model of Criminal Justice," *Social Problems* 25 (1978): 564; M. Radelet and G. Pierce, "Race and Prosecutorial Discretion in Homicide Cases," *Law & Society Review* 19 (1985): 587; Sabol, "Racially Disproportionate Prison Populations in the United States." For an overview of the ways this issue has continued to plague the American legal system, *see* "Developments in the Law, Race and the Criminal Process," *Harvard Law Review* 101 (1988): 1472.

20. Albert Bandura, "Mechanisms of Moral Disengagement," in *Origins of Terrorism: Psychologies, Ideologies, Theologies, States of Mind,* ed. W. Reich (New York: Cambridge University Press, 1989); C. Haney, "Violence and the Capital Jury: Mechanisms of Moral Disengagement and the Impulse to Condemn to Death," *Stanford Law Review* 49 (1997): 1447.

21. There is reason to believe that the ease with which Whites cognitively associate members of a racially stigmatized group with criminality has perceptual and memoric components. For example, in one study, participants who read crime stories that pictured White and African American perpetrators were more likely to incorrectly connect African Americans to the violent crimes. M. Oliver and D. Fonash, "Race and Crime in the News: Whites' Identification and Misidentification of Violent and Nonviolent Criminal Suspects," *Journal of Media Psychology* 14 (2002): 137. Of course, there is no reason to believe these tendencies are "hard-wired"; many social forces create and reinforce them. For a far-ranging discussion of this and a number of related issues, *see also* Kathryn Russell, *The Color of Crime: Racial Hoaxes, White Fear, Black Protectionism, Police Harassment, and Other Macroaggressions* (New York: New York University Press, 1998).

22. Lee Ross and Richard Nisbett, *The Person and the Situation: Perspectives of Social Psychology* (New York: McGraw-Hill, 1991).

23. *See also* Craig Haney, "The Good, the Bad, and the Lawful: An Essay on Psychological Injustice," in *Personality Theory, Moral Development, and Criminal Behavior,* ed. William Laufer and James Day (Lexington, MA: Lexington Books, 1983).

24. Nils Christie, *Crime Control as Industry: Towards Gulags, Western Style?* (London: Routledge, 1993), 134.

25. A detailed exposition of exactly what was known in the 1960s about these issues is beyond the scope of this book. At the core of the poverty-related social programs enacted during the War on Poverty was the assumption that "if poverty had its origin in circumstances too powerful for the individual to alter, then personal vices were more likely to be mechanisms for coping with

the environment than the root causes of the individual's woe." *See* David Zarefsky, *President Johnson's War on Poverty: Rhetoric and History* (University Park, AL: University of Alabama Press, 1986), 39. *See also* Michael Katz, *The Undeserving Poor: From the War on Poverty to the War on Welfare* (New York: Pantheon Books, 1990); Daniel Knapp and Kenneth Polk, *Scouting the War on Poverty: Social Reform Policies in the Kennedy Administration* (Lexington, MA: Heath Lexington Books, 1971). In addition, the President's Commission on Law Enforcement and the Administration of Justice filed a lengthy report in 1968 addressing the "challenge of crime in a free society." Among its central recommendations was to "prevent crime before it happens," which the Commission suggested could be done by "Eliminating social conditions closely associated with crime; improving the ability of the criminal justice system to detect, apprehend, judge, and reintegrate into their communities those who commit crimes; and reducing the situations in which crimes are most likely to be committed." President's Commission on Law Enforcement and Administration of Justice, *The Challenge of Crime in a Free Society* (New York: Avon Books, 1968), 40.

26. Statistics for the state of Washington compiled by the state's Sentencing Guidelines Commission indicated that Blacks made up 4% of the state's population but fully 37% of those sentenced under the three-strikes law. Scott Sunde, "Blacks Bear Brunt of '3 Strikes': Lesser Crimes Count Toward Life Sentence, and a Higher Imprisonment Rate Compounds Problem, *Seattle Post-Intelligencer*, February 20, 2001, http://seattlepi.nwsource.com/local/strk20.shtml. A California study showed that Blacks, who represent 6% of the California population, account for 31% of the state prison inmates but are 44% of three-strikes convicts. *See* Scott Ehlers, Vincent Schiraldi, and Jason Ziedenberg, *Still Striking Out: Ten Years of California's Three Strikes* (Washington, DC: Justice Policy Institute, March 2004).

27. Brown v. Board of Education of Topeka, 892 F.2d 851, 886 [10th Cir. (Kan.) 1989]. These were the words used by the 10th Circuit Court of Appeals—nearly 35 years after the original *Brown v. Board of Education* case had ordered that desegregation be accomplished "with all deliberate speed" [Brown v. Board of Education, 349 U.S. 294, 301 (1955)]—when it ruled that the City of Topeka still had not sufficiently reduced preexisting racial divisions in the public school system.

28. Alphonso Pinkey, *The Myth of Black Progress* (Cambridge, England: Cambridge University Press, 1984).

29. Otto Kerner, *Report of the National Advisory Committee on Civil Disorders* (New York: Bantam Books, 1968), which I referenced in endnote 57 in chapter 3 of this volume.

30. For example, poverty rates in general, as well as the percentage of children living in poverty, were cut by half between 1960 and the early 1970s. *See* Michael Katz, *The Undeserving Poor: From the War on Poverty to the War on Welfare* (New York: Pantheon, 1989); James Patterson, *America's Struggle Against Poverty, 1960–1985* (Cambridge, MA: Harvard University Press, 1986); John Schwarz, *America's Hidden Success: A Reassessment of Public Policy from*

Kennedy to Reagan (New York: W.W. Norton, 1986); and Jill Quadagno, *The Color of Welfare* (New York: Oxford University Press, 1995).

31. Gary Orfield, "Separate Societies: Have the Kerner Warnings Come True?" in *Quiet Riots: Race and Poverty in the United States*, ed. Fred Harris and Roger Wilkins (New York: Pantheon, 1988), 103.

32. Quadagno, *The Color of Welfare*, 176.

33. Harrell Rodgers, "Fair Employment Law for Minorities: An Evaluation of Federal Implementation," in *Implementation of Civil Rights Policy*, ed. Charles Bullock and Charles Lamb (Monterey, CA: Brooks Cole, 1984).

34. C. Hirschman and M. Wong, "Socioeconomic Gains of Asian Americans, Blacks, and Hispanics: 1960–1976," *American Journal of Sociology* 90 (1984): 584, 595. *See generally* Andrew Hacker, *Two Nations: Black and White, Separate, Hostile, and Unequal* (New York: Charles Scribner, 1991).

35. K. Crenshaw, "Race, Reform and Retrenchment: Transformation and Legitimation in Antidiscrimination Law," *Harvard Law Review* 101 (1988): 1331, 1332.

36. J. Feagin, "Slavery Unwilling to Die: The Background of Black Oppression in the 1980s," *Journal of Black Studies* 17 (1986): 173.

37. Fred Harris and Roger Wilkins, ed., *Quiet Riots: Race and Poverty in the United States* (New York: Pantheon, 1988).

38. Reynolds Farley, *Blacks and Whites: Narrowing the Gap?* (Cambridge, MA: Harvard University Press, 1984), 52. The "race to incarcerate" is Marc Mauer's term for the period of rapid prison growth during the last several decades of the 20th century. *See* Marc Mauer, *The Race to Incarcerate* (New York: W. W. Norton, 1999).

39. As one group of analysts concluded, "The gap between the earnings of white and African American males has been remarkably persistent: the only moments when it has really narrowed have been at the end of a long boom of growth, as in the early 1970s and the late 1990s." Angela Glover-Blackwell, Stewart Kwoh, and Manuel Pastor, *Searching for the Uncommon Ground: New Dimensions on Race in America* (New York: W. W. Norton, 2002), 92.

40. Cited in Christopher Jencks, *Rethinking Social Policy: Race, Poverty, and the Underclass* (Cambridge, MA: Harvard University Press, 1992), 35.

41. Farley, *Blacks and Whites*, 62.

42. Ibid., 154.

43. James Mingle, *Focus on Minorities: Trends in Higher Education Participation and Success* (Denver: Education Commission of the States, 1987). *See also* William Johnson and Arnold Packer, *Workforce 2000: Work and Workers for the 21st Century* (Washington, DC: U.S. Department of Labor, 1987, xx, which concluded that "Non-whites will make up 29 percent of the new entrants into the labor force between now and the year 2000, twice their current share of the workforce. Although this large share of a more slowly growing workforce might be expected to improve the opportunities for these workers, the concentration of blacks in declining central cities and slowly growing occupations makes this sanguine outlook doubtful."

44. A variety of structural, procedural, and social psychological factors were at work during these years to preserve the racially imbalanced status quo and

thwart legal efforts in the post–Civil Rights era to change it. For example, some researchers found that although the Civil Rights Act of 1964 and the related enforcement efforts of the Equal Employment Opportunity Commission (EEOC) led to greater parity in wages paid to Black and White employees in certain entry-level jobs, firms regularly provided more on-the-job training to White employees so that their wages quickly advanced beyond those of their Black counterparts. *See* E. Lazear, "The Narrowing of Black–White Wage Differentials Is Illusory," *American Economic Review* 69 (1979): 553. Other researchers thoughtfully catalogued the numerous ways in which various structural barriers translated into hostile social psychological environments that confronted minority job applicants and employees in the workplace. *See* T. Pettigrew and J. Martin, "Shaping the Organizational Context for Black American Inclusion," *Journal of Social Issues* 43 (1987): 41.

45. Thomas Edsall and Mary Edsall, *Chain Reaction: The Impact of Race, Rights, and Taxes on American Politics* (New York: Norton, 1991), 161, quoting John N. Odom in 1987, executive director of Black Agency Executives, an association of black management and social services executives.

46. Ibid., quoting Mary Anne Devanna, research director of Columbia Business School's Management Institute.

47. Jill Quadagno, *The Color of Welfare*, 177.

48. The status of Latinos in the United States continues to be less well understood, for a variety of reasons. For one, many earlier statistical analyses of economic, educational, and criminal justice data were inconsistent in their coding of Latino/Hispanic ethnicity (including whether it was coded at all). In addition, because the Latino population in the United States is growing rapidly, the data may quickly become stale. Finally, language barriers at times compromise the representativeness and reliability of some of the data that are collected.

49. Franklin James, *Persistent Urban Poverty and the Underclass: A Perspective Based on the Hispanic Experience*. Paper presented at the Conference on Persistent Poverty Among Hispanics, Tomás Rivera Center, San Antonio, Texas, April 1988.

50. Joan Moore, *An Assessment of Hispanic Poverty: Is There a Hispanic Underclass?* Paper presented at the Conference on Persistent Poverty Among Hispanics, Tomás Rivera Center, San Antonio, Texas, April 1988.

51. "Latino Children in U.S. Mired in Poverty," *San Francisco Chronicle*, August 27, 1991, p. B-10, col. 1.

52. Moore, *An Assessment*.

53. Glover-Blackwell et al., *Searching for the Uncommon Ground*, 80.

54. Data cited in Moore, *An Assessment*.

55. *See* Glover-Blackwell et al., *Searching for the Uncommon Ground*, 148.

56. *See, e.g.,* Sheldon Danziger, Deborah Reed, and Tony Brown, *Poverty and Prosperity: Prospects for Reducing Racial/Ethnic Economic Disparities in the United States*, unpublished manuscript, University of Michigan, August 25, 2002. *See also* James Smith, "Race and Ethnicity in the Labor Market: Trends Over the Short and Long Term," in *America Becoming: Racial Trends and Their*

Consequences (vol. 2), ed. Neil Smelser, William Wilson, and Faith Mitchell (Washington, DC: National Academy Press, 2001).

57. Glover-Blackwell et al., *Searching for Uncommon Ground*, 148.

58. K. See, "Comments from the Special Issue Editor: Approaching Poverty in the United States," *Social Problems* 38 (1991): 427, 428.

59. *See, e.g.*, James Inciardi, *The War on Drugs: Heroin, Cocaine, Crime, and Public Policy* (Palo Alto, CA: Mayfield, 1986); James Inciardi, *The War on Drugs II: The Continuing Epic of Heroin, Cocaine, Crack, Crime, AIDS, and Public Policy* (Palo Alto, CA: Mayfield, 1992); Tonry, *Malign Neglect*.

60. A Bureau of Justice Statistics study that focused on the distribution of offenses committed by federal and state prisoners documented the changes that have occurred in the types of crimes for which people have been incarcerated in the United States since the mid-19th century. See Margaret Cahalan, *Historical Corrections Statistics in the United States, 1850–1984* [Bureau of Justice Statistics Bulletin NCJ-102529] (Rockville, MD: Bureau of Justice Statistics, December 1986).

61. In some instances, the classification of offenses themselves actually changed to reflect a corresponding shift in the seriousness with which a particular kind of crime was regarded. For example, robbery once was classified as *property crime* but eventually was shifted to the category of *violent crime*. *Public-order offenses*, also known as *moral charges*, once were defined to include vagrancy, liquor law violations, and drug offenses. Eventually, however, drug offenses were given a separate category of their own.

62. California—which, along with Texas, has the largest prisoner population in the country—mirrored these national trends. At the start of the decade of the 1980s, as the state began a period of unprecedented prison growth, the great majority of prisoners (62%) were incarcerated for crimes against persons (typically, robbery). Less than one third were sent to prison for property offenses, and only 6% were imprisoned for drug crimes. Over the course of the next 2 decades, however, the percentage of prisoners incarcerated for crimes against persons steadily declined and the number imprisoned for drug offenses rapidly increased. By the end of the decade of the 1980s, violent offenders no longer represented the majority of prisoners, and drug offenders had risen from 6% to nearly one quarter of all prisoners. These proportions have remained relatively stable, with property and drug offenders continuing to constitute over half the total number of California prisoners. The data from which these conclusions are drawn appear in a number of statistical reports compiled by the Data Analysis Unit of the California Department of Corrections, especially in a report entitled "Historical Trends, California Department of Corrections," summarizing trends over 20-year periods, beginning with 1976. It may be accessed electronically at http://www.cdc.state.ca.us/pdf/hist00.pdf.

63. Bureau of Justice Statistics, *Sourcebook of Criminal Justice Statistics, 1991* (Washington, DC: U.S. Department of Justice, 1991).

64. A. Blumstein, "Making Rationality Relevant—The American Society of Criminology 1992 Presidential Address," *Criminology* 31 (1993): 1.

65. Tonry, *Malign Neglect*, 107.

66. Barbara Meierhoefer, *The General Effects of Mandatory Minimum Prison Terms* (Washington, DC: Federal Justice Center, 1992).

67. Tonry, *Malign Neglect*, 115.

68. Ibid.

69. Bureau of Justice Statistics, *supra* note 7.

70. B. Poindexter, "The War on Crime Increases the Time: Sentencing Policies in the United States and South Africa," *Loyola of Los Angeles Journal of International and Comparative Law Review* 22 (2000): 375, 397; "The U.S. sentencing scheme has been found to disproportionately affect African-Americans outside the Three-Strikes realm because of sentencing laws like those distinguishing between 'crack' and powder cocaine. 'The sentencing disparities between powder cocaine and crack cocaine have been well documented, showing that punishments for these two forms of the same drug are correlated with the race of the user. . . .'" (footnotes and internal citations omitted).

71. P. Johnson, "At the Intersection of Injustice: Experiences of African American Women in Crime and Sentencing,"*American University Journal of Gender and the Law* 4 (1995): 1, 56.

72. *See, e.g.,* United States v. Walls, 841 F. Supp. 24 (D.D.C. 1994), remanded in part, 70 F.3d 1323 (D.C. Cir. 1995), and E. Rodriguez and J. Murawski, "Federal Judge: Crack Sentences Unconstitutional; 'Cruel and Unusual' Ruling Opens Door for Other Challenges," *Legal Times*, January 31, 1994, p. 1.

73. *See, e.g.,* U.S. v. Watkins, 179 F.3d 489, 504 (2d Cir. 1999) (8th Amendment not violated by 100-to-1 sentencing ratio for crack vs. powder cocaine); U.S. v. Alton, 60 F.3d 1065, 1070 (3d Cir. 1995) (equal protection not violated by disparate impact of severe penalties for crack cocaine offenses on African Americans); U.S. v. Hayden, 85 F.3d 153, 157 (4th Cir. 1996) (equal protection not violated by sentencing disparity between crack and powder cocaine); U.S. v. Alix, 86 F.3d 429, 437 n.5 (5th Cir. 1996) (same); U.S. v. Dunlap, 209 F.3d 472, 480–481 (6th Cir. 2000) (no constitutional violation stemming from 100-to-1 statutory sentencing disparity between crack and powder cocaine); U.S. v. Westbrook, 125 F.3d 996, 1010 (7th Cir. 1997) (same); U.S. v. Smith, 82 F.3d 241, 244 (8th Cir. 1996) (neither equal protection nor due process violated by sentencing disparity between crack and powder cocaine); U.S. v. Jackson, 84 F.3d 1154, 1161 (9th Cir. 1996) (equal protection not violated by sentencing disparity between crack and powder cocaine); U.S. v. Turner, 928 F.2d 956, 960 (10th Cir. 1991) (due process not violated by sentencing disparity between crack and powder cocaine); U.S. v. Matthews, 168 F.3d 1234, 1250–1251 (11th Cir. 1999) (equal protection not violated by crack cocaine sentencing guidelines).

74. Indeed, as one commentator put it, "nothing undermines the perception of racial fairness in the criminal justice system more than disparate sentencing for conviction of crack versus powdered cocaine." A. Bullock, "Challenges Facing the Profession: Perceptions of Divided Justice," *Suffolk University Law Review* 33 (1999): 1, 5.

75. J. Inciardi, "Drug-Involved Offenders: Crime-Prison-Treatment," *Prison Journal* 73 (1933): 253, 253.

76. For example, one review of the literature indicated that "the hypothesis that smoked cocaine is more likely to lead to addiction than is an equal dose used intranasally has never been tested on either animals or humans." In addition, patterns of use among humans suggest that the differences in "continuation rates" between the two drugs (i.e., their addictive potential) are relatively small, and in any event, they appear to be the result of "differences in the social circumstances of users themselves" (i.e., that crack is more available in areas where people's life circumstances make drug distribution and use more likely). *See* John Morgan and Lynne Zimmer, "The Social Pharmacology of Smokeable Cocaine: Not All It's Cracked Up to Be," in *Crack in America: Demon Drugs and Social Justice*, ed. Craig Reinarman and Harry Levine (Berkeley, CA: University of California Press, 1997), 143.

77. Jeff Grogger, "An Economic Model of Recent Trends in Violence," in *The Crime Drop in America*, ed. Alfred Blumstein and Joel Wallman (New York: Cambridge University Press, 2002).

78. William Chambliss, "Policing the Ghetto Underclass: The Politics of Law and Law Enforcement," *Social Problems* 41 (1994): 177, 183. *See also* King, "The Impact of Incarceration on African American Families: Implications for Practice," 145.

79. *See, e.g.*, the discussion of these issues in Nancy Walker, Michael Senger, Francisco Villarruel, and Angela Arboleda, *Lost Opportunities: The Reality of Latinos in the U.S. Criminal Justice System* (Washington, DC: National Council of La Raza, 2004).

80. John Scalia, *Federal Drug Offenders, 1999 with Trends 1984–99* [Bureau of Justice Statistics Special Report NCJ 187285] (Washington DC: U.S. Department of Justice, August 2001).

81. Studies show no consistent relationship between law enforcement efforts made in the War on Drugs and decreased drug use. In fact, recent data suggest a continued increase in use for some groups and some drugs. For example, one nationwide government study done in 2001 reported significant increases in the percentage of persons 12 years or older who were estimated to have used illicit drugs over the figures reported the previous year. The survey also found "statistically significant increases between 2000 and 2001 in the use of particular drugs or groups of illicit drugs, such as marijuana . . . cocaine . . . and the nonmedical use of pain relievers . . . and tranquilizers." Substance Abuse and Mental Health Services Administration, *Results from the 2001 National Household Survey on Drug Abuse: Volume I. Summary of National Findings*, Office of Applied Studies, NHYSDA Series H-17, DHHS Publication No. SMA 02-3758 (Rockville, MD: SAMHSA, 2002), 1.

82. *See* Matthew Durose and Patrick Langan, *Felony Sentences in State Courts, 2002* [Bureau of Justice Statistics Bulletin NCJ 206916] (Washington, DC: Department of Justice, December 2004).

83. Indeed, by the start of the 21st century, only 24% of the persons incarcerated in the federal prison system for drug offenses were White. This contrasted with fully 40% who were Black and 33% who were Latino. See Scalia, *Federal Drug Offenders*.

84. Juanita Diaz-Cotto, *Gender, Ethnicity, and the State: Latina and Latino Prison Politics* (Albany, NY: State University of New York Press, 1996), 115.

85. Francisco Villarruel and Nancy Walker, *Donde Esta La Justicia? A Call to Action on Behalf of Latino and Latina Youth in the U.S. Justice System* (Washington, DC: Building Blocks for Youth, 2002).

86. Eileen Poe-Yamagata and Michael Jones, *And Justice For Some* (San Francisco: National Council on Crime and Delinquency, 2000), 11.

87. This practice was approved by the U.S. Supreme Court in Richardson v. Ramirez, 418 U.S. 24, 41–56 (1974).

88. *See, e.g.,* a joint report by The Sentencing Project and Human Rights Watch, *Losing the Vote: The Impact of Felony Disenfranchisement in the United States* (Washington, DC: Sentencing Project, 1998). For two law review notes highly critical of the practice, *see* A. Shapiro, "Challenging Criminal Disenfranchisement Under the Voting Rights Act: A New Strategy," *Yale Law Journal* 103 (1993): 537 (referring to "the intentionally racist use of criminal disenfranchisement throughout the South a century ago" and arguing that contemporary "criminal disenfranchisement laws have a disproportionate impact on minority offenders"); and Note, "The Disenfranchisement of Ex-Felons Citizenship, Criminality, and the 'Purity of the Ballot Box,'" *Harvard Law Review* 102 (1989): 1300. *See also* Jeremy Travis's discussion of this and related issues: Jeremy Travis, "Invisible Punishment: An Instrument of Social Exclusion," in *Invisible Punishment: The Collateral Consequences of Mass Imprisonment*, eds. Marc Mauer and Meda Chesney-Lind (New York: W.W. Norton, 2001).

89. See the estimates and references cited in "Developments in the Law, The Law of Prisons," *Harvard Law Review* 115 (2002): 1838, 1940 (and footnotes cited therein).

90. *See* The Sentencing Project/Human Rights Watch Report, *Losing the Vote*.

91. N. Demleitner, "Internal Exile: The Need for Restrictions on Collateral Sentencing Consequences," *Stanford Law and Policy Review* 11 (1999): 153.

92. Note, *"Losing the Vote,"* 1310.

93. *See, e.g.,* E. Lotke and P. Wagner, "Prisoners of the Census: Electoral and Financial Consequences of Counting Prisoners Where They Go, Not Where They Come From," *Pace Law Review* 24 (2004): 587. For a broader discussion of these and other problems associated with minority overrepresentation in prison, as well as a set of potential solutions, *see* G. Ward and M. Marable, "Toward a New Civic Leadership: The Africana Criminal Justice Project," *Social Justice* 30 (2003): 89.

94. E. Blumenson and E. Nilsen, "How to Construct an Underclass, Or How the War on Drugs Became a War on Education," *Journal of Gender, Race and Justice* 6 (2002): 61, 65.

95. Asserting that drug dealers were "increasingly imposing a reign of terror on public and other federally assisted low-income housing tenants," Congress in 1988 passed the Anti-Drug Abuse Act of 1988. § 5122, 102 Stat. 4301, 42 U.S.C. §11901(3) (1994 ed.). Title 42 U.S.C. § 1437d (1) (6).

96. This practice was recently upheld by the U.S. Supreme Court in Department of Housing and Urban Development v. Rucker, 122 S.Ct. 1230 (2002).

97. Public Law No. 104-193 §115 (August 22, 1996).
98. Black and Latino children are already 3 times more likely to live below the poverty line. *See* Glover-Blackwell et al., *Searching for the Uncommon Ground*, 95. Given the differential drug enforcement policies discussed earlier, laws that disqualify persons from receiving public assistance and welfare benefits because of drug offenses are likely to further impoverish minority groups. If drug use is related to conditions of poverty and despair, then these policies seem likely to worsen the problem they were intended to solve. For a discussion of some of the other ways in which the application of these laws not only adversely affects African Americans but also undermine the ability of drug offenders to overcome their addictions (in part by making it more difficult for them to avail themselves of treatment opportunities), see Gwen Rubinstein and Debbie Mukamal, "Welfare and Housing—Denial of Benefits to Drug Offenders," in *Invisible Punishment: The Collateral Consequences of Mass Imprisonment*, ed. Marc Mauer and Meda Chesney-Lind (New York: W. W. Norton, 2002).

II

PRISON AS
CRIMINOGENIC CONTEXT

5

CONTEXT MATTERS: SOCIAL HISTORY, CIRCUMSTANCE, AND CRIME CAUSATION

What about those offenders who have suffered so much beforehand in life that they, in a way, have been punished long before they committed the crime they now have to be punished for? . . . I do not know. But I do know that I cannot accept a system for the ranking of values which by implication makes all these distinctions—and thereby the values they express—of negligible importance.

—Nils Christie[1]

What social psychology has given to an understanding of human nature is the discovery that forces larger than ourselves determine our mental life and our actions—that chief among these forces . . . [is] the power of the social situation.

—Mahzarin R. Banaji[2]

This chapter explores a core irony in American prison policy over the last several decades: As the United States became increasingly devoted to harsh policies of imprisonment—some consequences of which I described in the previous two chapters—the discipline of psychology was undergoing a revolution in thinking that drastically changed our perspective on the causes of crime and the psychological effects of prison pain. For the first time in the modern history of corrections, contemporary psychological theory challenged the logic of approaching crime control exclusively through the imprisonment of individual lawbreakers. Moreover, it directly contradicted the belief that what happened to people in prison—how they were treated, under what conditions, and for how long—did not much matter.

The new insights that I review in this chapter—ones emphasizing the importance of past and present context—were developed and refined over the last several decades. Yet, they played literally no role in the crime control strategies and policies of mass imprisonment that were devised

127

and implemented over exactly the same period. Despite the public policy implications of the new contextual model of behavior, it was ignored in precisely those policymaking arenas where its influence should have been felt. Instead, a renewed emphasis on the role of individual and presumably unencumbered free choice in criminal behavior was used to support harsh criminal justice and prison policies.

Criminal behavior thus continued to be treated as though it were the exclusive product of internal causes, and social and economic circumstances were regarded as irrelevant to the control of crime. This narrow and scientifically outmoded view of crime causation was embraced with, if anything, more enthusiasm than in the past. Correspondingly, attempts to transform criminogenic environments were increasingly portrayed as futile and misguided. Politicians urged, and policymakers devised, strategies of crime reduction that focused exclusively on identifying, containing, and incapacitating as many individual criminals as possible, punishing them with the utmost harshness, and largely ignoring the long-term psychological consequences of such treatment. Beginning in the mid-1970s, the criminal justice system began to move rapidly and decisively to do exactly those things.

The alleged demise of rehabilitation as a goal and justification for incarceration contributed significantly to these trends. Claims that prison rehabilitation programs everywhere were badly failing were used to support an antiquated and unfounded argument that criminality was an intractable trait and that the predisposition to offend would not yield even in the face of the most powerful and well-designed correctional programs. In essence, advocates of increasingly harsh prison policies contended that criminals were too innately bad to be changed for the better, no matter how potent the new therapeutic circumstance or program-oriented situation in which they were placed in prison.

By implication, prisoners were portrayed as much worse and tougher than the penal institutions to which they were being sent. That is, because prisoners' bad characters were thought to be too resilient to be changed for the better in these settings, they likely could not be harmed by them either. Thus, as the roots of criminal behavior increasingly were portrayed as residing in the extraordinarily strong and unmodifiable character of prisoners, "liberal" concerns over the potentially harmful effects of prison conditions came to be seen as exaggerated and misplaced. Soon, the nation witnessed the implementation of prison policies that were based on pure politics rather than valid theory or data.

Throughout the 1980s, as one commentator noted, "scholars who continue[d] to investigate social explanations" for crime were continually placed on the defensive by voices that called for a return to individualistic theories of criminal behavior.[3] But this renewed individualism was not restricted to crime control and prison policies. This was the same period during which *laissez faire* critiques of social welfare programs were embraced, and a range of economic policies were justified with rhetoric that was steeped in a 19th-century worldview. There was a broad public and political synergy between policies and programs that shifted governmental priorities from social welfare to social control.

It is not surprising that the emphasis on free will and personal autonomy lent itself to crime control policies that focused exclusively on individual responsibility and blame. Indeed, the voices calling loudly for a strengthening of these individualistic and punitive approaches to crime control tended "to see criminals as fundamentally different from other people—less bound by culture and less rational in their behavior" and to explain high crime rates in certain geographical areas in terms of "the movement of already deviant individuals and families into those localities rather than as the result of economic and social disadvantages affecting particular groups and areas."[4]

The last several decades of the 20th century saw a vigorous campaign of large-scale incarceration, pursued in the name of incapacitating and punishing the greatest number of wrongdoers possible. As I noted in chapter 3, prison populations skyrocketed, with a corresponding lack of concern over the particular conditions of confinement to which they were being sent. Even though the overwhelming majority of prisoners eventually would be released back into free society, little thought was given to the potentially harmful consequences of their long-term incarceration. However, as I suggest in this chapter, in light of what we know about the importance of social history and context in understanding the causes of crime and the consequences of harsh and uncaring treatment, that policy was premised on a fundamentally flawed set of behavioral assumptions.

THE CONTEXTUAL REVOLUTION IN PSYCHOLOGY[5]

The pervasive individualism that has characterized prison policy over much of the last 2 centuries, and which turned especially pessimistic and punitive over the last 3 decades, is now markedly at odds with contemporary psychological theory. At the outset of the era of mass imprisonment, Albert Bandura noted that traditional, largely individualistic theories of moral action typically assumed that behavioral standards routinely operated as internal mechanisms, controlling behavior from within by governing future actions and guiding subsequent choices. Persons were supposed to be restrained from reprehensible or illegal conduct through the operation of this internal moral compass, irrespective of the contexts in which they found themselves. However, Bandura observed, "the testimony of human behavior . . . contradicts this view."[6]

Even earlier, Stanley Milgram had provided classic demonstrations of the power of social settings to elicit extreme behavior. Milgram's research was conceived and interpreted in terms of *obedience*—the willingness of people to comply with extraordinary demands made by authority figures. But it also demonstrated the capacity of otherwise normal, psychologically healthy persons to engage in extremely aggressive and apparently hurtful behavior in response to the demands of the setting in which they had been placed. Milgram's conclusion—that "under certain circumstances, it is not so much the kind of person a man is as it is the kind of situation in which he is placed that determines his actions"[7]—had broad implications that extended to many other realms of social life, including crime and punishment.

Indeed, increased recognition of the importance of the situational and contextual determinants of behavior has occurred in many different areas of psychology over the last several decades. For example, "explaining the behavior of particular individuals" is now understood to require "not only psychological theory but also situational, biographical, and historical information."[8] As social psychologists Lee Ross and Richard Nisbett summarized,

> What has been demonstrated through a host of celebrated laboratory and field studies is that manipulations of the immediate social situation can overwhelm in importance the type of individual differences in personal traits or dispositions that people normally think of as being determinative of social behavior.[9]

One of those "celebrated" laboratory studies was conducted by Phillip Zimbardo, Curtis Banks, and myself, and it has some direct relevance to the issues that are addressed later in this book. We found that the behavior of a sample of otherwise normal, psychologically healthy young men was dramatically altered when they were placed in a simulated prison environment and randomly assigned to the role of either a prisoner or a guard. Their role-driven actions emerged rapidly and were extreme. Most of the "guards" became aggressive and abusive in the treatment of the "prisoners," who in turn were psychologically distressed by the experience to such a degree that nearly half of them had to be released because they suffered acute emotional breakdowns. None of the personality or attitudinal measures used in the study explained the behavior of the participants, which seemed to occur entirely as a function of the extreme nature of the environment in which they had been placed.[10]

However, empirical findings and theoretical insights like these extended well beyond the subdiscipline of social psychology. In fact, virtually every area of empirical psychology now recognizes the importance of social context and situation in making sense of the phenomena once studied in sterile laboratory settings. For example, the shape of contemporary cognitive psychology was changed when prominent researchers like Ulric Neisser began to emphasize the importance of examining human memory in everyday situations and "natural contexts." One of those researchers was even led to declare that "context is everything" in the study of memory and cognition.[11]

Indeed, Michael Spivey and his colleagues have suggested that the immediate visual context is often used by listeners to resolve linguistic ambiguities, and the Spivey team and others have speculated that people actually use the external environment as "storage bins" for information and memories that are not essential or possible for us to represent internally.[12] Whatever else these emerging paradigms reflect, they signal a decentering of the individual perceiver, who is now no longer seen as the exclusive repository of images of the external world but is rather highly dependent on that world to function as an "external memory store" to assist his or her internal cognitive processing.[13]

The important influence of social context on cognitive processes was recognized over the last several decades by numerous researchers in other areas of psychology who studied a wide range of related topics. For example, psychologists who specialized in cognitive development increasingly emphasized the importance of social and cultural context in setting the broad but crucial parameters within which children learn to think and develop intellectually. My Santa Cruz colleague Barbara Rogoff has been one of the leaders in documenting the nature and application of this context-based process.[14] Psycholinguists, including another of my colleagues, Raymond Gibbs, have argued that our use of metaphors to structure concepts is strongly shaped by how we "culturally conceptualize situations" and "by our interactions with social/cultural artifacts around us." Gibbs observed that "the cognitive models we create surely extend beyond the individual."[15]

Similarly, a recent collaboration between distinguished law professor Anthony Amsterdam and renowned cognitive psychologist Jerome Bruner examined the categorizing, narrative, and rhetorical practices of law and lawyers. Underscoring a fundamental social contextualist point, the authors began their extended analysis of these issues by noting that

> everything that human beings do . . . is in some sense specialized, reflecting the particular roles people are playing, the specific aims they are pursuing, the context-dependent position they occupy in their society. In that sense, one can give no general account of human pursuits.[16]

And they ended it by observing that "there always remains the wild card of *all* interpretation—the consideration of *context*, that ineradicable element in meaning-making."[17]

Even in personality psychology itself—for obvious reasons likely to be one of the last bastions of psychological individualism—Walter Mischel's thoughtful summary of the state of the field in the 1990s acknowledged that "context sensitivity and discriminativeness across situations" are "the rule rather than the exception for most social behavior."[18] In fact, Mischel is as clear about this now as he was more than a generation ago: "One of the core conclusions that needs to be drawn from 50 years of research is that the situation of the moment plays an enormously powerful role in the often automatic activation and regulation of complex human social behavior."[19] And in clinical psychology, one theorist's social contextualist suggestion a quarter-century ago, that "clinical psychology is a form of social engineering,"[20] is a perspective that present-day reviewers now acknowledge "has had a significant impact on clinical science."[21]

To take just one example of how clinical science has been influenced by this paradigm shift, a therapeutic approach termed *relapse prevention* has been successful in solving the difficult clinical problem of treating alcohol and drug addictions on a long-term basis. It does so by focusing on "the dynamic interactions between multiple risk factors and situational determinants" of the addiction-related behavior.[22] Specifically, therapists concentrate on "the goal of identifying and preventing high-risk situations for relapse," so that patients learn to recognize and respond appropriately to (often by avoiding) various contextual cues that are associated with their addictive behavior.[23] Although the therapist still concentrates on individual patients, the focus clearly has shifted outward—to the situations and circumstances that influence their actions.

These empirical and theoretical insights from across a wide range of specialties in contemporary psychology are the basis on which a new psychological model of the person has been constructed that emphasizes the role of past and present social contexts in shaping and influencing all forms of social behavior. This contemporary psychological framework has profound implications for rational crime control policy and for the development of intelligent limits to prison pain. Fashioning a fair and effective societal response to crime requires a valid understanding of its nature and origins. Too often in the history of imprisonment—and certainly over the last several decades in which crime and punishment have been so highly politicized—prison policy has been premised on myth and what we now recognize as mistaken assumption.

Indeed, a contemporary social contextual understanding of behavior represents an important, definitive challenge to the antiquated, individualistic notions that have guided past thinking about crime and punishment. The last several decades have produced more systematic knowledge of, and empirically based insights into, the nature of criminality than any previous period in history. These contemporary analyses of the origins of social and criminal behavior call the recent overdependency on imprisonment directly into question. As more valid models of behavior emerge and eventually are integrated into criminal law and other parts of the criminal justice system, prison is destined to become less central in any overarching and effective strategy of crime control. The remainder of this chapter reviews some of the empirical research that provides the basis for this alternative framework and the emerging challenges to which it gives rise.

CRIMINOGENIC LIVES: THE ROLE OF SOCIAL HISTORICAL FACTORS

The attention now devoted by psychologists to the study of the entire life course reflects awareness of what one researcher has termed "the reality imperatives—situational demands, opportunities, and barriers" that shape our lives.[24] Few contemporary psychologists would disagree that human behavior must be examined in context because "individuals are embedded in a changing social, cultural, and economic environment, as well as being products of a life history of events, beliefs, relationships, and behavior."[25] To be sure, the work of developmental contextualists has greatly increased our understanding of the importance of social context in shaping the individual life course: "A given organismic attribute only has meaning for psychological development by virtue of . . . its relation to a particular set of time-bound, contextual conditions."[26]

Several decades of psychological study and analysis now support the proposition that childhood events and developmental contexts—what I call social historical factors—profoundly influence and affect adult behavior—including criminality. This emphasis on the background experiences and early childhood development of persons who have committed criminal offenses also connects directly with a renewed emphasis in the discipline of psychology on the use of social historical research techniques,[27] or what is sometimes termed "the study of lives."[28] It is based in part on the vast and growing literature on the importance of past and present social contexts in understanding human behavior,[29] as well as on studies of the ways in which certain kinds of past experiences can shape and influence human development over the entire life course.[30] As one researcher has noted, the social or life history approach "implies a holistic stance to social reality" and is the "method of choice when complex human events are at stake, when inquiries into the subjective realm of human beliefs, motives and actions in complex social matrices are involved."[31] This method is in many ways uniquely suited to provide insights into how the backgrounds of criminal offenders have helped to shape their character, influence the course of their development, and affect their actions as adults.

Psychologists have long known that children need to be provided with "dependable attachment, protection, guidance, stimulation, nurturance, and ways of coping with adversity"[32] during their early years of growth and development. But we also now know that many persons who commit crimes as adults have lacked most—or all—of these things in their early lives. The two facts are not unrelated. As I discuss later in this chapter, evidence that a great many persons who engage in adult criminal behavior once lived in abject poverty, frequently were the victims of physical or emotional abuse and chronic neglect, and were exposed to a variety of other painful experiences as children has important implications for crime control and prison policy.

Two decades ago, developmental psychologists Ann Masten and Norman Garmezy proposed an extremely useful framework with which to identify and understand psychologically critical events that occur in the course of an individual life history. Their "risk factors" model focuses on those events whose presence in one's background indicates "a higher probability for the development of a disorder" later in life. The factors represent "risk" because they are statistically associated with a higher likelihood of subsequently experiencing one or another kind of psychological problem.[33] In addition, under their rubric, *stressors* refer to "any change in the environment which typically—i.e., in the average person—induces a high degree of continual tension and interferes with normal patterns of response."[34] As much of the literature that I summarize in this chapter indicates, much crime is committed by persons whose life histories have been pervaded by such risk factors and whose adult lives also surround them with severe tension-producing environmental stressors. The combination of these forces inhibits the development and maintenance of prosocial and law-abiding patterns of behavior.

Indeed, Masten and Garmezy made precisely this connection in their seminal work: "Children who pursue delinquent careers may have been exposed to very severe stresses and harmful life events, genetic disadvantage, inappropriate parental models, selective reinforcement by parents of the child's maladaptive behavior, and chronic low self-esteem."[35] When added up over the course of a single life, these multiple risk factors form a whole that is greater than the individual parts; their aggregate effects can have profound consequences for a wide range of problematic adult behaviors, including adult criminal behavior.

For example, in recent years, increased attention has been given to the mechanisms by which the structural variable of poverty produces significant psychological consequences for children who experience it. We know that poverty forces family members to adapt to scarcity in ways that affect interpersonal relationships and, in turn, child development. One ethnographer studying children growing up in a poor urban neighborhood acknowledged their impressive resourcefulness in coping with poverty, but was nonetheless forced to conclude that these admirable adaptive skills were still "no match for the physical toll of poverty and its constant frustrations and humiliations."[36]

Among other things, researchers have documented the ways in which economic hardship produces psychological distress for both parents and children. This distress undermines parents' ability to provide nurturant care and increases tendencies toward inconsistent discipline that, in turn, are associated with increased depression, drug use, and delinquency for their adolescent children. In addition, the sheer stress of poverty makes parents more vulnerable to negative life events of all sorts, and this further undermines their capacity for supportive and involved parenting.[37]

Economic hardship can also worsen or exacerbate a parent's own preexisting emotional problems and personal vulnerabilities. Scarce resources mean that such long-standing problems are likely to go unaddressed and that instability within the family itself is likely to increase. Thus, poverty does great damage to children through their parents—by forcing their parents to grapple with a staggering number of day-to-day problems that eventually may overwhelm them, compromising their own well-being, and undermining their ability to serve in consistent caretaker roles. Family turmoil and chronic transience often result.

Poverty also may introduce other forms of chaos and instability into the lives of children who experience it. Poor parents often change residences to escape creditors or to leave deteriorating and conflictual social and personal relationships behind. Some move for no apparent reason at all. The children who are captives of these patterns of instability often have little or nothing in their lives that is constant or that lasts long enough to allow them to make genuine emotional investments. Some lack the psychological permanence that is needed to structure their internal lives and to use the structure as the basis on which to build stable identities. Thus, children in environments that are not only deprived but also chaotic and unpredictable, often show the greatest adverse effects.

We know that many persons who engage in crime have experienced high levels of poverty and economic deprivation throughout their lifetimes, and psychological research has identified many of the intermediate steps along the pathway from this early experience to adult criminality. Among the long-term consequences of childhood poverty, researchers have documented the persistent despair and emotional distress that severe economic deprivation can inflict. One national survey found that welfare status or perceived financial stress was significantly related to children's emotional and behavioral problems—specifically, to higher levels of depression, antisocial behavior, and impulsivity.[38] To the extent to which children who lack the resources and socialization to seek professional help for these emotional problems are tempted to cope by "self-medicating," early patterns of illicit drug use, subsequent higher rates of addiction, and eventual criminal behavior are likely to emerge.

Poverty is also directly related to other risk factors that are known to have long-term adverse—and criminogenic—effects. For example, we now know that persistent poverty is predictive of severe and recurrent child abuse. Poor communities tend to lack organized community services designed to alleviate stressors that contribute to child abuse. Instead, most poor families are "systematically shunted into community systems which are predominately punitive and regulatory, and conversely diverted away from those systems which are supportive and enhancing of parental role performance."[39]

In fact, one group of researchers concluded that long-term or chronic poverty was systematically related to patterns of repeated maltreatment. Thus, children who were abused on multiple occasions were more likely to live "in families with intergenerational histories of poverty."[40] They also lived in families "with a generalized history of violence, which in some cases explained their parents' criminal histories."[41] The long-term poverty created a larger context for the abuse, violence, and criminality in which the children were reared: "The problems of these families, then, are inextricably tied to both past and present experiences of economic deprivation and associated antisocial behaviors."[42] Indeed, the researchers concluded that "violence does occur at all income levels but it is more often repeated among the persistently poor."[43]

Over the long run, these effects tend to recur and reappear from one generation to the next. Thus, poverty may beget violence that—particularly if it leads to incarceration—often begets continuing poverty for the next generation of children. This fact may help to explain the comparatively higher rates of child maltreatment that have been reported in African American families, in which poverty tends to be chronic and structurally embedded rather than transitory. For example,

> Black children suffer disproportionately from virtually every form of stress affecting full and healthy development. Too many black children live in conditions of poverty that deprive them of necessary medical care, adequate housing, food, and clothing. Yet none of these stressors is more threatening to the healthy development of black children and to the stability of their families than interfamilial child abuse.[44]

The linkages from childhood poverty to adult crime and violence may appear complicated, but they are rarely difficult to understand. In addition to the role that poverty plays in increasing instability and despair, in undermining self-esteem, in forcing the undersocialization of children, and in interfering with consistent and nurturant parenting—all of which put children at greater risk of delinquent behavior—we know that poverty results in increased levels of frustration. Indeed, chronic poverty can result in chronic frustration. Depending on the circumstances—particularly the reasons a person perceives that his or her desired goals are persistently blocked—

such frustration may produce greater levels of "angry aggression."[45] Numerous studies provide empirical support for the commonsense proposition that the kind of frustration that makes people angry also often leads to subsequent aggression. In extreme cases, this may help to account for the relationship that researchers have found between adult poverty and homicide.[46]

In addition to poverty, material deprivation, and chronic instability, the social histories of many criminal defendants are characterized by a host of other risk factors. Child abuse or *maltreatment* has been defined variously as "the degree to which a parent uses negative, inappropriate control strategies with his or her child"[47] or "acts of omission or commission by a parent or guardian that are judged by a mixture of community values and professional expertise to be inappropriate and damaging."[48] Whichever definition is used, child maltreatment has been widely recognized as an important social problem since at least the 1960s.[49]

The long-term psychological consequences of child maltreatment now are very well understood. We know that child abuse can be psychologically destructive and, depending on its nature and severity, can produce profoundly disabling long-term effects in those who are its victims.[50] Indeed, as early as the 1970s, the pattern by which a "battered child tends to become a battering parent" was well enough established to be referred to as the *classical battered-child syndrome*.[51] But we also knew by then that the later problematic effects of such mistreatment were more general in nature.

Although it is difficult to predict precisely which of the harmful effects of maltreatment any particular child will manifest later in life, studies show that juveniles who have become involved in delinquency "have endured child abuse and neglect at far greater rates than estimates for the population as a whole and for the low-income groups in particular."[52] Indeed, by the late 1960s and early 1970s, researchers already had identified the connection between child abuse and subsequent criminal behavior.[53] By the mid-1970s, the entry in the *Textbook of Pediatrics* that dealt with child abuse contained this stark observation: "The untreated [abusive] families tend to produce children who grow up to be juvenile delinquents and murderers, as well as the batterers of the next generation."[54]

It is now a widely accepted scientific fact that abused children are much more likely to engage in violence as adults, giving rise to what has been called a *cycle of violence*.[55] Developmental psychologists and others understand that although extreme physical punishment may produce conformity in the immediate instance in which it is administered, it tends to increase the probability of deviance later in life, including delinquency in adolescence and violent crime as an adult.[56] In a society whose criminal justice system has resorted to harsh punishment so quickly in recent years, it is of no small consequence to note that those who have been neglected and abused as children have a higher likelihood of arrests for delinquency, adult criminality, and violent criminal behavior.[57] This relationship is not restricted to one particular ethnic or racial group. Thus, in general, "abused and neglected children demonstrate increased risk of becoming adult criminals and of becoming adult violent criminals. . . ."[58]

There are broad contextual explanations for the interpersonal transmission of violence. We know that family environment is "a key factor in understanding the etiology and maintenance of aggressive behavior," and several researchers have suggested that patterns of behaving like these are transmitted from one generation to another implicitly through modeling. That is, "children learn to aggress by observing aggression, particularly that of their parents who are familiar and powerful models."[59] As one early reviewer put it, harsh punishment "both frustrates the child and provides him a model" with which to discharge that frustration.[60] Similarly, Joan McCord has suggested that aggressive parental behavior tends to recur in the children who are exposed to it in part because aggressive fathers are likely to create the social environments conducive to aggressive behavior.[61]

Other aspects of a child's life may worsen the effects of this abuse or act as additional risk factors that must be overcome. For example, many children who suffer abuse at the hands of family members also live in communities in which they are exposed to violence outside the home. Indeed, one study concluded that children who grew up in urban housing projects were exposed to traumatic violence comparable to that experienced by children who lived in "war zones," and that many of them had the same kinds of psychological sequelae and needed the same kinds of treatment as their battle-scarred counterparts.[62] Moreover, notwithstanding the progress made since the 1960s in quelling overt expressions of racism in this society, it has been noted that significant numbers of African American and Latino children "still encounter expressions of racial hatred, live in racially segregated neighborhoods, and endure the suspicion widespread among many people in positions of authority."[63] Thus, in addition to the community violence to which they are exposed, they must cope with the long-term stress and microaggression to which racism has subjected them.

Taken collectively, *these* are the deep roots of crime and violence in our society. The basic causal connections have been well established in study after study, confirming the existence of these unfortunate cycles—ones that begin at home and ones in which many lawbreakers have become deeply enmeshed. The psychological focus on risk factors allows us to better identify the ways in which the social histories of persons who have committed crimes differ from those of most law-abiding citizens. Appreciating the long-term, cumulative effects of these risk factors often helps to account—in psychological rather than legal terms—for a person's presence in a courtroom or a prison yard.

JUVENILE INSTITUTIONALIZATION: STATE-SANCTIONED RISK FACTORS

In addition to poverty and parental maltreatment, many persons convicted of adult criminal offenses have been exposed to another set of powerful but often overlooked risk factors in their backgrounds and social histories. As children, many of them have been confined in juvenile institutions where they have been subjected to psychologically harmful conditions that are severe enough to produce long-term damage. These extreme experiences can greatly increase the likelihood that they will have subsequent emotional problems, engage in further delinquent behavior, and commit adult crimes later in life. Thus, notwithstanding the benefits of juvenile justice system interventions that are properly designed and caring, many young persons are subjected to traumatic forms of institutional mistreatment that act as risk factors for later criminal behavior.[64]

Research on juvenile facilities documents the fact that far too many children placed there are subjected to "the corrosive and brutalizing inhumanity of custodial institutions," where they are abused again, this time within "a culture of bullying, intimidation and almost routine self harm" that prevails inside the places they are sent.[65] In these cases, the experience of juvenile institutionalization adds to the cumulative effects of years of prior exposure to the kind of criminogenic risk factors I discussed in the previous section.

For children who are subjected to even earlier state intervention in the form of foster care placements, this pattern may begin when they are relatively young—long before any delinquent behavior has occurred. Studies of children who have been placed in the child welfare system indicate that they suffer from a host of untreated problems that, in fact, may be exacerbated by poor-quality foster care. It is not surprising that many of them eventually are placed in juvenile justice institutions.

For example, one researcher found that children in foster care were twice as likely to have been held back a grade, were 4 times as likely to have been expelled from school, and, even by age 17, to read at about a seventh-grade level. The children in this study were more likely to have had contact with the legal and mental health systems—more than one third had spent at least a night in a correctional facility, and one quarter reported having been prescribed psychotropic medications. Moreover, they typically were subjected to multiple foster care placements, and nearly 40% had been in four or more foster homes. Most of these placement changes required the children to move to different schools as well as residences, creating social and academic instability.[66]

Each early institutional intervention can increase the likelihood that a subsequent one will occur. Children who leave harmful foster care placements are at greater risk of behavioral problems that, in turn, lead to incarceration in juvenile justice system institutions. Unfortunately, few juvenile institutions are structured to address the lasting effects of previous trauma. Indeed, in many parts of the country, the older that children become and the deeper into the system they travel, the worse the conditions and the treatment to which they will be exposed. For example, one study of the California Youth Authority—the part of the state's juvenile justice system to which older children are sent—reached the "specific and urgent" recommendation in the mid-1980s that "our present system for dealing with youthful offenders needs drastic overhauling," in large part because of the extent to which it "return[ed] to freedom young men and women who have been brutalized by their institutional experience."[67]

But these critical conclusions are not restricted to a single state or to a particular time. In the mid-1970s, the National Advisory Commission on Criminal Justice Standards and Goals noted that juvenile justice institutions in the United States were not effective in accomplishing much of anything other than punishing young offenders. They did not appear to deter juveniles from future crime, and although they gave the impression of protecting the community, "the protection does not last." The Commission concluded that such places may "relieve the community of responsibility by removing the young offender, but they make successful integration unlikely. They change the committed offender, but the change is more likely to be negative than positive."[68]

Similarly, a major study sponsored by the Department of Justice and published in the early 1980s reached a number of conclusions on the effects of juvenile institutions.[69] It was published at around the time when criminal justice policies in general were becoming harsher and support for punishment-oriented responses to juvenile as well as adult crime was on the rise. Perhaps the most dramatic findings pertained to the lack of overall effectiveness of the juvenile justice system: "With few exceptions, intervention by the agencies of social control does not play even a moderate role in decreasing the seriousness of adult contacts."[70] In fact, the author of the study reported not only that the juvenile justice system was failing to accomplish anything positive but also that it appeared to be counterproductive: "To place youth in the 'troublemaker' category early in their school careers may only result in treatment which maximizes the fulfillment of the prophesy."[71]

Thus, children who were brought into the juvenile system were doing significantly worse than those with comparable offenses who were not:

> It is apparent that the consequences of processing have been continuing misbehavior and continuing involvement while similar persons who have not become so heavily involved in the system are less likely to

continue to engage in behavior which results in their names appearing in the public records.[72]

The careful design of the research made its conclusions about the long-term negative consequences of juvenile institutionalization difficult to ignore. Yet that appeared to be exactly what happened.

Thus, 16 years later the American Bar Association and the U.S. Department of Justice issued a joint report on the state of juvenile justice institutions in the United States. Echoing the very concerns expressed in the nationwide study conducted in the early 1980s, it acknowledged that institutions in the late 1990s were "increasingly overcrowded" and "significantly deficient," and incarcerated a disproportionate number of minority young offenders for property and drug-related crimes.[73] Areas of concern included what the authors described as "well documented deficiencies" in conditions of confinement, the nature and quality of treatment and educational services, security, and suicide prevention. As they noted, "subjecting youth to abusive and unlawful conditions of confinement serves only to *increase rates of violence and recidivism and to propel children into the adult criminal justice system.*"[74]

In this sense, then, involuntary confinement in poorly run juvenile correctional facilities is a risk factor for adult criminality. Damaging institutional experiences—ones that the children certainly did not choose—can adversely affect their future behavior. The sad irony is obvious: Children may be made worse by the very institutions charged with the responsibility of making them better. Moreover, in this instance, the criminogenic risk factors have been created and imposed directly by the state rather than by an abusive parent or family member. Yet, the long-term consequences are equally predictable.

CRIMINOGENIC CONTEXTS:
THE ROLE OF IMMEDIATE SITUATIONS

Modern psychological theory has established another important component to the relationship between social context and criminal behavior. Unlike the previous sections in which I reviewed studies that focused on accumulated past contexts—the developmental risk factors that are embedded in social and institutional histories—this section concentrates on the more immediate influence of the present situations or settings in which criminal behavior occurs.

In the broadest terms, we now know that the structure of the situation in which behavior transpires can exert a powerful influence over the shape and direction of that behavior. Crime is no exception to this general rule. That is, crime often occurs as much because of the characteristics of the situation or setting where it takes place as the characteristics of the people who engage in it.

There are several senses in which this can be true. In some instances, the *criminogenic*, or crime-producing, context consists of microevents—immediate provocations, affronts, or inducements—that help to precipitate criminal acts. In other instances, the criminogenic environment is broader and more atmospheric in nature. That is, there are certain kinds of communities and neighborhoods in which the behavioral norms and expectations, the available opportunity structures, and the frequency and salience of interpersonal conflicts combine to greatly increase the likelihood that their residents will engage in criminal behavior. Criminogenic contexts need to be understood in all of these ways—as focused, immediate, and acute, as well as broad, atmospheric, and chronic.

In addition, as I discuss at the end of this chapter, social history and present context are closely intertwined. The prevalence of social historical risk factors is greatest in those neighborhoods and communities where criminogenic contexts and influences are widespread and severe. Moreover, the individual adaptations that we make to difficult life circumstances are shaped by our past history and may intensify in powerful ways the effects of background criminogenic factors. That is, attempts to overcome the stress in one's life are shaped by background and history. Thus, people who were subjected to many risk factors earlier in life may find that they lack the personal resources and resiliency to cope effectively with the stressors that they encounter later on. Moreover, poor adaptive skills not only fail to solve current problems but also may make the effects of past trauma more powerful, creating new problems of their own. Drug use is a good example of an attempt to cope with life stress that frequently worsens rather than ameliorates it, and often increases the likelihood of subsequent criminal behavior.

The importance of taking present context into account in attempts to understand and predict behavior is routinely recognized in many professional environments. In fact, in forensic settings that require decision makers to attempt to predict future violent behavior, traditional models of clinical judgment are now being called into question and criticized for assuming that "behavior is largely independent of context." Researchers concede that the narrowly individualistic approach used in the past makes the models "poorly suited" to the task of "assessing risk in order to effectively manage potentially violent patients in the community."[75] Instead, there is increasingly widespread recognition of the value of what has been called a *conditional* model of violence prediction. In this model, the "enduring features of the patient's life situation" and the range of "foreseeable events or stressors" that he or she is likely to encounter are among the important contextual factors that mental health professionals are encouraged to take explicitly into account.[76]

Indeed, more sophisticated contemporary approaches to violence prediction and violence risk assessment have already begun to incorporate an explicitly contextual, or *ecological*, perspective into what were previously highly individualistic, purely person-centered inquiries. "The advantage of such an ecological approach is to increase emphasis on social and situational factors that may, in conjunction with individual characteristics, exacerbate or protect against the occurrence of violent behavior."[77] Of course, the same approach used to predict future violent or criminal behavior appropriately can be used to understand and evaluate past criminality as well. This new perspective promises to modify the way we think about crime control strategies, legal culpability, and prison policy. Seeing violent behavior as a product of the situation in which it occurs should provoke a reexamination of exclusively individual-centered approaches to reducing crime, the narrow doctrines by which moral blame for wrongdoing is ascribed, and the overall logic or rationale for the especially harsh punishment of criminal acts.

Much of the research on the contextual determinants of crime has been conducted by social psychologists, who, by training, tend to focus more on situational than dispositional influences on behavior. For example, contrary to traditional claims that violence occurs "mainly out of people's persistent internal drives," social psychologist Leonard Berkowitz has long maintained that human aggression is "largely reactive, a response to situational conditions."[78] Berkowitz acknowledged that some persons may be more likely to respond aggressively than others, but has been quick to add that "appropriate situational stimuli" are virtually always required to provoke the violent reaction.[79] More specifically, he has argued that situations in which persons are frustrated or thwarted in achieving their goals generally raise the probability that aggression of some sort will occur.[80]

Research by social psychologist Philip Zimbardo and others on what has been termed *deindividuation* and *depersonalization* similarly indicates that when people live and interact under conditions of relative anonymity, or when they are in situations in which their sense of self-awareness and concern for social evaluation are reduced, they are, in turn, more likely to engage in aggression.[81]

Henry Steadman has been instrumental in advancing an explicit situational approach to violence in which the characteristics of the immediate circumstances under which violent behavior occurs are carefully analyzed. For example, in one study he examined the situational determinants of certain extreme forms of violent crime—specifically, homicides and assaults that were not committed as incidental to some other crime and that were serious enough to result in incarceration.[82] When these violent encounters were subjected to a microanalysis in which both the motives of the perpetrators and the sequence of events that immediately preceded the aggressive behavior were examined, several characteristic patterns emerged.

Steadman found that the violence was often precipitated by an *identity attack*—an insult or challenge to the perpetrator's sense of self. This identity attack was followed by an escalating pattern in which the victim attempted to verbally influence the antagonist. When these initial influence attempts failed, they led to threats that were followed by expressions of intentions to retaliate. In the final stages of the violent encounter, the verbal conflict ended and a physical conflict began. Steadman found that both the perpetrators and victims of this kind of violence shared a self-concept that seemed to require them to counterattack and retaliate when aggressed against. Whether they had been socialized to embrace the norms of violent retaliation—perhaps in institutional settings, where this pattern is widespread—or lived in circumstances in which they had little else from which to derive self-esteem than their ability to forcefully demand "respect," the response seemed automatic once the conflict had escalated beyond a certain point. Obviously, the greater the number of people who are socialized in this way in a particular neighborhood or community, the greater the likelihood of such violent encounters.

Also, as perhaps would be expected, Steadman found that violence was more likely to occur in situations in which one of the participants had a weapon. Surprisingly, the person who initially possessed the weapon more typically was the one who was victimized in the violent encounter itself. Nonetheless, the social contextual implication is obvious: Ease of access to weapons increases levels of violence. Social settings, neighborhoods, and communities where people feel they are in danger and need weapons for self-protection also may set in motion a self-fulfilling prophecy whereby the weapons themselves increase the likelihood that they will be used.

Other contextual models of criminality have focused on what researchers have termed *criminal embeddedness*, or the degree to which the places where people live immerse them in a network of interpersonal relationships that increase their exposure to crime-prone role models. In some instances this network includes what are in essence tutelage relationships in which persons with little or no criminal experience are influenced in a direct way by more sophisticated criminal actors who are present in the neighborhoods where they live.[83] Indeed, the process of "getting into street crime" requires some of the very same social skills that lead to success in other contexts—in particular, a heightened sensitivity to people and the ability to learn effectively from others. However, the goals to which those skills are applied—criminal or not—are shaped largely by the context in which someone is embedded.

Many contextual models of criminal behavior are more global and less microanalytic in nature. For example, a group of sociological researchers has used the term *neighborhood disadvantage* to describe the nexus or cluster of interrelated ecological factors that often accompany poverty and amplify its negative effects on individual development as well as adult behavior.[84] These factors help to disrupt the social organization of the neighborhood, undermine the creation of shared community norms, and weaken any generalized or collective support for positive family socialization.

Neighborhood disadvantage can be criminogenic in several ways. For example, high rates of unemployment can adversely affect homelife and the prevalence of single-parent families in neighborhoods may minimize the amount of time that children spend with positive role models. Disadvantaged neighborhoods are also often characterized by extreme levels of transience and mobility that contribute to an overall sense of impermanence and disorganization that, in turn, undermines the development of stable, consistent, and consensual community norms against engaging in criminal behavior.

Finally, although they are conceptually distinct and can be analytically separated, the two broad categories of criminogenic influences I have discussed in this chapter—traumatic social histories and criminogenic situations—are highly interconnected and co-occurring in real life. There are several obvious ways in which this is so. For one, many victims of early childhood mistreatment are concentrated in neighborhoods that also are plagued by criminogenic social conditions. Not only are these people more vulnerable to structural disadvantage (because they are more likely to lack the personal resources to overcome it), but they are more likely to encounter criminogenic circumstances throughout their life course. For example, poverty not only is a risk factor in its own right, and correlated with other risk factors (such as child maltreatment) but also is directly related to criminogenic circumstances like neighborhood disadvantage.

The consequences of early childhood deprivation and maltreatment typically reverberate through the life course of many criminal defendants. Early trauma predisposes children to social and emotional problems that may continue to plague them as adolescents and young adults. Absent positive, sustained, and nurturing interventions—precisely the kind of interventions that, because of the limited access to high-quality social services and therapeutic resources in the communities where they live, these children are unlikely to obtain—their problems tend to persist into adulthood. This means they will be less able to overcome, manage, or negotiate the interpersonally complex and challenging situations that they encounter. They may be unable to find nurturant or sustaining relationships to buffer them from the structural hardship that surrounds them, and their ability to create healthy and competent adult identities may be correspondingly compromised.

Past experience can shape the context of present decision making and also often leads to the development of problematic patterns and styles of coping with difficult situations that are, as I noted previously, self-fulfilling in nature. That is, many of the adaptive reactions acquired in the attempt to overcome bad situations are so counterproductive that they elicit the very same kind of negative treatment that produced them, or increase the likelihood that the very outcome that the person seeks to avoid will occur. For example, some adolescents react to the painful memory of past mistreatment and rejection with avoidance behavior—by pushing people away, becoming aggressive, or acting emotionally distant. But these adaptations can lead to further hostile treatment by others and even more interpersonal rejection. A pattern of ever-escalating misbehavior and social disconnection from others is more likely to ensue.[85]

THE CRIMINOGENICS OF RACE AND ETHNICITY IN A DIVIDED SOCIETY

In the last chapter, I discussed some of the race-based structural inequalities that racial and ethnic minorities—especially African Americans—continue to confront in our society and that help to account for minority overrepresentation in the criminal justice system. The persistence of large structural inequalities translates into differences in the day-to-day lives of minority citizens. Among other things, it means that normative social and institutional histories and present life circumstances still vary by race in the United States, and do so in ways that create large disparities in exposure to a wide range of criminogenic factors. I also suggested that recent legal reforms that systematically excluded these structural factors from consideration at the time of criminal sentencing exacerbated a long-standing historical pattern of racial disproportions in prison.

In the final section of this chapter, I briefly discuss just some of the ways that race and ethnicity are intertwined in our society with circumstances and situations that are criminogenic in nature. Indeed, in an observation with direct implications for understanding the causes of crime and the fairness of punishment, William Julius Wilson has argued that "the social problems of urban life in the United States are, in large measure, the problems of racial inequality."[86] Wilson suggested that centuries of discrimination and prejudice produced racial divisions in the labor force that continued to disadvantage minorities through the 1980s. These divisions were exacerbated by impersonal economic shifts of the sort that regularly occur in advanced industrial societies. But in a society in which economic marginality was so closely tied to race, their effects rippled through minority communities with more destructive consequences than others.

Thus, Wilson cited data showing that "Blacks have experienced a deterioration of their economic position on nearly all the major labor-market indicators" through the mid-1980s.[87] He suggested that a social transformation had occurred in which "a disproportionate concentration of the most disadvantaged segments of the urban Black population" had produced "a social milieu significantly different from the environment that existed in these communities several decades ago."[88] Wilson concluded that this dynamic was responsible for the creation of what he termed a *tangle of pathology* that plagued the American inner city.[89]

Modern psychological theory tells us that this "tangle" is made of structural and social contextual components, as this chapter has attempted to make clear. But we also know that these structural and social contextual components have psychological consequences for those who experience them. Psychologists understand that the racial disparities and interpersonal racism to which persons of color continue to be exposed in our society are, to say the least, "stressful."[90] For example, economic disadvantage creates high levels of chronic frustration and places people inside circumstances that are filled with barriers that thwart socially prescribed, widely shared goals. Moreover, race-based economic disadvantage increases exposure to other criminogenic circumstances like neighborhood disadvantage and criminal embeddedness.

Other analysts have suggested that African Americans, especially, are subjected to what have been termed *microaggressions*—the "subtle, stunning, often automatic, and non-verbal exchanges which are 'put downs' of blacks" by Whites who may use them "unintentionally" but nonetheless persistently.[91] Over time, exposure to these kinds of experiences takes a psychological toll. Among other things, "self perceived experiences of racial discrimination are associated with increased psychiatric symptoms, clinical disorder, and lowered levels of subjective well-being."[92] Indeed, the direct or anticipated experience of racism is associated with depression, generalized dissatisfaction with life, decreased self-esteem, and other emotional problems.[93]

Thus, Wilson's tangle has a clear economic and social basis that produces psychological effects. Nonetheless, it continues to be ignored in policy discussions about crime control and decisions to incarcerate those persons who have been caught in its grasp.[94]

As I noted in the last chapter, racial differentials in the number of young persons who are confined inside juvenile justice institutions adds another long-term dimension to the problem. Like their adult counterparts, Black and Latino juveniles are more likely to be arrested, retained in jail, bound over to adult court, convicted, and given longer prison sentences than Whites. The disparities are substantial—for example, African American juveniles are between 6 and 9 times more likely than Whites to be sentenced to juvenile prisons (depending on whether it is their first or a subsequent incarceration). Moreover, once incarcerated, Black and Latino children spend, on average, 25% to 50% longer in juvenile institutions than do Whites.[95]

Because the negative effects of early institutionalization are highly criminogenic,[96] such disproportions—both in the likelihood of being incarcerated and in the amount of time spent in juvenile institutions—help to ensure that an unusually large number of young, minority men will eventually enter an adult prison. Add to this the secondary effects of incarceration—the social and economic disruption that high rates of imprisonment produce in families, neighborhoods, and communities[97]—and the long-term implications of the problem of minority overrepresentation in the juvenile justice system become clearer.

There is a final cost that the racial dynamic at the core of our current crime control policies incurs. Policies of harsh punishment—whereby increased levels of pain are meted out by one segment of the population and directed primarily at another—contribute to a degraded and diminished view of persons who are targeted in this way. The last 2 decades in the United States have witnessed a growing racial divisiveness that has crystallized around issues of crime and punishment. Ignoring the effects of racially discriminatory criminal justice decision making and race-based inequalities in exposure to criminogenic social conditions subtly promotes the inference that there are essential—perhaps even innate—differences in criminality between racial groups. Combined with some of the psychological processes that I discussed in the last chapter, this is likely to have indirect criminogenic consequences of its own.

CONCLUSION

The contextual model of behavior I have summarized in this chapter is one that counsels moderation and restraint in our approach to punishment and the levels of prison pain that are routinely inflicted on persons who have committed criminal acts. It should lead us to question both the wisdom and fairness of using the increased pains of imprisonment as our primary strategy of crime control. Imposing severe punishments on persons whose developmental histories and present life circumstances increased the likelihood that they would engage in the criminal behavior for which they are being punished incurs substantial costs. Yet, now we understand why it is unlikely ever to achieve its intended crime-reducing effects.

Thus, as many of the studies that I reviewed in this chapter confirm, exposure to a significant number of risk factors at earlier stages of someone's life is more than just unfortunate or regrettable; it also can be deeply criminogenic. The risk factors may be produced by structural forces like chronic poverty or severe economic hardship and deprivation, or by more direct forms of mistreatment, like parental neglect and physical or emotional abuse. They can even include institutional harms inflicted on children who are incarcerated in uncaring, hurtful juvenile facilities. In any event, because criminal behavior is shaped and influenced by the social and institutional histories of its perpetrators, addressing early childhood and adolescent experiences should become an important priority in developing effective strategies of crime control.

In addition, research conducted over the last several decades underscores the importance of factoring the immediate situation or present circumstances into this equation. Like all social behavior, crime is influenced by the context in which it occurs. Certain situations have criminogenic features that increase the likelihood that crime will occur. They include communities that are plagued by high levels of instability and deindividuation, where residents are more likely to encounter interpersonal provocation and stress, where crime and criminal lifestyles are already widespread, and where other forms of neighborhood disadvantage persist, increase the probability of criminal behavior.

Clearly, the fact that crime occurs as much because of the characteristics of past or present social situations or settings as the characteristics of the persons who commit it represents a rational basis for limiting the excessive dependency on imprisonment that has arisen over the last several decades. A more balanced approach would include redirecting governmental resources toward the contextual targets where they are likely to do the most good. No thoughtfully devised, psychologically informed crime control and prison policy would persist with the past exclusive emphasis on the harsh punishment of individuals in the face of compelling theory and data that illustrate the significant ways in which social contextual variables influence their criminality. And, it would seem, no society that genuinely values fairness and social justice can continue to imprison such large numbers of its citizens on the basis of behavioral premises that are no longer valid.

One final implication of the modern psychological theory discussed in this chapter frames the issues that are addressed in the several chapters that follow. There is scarcely a more powerful social context or setting in our society than prison. If context matters, then the *institutional* context of prison itself has potentially harmful effects on persons exposed to it. There is much evidence that, far from merely being merely unpleasant, the pains of imprisonment can transform prisoners, impede their development, undermine their overall well-being, and negatively affect their potential for postprison adjustment.

What we now know about the power of contextual factors to shape behavior and redirect life paths should sensitize policymakers to potential costs of prison pain. The personal and social consequences of imprisonment would be weighed more heavily in a model of crime control in which context matters. In any event, the potential criminogenic effects of subjecting people to painful, sometimes traumatic experiences for long periods of time in the course of their incarceration can no longer be ignored. In the next several chapters I discuss some of the ways in which people are influenced and affected by the experience of imprisonment, how they cope with the stress of living in unusual and extreme correctional environments, and the various ways in which prisons themselves have begun to "behave badly" in the face of powerful forces that have compromised their orderly operation and distorted their mission.

NOTES

1. Nils Christie, *Limits to Pain* (Oxford, England: Martin Robertson, 1982), 45.
2. M. Banaji, "Ordinary Prejudice," *Psychological Science Agenda* 14 (2001): 8, 8.
3. Mercer Sullivan, *"Getting Paid": Youth Crime and Work in the Inner City* (Ithaca, NY: Cornell University Press, 1989), 3. I should note that, despite what I say in this chapter about the emerging social contextual perspective and the burgeoning literature on the social historical and situational causes of crime, some of the voices to which Sullivan refers came from within psychology and a few of them were given credence by politicians, policymakers, and members of the public during this era. For example, some highly publicized, but badly flawed, research by psychiatrist Samuel Yochelson and psychologist Stanton Samenow suggested that criminals were a "breed apart," who, "without exception," all thought alike, and whose behavior was the product of little more than their willful badness. Samuel Yochelson and Stanton Samenow, *The Criminal Personality*, vol. 2. (New York: Jason Aronson, 1977), 5. Psychologist Sarnoff Mednick's research was discussed in the press even before it was published and was used to suggest that there was some kind of innate defect in the genetic makeup of criminals. *See* D. Perlman, "New Study Links Crime to Heredity," *San Francisco Chronicle* (January 12, 1982): 6; and S. Mednick, W. Gabrielli, and B. Hutchings, "Genetic Influences in Criminal Convictions: Evidence From an Adoption Court," *Science* 224 (1984): 891, 892. This is not the time or place to systematically critique Yochelson and Samenow's work or, in Mednick's case, to discuss the misleading ways in which it was characterized in the media, except to say that, in both instances, the messages were seriously out of synch with advances being made in mainstream psychology on the contextual determinants of behavior. There is much precedent for using a narrow brand of psychological individualism—whether it is part of the scientific

mainstream or not—to support the criminal justice status quo. *See* C. Haney, "Psychological Theory and Criminal Justice Policy: Law and Psychology in the 'Formative Era,'" *Law and Human Behavior* 6 (1982): 191.

4. Sullivan, *"Getting Paid,"* 2.

5. For a more extended discussion of many of the issues I discuss here, *see* C. Haney, "Making Law Modern: Toward a Contextual Model of Justice," *Psychology, Public Policy, and Law,* 7 (2002): 3–63.

6. Albert Bandura, *Behavior Theory and the Models of Man.* Presidential Address given at the meeting of the American Psychological Association, New Orleans, (August 1974), 7.

7. S. Milgram, "Some Conditions of Obedience and Disobedience to Authority," *Human Relations* 18 (1965): 57, 75.

8. P. Manicas and P. Secord, "Implications for Psychology of the New Philosophy of Science," *American Psychologist* 38 (1983): 399.

9. Lee Ross and Richard Nisbett, *The Person and the Situation: Perspectives of Social Psychology* (New York: McGraw-Hill, 1991), xiv.

10. This study was first published in C. Haney, W. Banks, and P. Zimbardo, "Interpersonal Dynamics in a Simulated Prison," *International Journal of Criminology and Penology* 1 (1973): 69. The relationship of the results to actual prison environments was discussed in somewhat greater detail in Craig Haney and Philip Zimbardo, "The Socialization into Criminality: On Becoming a Prisoner and a Guard," in *Law, Justice, and the Individual in Society: Psychological and Legal Issues,* ed. June Tapp and Felice Levine (New York: Holt, Rinehart & Winston, 1977).

11. Susan Engel, *Context Is Everything: The Nature of Memory* (New York: Worth, 1999). *See also* Ulric Neisser and Ira Hyman, ed., *Memory Observed: Remembering in Natural Contexts,* 2d ed. (New York: Worth, 1999).

12. *See, e.g.,* D. Richardson and M. Spivey, "Representation, Space, and Hollywood Squares: Looking at Things That Aren't There Anymore," *Cognition* 76 (2000): 269; M. Spivey, M. Tanenhaus, K. Eberhard, and J. Sedivy, "Eye Movements and Spoken Language Comprehension: Effects of Visual Context on Syntactic Ambiguity Resolution," *Cognitive Psychology* 45 (2002): 447.

13. J. O'Regan, "Solving the 'Real' Mysteries of Visual Perception: The World as an Outside Memory." *Canadian Journal of Psychology* 46 (1992): 461.

14. Barbara Rogoff, *Apprenticeship in Thinking: Cognitive Development in Social Context* (New York: Oxford University Press, 1990).

15. R. Gibbs, "Taking Metaphor out of Our Heads and Putting It Into the Cultural World," *Current Issues in Linguistic Theory* 175 (1992): 145, 162.

16. Anthony Amsterdam and Jerome Bruner, *Minding the Law* (Cambridge, MA: Harvard University Press, 2000), 3.

17. Ibid., 287. And in between these observations, among many other things, they noted, "Human utterances are heard, understood, and processed in a situational context. Most of the things people say to one another are incomprehensible when parsed solely in accordance with the rules of grammar, dictionary definitions, and codes of formal logic. Their uptake is a product of interpretive

activity conditioned by the nature and specific circumstances of the communicative setting" (ibid., 167).

18. Walter Mischel, "Personality Dispositions Revisited and Revised: A View After Three Decades," in *Handbook of Personality: Theory and Research*, ed. Lawrence Pervin (New York: Guilford Press, 1990), 130.

19. Walter Mischel, "Was the Cognitive Revolution Just a Detour on the Road to Behaviorism? On the Need to Reconcile Situational Control and Personal Control," in *The Automaticity of Everyday Life, Advances in Social Cognition*, vol. 10, ed. Robert Wyer (Mahwah, NJ: Lawrence Erlbaum, 1997), 183. He continued, "The significance of the situation in the regulation of human social behavior remains formidable, even after three decades of cognitive revolution" (ibid.).

20. Sharon Brehm, *The Application of Social Psychology to Clinical Practice* (Washington, DC: Hemisphere Publishing, 1976), 226.

21. J. Jacobson and G. Weary, "The Application of Social Psychology to Clinical Practice: A Catalyst for Integrative Research," *Contemporary Psychology*, 41 (1996): 1173, 1175.

22. K. Witkiewitz and G. Martin, "Relapse Prevention for Alcohol and Drug Problems: That Was Zen, This Is Tao," *American Psychologist* 59 (2004): 224 224. A meta-analytic review of some 26 studies showed that relapse prevention techniques reduced substance abuse and improved psychosocial adjustment. *See* J. Irvin, C. Bowers, M. Dunn, and M. Wang, "Efficacy of Relapse Prevention: A Meta-Analytic Review," *Journal of Consulting and Clinical Psychology* 67 (1999): 563.

23. A *high-risk situation* is defined as "a circumstance in which an individual's attempt to refrain from a particular behavior (ranging from any use of a substance to heavy or harmful use) is threatened." Witkiewitz and Martin, "Relapse Prevention," 224–225.

24. Phyllis Moen, "Introduction," in *Examining Lives in Context: Perspectives on the Ecology of Human Development*, ed. Phyllis Moen, Glenn H. Elder, and Kurt Luscher (Washington, DC: American Psychological Association, 1995), 5.

25. Ibid., 6.

26. R. Lerner and M. Kauffman, "The Concept of Development in Contextualism," *Developmental Review* 5 (1985): 309, 324; *See also* Urie Bronfenbrenner, *The Ecology of Human Development* (Cambridge, MA: Harvard University Press, 1979); Urie Bronfenbrenner, "Ecological Systems Theory," in *Annals of Child Development—Six Theories of Child Development: Revised Formulations and Current Issues*, ed. Ross Vasta (Greenwich, CT: JAI Press, 1989); Richard Lerner, *On the Nature of Human Plasticity* (New York: Cambridge University Press, 1984); Richard Lerner and Jacqueline Lerner, "Organismic and Social Contextual Bases of Development: The Sample Case of Adolescence," in *Child Development Today and Tomorrow*, ed. William Damon (San Francisco: Jossey-Bass, 1989).

27. *See, e.g.*, Glen Elder, "Social History and Life Experience," in *Present and Past in Middle Life*, ed. Dorothy Eichorn, John Clausen, Norma Haan, Marjorie Honzik, and Paul Mussen (New York: Academic Press, 1981); Jaber Gubrium and James Holstein, "Biographical Work and New Ethnography," in *Interpreting*

Experience: The Narrative Study of Lives, ed. Ruthellen Josselson and Amia Lieblich (Thousand Oaks, CA: Sage, 1995).

28. *See, e.g.*, Donald Polkinghorne, "Narrative Knowing and the Study of Lives," in *Aging and Biography: Explorations in Adult Development*, ed. James Birren, Gary Kenyon, Jan-Eric Ruth, Johannes Schroots, and Torbjorn Svensson (New York: Springer, 1996); Robert White, "Exploring Personality the Long Way: The Study of Lives," in *Personality Structure in the Life Course: Essays on Personology in the Murray Tradition*, ed. Robert Zucker, Albert Rabin, Joel Aronoff, and Susan Frank (New York: Springer, 1992).

29. *See, e.g.*, Walter Mischel, *Personality and Assessment* (New York: Wiley, 1968); Moen, Elder, and Luscher, *Examining Lives in Context*; Ross and Nisbett, *The Person and the Situation*.

30. *See, e.g.*, A. Caspi, D. Bem, and G. Elder, "Continuities and Consequences of Interactional Styles Across the Life Course," *Journal of Personality* 57 (1989): 375; Martin Richards and Paul Light, ed., *Children of Different Social Worlds: Development in a Social Context* (Cambridge, MA: Harvard University Press, 1986); L. Sroufe, B. Egeland, and T. Kreutzer, "The Fate of Early Experience Following Developmental Change: Longitudinal Approaches to Individual Adaptation in Childhood," *Child Development* 61 (1990): 1363.

31. K. Ortiz, "Mental Health Consequences of Life History Method: Implications From a Refugee Camp," *Ethos* 13 (1985): 99, 100.

32. D. Hamburg, "The American Family Transformed," *Society* 30 (1993, January–February): 60, 60.

33. Ann Masten and Norman Garmezy, "Risk, Vulnerability and Protective Factors in Developmental Psychopathology," in *Advances in Clinical Child Psychology*, ed. Benjamin Lahey and Alan Kazdin (New York: Plenum, 1985), 3.

34. Ibid., 6.

35. Ibid., 25.

36. Carl Nightingale, *On the Edge: A History of Poor Black Children and Their American Dreams* (New York: Basic Books, 1994), 55.

37. *See, e.g.*, A. Kaiser and E. Delaney, "The Effects of Poverty on Parenting Young Children," *Peabody Journal of Education* 71 (1996): 66; *see also* V. McLoyd, "The Impact of Economic Hardship on Black Families and Children: Psychological Distress, Parenting, and Socioeconomic Development," *Child Development* 61 (1990): 311.

38. *See, e.g.*, D. Takeuchi, D. Williams, and R. Adair, "Economic Distress in the Family and Children's Emotional and Behavioral Problems," *Journal of Marriage and the Family* 53 (1991): 1031.

39. J. Giovannoni, "Parental Mistreatment: Perpetrators and Victims," *Journal of Marriage and the Family* 33 (1971): 649, 649.

40. C. Kruttschnitt, J. McLeod, and M. Dornfeld, "The Economic Environment of Child Abuse," *Social Problems* 41 (1994): 299, 309.

41. Ibid., 310

42. Ibid.

43. Ibid.

44. Ruby Lassiter, "Child Rearing in Black Families: Child-Abusing Discipline?" in *Violence in Black Families*, ed. Robert Hampton (Lexington, MA: Lexington Books, 1987), 39. *See also* J. Daniel, R. Hampton, and E. Newberger, "Child Abuse and Accidents in Black Families: A Controlled Comparative Study," *American Journal of Orthopsychiatry* 53 (1983): 645; V. McLoyd, "The Impact of Economic Hardship."

45. *See, e.g.*, L. Berkowitz, "The Frustration–Aggression Hypothesis: Examination and Reinterpretation," *Psychological Bulletin* 106 (1989): 59.

46. *See, e.g.*, L. Huff-Corzine, J. Corzine, and D. Moore, "Deadly Connections: Culture, Poverty, and the Direction of Lethal Violence," *Social Forces* 69 (1991): 715; K. Williams, "Economic Sources of Homicide: Reestimating the Effects of Poverty and Inequality," *American Sociological Review* 49 (1984): 283.

47. David Wolfe, *Child Abuse: Implications for Child Development and Psychopathology* (Newbury Park, CA: Sage, 1987), 25.

48. James Garbarino, "The Incidence of and Prevalence of Child Maltreatment," in *Family Violence*, ed. Lloyd Ohlin and Michael Tonry (Chicago: University of Chicago, 1989), 220.

49. For example, here is a sample of articles and book chapters published on the topic of child abuse during the 1960s: E. Bennie and A. Sclare, "The Battered Child Syndrome," *American Journal of Psychiatry* 125 (1969): 975; R. Birrell and J. Birrell, "The Maltreatment Syndrome in Children: A Hospital Survey," *Medical Journal of Australia* 522(23) (1968): 1023; E. Elmer, "Abused Children and Community Resources," *International Journal of Offender Therapy* 11 (1967): 16; Vincent J. Fontana, "Further Reflections on Maltreatment of Children," *New York State Journal of Medicine* 68 (1968): 2214; D. Gil, "Physical Abuse of Children: Findings and Implications of a Nationwide Survey," *Pediatric Supplement* 44 (1969): 857; Ray Helfer and Ruth Kempe, ed., *The Battered Child* (Chicago: University of Chicago Press, 1968). *Cf.* Newberger and Bourne's 1978 observation that "child abuse has emerged in the last fifteen years as a visible and important social problem." E. Newberger and R. Bourne, "The Medicalization and Legalization of Child Abuse," *American Journal of Orthopsychiatry* 48 (1978): 593, 593.

50. *See, e.g.*, Leonard Shengold, *Soul Murder: The Effects of Childhood Abuse and Deprivation* (New Haven, CT: Yale University Press, 1989).

51. M. Lystad, "Violence at Home: A Review of the Literature," *American Journal of Orthopsychiatry* 45 (1975): 328, 334 (emphasis added). For examples of published reports from the previous decade that described this relationship, *see* G. Curtis, "Violence Breeds Violence—Perhaps?" *American Journal of Psychiatry* 120 (1963): 386; L. Eron et al., "Social Class, Parental Punishment for Aggression, and Child Aggression," *Child Development* 34 (1963): 849; L. Kopernik, "The Family as a Breeding Ground of Violence," *Corrective Psychiatry and the Journal of Social Therapy* 10 (1964): 10; M. Lefkowitz, L. Walder, and L. Eron, "Punishment, Identification, and Aggression," *Merrill-Palmer Quarterly* 9 (1963): 159; L. Silver, C. Dublin, and R. Lourie, "Does Violence Breed Violence? Contributions from a Study of the Child Abuse Syndrome," *American*

Journal of Psychiatry 126 (1969): 152; Marian Radke-Yarrow, John Campbell, and Roger Burton, "Theories and Correlates of Child Aggression," in *Child Rearing: An Inquiry Into Research and Methods*, ed. Marian Radke-Yarrow, John Campbell, and Roger Burton (San Francisco: Jossey-Bass, 1968).

52. Ibid., 251.

53. *See, e.g.*, D. Sargent, "The Lethal Situation: Transmission of Urge to Kill From Parent to Child," in *Dynamics of Violence*, ed. Jan Fawcett (Chicago: American Medical Association, 1971); Silver, Dublin, and Lourie, "Does Violence Breed Violence?"

54. B. Schmitt and C. Kempe, "Neglect and Abuse of Children," in *Nelson Textbook of Pediatrics*, ed. Victor Vaughan and R. James McKay (Philadelphia: W.B. Saunders, 1975), 107.

55. K. Dodge, J. Bates, and G. Petit, "Mechanisms in the Cycle of Violence," *Science* 250 (1990): 1678; C. Widom, "Child Abuse, Neglect, and Adult Behavior: Research Design and Findings on Criminality, Violence, and Child Abuse," *American Journal of Orthopsychiatry* 59 (1989): 355; C. Widom, "The Cycle of Violence," *Science* 244 (1989): 160.

56. *See, e.g.*, M. Straus, "Discipline and Deviance: Physical Punishment of Children and Violence and Other Crime in Adulthood," *Social Problems* 38 (1991): 133.

57. B. Rivera and C. Widom, "Childhood Victimization and Violent Offending," *Violence and Victims* 5 (1992): 19.

58. Ibid., 20.

59. D. Doumas, G. Margolin, and R. John, "The Intergenerational Transmission of Aggression Across Three Generations," *Journal of Family Violence* 9 (1994): 157, 157–158.

60. Lystad, "Violence at Home," 330.

61. Joan McCord, "Aggression in Two Generations," in *Aggressive Behavior: Current Perspectives*, ed. L. Rowell Huesmann (New York: Plenum, 1994).

62. N. Dubrow and J. Garbarino, "Living in the War Zone: Mothers and Young Children in a Public Housing Development," *Child Welfare* 68 (1989): 3. *See also* Joan McCord's introductory chapter on urban violence and the chapters that follow it: Joan McCord, "Inner City Life: Contributions to Violence," in *Violence in Urban America: Mobilizing a Response*, ed. National Research Council, (Washington, DC: National Academy Press, 1994).

63. Nightingale, *On the Edge*, 10. *See also* Elijah Anderson, *Streetwise: Race, Class, and Social Change in an Urban Community* (Chicago: University of Chicago Press, 1990); Geoffrey Canada, *Fist, Stick, Knife, Gun: A Personal History of Violence in America* (Boston: Beacon Press, 1995); Daniel Coyle, *Hardball: A Season in the Projects* (New York: G. P. Putnam, 1993); Alex Kotlowitz, *There Are No Children Here* (New York: Doubleday, 1991); Luis Rodríguez, *Always Running, La Vida Loca: Gang Days in L.A.* (Willimantic, CT: Curbstone Press, 1993).

64. For early research on positive outcomes in juvenile facilities, see J. Simpson, T. Eynon, and W. Reckless, "Institutionalization as Perceived by the Juvenile Offender," *Sociology and Social Research* 48 (1963): 13.

65. B. Goldson, "'Children in Need' or 'Young Offenders'? Hardening Ideology, Organizational Change and New Challenges for Social Work with Children in Trouble," *Child and Family Social Work* 5 (2000): 255, 258.

66. Monica Davey, "Youths Leaving Foster Care Are Found Facing Obstacles," *New York Times*, February 24, 2004, p. A10, reporting on several studies by Mark Courtney and his colleagues. See also Mark Courtney, Sherri Terao, and Noel Best, *Midwest Evaluation of the Adult Functioning of Former Foster Youth: Conditions of the Adult Preparing to Leave State Care in Illinois* (Chicago: Chapin Hall Center, University of Chicago, 2004); Mark Courtney et al., *The Educational Status of Foster Children. Issue Brief* (Chicago: Chapin Hall Center, University of Chicago, 2004). Available at www.about.chapinhall.org (last visited July 1, 2005).

67. Steve Lerner, *Bodily Harm: The Pattern of Fear and Violence at the California Youth Authority* (Bolinas, CA: Commonweal Research Institute, 1986), 46. *See also* Dwight Abbott, *I Cried, You Didn't Listen: A Survivor's Expose of the California Youth Authority* (Los Angeles: Feral House, 1991); Barry Krisberg and James Austin, *Reinventing Juvenile Justice* (Thousand Oaks, CA: Sage Publications, 1993). Little was done to heed the criticism contained in these commentaries. In fact, a series of expert reports were released in late 2004 that described adverse, harmful conditions and practices in the Youth Authority, leading to a federal judge's appointment of a special master to oversee sweeping reforms. These reports and a consent decree reached in the case can be viewed on the Prison Law Office Web site at www.prisonlaw.com.

68. National Commission on Criminal Justice Standards and Goals, *Task Force Report on Corrections* (Washington, DC: Government Printing Office, 1973), 597.

69. Lyle Shannon, *Assessing the Relationship of Adult Criminal Careers to Juvenile Careers: A Summary* (Washington, DC: U.S. Department of Justice, Office of Juvenile Justice and Delinquency Prevention, 1982).

70. Ibid., 8.

71. Ibid., 13.

72. Ibid., 15. Shannon made several additional, important observations. For one, "Court effectiveness involves an understanding of the life experiences that have brought [the juveniles] to court" (ibid., vi). He also reported a familiar pattern of racial disparity: "No matter which measure of frequency or seriousness of police contacts was utilized . . . black males had the most contacts and most serious involvement with the police" (ibid., 1).

73. Patricia Puritz and Mary Ann Scali, *Beyond the Walls: Improving Conditions of Confinement for Youth in Custody* (Washington, DC: U.S. Department of Justice, 1998), xi.

74. Ibid. (emphasis added). The tendency for institutional placements to become punitive and excessively controlling—even those that initially are conceived as less restrictive alternatives—seems widespread. Teresa O'Neill's study of *secure accommodation*—the quaint British term for facilities in which children too young to be imprisoned were housed—showed that these units were soon

dominated by a concern for control that quickly led to the use of serious sanctions (e.g., locking the children in their rooms, taking away all of their possessions, and sometimes even turning off the electricity in the unit). O'Neill's interviews suggested that even the staff members who participated in the widespread "macho" staff culture understood that secure accommodation was not an effective way to deal with the troubled children who were placed under their control. Teresa O'Neill, *Children in Secure Accommodation: A Gendered Exploration of Locked Institutional Care for Children in Trouble* (London: Jessica Kingsley, 2001).

75. J. Skeem, E. Mulvey, and C. Lidz, "Building Mental Health Professionals' Decisional Models Into Tests of Predictive Validity: The Accuracy of Contextualized Predictions of Violence," *Law and Human Behavior* 24 (2000): 607, 609.

76. Ibid.

77. E. Silver, E. Mulvey, and J. Monahan, "Assessing Violence Risk Among Discharged Psychiatric Patients: Toward an Ecological Approach," *Law and Human Behavior* 23 (1999): 237, 237.

78. See, e.g., Leonard Berkowitz, "Situational Influences on Aggression," in *Aggression and War: Their Biological and Social Bases*, ed. Jo Groebel and Robert Hinde (Cambridge, England: Cambridge University Press, 1989), 91.

79. Ibid.

80. Berkowitz used research conducted on the *classic frustration–aggression hypothesis* to explain violence in a number of real-world settings. See, e.g., Leonard Berkowitz, "The Study of Urban Violence: Some Implications of Laboratory Studies of Frustration and Aggression," *American Behavioral Scientist* 11 (1968): 14. Since that early work, he and others have modified the original frustration–aggression hypothesis to argue that frustration generally increases the tendency to aggress, although whether and how that aggression is expressed will vary as a function of the situation in which the frustration is experienced. See, e.g., Richard Felson, "Kick 'em When They're Down: Explanations of the Relationship Between Stress and Interpersonal Aggression and Violence," *Sociological Quarterly* 33 (1992): 1.

81. See, e.g., S. Prentice-Dunn and R. Rogers, "Effects of Deindividuating Situational Cues and Aggressive Models on Subjective Deindividuation and Aggression," *Journal of Personality & Social Psychology* 39 (1980): 104; Steven Prentice-Dunn and Ronald Rogers, "Deindividuation and the Self-Regulation of Behavior," in *Psychology of Group Influence*, ed. Paul Paulus (Hillsdale, NJ: Erlbaum, 1989); L. Taylor, E. O'Neal, T. Langley, and A. Butcher, "Anger Arousal, Deindividuation, and Aggression," *Aggressive Behavior* 17 (1991): 193; P. Zimbardo, "The Psychology of Evil: A Situationist Perspective on Recruiting Good People to Engage in Anti-Social Acts," *Japanese Journal of Social Psychology* 11 (1995): 125.

82. R. Felson and H. Steadman, "Situational Factors in Disputes Leading to Criminal Violence," *Criminology: An Interdisciplinary Journal* 21 (1983): 59.

83. See, e.g., B. McCarthy and J. Hagan, "Getting Into Street Crime: The Structure and Process of Criminal Embeddedness," *Social Science Research* 24 (1995): 63.

84. D. Elliott, W. Wilson, D. Huizinga, R. Sampson, and B. Rankin, "The Effects of Neighborhood Disadvantage on Adolescent Development," *Journal of Research in Crime and Delinquency* 33 (1996): 389.

85. Gerald Patterson and his colleagues have done an excellent job teasing apart the sequence of developmental events by which children move from abusive backgrounds, to problematic styles of interpersonal behavior and, finally, to delinquency. *See, e.g.*, G. Patterson, B. DeBaryshe, and E. Ramsey, "A Developmental Perspective on Antisocial Behavior," *American Psychologist* 44 (1989): 329, 331. *See also* G. Patterson and T. Dishion, "Contributions of Families and Peers to Delinquency," *Criminology* 23 (1985): 63.

86. William Julius Wilson, *The Truly Disadvantaged: The Inner City, the Underclass and Public Policy* (Chicago: University of Chicago Press, 1987), 20.

87. Ibid., 42.

88. Ibid., 58.

89. Ibid., 21.

90. *See, e.g.*, R. Clark, N. Anderson, V. Clark, and D. Williams, "Racism as a Stressor for African Americans: A Biosocial Model," *American Psychologist*, 54 (1999): 805.

91. Peggy Davis, "Law as Microaggression," *Yale Law Journal* 98 (1989): 1559, 1565, quoting psychiatrist Chester Pierce, who first coined the term. *See* Chester Pierce, "Offensive Mechanisms," in *The Black Seventies*, ed. Floyd B. Barbour (Boston: Porter Sargent Publisher, 1970).

92. Sheldon Danziger, Deborah Reed, and Tony Brown, *Poverty and Prosperity: Prospects for Reducing Racial/Ethnic Economic Disparities in the United States* (Geneva: United Nations Research Institute for Social Development, 2004), 23 (summarizing the results of various psychological studies).

93. *See, e.g.*, C. Broman, "Race-Related Factors and Life Satisfaction Among African Americans," *Journal of Black Psychology* 23 (1997): 36; T. Brown et al., "'Being Black and Feeling Blue': Mental Health Consequences of Racial Discrimination," *Race and Society* 2 (1999): 117; H. Landrine and E. Klonoff, "The Schedule of Racist Events: A Measure of Racial Discrimination and a Study of Its Negative Physical and Mental Health Consequences," *Journal of Black Psychology* 22 (1996): 114; R. Rumbaut, "The Crucible Within: Ethnic Identity, Self Esteem, and Segmented Assimilation Among Children of Immigrants," *International Migration Review* 28 (1994): 748; J. Taylor and B. Jackson, "Evaluation of a Holistic Model of Mental Health Symptoms in Black American Women," *Journal of Black Psychology* 18 (1990): 19; and V. Thompson, "Perceived Experiences of Racism as Stressful Life Events," *Community Mental Health Journal* 32 (1996): 223.

94. It is true that the economic boom of the 1990s was "deep" enough to have a real impact on minority unemployment and poverty rates. However, even at the end of the 1990s, 23.6% of African Americans and 22.8% of Latinos still were living below the poverty line. The relatively brief period of improvement in their economic status that occurred during the 1990s did not reverse or eradicate the sense of despair that had been generated by many decades of marginalization and little or no expectation that economic progress would be

sustained. As one study recently summarized, "African American families not only have lower levels of wealth and security, but they also have low expectations about their prospects for attaining racial equality in economic well being." Danziger, Reed, and Brown, *Poverty and Prosperity*, 20. Moreover, the comparatively lower levels of educational opportunity raised concerns about whether the decrease in unemployment could be sustained: "Despite a robust economic boom in the 1990s, the employment prospects and earnings levels of less-educated workers remain tenuous. Through no fault of their own, they face much bleaker labor market prospects than did their counterparts in the years from the late 1940s through the early 1970s when the economy was booming for workers at all skill levels" (ibid., 35).

95. *See, e.g.*, Eileen Poe-Yamagata and Michael Jones, *And Justice for Some* (San Francisco: National Council of Crime and Delinquency, 2000). *See also* the discussion of this and related issues in chapter 4, this volume.

96. *See, e.g.*, D. Conley, "Adding Color to a Black and White Picture: Using Qualitative Data to Explain Racial Disproportionality in the Juvenile Justice System," *Journal of Research in Crime & Delinquency* 31 (1994): 135; M. Wordes, T. Bynum, and C. Corley, "Locking Up Youth: The Impact of Race on Detention Decisions," *Journal of Research in Crime & Delinquency* 31 (1994): 149.

97. *See, e.g.*, C. Haney, "The Social Context of Capital Murder: Social Histories and the Logic of Mitigation," *Santa Clara Law Review* 35 (1995): 547; R. Sampson, "Urban Black Violence: The Effect of Male Joblessness and Family Disruption," *American Journal of Sociology* 93 (1987): 348.

6

SURVIVING THE SOCIAL
CONTEXT OF PRISON

Next to killing, imprisonment is the strongest measure of power at the disposal of the state. . . . Nothing is so total, in constraints, in degradation, and in its display of power, as is the prison.

—Nils Christie[1]

The fact that the very word "pain" has its etymological home in "poena" or "punishment" reminds us that even the elementary act of naming this most interior of events entails an immediate mental somersault out of the body into the external social circumstances that can be pictured as having caused the hurt.

—Elaine Scarry[2]

Prisons are concrete-and-steel embodiments of our society's commitment to psychological individualism and the dispositional view of human behavior on which it is based. The extraordinary dependence on imprisonment that has occurred in the United States over the last several decades reflects the persistent belief that crime can be reduced primarily by locking up individual lawbreakers and doing little else. As I noted in the last chapter, this approach came at the expense of more psychologically informed alternative strategies that might have targeted traumatic social histories and criminogenic social conditions instead. Despite compelling evidence that the behavioral assumptions on which this narrow crime control policy is premised were badly flawed, it remains firmly in place.

As I discuss in this chapter, prison is itself a powerful social context that can have destructive, even criminogenic, consequences on the persons confined there. The failure to fully appreciate these negative effects is one of the unfortunate legacies of psychological individualism and the belief that, just as they would be in the freeworld, prisoners are fully autonomous free agents who are largely impervious to their surroundings. This 19th-century view of behavior allowed early prison advocates to account for the failures of the first carceral regimes in terms of the intractable character of their captives rather than the inhumane conditions of confinement to which they were subjected. The devastating effects of prison life could be minimized or ignored because of a willingness to assume that the deteriorated state of the prisoners was somehow a result of their preexisting depraved or pathological natures.

However, now that the importance of social contextual influences on behavior is acknowledged more broadly, prison conditions themselves—and the pains of imprisonment that accompany them—also must be taken more seriously and analyzed more carefully. Among other things, this new perspective should sensitize legal decision makers and policymakers to the ways in which the setting of prison and the nature of prison life can shape prisoner behavior. Adapting to the realities of prison life may change a prisoner's habits of thinking and acting in ways that will persist long after his or her incarceration has ended. Badly run, unduly harsh, and especially uncaring prisons force prisoners to adjust to adverse situational contingencies in ways that are likely to have counterproductive, dysfunctional long-term consequences.

Because there are only so many ways to repressively and involuntarily confine large numbers of people in a relatively small space for prolonged periods of time, many aspects of the prison environment itself are more or less dictated by the task at hand. This is one of the reasons that the basic structure of prison has been so resistant to change. Indeed, few if any social institutions in our society have retained so much of their original 19th-century form. Thus, at the start of the 21st century, our otherwise technologically advanced and sophisticated society still responds to crime largely by locking human beings in cages.

However, the longevity of the prison form should not be mistaken as a sign of its effectiveness. Although prisons have a long history, it is one filled with controversy and debate. Many commentators have argued that prisons are painfully unhealthy places for guards and prisoners alike. Others have concluded that there is little evidence that the human, social, and economic price we continue to pay for prisons can be fully justified by the ends they effectively serve. In many ways, for many people, prisons still represent what Foucault called "the detestable solution, which one seems unable to do without."[3]

I believe that one reason we seem unable to do without them is that we remain stubbornly wedded to the individualistic view of human behavior on which they are based. In this chapter, then, I look carefully at some of the aspects of imprisonment that make it a "detestable solution," and I do so from an alternative, more psychologically informed perspective. Applying a social contextual framework to the prison environment provides a more realistic look at its psychological effects and its potential harms.

MEASURING PRISON PAIN

In the closing decades of the 20th century, an empirical consensus of sorts emerged among many penologists and prison policymakers to the effect that imprisonment per se appeared to inflict relatively little measurable psychological harm—at least in well-run prisons and for the most resilient prisoners. The view was perhaps a reflection of the individualism of the times and perhaps also a form of wishful thinking in the face of the unprecedented influx of prisoners who crowded into prisons everywhere. In any event, Hans Toch accurately summarized it, noting that "though *some* inmates experience tangible stress, which is destructive and disabling for them, most inmates somehow adapt to prison and remain comparatively healthy and sane behind walls."[4]

However, it is important to note that, even then, the debate over the psychological effects of imprisonment revolved around how much harm was inflicted rather than how much benefit was produced. Moreover, proponents of the prison status quo seemed relieved to learn that prisons did not harm literally everyone who was confined in them. For example, prison expert Frank Porporino summarized the literature on prison effects this way: "The evidence indicates that imprisonment is not generally or *uniformly devastating*. . . . Imprisonment, in and of itself, does not seem *inevitably* to damage individuals."[5] Nonetheless, even analysts who concluded that incarceration was not uniformly devastating or inevitably damaging did not deny its potential to do harm. Thus, Porporino also conceded that

> relationships with family and friends can be severed . . . particular vulnerabilities and inabilities to cope and adapt can come to the fore in the prison setting, [and] the behavior patterns and attitudes that emerge can take many forms, from deepening social and emotional withdrawal to extremes of aggression and violence.[6]

Of course, statements to the effect that not everyone who passes through prison is irreparably harmed, devastated, or made insane by the experience represent fairly faint praise. Yet, this tepid endorsement also must be qualified in several important respects. The first is that not all prisons are equally benign. Notwithstanding the tendency among commentators to talk about prison as if it were some sort of Weberian ideal type, conditions of confinement vary widely along critical dimensions that can render one prison fundamentally different from—and more or less harmful than— another. Indeed, the effects of confinement in, say, a relatively well-run, program-oriented minimum-security prison cannot be generalized to those suffered in a dangerously overcrowded or brutally mismanaged maximum-security prison.[7] When scholars, researchers, and policymakers refer to these very different kinds of facilities—or to prisons in general—as though they were the same, they blur critically important distinctions. Implying that what happens (or not) in one kind of prison necessarily applies in another is simply incorrect.[8]

In this regard, it is not surprising that Canadian scholars have tended to provide the strongest defenses of the prison status quo. Canadian prisons historically have experienced relatively few of the most serious problems that have regularly plagued many prisons in the United States. For example, in 1989, when scores of American prisons were in the midst of massive overcrowding crises, and legislators and correctional administrators across the country were forced to respond to court orders requiring them to reduce populations and build more institutions, a Canadian commentator observed that "The problem of prison overcrowding is not yet as compelling in Canada as it is in the United States. For instance, *no* Canadian custodial institutions are under a court order for failing to provide acceptable living conditions because of overcrowding."[9]

Similarly, in the 1980s Canadian researcher Peter Suedfeld offered stirring defenses of what he understood to be "solitary confinement in prison." His comments were featured prominently in some debates in the United States, where a controversial policy to increase the use of solitary confinement was being implemented. Yet, Suedfeld also made a point of conceding that whenever long-term isolation also entailed mistreatment by guards and the loss of educational, vocational, and recreational activities, it was likely to produce harmful effects.[10] Unfortunately, the potentially harmful conditions and treatment about which he cautioned were precisely what many prison experts in the United States were concerned were becoming routine in many solitary confinement units, and exactly why they had voiced criticisms of the practice. Suedfeld and his opponents in this debate appeared to be talking about the same thing when they referred to "solitary confinement," but they were not.

In addition to this confusion over comparable terminology, empirical studies of the pains of imprisonment have been limited by the lack of meaningful techniques with which to measure the phenomenon. That is, the variability and subjectivity of psychological pain have impeded the development of a standardized metric with which to gauge it. Moreover, attempts to document the harmful effects of long-term imprisonment continue to be complicated by the fact that people tend to adapt over time to the suffering they endure. Simply put, the human psyche abhors the sensation of constant pain. Because—like all people—prisoners can tolerate only so much suffering before attempting to transform the experience to reduce its painfulness, it is difficult to accurately measure the effects of the chronic cruelty of prison life.

When people are able to make effective use of the psychological mechanism by which the experience of chronic pain is muted or dampened, long-term exposure to cruel conditions may lead to less self-reported psychological suffering. But it is difficult to argue that this numbing process does not come at a significant psychic cost. The inability to capture this phenomenon with the techniques commonly used to measure suffering helps to account for some of the masking of long-term prison effects—the argument that, somehow, most people manage to "adjust," more or less.

Moreover, most studies of the effects of long-term imprisonment assess its effects in the very context where prisoners are forced to adapt and attempt to achieve a tolerable psychological state—inside prison itself. Arguably, a much more meaningful test of the ways that the pains of imprisonment have transformed prisoners would occur *after* their release, when the full extent of the psychological changes brought about by the atypical and severe environment of prison would be more apparent. As I suggest later in this chapter, research focusing on that point in the process of measuring change indicates that the experience of imprisonment is anything but benign.

In related ways, studies of prison effects often reflect an excessive focus on quantitative indices of suffering. These approaches lead researchers to ignore more subtle, yet profound, changes that destructive prison conditions can produce.[11] Especially in light of the complex interpersonal dynamics and politically charged demand characteristics that may come into play in many prison environments, where prisoners do not want to "cop out" and admit to suffering or pain—and certainly not to persons who are viewed as part of "the system"—it often is difficult to know how to interpret studies that purport to show no effects from exposure to conditions that we know otherwise would be harmful and damaging. Moreover, there certainly is no reason that numerical measurements of the pains of imprisonment *necessarily* produce more valid representations of prison effects than more subjective accounts provided by more interpretive researchers who use observation and interview methodologies.

One example of the narrow, quantitative approach that has characterized the study of prison effects is found in a widely cited literature review by Canadian researchers James Bonta and Paul Gendreau. Published in 1990, when incarceration rates already were at an all-time high and policies of mass imprisonment had received critical academic scrutiny, the review seemed to minimize concerns over the negative psychological consequences of the prison experience. Indeed, the authors argued that careful empirical research simply "failed to uncover . . . pervasive negative effects of incarceration."[12] But, to reach these conclusions, Bonta and Gendreau had to exclude much valuable research from their discussion of the psychological effects of imprisonment.

Specifically, they systematically ignored many of the studies that had reached some of the most negative conclusions because, as the authors put it, they were not "empirical" enough. However, by "insufficiently empirical"

Bonta and Gendreau meant simply that the research they excluded lacked quantitative indices of suffering.[13] For example, in discarding the results of one well-known observational and interview study done by British research-ers Stanley Cohen and Laurie Taylor, Bonta and Gendreau claimed that the former's research "did not provide *empirical* evidence for psychological or behavioral deterioration."[14]

In fact, Cohen and Taylor's research on a special security wing in an English maximum-security prison was clearly an empirical study, one that was based on extensive in-prison contact with prisoners, unstructured group interviews, the prisoners' autobiographical writing and reactions to liter-ature, and direct feedback about the researchers' conclusions from the prisoners themselves. As Cohen and Taylor noted, "these research methods were not chosen by default. They were the best ways that we knew to obtain a phenomenological picture of life in E-Wing for maximum security prisoners."[15]

Bonta and Gendreau's narrow definition of empirical evidence also led them to ignore numerous classic sociological works on prisons that documented the severe effects that certain conditions of confinement had on inmates.[16] Using only quantitative indices of prison pain also meant that they overlooked a number of highly instructive journalistic and autobio-graphical accounts of imprisonment. Moreover, by narrowly limiting defini-tions of the negative effects of imprisonment—specifically looking only at "behaviors that threatened the physical welfare of the offender (e.g., aggres-sive behavior, suicide) and indicators of physiological stress levels (e.g., elevated blood pressure) and psychological distress (e.g., depression)"[17]— they disregarded many of the broad and subtle ways that prison changes people and causes them pain. Finally, of course, by concentrating only on in-prison changes and effects—like most researchers who addressed these issues at that time—Bonta and Gendreau could not examine whether and how prison produced psychological changes that would prove dysfunctional or disabling upon release of the prisoner.

Although legitimate concerns over the subjectivity and potential biases of less controlled studies of the effects of imprisonment should not be summarily dismissed, a wholesale rejection of the reflective observations that they contain seems equally unwarranted. The classic sociological analy-ses and journalistic and autobiographical accounts of prison life include a number of sensitive insights about the debilitating aspects of incarceration. They are too consistent to ignore, and among other things, they certainly contradict claims that imprisonment is a psychologically neutral experi-ence.[18] In fact, many of the firsthand, autobiographical accounts of prison life were written by persons whose experiences appeared to have profoundly transformed them. In some instances, the published stories themselves were conceived by their authors as one way to exorcise the demons that they felt prison had instilled in them. Victor Serge, for example, wrote that prison "burdened me with an experience so heavy, so intolerable to endure" that, long after his release, he felt compelled to write his first book "to free myself from this inward nightmare."[19]

Indeed, some of the most subtle, yet profound, adaptations that prisoners make to prison life are unlikely to be reflected in check marks on the type of research questionnaires that lend themselves to quantitative analysis. As Cohen and Taylor observed, standard personality inventories and questionnaires of the sort commonly used in "objective" studies of prisons often are not appropriate for longer-term inmates:

> There's not much point in asking a man who's been inside for ten years and faces another twenty, whether or not he can "easily get some life into a rather dull party" (to quote item 51 of the widely used Eysenck Personality Inventory).[20]

Moreover, most of the available standardized questionnaires have been developed for use in more mundane contexts, and normed with persons who share few background experiences with prisoners. Yet, researchers rarely acknowledge or discuss the limitations brought about by the use of these instruments with prisoners in such an extraordinary setting as prison.

As I suggested previously, a more meaningful analysis of the psychological pains of severe prison conditions might focus instead on the extreme adaptations prisoners undergo to survive, and the deeper changes in their value systems and worldviews that invariably result. Sociological and ethnographic accounts of prison life are among the few available sources of information about these more complex and dynamic transformations. We still lack research instruments that can quantify the psychological effects of entering a world in which survival may depend on achieving total emotional control, constantly maintaining a high level of suspicion and hypervigilance, and striving for mastery over the intricacies of interpersonal deceit. Similarly, no standardized tests that I know can measure the precise consequences of being surrounded by models of aggressive domination, or calibrate the identity transformations that take place inside many prisoners who are treated as categorically untrustworthy, worthless, and unpredictably and inexplicably violent. But that does not mean that these core aspects of the prison experience fail to produce pain or harm or significant psychological consequences that can be accurately described and thoughtfully analyzed.

THE PSYCHOLOGICAL TOLL OF INCARCERATION

Despite the narrowness of the quantitative measures that are used in traditional psychological studies of the pains of imprisonment, they nonetheless *do* provide a limited database with which many specific negative effects can be catalogued. For example, despite Bonta and Gendreau's assertion that prisons were not particularly harmful to the prisoners in the studies they summarized, they also made the following empirically documented concessions: that "physiological and psychological stress responses . . . were very likely [to occur] under crowded prison conditions";[21] that "a correlation [has been found] between population density and misconduct [when age is used as a moderator variable]";[22] that there is "a significant relationship between crowding and post-release recidivism";[23] and that "high inmate turnover [in some prisons has been found to predict] inmate disruptions."[24]

Bonta and Gendreau also acknowledged that "as sentence length or exposure to crowded situations increase so does the risk for misconduct";[25] that "when threats to health come from suicide and self-mutilation, then inmates are clearly at risk";[26] that "in Canadian penitentiaries, the homicide rates are close to 20 times that of similar-aged males in Canadian society";[27] and that "a variety of health problems, injuries, and selected symptoms of psychological distress were higher for certain classes of inmates than probationers, parolees, and, where data existed, for the general population."[28]

Moreover, even this narrowly framed review of the literature on the effects of imprisonment acknowledged that studies showed long-term incarceration to result in "increases in hostility and social introversion . . . and decreases in self-evaluation and evaluations of work and father";[29] that imprisonment produced "increases in dependency upon staff for direction and social introversion," a tendency for prisoners to prefer "to cope with their sentences on their own rather than seek the aid of others,"[30] "deteriorating community relationships over time,"[31] and "unique difficulties" with "family separation issues and vocational skill training needs"[32]; and that some researchers have speculated that "inmates typically undergo a 'behavioral deep freeze'" such that "outside-world behaviors that led the offender into trouble prior to imprisonment remain until release."[33]

Finally, despite their assertion that the pains of imprisonment commonly were exaggerated in many descriptions of prison life, Bonta and Gendreau further reported that there were "signs of pathology for inmates incarcerated in solitary for periods up to a year";[34] that higher levels of anxiety have been found in inmates after 8 weeks in jail than after 1;[35] that increases in psychopathological symptoms occurred after 72 hours of confinement;[36] and that death row prisoners have been found to have "symptoms ranging from paranoia to insomnia" and "increased feelings of depression and hopelessness" and "powerlessness," and to be "fearful of their surroundings, and . . . emotionally drained."[37]

Thus, even this highly selective literature review that seemed to defend the correctional status quo included a long list of empirically documented and well-quantified negative effects. No careful reading of the cited results could lead to the conclusion that prisons were psychological healthy places in which to confine persons for long periods of time. Although concern over the harmful consequences of incarceration may have waned among politicians and citizens in general over the last several decades, along with a consensus among some penologists and correctional policymakers that prisons were not uniformly devastating to every prisoner, this was *not* because prison conditions had improved significantly or because there was new and convincing scientific evidence to show that imprisonment did little or no damage to the persons who were subjected to it.

Instead, as I noted earlier, a different set of influences was at work to divert attention from the harshness of prison life and sidetrack discussions of its harmful effects. As Jonathan Willens summarized it, because prisoners were depicted as "brutal, hardened criminals," it was possible to ignore their inhumane treatment and minimize the long-term consequences of harsh confinement. Moreover, as prison itself came to be defined as "inherently dangerous and violent," without any mandate to provide positive programming intended to benefit prisoners, almost anything could be done in the name of institutional security, including practices "which are themselves dangerous and violent." A "new legal prison" emerged that, as Willens put it, "legitimates attacks on the prisoners, attacks on his space, his property, his body, and his pride." [38]

Widespread stereotypes that cast prisoners in subhuman terms implied that they did not warrant the same minimal considerations—or deserve the same limits to the level of pain and harm to which they legitimately could be subjected—as other persons. However, these views are at odds with what we know about the psychological effects of the conditions under which prisoners are kept and to which they are required to adapt. Understanding prison as a powerful social context in its own right and examining the mechanisms that prisoners must use to survive in such places provides some insight into where and how these institutional settings and situations will need to be changed to minimize their harmful effects.

COPING WITH THE STRESS OF IMPRISONMENT

A half-century ago, Gresham Sykes wrote that "life in the maximum security prison is depriving or frustrating in the extreme."[39] Little has changed inside contemporary American prisons to alter that view. Extreme deprivations and stark power differentials still characterize most correctional environments. They generate and provoke a wide range of strong human emotions, including frustration, anger, fear, sadness, and resentment. The concentration of these emotions in one relatively small place from which there is no escape and few release valves—prison itself—has potentially explosive consequences. Of course, prisons are structured to keep these self-generated forces repressively in check. To do so, prison staff and administrators attempt to strike a delicate psychological balance. On the one hand, prisoners are forcefully dominated and severely deprived by their conditions of confinement. On the other hand, if the controls are too severe or the deprivations too complete, prisoners may break down, rebel, or become unmanageable in other ways, and the balance will be lost.

For prisoners hoping to survive the experience, the necessary psychological balancing is very different. As Hans Toch and Kenneth Adams have acknowledged, the "dictum that prisons are stressful cannot be overestimated."[40] Many studies of the psychological effects of incarceration have focused on prisoner adaptation, survival skills, or methods of coping in the face of severely stressful conditions.[41] Although many inmates do survive even the most severe conditions of confinement, they do so with little assistance from prison officials, who rarely acknowledge or explain the effects of these stressful conditions, let alone regularly take action to meaningfully address and ameliorate them for prisoners.

Of course, prisoners have little choice but to attempt to adapt to prison life. Yet, mastering the psychological rigors of prison does little to facilitate successful reintegration into the freeworld. Most prisoners must negotiate the tensions between their preprison identity, the person who they appear to be in prison, and, finally, the one they actually become.[42] Many are unable to successfully manage these profoundly complicated identity shifts. Moreover, the ability to successfully adapt to certain prison contexts may be inversely related to subsequent adjustment in the community. That is, as one study showed, "Inmates who adjusted most successfully to a prison environment actually encountered the most difficulty making the transition from institutional life to freedom."[43]

Nonetheless, of course, prisoners must accommodate to the many painful and stressful aspects of imprisonment. Research on the effects of general environmental stress emphasizes that its negative impact is amplified by perceived threat and reduced by the perception of control.[44] That is, stress is made worse when people perceive themselves to be in psychologically or physically threatening conditions, and lessened when they perceive themselves to have more control over their environment. Accordingly, prisons represent an unfortunate combination—a situation characterized both by high threat and low control—that intensifies the level of psychological stress.

Moreover, as inflicting pain was accepted as a legitimate goal of imprisonment over the last several decades, adverse prison conditions and potentially harmful forms of treatment came to be regarded as normative and otherwise unproblematic. In this context, many prisoners lost confidence in their ability to redress grievances through administrative mechanisms or procedures. In many parts of the country, prisoners lack legal representation, and effective outside intervention to address their hardships is rare or nonexistent. In addition, the increased length of prison sentences that were meted out over the last several decades meant that many prisoners experienced these harsh conditions for very long periods of time. Thus, short-term strategies used to manage acute prison stress naturally evolved into chronic lifestyles.

Stress that is extreme and endured on a long-term basis is more than unpleasant; it can result in permanent damage. Frederick Hocking's classic review of the psychological consequences of exposure to extreme environmental stress led him to conclude that it "may result in permanent psychologic disability." And, although persons vary in their ability to adjust to and tolerate different amounts of stress, "subjection to prolonged, extreme stress results in the development of 'neurotic' symptoms in virtually every person exposed to it. . . ."[45] Individual difference variables—"constitutional factors, patterns of child rearing, and preexisting personality characteristics"—appear to influence how long a person can withstand prolonged, extreme stress, not whether they eventually succumb.[46]

Thus, the psychological mechanisms used in response to high levels of prison stress can take a severe psychological toll, and the longer the duration and the more intense the stressful conditions to which prisoners must adapt, the greater are the consequences. In addition to severely overcrowded conditions, high levels of idleness, inadequate mental health care, and the like—all of which have become widespread and represent the norm in a number of prison systems—there are even more extreme forms of prison stress with which many prisoners must cope. Although physical brutality certainly is not as commonplace as it once was, when courts literally refused to intervene behind prison walls,[47] some prisoners nonetheless are subjected to forms of extreme degradation, humiliation, and even physical mistreatment.

Extreme conditions of confinement and staff mistreatment are not relegated to a few antiquated prison regimes that are regarded as throwbacks to some bygone era. As one federal judge observed in the mid-1990s with respect to California's supposedly "state-of-the-art" facility at Pelican Bay prison, "the prison setting offers a tremendous potential for abuse" by staff who have "powerful weapons and enormous manpower at their disposal, and exercise nearly total control over the inmates under their supervision."[48]

To be sure, some clear patterns emerge among persons forced to adapt to extreme prison stress. However, several caveats are in order. For one, the adaptations that I describe in this section and the next are neither mutually exclusive nor universally employed. That is, prisoners may manifest one or more of these patterns simultaneously, or shift between them over time. Prisoners who are psychologically resilient and who are housed in well-run institutions where prison stress does not reach such extreme levels may manifest few, if any, of them. Hans Toch has observed, and I would agree, that few of the effects of prison stress "are cross-sectional, immediate, and 'purely out there,' because personal susceptibilities that intersect with environments are built up through personal histories."[49] Nevertheless, several distinct adaptations to the social context of prison can be identified.

For example, many prisoners devote a substantial portion of their day-to-day existence to trying to minimize the very real risks and dangers of imprisonment. Vivid accounts of life inside prisons in the United States written over the last several decades acknowledge that many of them are truly dangerous and frightening places.[50] As an American Bar Association report published in the early 1990s told readers, simply and directly,

> As an inmate, you would be vulnerable. Because prisons are chronically understaffed and because of their design, it is presently impossible for correctional officers to continually observe what the prisoners are doing in their cells and elsewhere. If you therefore refused to share your personal possessions with another inmate, buy that inmate items requested from the prison commissary, have sex with the inmate, or do something else the inmate wanted you to do, you might get beaten up, stabbed, raped, or even killed.[51]

It is not surprising that prisoners in such environments may become obsessed with their own personal safety. They rely on constant and extreme forms of hypervigilance as a defense against victimization in the hostile world that surrounds them.

In a related way, some prisoners also learn to project a tough convict veneer that keeps all others at a distance. Indeed, as one prison researcher put it, many prisoners "believe that unless an inmate can convincingly project an image that conveys the potential for violence, he is likely to be dominated and exploited throughout the duration of his sentence."[52] Richard McCorkle's study of a maximum-security Tennessee prison attempted to quantify the kinds of behavioral strategies prisoners used to survive dangerous prison environments. He found that "fear appeared to be shaping the life styles of many of the men," that it had led over 40% of prisoners to avoid certain high-risk areas of the prison, and that about an equal number of inmates reported spending additional time in their cells as a precaution against victimization. At the same time, almost three quarters of the prisoners reported that they had been forced to "get tough" with another inmate to avoid victimization, and more than a quarter kept a "shank" or other weapon nearby with which to defend themselves. McCorkle found that age was the best predictor of the type of adaptation a prisoner took—younger prisoners were more likely to use aggressive avoidance strategies than older ones.

Shaping such an outward image of toughness requires prisoners to carefully monitor, dampen, and control their emotional responses. They struggle to suppress visible reactions to events around them.[53] Signs of vulnerability or a lack of control inside the immediate prison environment are potentially dangerous because they invite exploitation. As one experienced prison administrator once wrote, "Prison is a barely controlled jungle where the aggressive and the strong will exploit the weak, and the weak are dreadfully aware of it."[54] Prisoners also become remarkably skilled "self-monitors" who routinely calculate the way that every aspect of their outward behavior might be interpreted by the rest of the prison population. Ideally, such calculations will become second nature because the slightest miscue or hesitation might be misinterpreted by others. For example, even subtle indications of complicity with the prison administration may lead to ostracism or precipitate more serious forms of retaliation.

Toch and Adams put the matter somewhat differently, arguing that the threat of exploitation is "tangible" because "fear is equated with 'weakness,' and weakness earns contempt and invites aggression" in prison. Prisoners learn to target those who have already shown that they are susceptible to intimidation, a pattern that obviously worsens the plight of weaker prisoners.[55] It follows, then, that prisoners will adapt to these contingencies by attempting to avoid the appearance of susceptibility to intimidation at all costs.

Prisoners who labor at both an emotional and behavioral level to develop a "prison mask" that is unrevealing and impenetrable risk alienation from themselves and others. That is, they may develop an emotional flatness that becomes chronic and debilitating in social interactions and in their personal relationships. Some will find that they have created a permanent and unbridgeable distance between themselves and other people. Others find that the risks associated with open, genuine communication are too great; their prison experience leads them to withdraw from authentic social interactions altogether.[56] Some prisoners seek safety in social invisibility. They become as inconspicuous and unobtrusive as possible by disconnecting completely from others. These prisoners may retreat deeply into themselves, trust virtually no one, and adjust to prison stress by leading isolated lives of quiet desperation.[57]

This kind of self-isolating dynamic is exacerbated by the enormous strain that imprisonment places on family and other personal relationships.[58] Financial and interpersonal hardships that are imposed on loved ones and the significant practical difficulties that are encountered in the course of most prison visiting (that can range from mere inconvenience to outright humiliation) may take a significant and sometimes decisive toll on already fragile connections some prisoners have to family members, intimates, and the outside world in general.[59] Visitors unaware of the day-to-day stress of imprisonment, the cumulative effect of the daily humiliations and degradations of prison life, and the mood swings that these uncontrollable events can precipitate in prisoners may be taken aback by their unpredictability or by learning that contact with the outside world sometimes is more painful than it is pleasant. Yet for some prisoners, self-imposed isolation—pushing others away—paradoxically functions as a defensive reaction to the anticipated loss of social support.[60]

In another paradox of prison life, idleness and inactivity often lead to chronic tiredness or lethargy. Prisoners talk about "pulling time," as if it were a weight; among other things, the heaviness to which they refer comes from the lack of meaningful activities in which to engage and the monotony of their surroundings and daily routine. Victor Serge was especially sensitive to the disjuncture between the weight of prison time and the pace of the freeworld: "The contrast between this vacant, empty prison time and the intense rhythm of normal life is so violent that it will take a long and painful period of adaptation to slow down the pulse of life. . . ."[61]

As I discuss in more detail later in this chapter, many prisoners become increasingly dependent on the structure and procedures of prison to initiate and organize their behavior. However, in extreme cases the complete loss of personal initiative leads to lethargy or even depression. It is not surprising that long-term prisoners are particularly vulnerable to this kind of despondency. Indeed, Taylor wrote that the long-term prisoner "shows a flatness of response which resembles slow, automatic behavior of a very limited kind, and he is humorless and lethargic."[62] In fact, Jose-Kampfner has analogized the plight of long-term women prisoners to that of persons who are terminally ill, whose experience of this "existential death is unfeeling, being cut off from the outside . . . [and who] adopt this attitude because it helps them cope."[63]

ON PRISONIZATION AS COPING

In addition to the patterns of coping I described in the preceding section—hypervigilance, projecting a tough convict veneer, suppressing outward signs of emotion, and becoming generally distrustful of others—there is a more general process at work as prisoners adjust to the rigors of prison life. The term *institutionalization* is used to describe ways in which inmates are shaped and transformed by the institutional environments in which they live. George Herbert Mead once noted that "a person is a personality because he belongs to a community, because he takes over the institutions of that community into his own conduct."[64] If so, then a prisoner's personality is shaped by the institutional contingencies to which the community of prison requires him to adapt.

Called *prisonization* when it occurs in correctional settings, the process has been studied extensively by sociologists, psychologists, psychiatrists, and others.[65] In his classic formulation, sociologist Donald Clemmer defined prisonization as "the taking on in greater or less degree of the folkways, mores, customs, and general culture of the penitentiary,"[66] but there are important psychological components to the process as well. Just like the previously discussed coping mechanisms, these changes are natural and normal adaptations made by prisoners in response to the unnatural and abnormal conditions of prison life. Of course, even these normal responses may become problematic if they are taken to extremes, or become so chronic and deeply internalized that they persist even though surrounding conditions have changed. Like most gradual transformations, prisonization does not require conscious awareness or mean that prisoners make a "choice" to allow themselves to be changed in these ways.

It is not surprising that during the initial period of incarceration, most prisoners find the harsh and rigid institutional routine, deprivations of privacy and liberty, stigmatized status, and sparse living conditions to be stressful, unpleasant, and difficult to tolerate. As prison researcher Edward Zamble put it simply, "It would appear that the beginning of the term [of imprisonment] induces considerable psychological discomfort. . . ."[67] However, over time, they come to accept the many aspects of prison life that they cannot change. Indeed, as Zamble noted, "the constancy of the prison environment leads to a slow and gradual amelioration."[68]

The process of gradually ameliorating is not necessarily neutral or benign. Zamble and others have suggested that this process "does not induce widespread behavior change," but instead results in a kind of "behavioral *deep freeze*."[69] However, I believe this misapprehends the nature of the process by which persons adjust to the atypical and powerful prison environment. The "deep freezer" of the prison is an extreme social context that imposes unique and severe contingencies on prisoners that govern their behavior.

Once they have adapted to these contingencies, many prisoners find that their new behavior patterns are not easily "unfrozen." Moreover, the benign-sounding term *amelioration* does not necessarily capture the painfulness of the process, the losses that occur in the course of the transformation, or the distortions in the habits of thinking and acting that are required to bring it about. Prisoners who try to actively resist the process may suffer severe negative consequences—applied by the prison administration or even by other inmates—and their very psychological survival may be placed at risk. In any event, widespread and deep-seated behavior change certainly occurs; it is the very purpose of the process.

There are several important dimensions to the process of prisonization. Among other things, penal institutions typically force people to give up the power to make most of their own choices and decisions. However, this seemingly reasonable practice is taken to extreme lengths: Prisoners must relinquish control over the most basic and mundane aspects of their daily existence. They generally have no choice over when they get up or turn their lights out; when, what, or where they eat; and whether and for how long they shower or make a phone call. These and most of the other countless daily decisions that citizens in the freeworld make on a day-to-day basis and naturally take for granted are made by others in prison. Prisoners typically feel infantalized by this loss of control. However, over time, as they adapt to the erosion of personal autonomy, the fact that others routinely decide these things begins to seem increasingly "natural."

As prisonization continues, prisoners come to *depend* on institutional decision makers to make choices for them, and to rely on the structure and routines of the institution to organize their daily activities. Years spent having others make their decisions, organizing and directing their behavior and otherwise exercising control over the course of their lives, accustoms them to it. Indeed, the loss of autonomy and the corresponding dependency on prison structure may become so complete that some prisoners are troubled and even traumatized by the unstructured and unpredictable nature of the freeworld settings to which they return. In extreme cases they may lose the capacity to initiate activity, to use their own judgment to make effective decisions, or to engage in planful behavior of any kind.

Most prisoners live in correctional institutions that deny them basic privacy rights and are confined in facilities that place an extremely heavy emphasis on security and control. A little more than one in four prisons in the United States is classified as maximum security, and nearly 40% of the nation's inmates are housed in such places.[70] These institutions tend to be large—the great majority house over 750 prisoners—and they typically are surrounded by high double fences or walls, with armed guards in observation towers.[71] In addition to the external physical constraints, prisons implement an elaborate network of rules and use multiple structures, devices (e.g., locks, grills, handcuffs, chains), and control mechanisms of all sorts to keep behavior inside the institution in check.

Over time, however, many prisoners become dependent on these limiting structures and procedures to constrain their actions. Rather than relying on internal organization, or what is commonly referred to as *self-control*, to guide and restrain prisoners' conduct, institutions shape inmate decision making around external limits and constraints. In a related way, prisoners also get used to, come to expect, and then find that they depend on the routine and continuous surveillance to which they have been subjected. Of course, they assume that certain violations of the elaborate network of numerous rules in which they are immersed will be punished—often swiftly and, depending on the nature of the violation, severely. They also expect that the very clear boundaries with which they are surrounded will be enforced, with equal vigor. However, many prisoners come to rely on these external forms of monitoring as a way of controlling their own behavior and that of others.

Prisonization creates so much dependency on external limits and constraints that internal controls may atrophy or, in the case of especially young inmates, fail to develop at all. Like the ability to initiate behavior, the capacity to exercise self-control diminishes under conditions where it is rarely used or needed. If and when the external limits on which prisoners are forced to become dependent are removed, however, they may find that they are less able to make appropriate choices, exercise personal judgment, or refrain from behavior that ultimately is harmful or self-destructive.

Prisoners also must adjust to extremely deprived and diminished living conditions. Each prisoner typically lives in a small, cramped, sparsely furnished, and sometimes badly deteriorating and poorly maintained living space. Notwithstanding the extensive prison construction programs that were undertaken over the last several decades in the United States, fully one quarter of the nation's prisoners in the year 2000 were housed in facilities that were 50 or more years old. In fact, 80,000 prisoners were still confined in prisons that were constructed a century ago.[72] Whatever the age of the facilities in which they are kept, most maximum-security prisoners live in cells that are about 60 square feet in dimension—a space that is roughly the size of king-size bed. It contains a prisoner's bunk, a toilet, a sink, and, typically, a cabinet or closet where all of the inmate's personal possessions must be stored.

In addition, most share this space with another person (whose bunk and personal possessions also must fit into the cell). Prisoners who are double-celled sometimes have little or no control over the identity of the person who shares these extremely small living spaces with them and with whom they must negotiate the intimate daily contact that these close quarters require.[73] Although most prisoners do not stay around the clock in these cramped spaces, high levels of overcrowding and the lack of rehabilitation programs have combined to further reduce already limited opportunities for meaningful out-of-cell activities in maximum-security prisons. Moreover, in prisons that are plagued by violent conflict, prisoners are "locked down," and they may remain in their cells continuously—sometimes for months at a time—until normal movement is restored.

The degraded conditions under which prisoners live serve as constant reminders of their compromised and stigmatized social status and role. A diminished sense of self-worth and personal value may result. In extreme cases of prisonization, the symbolic meaning that can be inferred from this externally imposed substandard treatment and these degraded circumstances is internalized. That is, prisoners may come to think of themselves as the kind of person who deserves no more than the degradation and stigma to which they have been subjected while incarcerated.[74] This degraded identity may be difficult or impossible to relinquish upon release from prison, especially if prisoners return to communities where they continue to be marginalized or stigmatized by others.

Indeed, many people come to prison already having begun to think of themselves as marginal, as outlaw, or "other." In any event, prison tends to foist such an identity on new arrivals and then "fix" or harden it by virtue of the way prisoners subsequently are treated, referred to, and looked upon by many staff members. For some, this prison identity will include a deep sense of damage, deviance, and even moral failure. Whether deserved at some level or not, these are not senses of self that are likely to enable someone to successfully reenter the freeworld. Thus, the experience of imprisonment instills its own sense of stigma, an often internalized version that compounds the effects of the social stigma that prisoners will almost undoubtedly encounter in the larger society as a result of their ex-convict status.

Prisons are also characterized by elaborate *informal* rules and norms that are part of the unwritten, but essential, culture and code that prevail inside prison and among prisoners themselves. Like the formal rules of the institution, these, too, must be abided; there are very real and often severe consequences when violations occur. Some prisoners, eager to defend themselves against what they perceive as constant dangers and deprivations of the surrounding environment, may fully embrace and internalize as many of these informal norms as possible. The norms of the prisoner culture can be harsh, exploitative, and even predatory. Particularly in poorly run maximum-security prisons, where the informal prisoner culture becomes especially strong, many prisoners—those who cannot devise one or another strategy to somehow appear aloof or uninvolved—face a stark choice between becoming a victim or victimizer.

Because many of the basic human needs and desires that are taken for granted in the freeworld—the need to recreate, work, and love—are ignored, suppressed, or greatly compromised in prison, prisoners seek alternative ways of fulfilling them. For example, few prisoners have access to gainful employment, where they can obtain meaningful and marketable job skills or earn adequate compensation. In many places, "work" consists of menial tasks that they perform for only a few hours a day. Similarly, with rare exceptions—in those very few states that permit conjugal visits—prisoners are prohibited from sexual contact of any kind. As a result of these restrictions and prohibitions, prisoners are drawn closer to an illicit-inmate culture where substitute experiences can be found. To many prisoners, this illicit culture and accompanying underground economy appear to offer the best way to tolerate and survive their otherwise deprived and degraded conditions.

Ironically, in prisons where treatment is particularly severe and the day-to-day deprivations of prison life are especially extreme, the power and importance of the informal prisoner culture expands. That is, the less access prisoners have to meaningful programming opportunities and other institutionally sanctioned activities in which to become invested and engaged, the more likely an alternative and oppositional prisoner culture is to emerge. Among other things, this means that some prisoners will rely on prison gangs or cliques to provide support, comradeship, protection, and access to activities and other goods and services that they perceive cannot be obtained any other way. And, as the informal gang culture grows stronger, the choice to refrain or completely withdraw from it is more difficult to make. Prisoners in these places either actively participate or devise a way to carefully negotiate a precarious, and at times very risky, neutral status.

As I noted earlier, signs of weakness or vulnerability may invite exploitation in prison, and prisoners are reluctant to show genuine emotion or interpersonal intimacy. Prisoner culture strongly reinforces this norm and helps to turn it into a self-fulfilling prophecy as well as a survival strategy. That is, in many prison settings, the failure to exploit weakness is itself seen as a sign of weakness and an invitation to exploitation by others. In men's prisons especially, these values and orientations may promote a kind of hypermasculinity in which force and domination are glorified.

Of course, prisoners struggle to preserve their sense of self and maintain self-respect in a larger context of constant subordination. For some, an exaggerated need to preserve one's "manhood" results, constructed in a prison environment that constantly undermines and even obliterates it. Some prisoners embrace these expectations by promoting their own reputation for toughness, adopting an orientation in which even seemingly insignificant insults, minor affronts, or the slightest signs of disrespect must be responded to quickly and decisively, sometimes even with deadly force. As one prison observer put it, "The cultural rules for recouping manhood arise out of an environment of stress, loss, and deprivation."[75] It is also understandable that in such an environment—one characterized by enforced powerlessness and social deprivation—men and women prisoners confront distorted norms of sexuality in which dominance and submission often become entangled with and mistaken for the basis of intimate relations. These behaviors may become the vehicles through which all close personal or intimate connections are established.

Prisoners who internalize these habits, values, and perspectives—all normal reactions to an abnormal situation—will experience great difficulty transitioning back to freeworld norms. A tough veneer that precludes seeking help for personal problems, the generalized mistrust that comes from the fear of exploitation, and a tendency to strike out in response to minimal provocations are highly functional in many prison contexts but problematic virtually everywhere else. In interactions with persons who know nothing about the norms and psychological effects of the place from which they come, prisoners may be perceived as unfeeling, distant, aloof, or cold; needlessly suspicious or even paranoid; and capable of impulsive, dangerous overreactions.

As I noted earlier, although prisoner culture is informal, its norms often are very forcefully imposed and its effects on prisoners are powerful and long lasting. Socialization into the habits of thinking and acting that are required to fit into this culture may contribute as much to the prisonization process as adaptations to the rules, routines, and structure that are formally imposed by the institution. These habits of thinking and acting are equally difficult to relinquish upon release.

Prisonization may affect younger prisoners even more profoundly than others. Many enter these powerful socializing environments before they have acquired stable values of their own or developed the capacity to make adult judgments, choices, and decisions. Thus, they are more likely to shape their habits and beliefs around the structure of the institution and the norms of the prisoner culture in which they are immersed. Obviously, younger inmates who enter prison environments during more formative stages of their lives lack a preexisting identity that they can strive to regain when they leave the institutional structure and prison culture behind.

Finally, because prisonization occurs gradually and many of the psychological changes take place subtly over time, prisoners often are unaware of the depth and magnitude of the transformations that they have undergone. Because many have learned to ignore or mask their internal feelings and reactions, they struggle during the transition back to the freeworld to locate the source of the anxiety and disjuncture that they are experiencing. Because they have been taught to conceal emotions, problems, and vulnerabilities— even to themselves—it is difficult to acknowledge these things once they leave prison. A projected image of unproblematic postprison adjustment may belie a great deal of inner turmoil, stress, and fear that can jeopardize their successful return to the freeworld.

The impact of prisonization has increased during the last several decades. In addition to the greater numbers of people incarcerated, the *amount* of time served in prison has risen. Thus, the adaptations that most prisoners make in order to adjust to the prison context are no longer short term in nature.[76] For example, between 1986 and 1997, the average amount of prison time actually served by federal prisoners nearly doubled—from 15 months to 29 months. For drug offenders, it increased from 20 months to 43 months. The trends toward harsher federal sentences continued throughout this period so that, by 1997, about 70% of persons entering federal prison that year could expect to serve 5 years or more before being released.[77]

Although more difficult to pinpoint precisely, it appears that the trends in state sentencing have lagged somewhat behind the federal system but nonetheless paralleled them.[78] By 2002, prisoners were being sentenced, on average, to about 4.5 years (53 months) in prison.[79] In addition, in some

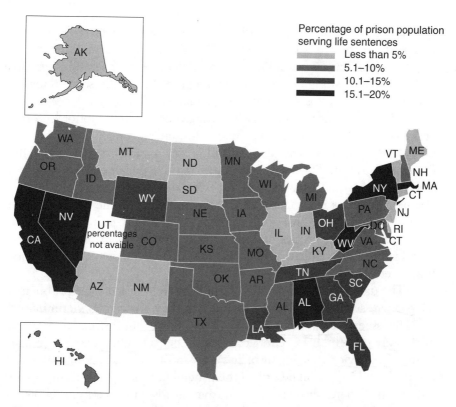

Figure 6.1. Percentages of prisoners serving life. Data from *The Meaning of "Life": Long Prison Sentences in Context*, by M. Mauer, R. King, and M. Young, May 2004, Washington, DC: The Sentencing Project. Adapted with permission of M. Mauer. See also http://www.soros.org/initiatives/justice/articles_publications/publications/lifers_20040511.

states there was an increase in the numbers of prisoners sentenced to *very* long prison terms. In fact, as Figure 6.1 illustrates, a number of states now have between 15% and 20% of prisoners serving "life" sentences. Overall, about 1 in 11 prisoners is serving life in a state or federal prison.[80] In the face of these long sentences, prisonization evolves from being merely a set of short-term adaptations to an actual long-term strategy of living.

PRISON CONDITIONS AND PRISON VIOLENCE

Situational analyses of misconduct and violent behavior in prisons have underscored the way actions are influenced by the context in which they occur.[81] Prison is experienced as a "pernicious assault on the self-esteem of the inmate,"[82] and many prisoners find it difficult to control hostile impulses in the face of this assault. Many prisoners silently feel frustrated and angry over arbitrary or abusive treatment or the deprived conditions under which they live. Others externalize their reactions and direct these negative emotions outward. Prisoners may channel their rageful, aggressive feelings by fantasizing about taking revenge to "even the score" later on, and some erupt explosively while still confined.

Although research is somewhat divided on whether a prior history of aggression predicts assaultive behavior while incarcerated,[83] or not,[84] especially stressful or provocative aspects of prison life increase the probability of violence overall. Placing prisoners who may have learned to react aggressively to frustration or conflict inside especially adverse conditions of confinement creates a particularly explosive mix.[85] Indeed, the combination of high levels of overcrowding, chronic idleness and a lack of meaningful programming opportunities, and the prevailing punishment-oriented correctional policies has resulted in many prisons becoming more dangerous places than ever before.[86]

The dangers and degradation of prison life have led some prisoners to adopt aggressive survival strategies in which they proactively victimize others. The issue of sexual assault in prison is a tragic, but instructive, example of the way that the harsh context of prison helps to elicit extreme, hurtful forms of behavior that, in turn, have severe, traumatic consequences for others. John Coggeshall described the general process by which this occurs: "In prison, inmates face antagonism from guards, violence from fellow inmates, and deprivation from incarceration itself. One method by which inmates retaliate is to humiliate and assault their fellow inmates sexually."[87] Thus, the frustration of sexual deprivation combines with the daily degradations of self to produce a perverse dynamic in which prisoners may acquire some degree of status through the sexual victimization of others. As one researcher put it, "Men who have been deprived of most avenues of self-expression and who have lost status by the act of imprisonment may resort to the use of sexual and physical power to reassert their uncertain male credentials."[88]

Estimates of the frequency of prison rapes vary widely. One report in the late 1960s indicated that sexual assault of those awaiting trial in Philadelphia was of near "epidemic" proportions.[89] Studies done in the 1980s estimated that about 9% of prisoners were sexually assaulted or were targets of sexual aggression.[90] The authors of one of these studies also speculated that sexual coercion or homosexual activity may lead to other forms of violence in prison, as prisoners retaliate for having been taken advantage of or compete with one another over desirable partners.[91]

More recent estimates suggest that over 20% of prisoners are coerced or persuaded into some form of sexual conduct while incarcerated.[92] In a mid-1990s study, researchers reported that about 22% of male prisoners had been victimized in this way (including 13% for whom the coerced sexual activity involved intercourse) and that, once having been victimized, prisoners were targeted for an average of nine nonconsensual incidents of sexual contact.[93] Others have noted that a sexual assault in prison often results in the victim being forced to "serve his assailant's needs for perhaps years thereafter."[94] Similarly, Coggeshall observed that "once an inmate has been forced to adopt a submissive lifestyle, the more intense the nightmare of domination becomes."[95]

Prison writer Wilbert Rideau provided an informed and equally unsettling account. He wrote that the "typical man walking into the average jail or prison in the nation" will find that "rape and sexual violence is as much a part of [his] pained existence as are the walls holding [him] prisoner."[96] Rideau also explained the difficulties that researchers confront in trying to obtain reliable estimates of the frequency with which this occurs: "Penal administrators rarely talk about the sexual violence that plagues their institutions, turning them into literal jungles. Prisoners are too involved to ever want to do anything more than forget it once they regain their freedom."[97] It is not surprising that the fear of sexual assault comes to dominate the lives of many prisoners,[98] and those who are victimized may experience profound psychiatric consequences once released.

Thus, although sexual aggression in prison appears to be highly situation specific, its consequences are not. One of the few studies of male rape victims outside of institutional settings concluded that men grappled with this kind of victimization in much the same way as women who had been raped. As would be expected, all of the respondents (selected because they had been the victims of adult rape that had occurred after the age of 16) reported that the rape had "a major detrimental effect on their lives."[99] Yet most of these victims had never reported the assault to anyone, and less than 10% reported it to the police. Almost all of the victims experienced long-term negative psychological consequences that included an increased sense of vulnerability, anger, loss of self-respect, conflicted sexual orientation, and emotional distancing. Roughly half reported long-lasting sexual dysfunction and rape-related phobias.

The consensus among researchers and clinicians is that "the consequences of sexual assault or coercive relationships are severe, no less within prison than without."[100] Clinicians who have described the psychiatric consequences of sexual assaults on male victims have concluded that most men experienced mood disturbances, problems in relationships with peers, and sexual difficulties as psychological sequelae to the assault.[101] Another group of researchers noted that, as in the case of women rape victims, men may experience posttraumatic stress disorder (PTSD) and its related symptoms.

Indeed, they suggested that, for men, there may be additional problems that are "related to cultural expectations of their roles."[102] They speculated that these problems would be worsened if the rapes occurred in a context like prison, where they were combined with other forms of chronic humiliation that violated the cultural roles that men were expected to assume and maintain. Moreover, although no one has studied it systematically, it seems likely that this aggressive sexual behavior will have long-term consequences for the perpetrators as well as the victims. That is, having engaged in these forms of sexual aggression—in response to the deprivations and pressures of prison life rather than preexisting preferences—may distort their sexual identity and their ability to create and maintain sexual intimacy outside of prison.

EXTREME REACTIONS TO PAINFUL CONDITIONS OF CONFINEMENT

Prison stress provides an extreme test of psychological strength and resiliency that some prisoners will fail. Many prisoners report that the initial period of incarceration is the most difficult and that their worst crises occur almost immediately. Acute psychiatric symptoms may emerge for the first time, or intensify in prisoners who enter prison with preexisting disorders. After this initial period, some prisoners adapt to the prison environment and the most obvious and severe symptoms may subside.[103] However, psychiatric problems persist in others and may become chronic. Moreover, there are some who move through the initial phases of incarceration seemingly intact, only to find themselves worn down by the constant psychological assault and stress of subsequent confinement. They experience more serious mental health problems in the later stages of incarceration.

As I discuss in detail in chapter 8, many inmates suffer identifiable and undiagnosable clinical disorders and syndromes in response to the harshness of prison life. Yet, there are some prison-related maladies that do not fit neatly into traditional diagnostic categories (perhaps because many of these categories are designed to describe forms of personal psychopathology that arise in relation to more normative social settings or situations). Instead, prison-related syndromes often emerge from the pathogenicity of this extreme situation. *Transient situational disturbance,* a disorder present in the second edition of the *Diagnostic and Statistical Manual of Mental Disorders (DSM)* that was in use until 1980, was defined as "an acute reaction to overwhelming environmental stress" that was expected to abate once the stress was diminished.[104] This important (albeit short-lived) diagnostic innovation focused attention on the clinical consequences of exposure to extreme situational stress or trauma of the sort that prison creates for many inmates.

Questions about the specificity of the diagnosis,[105] and recognition that situational traumas were not really transient—but produced chronic psychological problems that persisted long after exposure to the situation itself had ended—led to its revision.[106] PTSD is now used to describe a range of long-term trauma-related symptoms, including depression, emotional numbing, anxiety, isolation, hypervigilance, and related reactions.[107] More recently, Judith Herman and others have proposed that the diagnostic category of posttraumatic stress disorder be restructured to include what she termed *complex PTSD*, a disorder created by "prolonged, repeated trauma or the profound deformations of personality that occur in captivity."[108]

Unlike classic PTSD—which arises from relatively circumscribed traumatic events—complex PTSD occurs in response to more chronic exposure that is more closely analogous to the experience of imprisonment. Complex PTSD can result in protracted depression, apathy, and the development of a profound sense of hopelessness as the long-term psychological costs of adapting to an oppressive situation: "The humiliated rage of the imprisoned person also adds to the depressive burden. . . . During captivity, the prisoner can not express anger at the perpetrator; to do so would jeopardize survival."[109]

Whether they experience some form of PTSD or some other diagnosable psychological disorder, many prisoners do adapt to the pains of imprisonment by developing overt psychological symptoms—clinical depression, paranoia, and psychosis.[110] Nonetheless, as chapter 8 will elaborate, despite research conducted over the last 2 decades which indicates that somewhere between 12% and 24% of prisoners in the United States should be receiving psychiatric treatment,[111] no more than a fraction of that number are. Even fewer prisoners receive the kind of sustained and effective counseling and psychotherapy that they appear to need.

In extreme cases, some prisoners react to the psychic stresses of imprisonment by taking their own lives. Various studies have documented the much higher rates of prisoner suicide compared with that of the general population.[112] At least one study indicated that psychotherapeutic intervention could have a significant effect in reducing suicide rates,[113] and another noted that, despite causing the greatest number of prison fatalities, suicide was also "potentially the most preventable cause of death in prisons."[114]

Despite the predictable adverse mental health consequences of imprisonment, the punishment-oriented views that came to dominate American corrections in the later years of the 20th century have helped to create a knowledge gap of sorts: Too few prison staff members truly understand the psychological consequences of harsh confinement. Indeed, given the long period of time during which this punitive philosophy has prevailed—several decades now—a new generation of correctional workers is in place whose members have never known a time when prisons were intended primarily to help produce or promote positive change or otherwise do something beneficial for inmates. New employees have not often been trained to be sensitive to the psychologically harmful, potentially destructive characteristics of the prison settings that they oversee. Of course, those who fail to perceive the need for moderation in the treatment of prisoners also are less likely to initiate therapeutic intervention.

CONCLUSION

Prison is a powerful, often harsh, and potentially destructive social context. It transforms prisoners by forcing them to adopt problematic ways of thinking and acting to comply with the many institutional contingencies imposed on them. This compliance is essential to survive the psychological and physical demands of prison life. Yet, when prisoners use these adaptive mechanisms over long periods of time, many find them difficult to relinquish, even after they are no longer needed. Once useful and necessary, they prove troublesome, dysfunctional, and even disabling in the freeworld.

Moreover, the pains of imprisonment are too much for some prisoners to endure. Those who are unable to handle the stress of imprisonment may undergo severe forms of mental and emotional deterioration. The still common tendency to individualize and dispositionalize the root causes of what is perceived as deviant behavior helps to account for the relative lack of attention given to many of the most damaging effects of imprisonment. Nonetheless, over the last several decades, increasing numbers of prisoners have been exposed to conditions that pose significant psychological threats to their long-term stability.

Indeed, as I discuss in the next chapter, disruptive and problematic prisoner behavior that has been in large part *caused* by adverse prison conditions and harsh correctional practices, in turn, typically has been *blamed* on prisoners themselves. Thus, many prison systems have escalated the kind of punitive sanctions levied against those prisoners who have reacted overtly to the harsh conditions around them. In some places, policies and practices have been implemented that forcibly dominate prisoners and impose absolute compliance with rigid regimes at seemingly any cost. The result has been that, in certain ways and for certain prisons, incarceration has become more painful and psychologically destructive than in the past.

NOTES

1. Nils Christie, *Crime Control as Industry: Towards Gulags, Western Style?* (New York: Routledge, 1993), 23.
2. Elaine Scarry, *The Body in Pain: The Making and Unmaking of the World* (New York: Oxford University Press, 1985), 16.

3. Michel Foucault, *Discipline and Punish: The Birth of the Prison* (New York: Random House, 1977), 232.

4. H. Toch, "A Revisionist View of Prison Reform," *Federal Probation* (1981): 3, 3 (emphasis in original). *See also* L. Bukstel and P. Kilmann, "Psychological Effects of Imprisonment on Confined Individuals," *Psychological Bulletin* 88 (1980): 469.

5. F. Porporino, "Difference in Response to Long-term Imprisonment: Implications for the Management of Long-term Offenders," *The Prison Journal* 80 (1990): 35, 36 (emphasis added).

6. Ibid.

7. For example, compare the conclusions of a Canadian Prison Service employee who argued that "in reality, the evidence for a profound and incapacitating influence [of prison], that is both commonplace and severe, is scarce, if existent at all." J. Steven Wormith, "The Controversy Over the Effects of Long-Term Incarceration," in *Long-Term Imprisonment: Policy, Science, and Correctional Practice*, ed. Timothy Flanagan (Thousand Oaks, CA: Sage Publications, 1995), 55. *See also* E. Zamble, "Behavior and Adaptation in Long-term Prison Inmates: Descriptive Longitudinal Results," *Criminal Justice and Behavior* 19 (1992): 409.

8. One important distinction that can and should be made concerns the difference between maximum- and medium-security prisons, on the one hand, and minimum-security prisons, on the other. Most of what I say in this chapter and the next two about the context of imprisonment applies primarily to maximum- and medium-security prisons. These are places with a heavy emphasis on security and control, where prisoners are usually housed in cells (or, on occasion, dormitories). The facilities are generally surrounded by high walls or fences, with armed guards at the "security perimeters," and so on. Minimum-security facilities usually look and feel much less physically imposing, permit more freedom of movement, and vary much more widely in terms of day-to-day prisoner treatment. In any event, minimum-security prisons house fewer than 20% of prisoners confined in the United States. *See* James Stephan and Jennifer Karberg, *Census of State and Federal Correctional Facilities, 2000* (Washington, DC: Bureau of Justice Statistics, 2003), 7.

9. J. Brodeur, "Truth in Sentencing," *Behavioral Sciences & the Law* 7 (1989): 25, 34–35 (emphasis added).

10. *Cf.* P. Suedfeld, C. Ramirez, J. Deaton, and G. Baker-Brown, "Reactions and Attributions of Prisoners in Solitary Confinement," *Criminal Justice and Behavior* 9 (1982): 303, 333–334; *see also* P. Suedfeld, quoted in Michael Jackson, *Prisoners of Isolation: Solitary Confinement in Canada* (Toronto: University of Toronto Press, 1983), 79.

11. The clearest example of this can be found in J. Bonta and P. Gendreau, "Reexamining the Cruel and Unusual Punishment of Prison Life," *Law and Human Behavior* 14 (1990): 347.

12. Ibid., 348. What Bonta and Gendreau appeared to want to say was that, contrary to what "so many have assumed" about prisons (without specifying who the "so many" were), correctional institutions were not *always* harmful. However, given the political context in which this otherwise indisputable proposition

was made, "not always harmful" was easily translated into not often or not very harmful. Again, the substitution of one kind of prison—Bonta and Gendreau had mentioned that the kinds of institutions they were defending should be "humane"—for prisons in general seemed to provide broad academic support for the policies of increased levels and harsher forms of incarceration that were being implemented in many places.

13. Indeed, they insisted on what they called *objective measures* in studies that used "statistical tests" of the effects in question. Ibid., 349.

14. Ibid., 348 (emphasis added), referring to Stanley Cohen and Laurie Taylor, *Psychological Survival: The Experience of Long-term Imprisonment* (New York: Pantheon, 1972).

15. Cohen and Taylor, *Psychological Survival*, 37.

16. Including Donald Clemmer, *The Prison Community* (New York: Holt, Rinehart & Winston, 1958); Donald Cressey, *The Prison: Studies in Institutional Organization and Change* (New York: Holt, Rinehart & Winston, 1961); Erving Goffman, *Asylums: Essays on the Social Situation of Mental Patients and Other Inmates* (Garden City, NY: Anchor Books, 1960); Gresham Sykes, *The Society of Captives: A Study of a Maximum Security Prison* (Princeton, NJ: Princeton University Press, 1958); Gresham Sykes and Sheldon Messinger, "The Inmate Social System," in *Theoretical Studies of the Social Organization of the Prison*, ed. Richard Cloward (New York: Social Science Research Council, 1960; and Thomas Mathiesen, *Defences of the Weak: A Sociological Study of a Norwegian Correctional Institution* (London: Tavistock, 1965), as well as historical works that provide many similar insights, including Terence Morris and Pauline Morris, *Petonville: A Sociological Study of an English Prison* (London: Routledge & Kegan Paul, 1963).

17. Bonta and Gendreau, "Reexamining the Cruel and Unusual Punishment of Prison Life," 349.

18. See, e.g., Jack Abbott, *In the Belly of the Beast: Letters from Prison* (New York: Random House, 1981); Bruno Bettelheim, *The Informed Heart: Autonomy in a Mass Age* (New York: Free Press, 1971); Jimmy Boyle, *A Sense of Freedom* (Edinburgh: Canongate, 1977); Christopher Burney, *Solitary Confinement* (London: Clerke & Cockeran, 1952); Ann Cordilia, *The Making of an Inmate: Prison as a Way of Life* (Cambridge, MA: Schenkman, 1983); Bruce Danto, *Jail House Blues: Studies of Suicidal Behavior in Jail and Prison* (Orchard Lake, MI: Epic Publications, 1973); Ross Firestone, *Getting Busted: Personal Experiences of Arrest, Trial, and Prison* (New York: Douglas Books, 1970); Thomas Gaddis, *Birdman of Alcatraz* (New York: Random House, 1956); Rose Giallombardo, *Society of Women: A Study of a Women's Prison* (New York: Wiley, 1966); Anne Hamilton, *Angola: Louisiana State Penitentiary, A Half Century of Rage and Reform* (Lafayette, LA: Center for Louisiana Studies, 1990); Victor Hassine, *Life Without Parole: Living in Prison Today* (Los Angeles: Roxbury, 2004); George Jackson, *Soledad Brother: The Prison Letters of George Jackson* (New York: Bantam Books, 1972); Timothy Leary, *Jail Notes* (New York: Douglas Books, 1970); Nathan Leopold, *Life Plus 99 Years* (Garden City, NY: Doubleday, 1958); Howard Levy and Jerome Miller, *Going to Jail: The Political Prisoner* (New York:

Grove Press, 1971); Victor Serge, *Men in Prison*, trans. Richard Greeman (Garden City, NY: Doubleday, 1969).

19. Quoted in Richard Greeman's introduction to Serge's *Men in Prison*, p. xii. Serge remembered what he called the "icy moment" of arrest years after it happened. He crossed what he termed "the invisible boundary," after which "I was no longer a man but a man in prison. An inmate," 4.

20. Cohen and Taylor, *Psychological Survival*, 35.

21. Bonta and Gendreau, "Reexamining the Cruel and Unusual Punishment of Prison Life," 353.

22. Ibid.

23. Ibid., 354.

24. Ibid.

25. Ibid.

26. Ibid., 356.

27. Ibid.

28. Ibid.

29. Ibid., 357.

30. Ibid.

31. Ibid., 359.

32. Ibid., 360.

33. Ibid., 359.

34. Ibid., 361.

35. Ibid., 362.

36. Ibid.

37. Ibid., 361.

38. J. Willens, "Structure, Content and the Exigencies of War: American Prison Law After Twenty-Five Years 1962–1987," *American University Law Review* 37 (1987): 41, 133. Other writers have made the obvious, but often overlooked, connections between our conceptions of criminality and the kind of imprisonment that we think is appropriate or acceptable. One article—Martha Grace Duncan, "Slime and Darkness: The Metaphor of Filth in Criminal Justice," *Tulane Law Review* 68 (1994): 725, 729—suggested that there was a metaphorical connection as well. Duncan wrote that metaphoric descriptions of criminals as "scum" and "slime" not only have contributed to the view of criminals as diseased and contagious and made the increased use of segregation and quarantine more acceptable but also "may cause authorities to imprison criminals in places that are conceived as suitable filthy and malodorous" (ibid., 729). That is, because "criminals are commonly associated with slime, darkness, and foul odors" in public and political discourse, "their places of punishment must likewise reflect these qualities" (ibid., 755).

39. Gresham Sykes, *The Society of Captives*, 63.

40. Hans Toch and Kenneth Adams, *Acting Out: Maladaptive Behavior in Confinement* (Washington, DC: American Psychological Association, 2002), 230.

41. T. Flanagan, "Dealing with Long-term Confinement: Adaptive Strategies and Perspectives Among Long-term Prisoners," *Criminal Justice and Behavior* 8

(1981): 201; Robert Johnson, *Hard Time: Understanding and Reforming the Prison* (Monterey, CA: Brooks/Cole, 1987). Hans Toch's published work on these issues is notable, including Hans Toch, *Men in Crisis: Human Breakdowns in Prison* (Chicago: Aldine, 1975); Hans Toch, *Living in Prison: The Ecology of Survival* (New York: Free Press, 1977); Robert Johnson and Hans Toch, ed., *The Pains of Imprisonment* (Beverly Hills, CA: Sage, 1982); Hans Toch and Kenneth Adams, *The Disturbed Violent Offender* (New Haven, CT: Yale University Press, 1989). *See also* Edward Zamble and Frank Porporino, *Coping, Behavior, and Adaptation in Prison Inmates* (New York: Springer-Verlag, 1988).

42. T. Schmid and R. Jones, "Suspended Identity: Identity Transformation in a Maximum Security Prison," *Symbolic Interaction* 14 (1991): 415.

43. L. Goodstein, "Inmate Adjustment to Prison and the Transition to Community Life," *Journal of Research on Crime and Delinquency* 10 (1980): 246, 265.

44. *See, e.g.*, Gary Evans, ed., *Environmental Stress* (New York: Cambridge University Press, 1982).

45. F. Hocking, "Extreme Environmental Stress and Its Significance for Psychopathology," *American Journal of Psychotherapy* 24 (1970): 4, 23.

46. Ibid., 23.

47. In 1974, the U.S. Supreme Court famously declared that "there is no iron curtain drawn between the Constitution and the prisons of this country." Wolff v. McDonnell, 418 U.S. 539, 556–557 (1974). Although this declaration did not lead to the sweeping prison reforms some prisoners' rights advocates hoped it would, it is true that lawless prisons, many of them in the South, were brought under increasing legal control in the decades of the 1970s and 1980s in ways that reduced the most egregious forms of physical brutality to which many prisoners had been subjected. For example, in Ruiz v. Estelle, 503 F. Supp. 1265 (S.D. Tex. 1980, *aff'd* in part, *vacated* in part, 679 F.2d 1115 (5th Cir. 1982), *cert. denied*, 460 U.S. 1042 (1982), federal judge William Justice declared the rampant official violence in the Texas prison system (including the practice of using inmate "building tenders" to enforce prison rules—often by brutalizing other prisoners) unconstitutional.

48. Madrid v. Gomez, 889 F. Supp. 1146, 1160 (N.D. Cal. 1995).

49. H. Toch, "The Role of the Expert on Prison Conditions: The Battle of Footnotes in *Rhodes v. Chapman*," *Criminal Law Bulletin* 18 (1982): 38, 44.

50. *See, e.g.*, R. Blecker, "Haven or Hell? Inside Lorton Central Prison: Experiences of Punishment Justified," *Stanford Law Review* 42 (1990): 1149, 1202; Lee Bowker, *Prison Victimization* (New York: Elsevier, 1980); Leo Carroll, *Hacks, Blacks, and Cons: Race Relations in a Maximum Security Prison*. (Lexington, MA: Lexington Books, 1974); John Irwin, *Prisons in Turmoil* (Boston: Little Brown, 1980); Kelsey Kauffman, *Prison Officers and Their World* (Cambridge, MA: Harvard University Press, 1988); Steve Martin and Sheldon Ekland-Olson, *Texas Prisons: The Walls Came Tumbling Down* (Austin, TX: Texas Monthly Press, 1987); Roger Morris, *The Devil's Butcher Shop: The New Mexico Prison Uprising* (Albuquerque, NM: University of New Mexico Press, 1988); Wilbert Rideau and Ron Wikberg, *Life Sentences: Rage and Survival Behind Bars* (New York: Times Books, 1992).

51. Lynn Branham, *The Use of Incarceration in the United States: A Look at the Present and the Future* (Chicago: American Bar Association, April 1992), 13.

52. R. McCorkle, "Personal Precautions to Violence in Prison," *Criminal Justice and Behavior* 19 (1992): 160, 161.

53. Suppressing emotional reactions, especially in a tense and provocative environment like prison, may intensify rather than reduce the stress of confinement. For example, David d'Atri found that prisoners who suppressed hostile feelings (by, among other things, reporting that they never felt irritable or felt like fighting) and those who described their stay in prison in uniformly positive terms (for example, by characterizing their conditions of confinement as very comfortable and pleasant and the guards as good natured) had higher blood pressure levels than those who did the opposite. D'Atri interpreted this in terms of the repression of natural feelings of aggression. *See* David d'Atri, "Measuring Prison Stress," in *Confinement in Maximum Custody: Last Resort Prisons in the United States and Western Europe*, ed. David Ward and Ken Schoen (Lexington, MA: D.C. Heath, 1981).

54. Paul Keve, *Prison Life and Human Worth* (Minneapolis: University of Minnesota Press, 1974), 54.

55. Toch and Adams, *Acting Out*, 230.

56. *See, e.g.*, C. Jose-Kampfner, "Coming to Terms With Existential Death: An Analysis of Women's Adaptation to Life in Prison," *Social Justice* 17 (1990): 110; R. Sapsford, "Life Sentence Prisoners: Psychological Changes During Sentence," *British Journal of Criminology* 18 (1978): 128.

57. For an early account of one version of this adaptation, see Richard McCleery's study of maximum-security prisoners in North Carolina and Hawaii: Richard McCleery, "Authoritarianism and Belief Systems of Incorrigibles," in *The Prison*, ed. Donald Cressey (New York: Holt, Rinehart & Winston, 1961).

58. *See, e.g.*, A. Crosthwaite, "Punishment for Whom? The Prisoner or His Wife," "*International Journal of Offender Therapy* 19 (1975): 275; S. Fishman and A. Alissi, "Strengthening Families as Natural Support Systems for Offenders," *Federal Probation* 43 (1979): 16; Flanagan, "Dealing with Long-term Confinement."

59. *See, e.g.*, S. Friedman and T. Esselstyn, "The Adjustment of Children of Jail Inmates," *Federal Probation* 36 (1975): 27; D. Schneller, "Prisoners' Families: A Study of Some Social and Psychological Effects of Incarceration of the Families of Negro Prisoners," *Criminology* 12 (1975): 402.

60. For a discussion of the importance of maintaining family ties for both inprison and postprison adjustment, see C. Hairston, "Family Ties During Imprisonment: Do They Influence Future Criminal Activity?" *Federal Probation* 52 (1988): 48; C. Hairston, "Family Ties During Imprisonment: Important to Whom and for What?" *Journal of Sociology and Social Welfare* 18 (1991): 87.

61. Serge, "Men in Prison," 10.

62. A. Taylor, "Social Isolation and Imprisonment," *Psychiatry* 24 (1961): 373, 373. *See also* H. Levenson, "Multidimensional Locus of Control in Prison Inmates," *Journal of Applied Social Psychology* 5 (1975): 342, who found, not

surprisingly, that prisoners who were incarcerated for longer periods of time and those who were punished more frequently by being placed in solitary confinement were more likely to believe that their world was controlled by "powerful others." Of course, such beliefs are consistent with an institutional adaptation that undermines autonomy and self-initiative.

63. Jose-Kampfner, "Coming to Terms With Existential Death," 123.

64. George Herbert Mead, *The Social Psychology of George Herbert Mead* (Chicago: Phoenix Books, 1956), 239.

65. *See, e.g.,* Clemmer, *The Prison Community*; L. Goodstein, "Inmate Adjustment to Prison and the Transition to Community Life," *Journal of Research on Crime and Delinquency* 16 (1976): 246; R. Homant, "Employment of Ex-Offenders: The Role of Prisonization and Self-Esteem," *Journal of Offender Counseling, Services, & Rehabilitation* 8 (1984): 5; John Irwin, "Sociological Studies of the Impact of Long-Term Confinement," in *Confinement in Maximum Custody*, ed. David Ward and Ken Schoen (Lexington, MA: Lexington Books, 1981); B. Peat and T. Winfree, "Reducing the Intra-Institutional Effects of 'Prisonization': A Study of a Therapeutic Community for Drug-Using Inmates," *Criminal Justice and Behavior* 19 (1992): 206; C. Thomas and D. Peterson, "Comparative Organizational Analysis of Prisonization," *Criminal Justice Review* 6 (1981): 36. Institutionalization is by no means limited to prisoners. *See, e.g.,* Erving Goffman, *Asylums: Essays on the Social Situation of Mental Patients and Other Inmates* (New York: Anchor, 1961), examining the process as it occurs in mental patients; and D. Jansson, "Return to Society: Problematic Features of the Re-Entry Process," *Psychiatric Care* 13 (1975): 136, describing similar changes that took place in Peace Corps volunteers who encountered much difficulty reintegrating themselves back into U.S. society.

66. Clemmer, *The Prison Community*, 299. *See also* S. Olson, "Patterns of Infractions and Official Reactions to Institutional Regulations," *Social Science Quarterly* 54 (1973): 815. *See also* John Gibbs, "The First Cut Is the Deepest: Psychological Breakdown and Survival in the Detention Setting," in *The Pains of Imprisonment*, ed. Robert Johnson and Hans Toch (Beverly Hills, CA: Sage, 1982). For early descriptions of the relationship between time in prison and prisonization as an "inverted U" in which the effects of prisonization increase during one's stay in prison but begin to reverse themselves as prisoners come closer to the time of release, *see* Stanton Wheeler, "Socialization in Correctional Communities," *American Sociological Review* 26 (1961): 697; and P. Garabedian, "Social Role and Processes of Socialization in the Prison Community," *Social Problems* 11 (1963): 140.

67. Zamble, "Behavior and Adaptation in Long-term Prison Inmates," 420.

68. Ibid.

69. Ibid. (emphasis added)

70. *See* James Stephan and Jennifer Karberg, who wrote the U.S. Department of Justice 2000 census of state and federal correctional facilities, *Census of State and Federal Correctional Facilities, 2000*.

71. Stephan and Karberg, *Census of State and Federal Correctional Facilities, 2000*.

72. Ibid., 5. Prisoners who entered the prison system during the early years of the era of mass incarceration were even more likely to be housed in antiquated facilities. Thus, U.S. Department of Justice data released in 1988 indicated that, as recently as the early 1980s, fully 41% of the maximum-security prisons in operation had been built before 1925 and, according to 1984 statistics, one third of all of the nation's prisons were 50 or more years old. Although the massive prison construction programs that took place throughout the 1980s and 1990s have changed these percentages, as I noted in the text, many of those old prisons are still in operation.

73. Indeed, Bureau of Justice Statistics data from the 1980s indicated that only about one third of U.S. prisoners were single-celled. Bureau of Justice Statistics, *Population Density in State Prisons* (Washington, DC: U.S. Department of Justice, 1986), 1. Most maximum- and medium-security prisons constructed since then have been designed explicitly for double-celling.

74. These issues have been explored extensively in the past by sociologists. *See, e.g.*, R. Homant, "The Role of Prisonization and Self Esteem," *Journal of Offender Counseling, Services, and Rehabilitation* 8 (1984): 5; John Irwin, *The Felon* (Englewood Cliffs, NJ: Prentice-Hall, 1970); L. McCorkle and R. Korn, "Resocialization Within Walls," *The Annals*, 293 (1954): 88; C. Thomas and D. Peterson, "Comparative Organizational Analysis of Prisonization"; C. Tittle, "Institutional Living and Self-Esteem," *Social Problems* 20 (1972): 65; and R. Wulbert, "Inmate Pride in Total Institutions," *American Journal of Sociology* 71 (1965): 1.

75. J. Phillips, "Cultural Construction of Manhood in Prison," *Psychology of Men & Masculinity*, 2(2001): 13, 23.

76. These increases have occurred in part because of various sentencing reforms that require prison time for certain offenses, increase the length of sentences, mandate longer portions of sentences to be served before release is possible, and impose enhanced sentences for second or third offenses (including, in some cases, so-called third-strike life sentences).

77. These data can be found in William Sabol and John McGready, *Time Served in Prison by Federal Offenders, 1986–1997* [Bureau of Justice Statistics Special Report NCJ 170032] (Washington, DC: U.S. Department of Justice, June 1999). In the federal system, the increases in sentence length can be dated relatively precisely, with the advent of the Sentencing Reform Act of 1984 (that went into effect in November 1987). It required that prison sentences be meted out for many offenses for which probation often had been granted, increased the length of prison sentences for more serious offenses, and required prisoners to serve greater portions of their sentences before release. The effects were dramatic.

78. A variety of factors led states to follow the federal system's lead in increasing the average sentence lengths served. Among other things, so-called truth-in-sentencing laws were encouraged by a federal government–inspired incentive: To qualify for certain forms of federal assistance, states were required to adopt laws mandating that prisoners would serve longer portions of their terms— 85%—comparable to those required by federal law. Most states complied.

79. *See* Matthew Durose and Patrick Langan, *State Court Sentencing of Convicted Felons, 2002: Statistical Tables* [Bureau of Justice Statistics Special Report NCJ 208910] (Washington, DC: U.S. Department of Justice, May 2005), Table 1.3.

80. These data, and the data used to construct Figure 6.1, are found in Marc Mauer, Ryan Kind, and Malcolm Young, *The Meaning of "Life": Long Prison Sentences in Context* (Washington, DC: The Sentencing Project, May 2004). Most of the prisoners serving life will someday be released. The Sentencing Project estimates that lifers entering prison in 1997 will spend approximately 29 years in prison. However, more than a quarter of life sentences now meted out are "life without parole."

81. *See, e.g.*, Anthony Bottoms, William Hay, and J. Richard Sparks, "Situational and Social Approaches to the Prevention of Disorder in Long-Term Prisons," in *Long-Term Imprisonment: Policy, Science, and Correctional Practice*, ed. Timothy J. Flanagan (Thousand Oaks, CA: Sage Publications, 1995); F. Deroches, "Anomie: Two Theories of Prison Riots," *Canadian Journal of Criminology* 25 (1983): 173; A. Pfefferbaum and N. Dishotsky, "Racial Intolerance in a Correctional Institution: An Ecological View," *American Journal of Psychiatry* 138 (1981): 1057; P. Steinke, "Using Situational Factors to Predict Types of Prison Violence," *Journal of Offender Rehabilitation* 17 (1981): 119.

82. Flanagan, "Dealing with Long-term Confinement," 212.

83. *See, e.g.*, G. Gaes and W. McGuire, "Prison Violence: The Contribution of Crowding Versus Other Determinants of Prison Assault Rates," *Journal of Research in Crime and Delinquency* 22 (1985): 41; T. Flanagan, "Correlates of Institutional Misconduct Among State Prisoners," *Criminology* 21 (1983): 29.

84. *See, e.g.*, T. Adams, "Characteristics of State Prisoners Who Demonstrate Severe Adjustment Problems," *Journal of Clinical Psychology* 33 (1977): 1100; V. Cox, P. Paulus, and G. McCain, "Prison Crowding Research: The Relevance for Prison Housing Standards and a General Approach to Crowding Phenomena," *American Psychologist* 39 (1984): 1148; and S. Light, "The Severity of Assaults on Prison Officers: A Contextual Study," *Social Science Quarterly* 71 (1990): 267.

85. *See, e.g.*, Hans Toch, "Social Climate and Prison Violence," in *Prison Violence in America*, ed. Michael Braswell, Steven Dillingham, and Reid Montgomery (Cincinnati: Anderson Publishing, 1985); K. Wright, "The Violent and Victimized in the Male Prison," *Journal of Offender Rehabilitation* 16 (1991): 1.

86. Prisons in the United States appear to be especially dangerous. For example, one review indicated that during the height of the increase in imprisonment in the United States, the nation's prison homicide rate was roughly 14 times higher than that in English prisons. *See* E. Dooley, "Unnatural Deaths in Prison," *British Journal of Criminology* 30 (1990): 229.

87. John Coggeshall, "Those Who Surrender Are Female: Prisoner Gender Identities as Cultural Mirror," in *Transcending Boundaries: Multi-disciplinary Approaches to the Study of Gender*, ed. Pamela Frese and John Coggeshall (New York: Bergin & Garvey, 1991), 84; *see also* Wilbert Rideau, "Prison: The Sexual Jungle," in

Rage and Survival Behind Bars, ed. Wilbert Rideau and Ron Wikberg (New York: Times Books, 1992).

88. Michael King, "Male Rape in Institutional Settings," in Male Victims of Sexual Assault, ed. Gillian Mezey and Michael King (Oxford, England: Oxford University Press, 1992), 68–69.

89. A. Davis, "Sexual Assaults in the Philadelphia Prison System and Sheriff's Van," Transaction 6 (1968): 8. Davis also documented the systematic underreporting of sexual incidents in custodial settings: Of 2000 incidents that were estimated to have occurred in Philadelphia jails, only 156 were documented, 96 were reported, 64 appeared in official prison records, and 40 resulted in disciplinary action against those held responsible.

90. P. Gunby, "Sexual Behavior in an Abnormal Situation," Medical News 245 (1981): 215.

91. P. Nacci and T. Kane, "The Incidence of Sex and Sexual Aggression in Federal Prisons," Federal Probation 47 (1983): 31.

92. See, e.g., Daniel Lockwood, Prison Sexual Violence (New York: Elsevier, 1980). See, generally, C. Bell, M. Coven, J. Cronan, C. Garza, J. Guggemos, and L. Storto, "Rape and Sexual Misconduct in the Prison System: Analyzing America's Most 'Open Secret,'" Yale Law and Policy Review 18 (1999): 195; R. Dumond, "The Sexual Assault of Male Inmates in Incarcerated Settings," International Journal of the Sociology of Law 20 (1992): 135; and R. Dumond, "Inmate Sexual Assault: The Plague That Persists," Prison Journal 80 (2000): 407.

93. C. Struckman-Johnson, et al., "Sexual Coercion Reported by Men and Women in Prison," Journal of Sex Research 33 (1996): 67. Of course, female prisoners also are raped while incarcerated, sometimes by correctional staff. See Human Rights Watch, All Too Familiar: Sexual Abuse of Women in U.S. Prisons, http://www.hrw.org/summaries/s.us96d.html. For a study of a specific state in which women prisoners were retaliated against for having reported sexual abuse by staff, see Human Rights Watch, Nowhere to Hide: Retaliation Against Women in Michigan State Prisons (New York: Human Rights Watch, 1998).

94. King, "Male Rape in Institutional Settings," 68.

95. Coggeshall, 91.

96. Rideau, "Prison: The Sexual Jungle."

97. Ibid., 121.

98. See, e.g., Lockwood, Prison Sexual Violence; Anthony Scacco, Rape in Prison (Springfield, IL: Charles Thomas, 1975); and Donald Tucker, "A Punk's Song: View From the Inside," in A Casebook of Sexual Aggression, ed. Anthony Scacco (New York: AMS Press, 1982).

99. Gillian Mezey and Michael King, "The Effects of Sexual Assault on Men: A Survey of Twenty-Two Victims," in Confronting Rape and Sexual Assault, ed. Mary Odem and Jody Clay-Warner (Wilmington, DE: Scholarly Resources, 1998).

100. King, "Male Rape in Institutional Settings," 70.

101. *See, e.g.,* P. Goyer and H. Eddleman, "Same-Sex Rape of Nonincarcerated Men," *American Journal of Psychiatry* 141 (1984): 576.

102. F. Davison, I. Clare, S. Georgiades, J. Dival, and A. Holland, "Treatment of a Man With a Mild Learning Disability Who Was Sexually Assaulted Whilst in Prison," *Medical Science and the Law* 34 (1994): 346, 348.

103. *Cf.* John Gunn, "The Role of Psychiatry in Prisons and the Right to Punishment," in *Psychiatry, Human Rights and the Law,* ed. Martin Roth and Robert Bluglass (Cambridge, England: Cambridge University Press, 1978); T. Harding and E. Zimmerman, "Psychiatric Symptoms, Cognitive Stress and Vulnerability Factors: A Study in a Remand Prison," *British Journal of Psychiatry* 155 (1989): 36.

104. American Psychiatric Association, *Diagnostic and Statistical Manual of Mental Disorders,* 2d ed. (Washington, DC: American Psychiatric Association, 1968), 49.

105. *See, e.g.,* J. Looney and E. Gunderson, "Transient Situational Disturbances: Course and Outcome," *American Journal of Psychiatry* 135 (1978): 660, who supported the use of the diagnostic category. They concluded that the prognosis for those with the disorder was generally positive, but also recommended that the category be refined to more narrowly reflect reactions to identifiable life stress rather than exacerbation of preexisting disorders.

106. For a discussion of some of the chronic, rather than transient, reactions to situational stress, *see, e.g.,* N. C. Andreasen and P. Wasek, "Adjustment Disorders in Adolescents and Adults," *Archives of General Psychiatry* 37 (1980): 1166. For an interesting discussion of the progression from transient situational disturbance to PTSD, *see* D. Brom, R. J. Kleber, and E. Witztum, "The Prevalence of Posttraumatic Psychopathology in the General and the Clinical Population," *Israel Journal of Psychiatry and Related Sciences* 28 (1992): 53. The inclusion of PTSD in the *DSM–III* did not necessarily represent an inevitable extension of transient situational disturbance to acknowledge the longer lasting, persistent effects of exposure to extreme situations. For example, see an interesting sociological account that concluded, "PTSD is in DSM–III because a core of psychiatrists and veterans worked consciously and deliberately for years to put it there. They ultimately succeeded because they were better organized, more politically active, and enjoyed more lucky breaks than their opposition." *See* Wilbur Scott, "PTSD in DSM–III: A Case in the Politics of Diagnosis and Disease," *Social Problems* 37 (1990): 294, 307–308.

107. American Psychiatric Association, *Diagnostic and Statistical Manual of Mental Disorders,* 4th ed. (Washington, DC: American Psychiatric Association, 1994), 111. For more detailed discussions of the disorder, *see* C. P. Erlinder, "Paying the Price for Vietnam: Post-Traumatic Stress Disorder and Criminal Behavior," *Boston College Law Review* 25 (1984): 305; J. E. Helzer, L. N. Robins, and L. McEvoy, "Post-Traumatic Stress Disorder in the General Population," *The New England Journal of Medicine* 1317 (1987): 1630; A. B. Rowan, D. W. Foy, N. Rodriguez, and S. Ryan, "Posttraumatic Stress Disorder in a Clinical Sample of Adults Sexually Abused as Children," *Child Abuse and Neglect* 18

(1994): 51; John P. Wilson and Beverly Raphael, ed., *International Handbook of Traumatic Stress Syndromes* (New York: Plenum, 1993).

108. Judith Herman, "A New Diagnosis," in *Trauma and Recovery*, ed. Judith Herman (New York: Basic Books, 1992), 119. *See also* Judith Herman, "Complex PTSD: A Syndrome in Survivors of Prolonged and Repeated Trauma," in *Psychotraumatology: Key Papers and Core Concepts in Post-Traumatic Stress*, ed. George S. Everly, Jr., and Jeffrey M. Lating (New York: Plenum, 1995).

109. J. Herman, "Complex PTSD: A Syndrome in Survivors of Prolonged and Repeated Trauma," *Journal of Traumatic Stress* 5 (1992): 377, 382.

110. *Cf.* R. DeWolfe and A. DeWolfe, "Impact of Prison Conditions on the Mental Health of Inmates," *Southern Illinois University Law Journal* 1979 (1979): 497; Hans Toch, *Men in Crisis: Human Breakdowns in Prison* (Chicago: Aldine, 1975); Hans Toch, *Living in Prison: The Ecology of Survival* (New York : Free Press, 1977).

111. For a brief, but especially thoughtful, review of these issues, see T. Kupers, "Trauma and Its Sequelae in Male Prisoners: Effects of Confinement, Overcrowding, and Diminished Services," *American Journal of Orthopsychiatry* 66 (1996): 189. *See also* J. James, D. Gregory, R. Jones, and O. Rundell, "Psychiatric Morbidity in Prisons," *Hospital and Community Psychiatry* 31 (1980): 674; J. Metzner, G. Fryer, and D. Usery, "Prison Mental Health Services: Results of a National Survey of Standards, Resources, Administrative Structure, and Litigation," *Journal of Forensic Sciences* 35 (1990): 433; H. Steadman, S. Fabisiak, J. Dvoskin, and E. Holoagan, "Survey of Mental Disability Among State Prison Inmates," *Hospital and Community Psychiatry* 38 (1987): 1086.

112. R. Bland, S. Newman, R. Dyck, and H. Orn, "Prevalence of Psychiatric Disorders and Suicide Attempts in a Prison Population," *Canadian Journal of Psychiatry* 35 (1990): 407; M. Salive, G. Smith, and T. Brewer, "Suicide Mortality in the Maryland State Prison System, 1979 Through 1987," *Journal of the American Medical Association* 262 (1989): 365; J. Smialek and W. Spitz, "Death Behind Bars," *Journal of the American Medical Association* 240 (1978): 2563. *See also* Lindsay Hayes, "National Study of Jail Suicides: Seven Years Later," *Psychiatric Quarterly* 60 (1989): 7, to the effect that suicide rates in detention facilities are roughly 9 times higher than in the general population.

113. Dooley, "Unnatural Deaths in Prison."

114. Salive et al., "Suicide Mortality in the Maryland State Prison System, 1979 Through 1987," 368.

7

OVERCROWDING AND THE SITUATIONAL PATHOLOGIES OF PRISON

[Under the prevailing view] it is the criminal who first acted, he initiated the whole chain of events. The pain that follows is created by him, not by those handling the tools for creating such pain.

—Nils Christie[1]

Today we still build prisons according to the functional logic that emerged in the course of the nineteenth century. . . . These muted, functional buildings nevertheless project an eloquent and well understood symbolism which speaks of unshakeable authority, of stored-up power, and of a silent, brooding capacity to control intransigence.

—David Garland[2]

Modern prisons are largely about control—the control of prisoners, their behavior, the degrees of freedom with which they can act, their level of contact with the outside world, and so on. When prisons are at risk of losing this control, those in charge feel compelled to intervene. Applying the contextual model of behavior that I have advanced in this book—but applying it here to the prison itself—highlights the connection between prison conditions and the correctional acts and practices that occur within them. To be sure, the prison administrators who create and implement prison policies and the line staff who enforce them on a day-to-day basis are highly responsive to the context in which they work. In this sense, prisons can be made worse by forces over which correctional personnel have little control. The last several decades represent such a period.

Specifically, I argue in this chapter that extreme levels of overcrowding and high levels of idleness threatened to make prisons especially difficult to manage. Having too many prisoners put correctional authorities at risk of not being able to control any of them. Moreover, because prisoners now were sent to prison for the explicit purpose of being punished, the use of painful techniques to control and constrain them seemed to be a logical extension of the publicly acknowledged mission of the institution. In addition, the last several decades saw the rise of especially powerful political interest groups that urged a "get tough" approach to crime and punishment. They helped to generate an unusually strident ideology that both demonized prisoners and made the use of repressive techniques seemingly essential to their control.

The view that present-day prisoners represented a new or different "breed" of convict further facilitated their punitive treatment. As one otherwise sympathetic and knowledgeable commentator put it, "Conditions in the prisons may be better than in the nineteenth century, but the prisoners are twentieth-century prisoners. They are sullen and resentful. . . ."[3] By the early 1980s, correctional administrators and others were said to be "almost unanimous in their belief that prisons are receiving a more aggressive, more dangerous, more vocal, and less tractable offender,"[4] despite the lack of any systematic data to support the claims. To complement these views, the media in the 1980s and 1990s often depicted modern-day criminals and prisoners as "rapacious monsters"[5] who needed to be given longer prison sentences and placed in specialized, tougher institutions to be controlled.

Because of the political context in which they operated and the institutional mandates by which they were bound during this period, prison systems had few alternative strategies with which to respond to internal problems generated by these broad outside forces. Thus, law-and-order political agendas were translated into higher rates of incarceration, and legislatures were slow to match funding for prison construction or prisoner programs with the increasingly punitive laws they passed. Prison authorities accommodated in the ways they knew best. Historically, prison authorities have been trained and socialized to use punitive techniques to maintain control in the face of contextual forces acting to undermine it. Thus, when prison staff perceive a crisis or threat, they typically increase the amount of pain they dispense.

Indeed, in the pages that follow I suggest that the correctional decision makers who shaped prison policy and the officials and staff who implemented daily prison operations over the last several decades often reacted to the extraordinarily difficult circumstances with which they were confronted by creating a series of *situational pathologies*—taking actions that worsened the very problems that they were designed to address. Just as prisoners react adversely to the harsh contexts in which they are placed, and sometimes engage in ill-advised, counterproductive, and even destructive behavior, so, too, prison officials and staff members were compromised by the unique pressures under which they worked over the last several decades.[6] Innovation, humanitarian reform, and prisoner-oriented change were subjugated to security concerns, perceived custodial needs, and the pragmatics of control.

By adopting strategies of repression and harsh control, correctional authorities quickly transformed prisons into more difficult places for prisoners to tolerate and even to survive. The precarious balance between the basic human needs and wants of prisoners and the coercive imperatives of the prison was lost. Thus, any real understanding of the behavior of prison administrations, staff members, and prisons themselves during this period requires an analysis of the immediate contexts in which they acted.

OVERCROWDING: THE EMERGENCE OF A DESTRUCTIVE CORRECTIONAL NORM

As I noted in chapter 3, the massive influx of prisoners that began in the late 1970s and early 1980s produced a rate of growth in the U.S. prison population that researchers repeatedly characterized as unprecedented.[7] Among other things, this meant that prisons everywhere were—and many still are—dangerously overcrowded. According to the ACLU National Prison Project, by 1995 there were fully 33 U.S. jurisdictions under court order to reduce overcrowding or improve general conditions in at least one of their major prison facilities. Nine were operating under court orders that covered their entire prison system.[8] Even those correctional systems which avoided judicial scrutiny often were significantly overcrowded.

In fact, some prison systems grew so large so quickly, that it became difficult for prison officials to keep track of the names and locations of all of the facilities in their system, let alone to meaningfully supervise and oversee them. For example, New York now operates some 70 prisons scattered across the state; fully 52 of them were built over the last 25 years. During this same period, the prisoner population in the state increased nearly sixfold, from approximately 12,000 to more than 70,000.[9]

The two largest prison systems in the nation—California and Texas—experienced comparable rates of rapid growth. Over the last 30 years, California's prisoner population expanded eightfold (from roughly 20,000 in the early 1970s to its current population of approximately 160,000 prisoners). Funding for prisoner services and programming did not remotely keep pace, which meant that many more prisoners had to make do on much less. In Texas, over just the brief 5-year period between 1992 and 1997, the prisoner population more than doubled as nearly 70,000 more prisoners were added to the prison rolls. Indeed, during the mid-1990s Texas quickly achieved one of the highest incarceration rates in the nation, and the state now operates more than 100 prisons to accommodate this rapid expansion in its already sizable prisoner population.

Of course, systems that grow at such a rate are at risk of losing their organizational stability. Moreover, despite unprecedented prison construction programs that increased the capacity of many prison systems, most remain overcrowded. Overcrowding, in turn, exacerbates the chronic pains of imprisonment. It is not surprising that a large literature on overcrowding has documented a range of adverse effects that occur when prisons have been filled to capacity and beyond. As a group of prison researchers concluded in the 1980s, as this problem was just beginning to take shape, "crowding in prisons is a major source of administrative problems and adversely affects inmate health, behavior, and morale."[10] Two other early commentators concluded their review of the literature in much the same way, namely, that "with few exceptions, the empirical studies indicate that prison overcrowding has a number of serious negative consequences."[11] Although other variables may mediate or reduce the negative effects of crowding,[12] the psychological toll can be substantial. Thus, despite an occasional study that yields an inconclusive finding,[13] there is little reason to doubt that crowding significantly worsens the quality of institutional life and increases the destructive potential of imprisonment.

Among other things, we know that prison overcrowding increases negative affect among prisoners,[14] elevates their blood pressure,[15] and leads to greater numbers of prisoner illness complaints.[16] It is not surprising that exposure to "long-term, intense, inescapable crowding" of the sort that characterizes many prison environments results in high levels of stress that "can lead to physical and psychological impairment."[17] In addition, overcrowding has been associated with higher rates of disciplinary infractions. For example, one study concluded that in prisons "where crowded conditions are chronic rather than temporary and where people prone to antisocial behavior are gathered together, there is a clear association between restrictions on personal space and the occurrence of disciplinary violations."[18]

Overcrowding directly affects prisoners' mental and physical health by increasing the level of uncertainty with which they regularly must cope. One useful psychological model of the negative effects of overcrowding emphasizes the way in which being confined in a space that is occupied by too many people increases the sheer number of social interactions persons have that involve "high levels of uncertainty, goal interference, and cognitive load. . . ."[19] Thus, crowded conditions heighten the level of cognitive strain that persons experience by introducing social complexity, turnover, and interpersonal instability into an already dangerous prison world in which interpersonal mistakes or errors in social judgments can be fatal. Of course, overcrowding also raises collective frustration levels inside prisons by generally decreasing the resources available to the prisoners confined in them. The sheer number of things prisoners do or accomplish on a day-to-day basis is compromised by the number and density of people in between them and their goals and destinations.

CROWDING AND DEPRIVATION: CREATING A DYSFUNCTIONAL PRISON CONTEXT

Prisoners in overcrowded correctional settings interact with more unfamiliar people, under extremely close quarters that afford little or no privacy or respite, and are less likely to have their basic needs addressed or met. Indeed, overcrowding operates at an individual level to worsen the experience of imprisonment by literally changing the social context or situation to which prisoners must adapt on a day-to-day basis. In addition to these direct, individual-level effects, however, overcrowding changes the way the prison itself functions.

For one, prison systems responding to the press of numbers often forego the careful screening, monitoring, and management of vulnerable or problematic prisoners—in part because there are too many of them to properly assess and in part because the system lacks the capacity to address their special needs anyway. As one group of clinicians conceded, "Unfortunately, the prospect of screening inmates for mental disorder and treating those in need of mental health services has become a daunting and nearly impossible task in the present explosion of prison growth."[20] Unidentified and untreated prisoners with mental illness in mainline prison populations are themselves more likely to deteriorate and, in addition, to have a significant adverse effect on the prisoners with whom they must live and interact.

Over the last several decades, prison administrators reacted to unprecedented levels of overcrowding in other ways that altered the nature of the prison setting. Resources for already limited programming and other activities were reallocated to create bed space and maintain basic security. The prison overcrowding crisis in the United States coincided with the advent of a correctional philosophy that, in a sense, saw deprivation as a goal rather than a problem. Unprecedented amounts of unproductive inactivity and idleness resulted.

For example, overcrowded prison systems often fail to address even the most basic educational needs of their prisoners. Surveys of literacy levels in prisons throughout the United States have documented the magnitude of the problem. One national study concluded that about 7 out of 10 prisoners were either illiterate or functionally illiterate in 1992.[21] Another study reached similar conclusions about the California prisoner population in the mid-1990s. Some 20.8% of California prisoners read at below the third-grade level, and another 30% were only "marginally literate" by accepted educational standards.[22] Little was done to remedy these problems. By 2002, the California prison system housed over 150,000 prisoners, some two thirds of whom had been incarcerated before. Yet, according to the Department of Corrections, those prisoners, on average, *still* read at no more than a seventh-grade level.[23] Indeed, prisoners around the country have left prison—and returned—still lacking basic literacy skills.

In addition, prisoners in many correctional systems were placed on long waiting lists to obtain prison jobs, and some never did. By the start of the 1990s, the Bureau of Justice Statistics reported that nearly 40% of the nation's prisoners had no prison work assignments at all, and that another 40% were assigned to what were termed *facility support services* that included primarily laundry, kitchen, and building maintenance jobs. Only 7% were involved in prison industry programs in which their job experiences and skill development were likely to be transferable to the freeworld.[24] A decade later, a number of large prison systems still were reporting the same levels of idleness. For example, only a little more than half of all prisoners in California are employed in prison jobs of any kind.[25]

In addition to failing to provide basic educational and meaningful occupational opportunities, overcrowded prison systems were unable to make counseling programs fully available to prisoners to address preexisting mental health or substance abuse problems. They also failed to provide many prisoners with the kind of vocational training that they would need to obtain gainful employment once they were released. In many jurisdictions, truly useful educational and vocational training programs have become so scarce that only inmates who are close to their release dates can apply to enter them. As average prison sentences lengthen, long-term prisoners wait for many years before they are even eligible for the programs that are available.

There is widespread agreement among correctional experts that chronic idleness produces negative psychological and behavioral effects in prison. As far back as the 1980s, when trends toward overcrowding and the lack of prison programming had just begun, the U.S. General Accounting Office (now the Government Accountability Office) noted, "Corrections officials believe that extensive inmate idleness can lead to destructive behavior and increase violence within institutions. Moreover, idleness does little to prepare inmates for re-entry into society."[26] But this warning was largely ignored as the trends toward higher rates of incarceration intensified over the next several decades.

Idleness-related frustration increases the probability of interpersonal conflict and assaults in prison. Overcrowding simultaneously reduces the opportunities for staff to effectively monitor prisoner behavior and drastically limits the options to reduce animosities between prisoners by separating them or sending them to different facilities. Thus, there is less for prisoners to do, and there are fewer outlets to release the resulting tension, a decreased staff capacity to identify prisoner problems, and fewer options to solve them once they do. Among the negative behavioral effects that are likely to occur is the increased risk of victimization. For example, one prison researcher has noted that "in less well-regulated institutions in which prisoners have little recourse to protection or in which there may be collusion between dominant prisoners and staff to maintain the peace, sexual violence tends to be greater."[27] Others agree that overcrowded conditions in which prisoners have much idle time can contribute to a higher level of prison rapes.[28]

Prison overcrowding also can reverberate back through the criminal justice system, creating problems in local jails.[29] That is, prison officials may react to overcrowded conditions by attempting to slow the rate at which they are willing or able to receive new prisoners. In extreme cases, they may refuse to take them at all. But the jail overcrowding that results—as prisoners back up in the system, awaiting transfer to prison—is harmful in its own right. For example, "Large jail populations may create logarithmically increasing demand for services, with overcrowding speeding the deterioration of jail facilities and further taxing the ability of institutions to provide for basic human needs."[30]

Unlike prisons, jails are not structured for long-term confinement. Keeping prisoners there for longer periods of time means that they will be deprived even further of meaningful activity, programming, or needed services. In some cases, for some prisoners, the consequences are more dire. Thus, researchers have found that suicides are prevalent in jails with high ratios of inmates to staff members.[31] Jail overcrowding also may mean that increasing numbers of persons will enter the prison system already traumatized by their prior incarceration.

THE DYNAMICS OF DESPERATION:
CYCLES OF DYSFUNCTIONAL BEHAVIOR

Overcrowding appears to have especially adverse effects on the institutional behavior of younger inmates. Thus, one study of the Texas prison system found that

> The greater the proportion of young prisoners housed in the institution, the greater the infraction and assault rates. There is some evidence for an interaction effect between age and prison size. Younger inmates may be more susceptible to the problems and control structures in large prisons than older inmates.[32]

Another study obtained similar results, with overall correlations that revealed "a significant association between density and total assaults and assaults on inmates" such that the greater the density the more frequent the assaults. But researchers found that the relationship between crowding and violence was "strongest in the institutions housing young offenders."[33]

Age-related crowding effects are not surprising. Younger prisoners tend to be more volatile, more sensitive to their surroundings, and in general more likely to react aggressively to the tensions and conflicts that crowded conditions of confinement generate.[34] However, prison officials and staff members respond to these crowding-related infractions by punishing prisoners, often by placing them in disciplinary segregation units. The heightened reactivity of younger prisoners to the context of crowded living conditions means that greater numbers of them will be exposed to even harsher conditions in the segregated or isolated housing units where many eventually are confined.

A number of adverse and presumably unintended long-term consequences are likely to follow from this scenario. Prison officials typically use an inmate's disciplinary segregation status to bar him or her from participation in educational or vocational programming. Moreover, extended time spent in segregation places prisoners at risk of developing a host of adverse psychological reactions that are associated with long-term isolation.[35] The lack of even minimal forms of programming and exposure to potentially disabling solitary confinement jeopardizes subsequent adjustment in the mainline prison population as well as in the freeworld. And if and when these prisoners do return to prison at a later time, they may well find that their prior disciplinary status leads more readily to their classification as a present security risk, making them prime candidates for assignment to a segregation unit once again.

Not surprisingly, several studies have suggested that overcrowding is associated with increased recidivism. For example, at the start of the 1980s, David Farrington and his colleagues found a strong relationship between overcrowding and prison ineffectiveness in England: Prisoners released from overcrowded prisons were more likely to be recommitted for subsequent criminal infractions. The relationship could not be explained away by other variables, leading Farrington to recommend a reduction in prison overcrowding to improve the ability of prisons to reduce crime. By sending fewer people to prison, or by reducing the effective lengths of prison sentences, he argued, the effectiveness of imprisonment might be enhanced.[36]

Similarly, several years after Farrington's English study, Canadian researchers concluded that placing low-risk offenders in often overcrowded, high-security facilities resulted in high rates of reincarceration.[37] The rates were significantly higher than those of comparable low-risk offenders who had been placed in halfway houses. The researchers concluded that the failure to properly divert low-risk offenders from high- to low-security facilities—

something that overcrowded prison systems often lack the capacity to do—"may actually increase the risk of future recidivism."[38]

Thus, the way officials respond to a structurally caused behavioral problem that they did not create and are hard pressed to control—crowding-related disciplinary infractions—can jeopardize the long-term well-being of prisoners, create even more disruptive behavior later on, and, indirectly, increase crime.

MEASURING HARM IN UNSTABLE PRISON SYSTEMS

Quantitative studies of the effects of prison overcrowding actually may understate the real nature and magnitude of the problems that occur. There are several context-based reasons why this is so. Even though overcrowding research generally uses highly sophisticated statistical models, much of it is premised on a very simple theoretical assumption: Increases in social density are expected to produce corresponding increases in various indices of psychological stress and behavioral dysfunction. However, this model assumes that other things in the environment remain relatively stable, so that the effects of overcrowding per se can be measured. If the environment itself changes in response to overcrowding—as it certainly does in the case of prisons (and, frankly, most other complex social systems)—then isolating the precise psychological effects of increased social density becomes more difficult.

Thus, the way prison administrators, line staff, and prisons themselves behave, react, and change in response to overcrowded conditions may complicate, mask, or neutralize the real effects of overcrowding on prisoners. Because few if any correctional systems have stable measures of the quality of prison life, many of the attempts to accommodate overcrowding that I discuss later in this chapter may hide many of its most pernicious effects and lead administrators to conclude that the problems are less serious, or are being managed more effectively, than, in fact, they are.

For example, in response to the pressures of overcrowding (and in the attempt to minimize their negative consequences), prison authorities may decide to reclassify prisoners, transfer certain inmates to other institutions, place some others in different units within the same prison, or implement different kinds of security procedures, disciplinary rules, and housing policies. Any one of these administrative responses can alter the nature of the prison environment as well as the makeup of the prisoner population housed within it. There is no simple way to separate the effects of these institutional reactions to overcrowding from the effects of overcrowding itself.

In addition, prison staff members who are faced with increasingly overcrowded living conditions may modify the internal and somewhat subjective standards that they use to define and document disciplinary infractions. As Timothy Flanagan observed, "the processes that lead to charging an inmate with a disciplinary infraction are situational in nature—involving a complex interplay between inmate, officer, and the setting in which the interaction occurs."[39] This interplay is subject to many of the same variables that both create and are affected by overcrowding.

Moreover, overcrowded prison conditions may trigger litigation that heightens the level of scrutiny that is focused on the prison by outside evaluators. The threat or reality of external monitoring may affect the behavior of decision makers inside the prison. Thus, as Richard McCorkle noted, prison staff may fail to officially report assaults—out of a concern that "a high assault rate would reflect poorly on the administration's ability to govern the prison."[40] In this way, the outside legal scrutiny that overcrowding often precipitates may heighten concerns over how the prison is being governed and, in turn, discourage staff from reporting every infraction of which they are aware.

On the other hand, overcrowding may lead prisoners to react to certain events in ways that would mask its harmful effects. As McCorkle also observed, "most victims of prison violence never report their victimization."[41] However, when prisoners perceive the correctional staff to be apathetic to their plight, or doubt their ability to protect them from inmate reprisals, they are unlikely to report what is happening to them. Because overcrowding creates even less favorable staff-to-inmate ratios, it contributes to both the perception and reality of worsening staff responsiveness and may lower the amount of victimization that is reported.[42]

Finally, prison officials are charged with the responsibility of monitoring and responding to disruptive and dysfunctional behavior and overt signs of prisoner deterioration. They possess the power to radically alter the mix of prisoners and the particular conditions under which they are confined. Under ideal conditions, prisoners who experience the most adverse reactions to overcrowding would be transferred to other institutions or placed in specialized housing where they would be removed from the normal routines of the mainline prison setting. In theory, at least, they should end up in facilities that provide them with much-needed respite or, depending on the seriousness of their reactions, some form of psychological treatment or counseling. More often, however, these prisoners will be placed in disciplinary segregation or punishment units. Indeed, they will move from being in the midst of too many people to none at all. This kind of re-sorting of prisoners and changes in the conditions to which they are exposed may simultaneously worsen the actual effects of overcrowding yet complicate any attempt to precisely assess the damaging effects of housing many more people together than the prisons were designed to hold.

PRISONS BEHAVING BADLY: THE BROADER CONTEXT OF OVERCROWDING

A number of broader contextual forces are often at work that coincide with changes in levels of overcrowding and significantly affect the behavior of guards and prisoners. In turn, they further complicate any straightforward determination of the adverse effects of overcrowding and, simultaneously, make bad situations—inside and even outside of prison—somewhat worse. For example, Sheldon Eckland-Olson studied the consequences of a sweeping federal court order in the Texas prison system that both ended the violent reign of inmate "building tenders" and required the state to reduce and carefully monitor levels of overcrowding.[43] The building tenders had functioned for many years in the Texas system as surrogate guards, wielding tremendous power over other inmates, often operating without supervision or restraint. Moreover, at the time the federal court stopped the practice, the Texas system was becoming dangerously overcrowded and the building tenders played an important, albeit brutal and illegal, role in attempting to manage and suppress the underlying tension and unrest. The court's careful oversight of the entire statewide department of corrections was intended to monitor and respond to this growing problem.

Indeed, because the court ended the abusive building tender practice and required the prison system to reduce overcrowding (as well as to improve conditions in other respects), violence rates should have been reduced throughout the system. Yet, the opposite appeared to occur. There were several reasons for this unexpected turn of events. For one, in part out of resistance to the court order itself, many Texas prison guards were reluctant to step in and control prisoner violence themselves. Increasingly, prisoners were forced to protect themselves, and as they did, officially reported violence rates were elevated.

It is also likely that violence that had once occurred at the hands of building tenders under the previous regime—because it was officially sanctioned—was not characterized as violence at all or was reported much less frequently than it actually occurred. Under the old Texas system, then, the true amount of violence inside the prisons likely was not reflected in the official statistics. After the court order—which was much resented by the prison staff (who thought it gave inmates too many rights)—violence by prisoners was likely to be more conscientiously and accurately documented.

Moreover, the criminal justice system *in general* behaves in response to prison overcrowding in ways that sometimes undermine its overall effectiveness. For example, if overcrowded prisons mean that probation and parole services are overtaxed by rapid increases in the number of recently released prisoners—as most studies of these agencies indicate they are—then agents may be directed to provide less guidance and meaningful supervision, or to offer fewer services designed to help probationers avoid prison and assist parolees in making a successful transition back into the freeworld. This, too, acts to increase the long-term effect of overcrowding on subsequent reoffending.[44]

Finally, the unprecedented magnitude of overcrowding in American prisons—many now operate at close to twice their capacity—may have reached and exceeded a ceiling effect for demonstrating adverse consequences.[45] Indeed, the rated capacities of most prisons were never intended to provide for particularly generous or luxurious accommodations. Thus, prisons operating at close to double those rated capacities certainly experience a lack of more than just space—including shortages in their staffing patterns, available prisoner services, and programming opportunities.[46]

Prison systems that are faced with nearly double their maximum number of prisoners may adopt desperate measures that not only have especially harmful effects on prisoners but also make it extremely difficult to identify stable relationships between population levels and anything else. In this regard, consider the discovery made by one researcher who examined overcrowding in the California prison system: "bus housing." Because the prison system was in such short supply of available bed space, it began "running buses up and down the state's highways containing enough inmates to fill a complete prison."[47] Prisoners were entering the system and being sent on bus trips of several hundred miles, all the while destined for a facility next to the point where they started. Indeed, "One administrator lamented that if a single bus broke down on a given day, the institution would face a major disaster—inmates in the yard with no beds."[48] It is difficult to envision any model of prison overcrowding that would adequately account for the adverse effect that this or similarly extreme approaches to managing severe levels of overcrowding would have on prisoners.

Thus, as I say, the way prisons and prison systems behave in response to overcrowded conditions may intensify their adverse effects and, at the same time, make them more difficult to discern. In fact, in light of the number of mutually interacting and uncontrollable variables in many of these studies, it is surprising that consistent patterns of any kind emerge. Even when they do, the aggregate statistics may fail to capture the range and depth of harmful overcrowding effects and the underlying psychological dynamics that produce them.

IGNORING THE CRITICAL NEEDS OF PRISONERS
IN TIMES OF CRISIS

The unprecedented influx of prisoners over the last several decades has further compromised the already minimal and often superficial evaluation and classification of incoming prisoners. The seriousness of a prisoner's offense for which he or she was committed and the length of his or her sentence now largely determine classification levels and, as a result, dictate most housing assignments. This means that many fewer new inmates are meaningfully screened or given a careful diagnostic evaluation and what—in the days of rehabilitation—was referred to as a needs assessment. The task of assigning prisoners to facilities turns largely on whether and where there is available bed space, rather than any matching of individual prisoner needs with available programming resources.

Overcrowding and the lack of any overarching commitment to rehabilitation has meant that many prisoners go for long periods of time without engaging in any productive activities that would effectively prepare them to be released back to the freeworld. As I noted earlier in this chapter, in many prison systems, fewer than half the prisoners are involved in educational programs, vocational training, or meaningful jobs that provide them with transferable skills or useful work experience. In addition to the sheer number of prisoners who go without such assignments, the quality of the programs for those who are assigned is often undermined by the ratio of prisoners' needs to the resources devoted to meeting them. For example, here is how sociologist John Irwin characterized the vocational training programs in a medium-security California prison he recently studied—programs in which, even then, less than 20% of the prisoners were fortunate enough to be involved:

> Several conditions greatly weaken the efficacy of these vocational training programs, most important, the lack of funds and resources. Instructors report that they have great difficulty obtaining needed equipment and materials. . . . Instructors are fired, or they quit and are not replaced. . . . Further, the training programs are regularly interrupted by lockdowns [and inclement weather] during which prisoners cannot be released to the hill for vocational training.[49]

In addition, as I discuss in greater detail in the next chapter, even by the most conservative calculations, there are several hundred thousand prisoners who are badly in need of counseling and treatment for a variety of preexisting cognitive, emotional, and psychological problems. Most prison systems do a poor job of identifying such persons, let alone allocating the necessary resources with which to treat them. But there are many other prisoners with different kinds of special needs that go largely unaddressed because, among other things, overcrowded prison systems do not have the luxury of taking them into account.

For example, a number of states have discontinued their sex offender treatment programs. Indeed, most do not even separate sex offenders from other prisoners. In fact, in the mid-1990s the U.S. Department of Justice reported that only about a dozen prison systems in the United States provided any kind of separate housing facilities for sex offenders, and few if any of those had enough dedicated space to accommodate all of the sex offenders who were incarcerated in their respective institutions.[50] The issue of separate facilities is particularly important for these prisoners. Because they fear victimization in prison, sex offenders are reluctant to identify themselves or draw attention to the nature of the offense for which they were committed. Their participation in sex offender treatment programs, in the rare prison system that provides such treatment, often depends entirely on their being housed in a safe environment where they will not be targeted by mainline prisoners.

Nonetheless, as I noted, overcrowding and scarce resources have helped to ensure that most sex offenders now are housed in general prison populations, where few will receive any special therapy and many are likely to be singled out by other prisoners for special abuse and victimization. The number of such prisoners is not insignificant. For example, in 1995, Texas and California alone reported having about 25,000 sex offenders imprisoned, and, at that time, neither state operated any separate facilities for them[51] Concern over the lack of specialized housing and treatment for sex offenders should also be based on an appreciation of the distorted norms of sexuality that pervade many prisons. In fact, the typical maximum-security prison is a sexually dysfunctional environment whose atmosphere seems almost perfectly designed to exacerbate preexisting sexual problems of whatever kind.[52]

The failure of prison systems to provide effective treatment for sex offenders—not necessarily by choice but often as an accommodation to scarce resources—has created another long-term problem. Many citizens regard untreated sex offenders as potential threats to public safety and, in turn, enthusiastically support the enactment of so-called sexual predator laws. Accordingly, in many states, after sex offenders have completed their prison terms, they routinely are *civilly committed* to prison-like facilities. These commitments are justified supposedly because their untreated mental abnormality—the one that presumably led to their original offense but was ignored during their term of imprisonment—renders them a "danger." Although these laws have been challenged on constitutional grounds— including the contention that the conditions of their civil confinement are far more punitive than therapeutic—they have been upheld.[53] In effect, it appears they may result in a lifetime of incarceration for many sex offenders, in part because of the inability or unwillingness of prison systems to provide them with effective treatment at an earlier time.

One final and very different example of the way in which overcrowded and underfunded prison systems have ignored basic prisoner needs and created significant long-term problems involves the plight of Latino prisoners. Although there has been relatively little research focused specifically on them, they now represent a major segment of the prisoner population in the United States. In some jurisdictions they are a plurality of those incarcerated. In addition to their growing numbers, however, many Latino prisoners encounter special problems once they enter prison.[54] Specifically, Latino prisoners with lower levels of English proficiency are functionally excluded from the relatively few existing educational, vocational, and other kinds of prison training programs because such programs typically are not offered in Spanish.[55]

As one study showed, although African American and Latino prisoners together were given less favorable job assignments than their White counterparts, "the fact that many Latinos had few or no English language skills further limited the range of jobs and educational and vocational programs to which they were assigned."[56] Similarly, the lack of any significant number of bilingual prison staff has likely prevented many Latino prisoners in correctional facilities throughout the country from properly using medical and psychiatric services, prison law libraries, and other legal resources, and has even interfered with their ability to fully understand prison rules or to effectively defend themselves in prison disciplinary proceedings.

MAINTAINING CONTROL THROUGH FORCE AND INTIMIDATION

Overcrowding, widespread idleness, and the failure of many prison systems to address the basic needs of prisoners have changed the context of imprisonment. Prison administrators have been forced to anticipate and react to many volatile and potentially explosive situations. In many instances, their reactions have been predictable but also problematic, serving to increase the amount of prison pain dispensed and making already dangerous situations, in the long run, more so.

Indeed, in the face of extraordinary increases in the sheer numbers of prisoners, many prison administrators pressed for new tools with which to control and contain them. In most jurisdictions, any pretense of carefully managing the prison "careers" of inmates or effectively monitoring the quality of the conditions under which they were kept was sacrificed during the rapid expansion of the prisoner population. Recall that Malcolm Feeley and Jonathan Simon identified an emerging penological management style in which correctional decision makers thought about prisoners only in the "aggregate," as dangerous "populations" that needed to be "herded," rather than as individuals in need of personal attention. Indeed, in terms that captured both the dehumanized consciousness of the decision makers and the devalued status of the prisoners under their control, Feeley and Simon analogized the overcrowding-driven new penology as akin to a "waste management" function.[57]

Thus, rather than improving living conditions and investing in prison programs and meaningful activities in which prisoners could participate, most systems committed to harsh policies and procedures to maintain order and control. They also began to rely increasingly on sophisticated and expensive security hardware and surveillance technology. Metal detectors, X-ray machines, leg irons, waist chains, handcuffs, "black boxes,"[58] holding cages, violent prisoner restraint chairs, psychiatric screens, chain-link fences, concertina wire, tasers, stun guns, pepper spray, tear gas canisters, gas grenades, and, in some jurisdictions, mini 14- and 9-millimeter rifles, 12-gauge shotguns, and the like are used now *inside* the cellblocks of a number of maximum-security prisons.[59]

For example, in maximum-security prisons in California, guards armed with rifles are strategically positioned inside mainline housing units and authorized to respond to inmate disturbances with lethal force. Thus, even when they are asleep, prisoners are under what is euphemistically called "gun cover." In New York City, the city's large jail on Rikers Island has resorted to what has been characterized as an "iron hand" approach to regain and maintain order by "using an array of tools and tactics—from a huge S.W.A.T. team, to electric stun shields, to a program that aggressively prosecutes inmates for crimes committed inside the jail."[60]

But these iron hands have a decidedly modern, technological grip. At Rikers, for example, "stun devices—large plexiglass shield threaded with wires—deliver six-second bursts of 50,000 volts of electricity, and are used to incapacitate inmates and cut the risk of hand-to-hand violence." In the late 1990s the devices were being used, on average, about once a week in the jail. Guards there and elsewhere also use specially equipped chairs "with magnetic sensors that can search for bits of metal hidden in inmates' mouths and other body cavities."[61] Although many guards and prisoners at some facilities agree that the new combination of technology and toughness can bring about reductions in violence—at Rikers, what was described as "an almost eerie, 'Twilight Zone' calm"[62] was created inside the formerly chaotic jail—it fails to directly address any of the underlying causes of the tensions that precipitated the violence in the first place.

Nonetheless, of course, in the words of one Rikers guard, it "shows we're in charge."[63] Despite the modern technological veneer in which it is cloaked, this goal—showing who is in charge or in control, sometimes at whatever cost—remains at the core of much correctional thinking. In lieu of confronting the contextual causes of problematic prisoner behavior, harsh and repressive tactics are used to suppress it. The correctional equivalent of the "law of the instrument"[64] means that the sheer availability of the iron hand—technological devices, hardware, and weapons—is likely to increase its use, even in response to minor infractions that in past times, in the absence of these armaments, might have been resolved in less forceful ways.

Moreover, the prevailing punitive ideology in American corrections has served to make the use of repressive forms of control seem more necessary and justified, leading to another punitive correctional trend: Many prison systems are making more extensive use of a new form of disciplinary segregation, or *lockup*, unit. Presumably designed to limit and control violence by keeping prisoners isolated from one another, the practice confines them under especially harsh and deprived conditions for very long periods of time.

The use of long-term solitary confinement was tried and then abandoned in the 19th century, when its psychological effects were recognized as harmful and inhumane. Yet, in the last several decades of the 20th century, it returned in the form of the modern *supermax* prison.[65] The trend began slowly. Before the massive influx of prisoners in the mid-1970s, some prison systems were rethinking the role of solitary confinement entirely, and others were devising ways to limit the amount and duration of isolation they used. However, as increasing numbers of prisoners entered the criminal justice system later in that decade—and in each subsequent one—punitive segregation emerged as one of the primary mechanisms to control unprecedented numbers of chronically idle and potentially unruly inmates.

At first, existing prisons were converted to segregation units. Thus, in large maximum-security California prisons like San Quentin and Folsom, there were extended periods during the 1980s when half or more of the entire prisoner population was housed in units that were devoted to long-term lockup. Even though one psychiatrist who worked in these units described them as producing "an atmosphere of terror rarely seen elsewhere" in society,[66] it was not uncommon for prisoners to be confined in them for several years or more.

Eventually, so-called supermax prisons were specially constructed for the purpose of isolating prisoners over the long term (and, for some, even on a permanent basis). Prisoners in supermax are allowed out of their cells for only very brief periods (on average, 1–2 hours a day), and otherwise eat, defecate, and lead the remainder of their lives entirely within the confines of their individual cells. Anytime prisoners in these units are moved or transported for any reason, they first are chained through special "cuff slots" on the outside of the cells, even before their doors are opened. In many supermax units, inmates must exercise alone in small, specially de-signed "exercise cages." In the notorious "control unit" at the Marion federal penitentiary, the cages were placed inside the cellblocks themselves. Among other special security procedures, prison rules at many supermax prisons also require two or three guards to serve as escorts whenever a prisoner is moved inside the institution.[67]

Punitive segregation like this is not necessarily reserved for inmates who have committed serious disciplinary infractions. Many prison systems place suspected gang members and affiliates on "indeterminate" terms in their lockup units—whether they have or have not been convicted of any specific, overt behavioral infractions. They release them only after they have provided incriminating information about other suspected gang members. In addition, mainline prisoners can experience supermax-like conditions whether they have or have not been involved in violence or committed a disciplinary infraction. That is, whenever a serious violent incident erupts inside a prison, officials may "lock down" an entire cell block or whole facility, turning it into the equivalent of a segregation unit that confines everyone to his or her cell. These lockdowns can persist for weeks and months and, in the recent history of some institutions, have been in effect more often than not.

The severe conditions created inside the supermax prisons have not escaped legal commentary and critique. In a number of cases, judges have expressed concerns over the "stark sterility and unremitting monotony" of the interior design of these units, and the fact that prisoners housed there can "go weeks, months or potentially years with little or no opportunity for normal social contact with other people." They have observed that the sight of prisoners in the barren exercise pens to which they are restricted creates an image "hauntingly similar to that of caged felines pacing in a zoo,"[68] and acknowledged that "many, if not most" of the prisoners housed in supermax "experience some degree of psychological trauma in reaction to their extreme social isolation and the severely restricted environmental stimulation" to which they are exposed.[69] But they have permitted prison systems to continue to use them.

A basic understanding of self-fulfilling prophecies (by which the expec-tations of others elicit the anticipated behavior),[70] labeling theory (in which socially constructed labels come to shape and delimit the perceptions of self and others),[71] or psychologist Bonnie Strickland's classic research on surveillance and trust (showing that high levels of the former significantly impaired and impeded the latter)[72] highlights some of the ways in which inmates are likely to be adversely affected by this kind of treatment. Indeed, some prisoners will develop long-lasting psychological dependencies on these drastic and extreme forms of external control. Because surveillance and constraints like these are replicated nowhere else in society, their dependencies and other reactions may have severely disruptive consequences for the prisoners who eventually are released back into free society.

Of course, some of these social psychological processes operate in both directions. For example, staff members are aware of the general reputation of the prisoners housed inside the supermax units where they work and—given the extraordinarily harsh and deprived conditions that have been created there—may readily conclude that they have been given a mandate to engage in intimidating, painful, and even brutal forms of social control. The tendency for this kind of absolute power to corrupt the behavior of those who wield it has been demonstrated in the brief history of these units.

For example, in the *Madrid* case that focused on California's Pelican Bay supermax prison, the court found that "excessive force was used in a variety of circumstances and settings, from staff assaults on inmates to punitive cagings under harsh conditions," and that "the amount of force applied was so strikingly disproportionate to the circumstances that it was imposed, more likely than not, for the very purpose of causing harm. . . ."[73] The excessive force in question included numerous instances of beating prisoners with batons; firing tasers, .38-millimeter gas guns, and mace at them; forcibly removing them from their cells for offenses as minor as failing to return a food tray; hog-tying prisoners or placing them in fetal restraints for as long as 9 hours for infractions like kicking their cell doors; placing naked prisoners in outdoor holding cages where they were exposed to public view as well as inclement weather (heavy rain and winter cold) for hours at a time; and "unnecessary, and in some cases, reckless . . ." discharging of lethal firearms inside the cellblocks of the prison.[74]

In theory, at least, these units are supposed to control violent prisoners by placing them in environments where they cannot harm anyone. Thus, prison officials claim that supermax prisons reduce the overall level of violence in the prison system by taking the most violent persons out of the general mix of prisoners. Yet there is little real evidence to support this notion. Indeed, Howard Bidna's early study examining the effects of these high-security units—conducted long before Pelican Bay was constructed—concluded that "the levels of fatal violence and of assaults by inmates on staff in California prisons were not significantly altered by the implementation of the strict security policies."[75] Bidna also found that although the overall rate of stabbings in the general prisoner population decreased, the levels increased in the security housing units despite (or perhaps because of) the intensified security procedures.

A more recent study indicated that supermax confinement failed to achieve its primary goal of reducing systemwide violence. That is, quite apart from the adverse psychological effects of supermax conditions on prisoners who experience them for such unprecedented lengths of time, there is no empirical evidence to support the assertion that such extreme forms of long-term isolation reduce overall levels of aggression. Indeed, in terms that are consistent with the psychological framework I have advanced here, the authors of this study suggested that "patterns of inmate behavior will remain unchanged without addressing the context in which prison violence occurs and how inmates and staff interact in that context."[76]

THE CONTEXTUAL ORIGINS OF THE PRISON GANG

There is another dysfunctional and dangerous adaptation that prisoners and guards make to each other and to the chaotic conditions around them. In chapter 6, I discussed some of the psychological changes that prisoners in general undergo to survive the rigors of the prison environment. As I noted, these include the struggle to preserve a sense of identity and self-worth in a setting where these things are deeply undermined. In part to establish a system of meaning that is separate from the one imposed on them by the prison, prisoners develop their own internal culture and corresponding set of norms. Indeed, some prisoners devise entirely separate languages or *argots* with which to communicate and that, among other things, allow them to retain their separate identities apart from the institutions that house them.[77] All prisons have what Polish sociologist Pawel Moczydlowski termed a "hidden life," and particularly in prisons that impose especially harsh conditions and severe deprivations, the terms of that life can become extreme and distorted.[78]

However, as I have argued in this chapter, the situational pathologies of prison extend well beyond the direct adaptations of the prisoners to the extreme environments in which they are placed. They also include the way in which the prison context itself first helps to create problematic behavior among prisoners and then, because of the manner in which this behavior is responded to, exacerbates it. No phenomenon illustrates this complex and paradoxical interplay better than the rise of prison gangs over the last several decades.

People join gangs in prison for largely the same reasons they do in the larger society: "When faced with an external threat, people tend to band together in groups to protect themselves. . . . The degree to which individuals seek this kind of protection depends on both their internal sense of security and the intensity of the external threat."[79] Thus, there is a personal component to the impulse to align with a group in order to achieve an internal sense of psychological security—especially in environments "where the self is constantly vulnerable to the lack of respect." Particularly in those places in our society "where social domination is increasingly experienced in terms of personal failure," gang membership becomes a preferred "strategy to defend subjectivity. . . ."[80] In addition, there is a social aspect to the attraction of the gang: "The gang is a response to social disorganization: It produces order in a world of disorder."[81] Of course, both aspects help to explain why street gangs typically take root in neighborhoods where young people—because of poverty, race, or ethnicity—are denied larger cultural representation and otherwise become marginalized and excluded from meaningful participation in the larger society.

With this perspective in mind, the increase in the numbers and the importance of prison gangs over the last several decades is best viewed as a consequence—not a cause—of pathological prison conditions. A growing number of prisoners in the United States have adapted to deteriorating, deprived, and dangerous prison conditions through a collective response: by seeking strength, opportunities, and security in numbers through the formation of prison gangs.[82] More specifically, prisoners who feel personally powerless, threatened, and vulnerable are more likely to feel the need to align themselves with others, to organize for their own protection, and to enhance their own status and control through connections to more powerful groups. Especially among many prisoners whose backgrounds and social histories have been filled with trauma and insecurity, and who confront what appears (at least initially) to be a confusing, socially disorganized prison world, joining with others in common purpose seems to offer them a stable identity and a source of security. In short, gangs provide psychological and physical protection to those who feel they need it.[83]

Yet, the initial self-protective motives of recruits makes them vulnerable to powerful gang-related pressures directing them toward more nefarious ends. Paradoxically, in the long run, prison gangs endanger the well-being of prisoners who initially join in the hope of surviving the treacherous and deprived conditions in which they live in prison. They soon learn that, eventually, having been identified as a gang member virtually always results in a worsened rather than improved quality of prison life. Thus, what begins as a seemingly natural and even necessary adaptation to increasingly intolerable conditions may become ultimately self-defeating. In this sense, gang membership represents another example of what I termed earlier the *dynamics of desperation* that starts with the tendency of extreme prison environments to force increasingly narrow Hobson's choices on prisoners. As a result, many will pursue what at the time seem like necessary short-term adaptations that over time lead to harmful consequences, ones made difficult to foresee by mounting pressures to survive intolerable conditions.[84]

In addition, however, the prison system's characteristic response to these problems—many of which are institutionally created—exacerbates them, completing the cycle of situational pathology.[85] That is, by viewing gang membership as a reflection of individual deviance, something to be suppressed through punishment, prison systems not only ensure the gangs' continued existence but inadvertently enhance their power. Among other things, "by imposing harsh, even tortuous, conditions" in an attempt to suppress gang activity, prison officials intensify "the need for 'a sense of belonging,' which is what causes gang members to gravitate toward one another in the first place."[86]

Refusing to acknowledge and alleviate the harsh overall conditions that have contributed to the rise of gang activity means that the root causes of the problem will not be addressed. This conclusion is shared by others. Indeed, a National Institute of Corrections study of the causes of increased prison gang activity implicated the poor quality of life in contemporary prisons (including a lack of programs and work opportunities, widespread idleness, overly restrictive visiting policies, and overcrowded, unsafe, and poorly maintained facilities).[87] Nonetheless, most prisons have continued to ignore these contextual issues and instead to target only individuals— by isolating gang members in harsh punitive segregation units (nowadays, often in supermax prisons), where "they are forced to rely on each other for human contact and support, because there is no other source."[88] Again, by this flawed logic, the draconian measures that have been introduced in response to the threat posed by the gangs have served to increase their power.

THE LEGACY OF ADVERSE CONDITIONS:
RIOTS AND RECIDIVISM

In extreme cases, breakdowns in prison social organization can precipitate more collective forms of violence. To be sure, *prison riots*—defined by researchers as the loss of control of "a significant number of prisoners, in a significant area of the prison, for a significant amount of time"[89]—are rare. Most experts acknowledge that a unique set of precipitating conditions— including adverse conditions of confinement, social disorganization, and the loss of legitimacy by the prison administration itself—are required before a prison riot is likely to occur.[90] For example, one social scientist who studied the deadly 1980 riot at the Penitentiary of New Mexico concluded that the prison's "control structure . . . in the late 1970s mirrored the inmate social structure: both depended upon coercion and resulted in fragmentation into cliques. These gradual structural changes within the organization set the stage for the riot."[91]

Similarly, sociologist Bert Useem explained the same riot in terms of the disintegration of social organization within the institution that had occurred beforehand. In the preceding decade, the penitentiary had deteriorated from a benign and orderly facility into a prison that was "harsh, abusive, painfully boring, and without the 'regulatory mechanisms' that had been in place" in the early part of the decade. By the late 1970s, there was a great deal of idleness, and "inmates remained confined to their living units with little to do or look forward to." Prisoners became frustrated and hostile, "not only toward prison officials and guards, but also toward one another."[92] An extraordinarily unfortunate sequence of events allowed prisoners to gain control of the facility, and an explosive outpouring of pent-up emotion and violence ensued.

However, the observations that have been made about preexisting conditions at the Penitentiary of New Mexico in the late 1970s seem to apply, in varying degrees, to many prisons in the United States. If so, what accounts for the relative infrequency of prison riots? The extreme levels of force and intimidation that I discussed earlier in this chapter and the sophisticated forms of technological control that have been introduced in many facilities provide part of the explanation. Prisoner resentment, frustration, and conflict are adequately suppressed and sufficiently controlled so that organized expression or resistance is effectively thwarted. Yet, it would be a mistake to conclude that suppressing these pervasive prisoner reactions prevents them from taking a psychological toll or from being expressed *after* prisoners are released. Indeed, in the remainder of this section I argue that a broader, albeit less visible, set of problems has been brought about by deteriorating conditions and harsh treatment: postprison debilitation that virtually guarantees high levels of reoffending.

In fact, long before the trends toward overincarceration began in the mid-1970s, a number of early studies of recidivism appear to have documented at least some of the adverse criminogenic effects of incarceration. In one early study, for example, Leslie Wilkins cautiously questioned conventional wisdom and concluded that "the use of probation as treatment for a large proportion of cases which many courts would have sent to prison does not result in a greater proportion of reconviction."[93]

Another early but compelling study suggested that under certain circumstances the experience of imprisonment made the subsequent commission of crimes more, rather than less, likely. Charles Eichman conducted a natural experiment with Florida prisoners that was occasioned by the U.S. Supreme Court's decision in *Gideon v. Wainwright*,[94] in a ruling that resulted in prisoners who had been unrepresented at their criminal trials being released from custody. Eichman compared over a hundred prisoners freed "prematurely" because of the Court's decision with a matched sample of prisoners who had served their full sentences. After 2 years of unsupervised freedom, the early-release group was almost half as likely to have recidivated as those who had stayed through their full terms (14% vs. 25%).[95]

A similar but less dramatic difference was found by California researchers at the start of the decade of the 1970s when they compared probationers with persons released after serving terms of incarceration. They found that 34% of probationers in their study recidivated, compared with 51% of those who had been incarcerated, and that these differences persisted even after controlling for demographics, prior record, and offense.[96] Another such study—this one published in the mid-1970s, as the era of overincarceration was just beginning—reached virtually the same conclusion, namely, that "incarceration is no better than noninstitutional treatment at preventing recidivism and may actually be worse."[97]

In the mid-1980s, Joan Petersilia and her colleagues reported that persons in their study who had been imprisoned were more likely to be arrested than a matched group of probationers (72% vs. 63%), more likely to have charges filed against them (53% vs. 38%), and more likely to be reincarcerated (47% vs. 31%) over the 2-year period on which they focused.[98] A few years later, another group of researchers reported that the adverse effects of imprisonment differed depending on the kind of crime for which persons were incarcerated. Specifically, the study indicated that "the robber's response to time served [was] linear, with the probability of recidivating increasing monotonically with time served. Evidently, robbers who are punished more severely, in terms of length of imprisonment, are not more likely to adopt avoidance behavior."[99] More generally, they concluded that "offenders who become increasingly estranged from the legitimate world as their sentence lengthens are more likely to recidivate if their sentences are longer."[100]

Note that most of these studies were conducted in an earlier period when at least some attention still was being given to the goal of rehabilitation. In the modern era, in which pain has been made the purpose of imprisonment, studies showing that prisons may do more harm to prisoners than good seem to have less shock value. Yet, the overall pains of imprisonment—and, therefore, the potentially debilitating consequences that follow harsh confinement—are likely to have increased as a result of the new emphasis on punitive social control and longer terms of imprisonment. Prisoners are now exposed to harsh prison conditions overseen by prison officials attempting to manage far too many people, with far too little to do, who are incarcerated for far too long a period of time.

And there is much new evidence that, indeed, these harsh and painful contexts do matter. That is, it does matter when prisons are plagued by a surplus of situational pathologies as opposed to having concerted efforts made to help prisoners resist maladaptive institutional responses and to provide them with humane treatment and programming. Recall the results of the large-scale, federally sponsored study I discussed in chapter 3, in which the postprison success rates of persons released in 1994 compared unfavorably with those of persons released a decade earlier.[101] Whatever else the "get tough" policies had accomplished during these years, they had not produced prisons able to either better ensure the success of parolees or create a great enough deterrent effect to dissuade them from future crime.

Consistent with the contextual model of behavior around which much of this book has been structured, there is an emerging new psychology of "prison effects" that documents the painfulness of prison and its long-term harmful—even criminogenic—consequences. For example, Alison Liebling and her colleagues found that the measured levels of distress in the prisons they studied were "extraordinarily high."[102] In fact, in 11 of the 12 facilities they studied, the mean distress score among prisoners was above the threshold needed to inquire into whether a patient is suffering from a treatable emotional or psychological illness. Furthermore, the levels of distress varied in predictable ways, in part as a function of the quality of life in the prison environment (or the prisoners' experience of it). Thus, prisons whose "moral performance" was poor—ones rated low on social climate and other measures—also produced higher levels of distress among prisoners.[103]

In addition to research on the effects of the general social climate of prison, some recent studies have focused on the psychological consequences of particular forms of prison trauma. Of course, not only do prisons vary widely in terms of the kinds of experiences they create for prisoners—the point I made at the outset of chapter 6 that not all prisons are equally benign, painful, or capable of inflicting harm—but prisoners vary in terms of how they experience the same environments or events and how harmful and disabling seemingly identical prison experiences prove to be for them over the long term.[104] Thus, one study of prison distress focused on the degree to which having been victimized in prison led to depression and symptoms of posttraumatic stress.[105] The researchers found that a history of having been exposed to trauma and violence prior to coming to prison helped to explain their level of prison distress, but also that "prison victimization contributes to the occurrence of depressive and [posttraumatic stress] symptoms."[106] Indeed, they concluded that the experience of being victimized in prison *added* to the pains of the preexisting events to which the prisoner had been exposed. Especially because of the potential for posttraumatic stress symptoms to prove disabling on release, the authors recommended that "rehabilitative efforts should help inmates recover from trauma occurring inside and outside prison."

Evidence that high levels of prison distress and trauma translate into lasting problems for the prisoners who suffer them comes from a variety of sources. For example, in Adrian Grounds's psychiatric assessments of a group of long-term prisoners who had been exonerated and subsequently released, he recognized that the most serious psychological problems many prisoners would face were likely to occur *after* they left prison. Indeed, his assessments uncovered a pattern of disabling symptoms and severe psychological problems that paralleled findings from the trauma literature in psychology and psychiatry. Grounds concluded that the "extent of the suffering was profound."[107]

It is not surprising that the overcrowded conditions and anti-rehabilitation ethos that characterized the last several decades in American corrections appear to have greatly increased the criminogenic risks that persons must overcome following incarceration. Joan Petersilia summarized the results of research on the plight of those released from the kind of prisons I have described in this and in several previous chapters this way:

> The average inmate coming home will have served a longer prison sentence than in the past, be more disconnected from family and friends, have a higher prevalence of substance abuse and mental illness, and be less educated and less employable than those in prior prison release cohorts. Each of these factors is known to predict recidivism, yet few of these needs are addressed while the inmate is in prison or on parole.[108]

Finally, Paul Gendreau and his colleagues conducted a comprehensive meta-analytic study of the relationship between incarceration, length of confinement, and recidivism. They concluded that doing time in prison actually had a criminogenic effect. Indeed, not only did going to prison increase the chances of reoffending, but also, the more time served, the greater were the crime-producing consequences. Although the overall effects were modest in size, Gendreau and his colleagues concluded that "the enormous costs accruing from the excessive use of prison may not be defensible," and that the long-term societal impact—in terms of increased amounts of crime produced by more people going to prison for longer amounts of time—was particularly problematic "given the high incarceration rates currently in vogue in North America."[109]

Although there is certainly no systematic empirical proof of the proposition that literally all prisons have significant criminogenic effects, these studies underscore the fact there may be a strong crime control rationale for transforming prisons and reducing the magnitude of the pain that they inflict. As one veteran prison administrator acknowledged,

> I now think that my colleagues and I initially underestimated the negative effect of custody. We are now much more willing to say that even the research findings on recidivism affirm a widely shared belief that custody is best viewed as the last resort.[110]

On a more positive note, context matters in the opposite way as well. That is, as Liebling and her colleagues have shown, not only is it possible to measure the quality of prison life and to document that overall distress levels tend to be very high in general, but also, it does matter whether prisoners are treated well in prison. In particular, the quality of prison life and the nature of correctional treatment can compound or alleviate the vulnerabilities with which persons enter prison. This means that prisoners who are confined in safe and caring facilities and who experience fair treatment during incarceration experience a greater sense of well-being and are less likely to experience negative outcomes during incarceration.[111]

CONCLUSION

It is not difficult to understand the flawed logic by which dangerously overcrowded prison systems that were threatened with what many administrators feared was an inevitable loss of control would resort to unprecedented and oppressive forms of treatment. In institutions where two or three prisoners were forced to live in cells built for one, or where inmates were required to sleep in hallways or on gymnasium floors, many officials came to regard counseling sessions, mental health services, educational classes, vocational training programs, and the like as niceties that could be dispensed with until more basic concerns were addressed. But they went much further. Many of their ill-advised short-term responses to the uncontrollable influx of prisoners have changed the social context of prison, producing conditions that are often hurtful and potentially destructive in the long run. They have consequences that will be personally disabling for some prisoners and produce outcomes that are unintended and undesirable both for correctional systems themselves and for society at large.

Many of these situational pathologies now threaten to become functionally autonomous, permanent features of the contemporary prison. They appear to reflect an emerging correctional norm authorizing extreme forms of deprivation and repressive control at the discretion of prison staff and administrators. G. K. Chesterton once noted that perhaps the most horrible thing about public officials was not that they were wicked or stupid, but that they "simply have got used to it,"[112] that is, accustomed themselves to many of the worst things that they were called upon to do. The last several decades have witnessed a spiraling escalation of punishment in the form of repressive control, excessive surveillance, and punitive isolation in penal systems throughout the United States. The rising tide of punishment developed its own momentum. In what might be termed the *iron law of corrections*, a kind of criminal justice analog to Helson's adaptation-level theory[113] occurred in which the increasingly extreme endpoints on the continuum of severe punishment served as anchors that made harsher punishments more tolerable at all other points along the scale. The sobering descriptions of institutionally sanctioned repression and, in too many instances, even outright brutality that appear in accounts of life inside some American prisons may be easier to understand—although not to countenance—from this perspective.[114]

As I have noted, these harsh policies also emerged within a larger sociopolitical context in which the limits to the pain of imprisonment had been effectively neutralized or eliminated. On the one hand, correctional administrators were confronted by severe management problems that stemmed from unprecedented overcrowding that they neither had initiated nor were in a position to stop. On the other hand, a punitive political climate allowed them to make a range of expedient but extreme managerial decisions in the name of security and control. Not only were the pains of imprisonment largely unregulated but they had been made the very purpose of incarceration. The pressures to control prisoners through the application of greater levels of pain—force, intimidation, and emerging technologies of pain delivery—proved too great to resist. Many prisons have continued to behave badly in response.

Of course, modern psychological theory would argue for much greater sensitivity to the harmful prison effects that were produced, ensuring that the institutional responses to real and perceived disorder did not cause situations and contexts to deteriorate even further. But this perspective was not represented in the decision-making process that produced these policies. In addition, there were few barriers left in place to prevent the drift toward cruel treatment. Among other things, these punitive trends were facilitated by a number of legal rulings by decision makers—once looked to as a source of protection from state-sanctioned excessive punishment. Absent meaningful oversight or intervention, and little or no consistent enforcement of humane limits to prison pain in many jurisdictions, these forbidding places directed what David Garland called their "stored-up power" and "silent, brooding capacity to control" against many of those prisoners least able to withstand it.[115] In fact, as I discuss in the next chapter, even the most vulnerable prisoners—those who are mentally ill or developmentally disabled—were subjected to many of these punitive extremes.

NOTES

1. Nils Christie, *Limits to Pain* (Oxford, England: Martin Robertson, 1982), 46, 49.
2. D. Garland, "Punishment and Culture: The Symbolic Dimensions of Criminal Justice," *Studies in Law, Politics, and Society* 11 (1991): 191, 203.
3. Lawrence Friedman, *Crime and Punishment in American History* (New York: Basic Books, 1993), 316.
4. I. Barak-Glantz, "Who's in the 'Hole'"? *Criminal Justice Review* 8 (1983): 29, 29.
5. *See, e.g.*, "The Incorrigibles: They Rape and Molest. They Defy Treatment. How Can Society Protect Itself?" *Newsweek*, January 18, 1993, p. 48. This article is typical of the genre. It ends with the observation that "one way or another, society keeps searching for a way to protect itself. After all, the Constitution isn't a suicide pact," 50.
6. Of course, stressful prison conditions exert significant pressures on correctional officers as well as prisoners. Although this book concentrates on the effects of

the prison context on prisoners, the correctional staff is an extraordinarily significant component of that environment. Other scholars and researchers have systematically addressed the important question of how correctional officers are changed and transformed by the experience of working in prison. *See, e.g.,* Ted Conover, *Newjack: Guarding Sing Sing* (New York: Vintage Books, 2000); Gary Cornelius, *Stressed Out: Strategies for Living and Working With Stress in Corrections* (Laurel, MD: American Correctional Association, 1994); Elaine Crawley, *Doing Prison Work: The Public and Private Lives of Prison Officers* (Cullompton, England: Willan Publishing, 2004); P. Finn, "Correctional Officer Stress: A Cause for Concern and Additional Help," *Federal Probation* 62 (1998): 65; R. Huckabee, "Stress in Corrections: An Overview of the Issues. *Journal of Criminal Justice* 20 (1992): 479; Alison Liebling and David Price, *The Prison Officer* (Leyhill, England: Prison Service and Waterside Press, 2001); Alison Liebling, *Prisons and Their Moral Performance: A Study of Values, Quality, and Prison Life* (New York: Oxford University Press, 2004); and Lucien Lombardo, *Guards Imprisoned: Correctional Officers at Work* (New York: Elsevier, 1981).

7. *See, e.g.,* chapter 4, this volume.

8. American Civil Liberties Union, National Prison Project, *Status Report: State Prisons and the Courts* (Washington, DC: Author, 1995).

9. T. Conover, "Guarding Sing Sing," *The New Yorker*, April 3, 2000, p. 56.

10. V. Cox, P. Paulus, and G. McCain, "Prison Crowding Research: The Relevance for Prison Housing Standards and a General Approach to Crowding Phenomena," *American Psychologist* 39 (1984): 1148, 1150; Gilbert Gaes, "The Effects of Overcrowding in Prison," in *Crime and Justice: Annual Review* of Research, ed. Michael Tonry and Norval Morris (Chicago: University of Chicago Press, 1985); Paul Paulus, *Prison Crowding: A Psychological Perspective* (New York: Springer-Verlag, 1988).

11. T. Thornberry and J. Call, "Constitutional Challenges to Prison Overcrowding: The Scientific Evidence of Harmful Effect," *Hastings Law Journal* 35 (1983): 313, 351. Overcrowding studies at women's prisons showed similar effects. *See* B. Ruback and T. Carr, "Crowding in a Woman's Prison: Attitudinal and Behavioral Effects," *Journal of Applied Social Psychology* 14 (1984): 57.

12. *See, e.g.,* S. Ekland-Olson, "Crowding, Social Control, and Prison Violence: Evidence From the Post-*Ruiz* Years in Texas," *Law and Society Review* 20 (1986): 389.

13. *See, e.g.,* J. Bleich, "The Politics of Prison Crowding," *California Law Review* 77 (1989): 1125.

14. *See, e.g.,* P. Paulus, V. Cox, G. McCain, and J. Chandler, "Some Effects of Crowding in a Prison Environment," *Journal of Applied Social Psychology* 5 (1975): 86, 90. "The present study indicates that living under relatively crowded housing conditions in a prison produces both negative affect and a lower criterion of what constitutes overcrowding."

15. *See, e.g.,* D. D'Atri, "Psychophysiological Responses to Crowding," *Environment and Behavior* 7 (1975): 237: "The major hypothesis that there would be an association between degree of crowding and blood pressure, systolic and diastolic, was strongly supported," 247.

16. *See, e.g.*, G. McCain, V. Cox, and P. Paulus, "The Relationship Between Illness Complaints and Degree of Crowding in a Prison Environment," *Environment and Behavior* 8 (1976): 283, 288.

17. P. Paulus, G. McCain, and V. Cox, "Death Rates, Psychiatric Commitments, Blood Pressure, and Perceived Crowding as a Function of Institutional Crowding," *Environmental Psychology and Nonverbal Behavior* 3 (1978): 107, 115. *See also* Adrian Ostfeld, Stanislav Dasl, David D'Atri, and Edward Fitzgerald, *Stress, Crowding, and Blood Pressure in Prison* (Hillsdale, NJ: Lawrence Erlbaum, 1987).

18. E. Megargee, "The Association of Population Density, Reduced Space, and Uncomfortable Temperature with Misconduct in a Prison Community," *American Journal of Community Psychology* 5 (1977): 289, 295.

19. *See, e.g.*, V. Cox, P. Paulus, and G. McCain, "Prison Crowding Research," *American Psychologist* 39 (1984): 1148, 1159. *See also* E. Sieh, "Prison Overcrowding: The Case of New Jersey," *Federal Probation* 53 (1989): 41, for a brief review. For a discussion on the health risks of prison and jail overcrowding, *see* B. Walker and T. Gordon, "Health Risks and High Density Confinement in Jails and Prisons," *Federal Probation* 44 (1980): 53.

20. F. DiCataldo, A. Greer, and W. Profit, "Screening Prison Inmates for Mental Disorder: An Examination of the Relationship Between Mental Disorder and Prison Adjustment," *Bulletin of the American Academy of Psychiatry and Law* 23 (1995): 573, 574.

21. National Center For Education Statistics, *Literacy Behind Prison Walls* (Washington, DC: U.S. Department of Education, October 1994).

22. Gary Sutherland, *Reading Proficiency of Inmates in California Correctional Institutions* (Sacramento: California State University, 1997).

23. California Department of Corrections Web site, at http://www.cdc.state.ca.us/factsht.htm. Last visited December 30, 2002.

24. Kathleen McGuire and Ann Pastore, *Sourcebook of Criminal Justice Statistics, 1992* [U.S. Department of Justice, Bureau of Justice Statistics] (Washington, DC: U.S. Government Printing Office, 1993), 634.

25. Specifically, only 53.6% of the more than 150,000 California prisoners were employed in any type of work assignment at the end of the year 2002. California Department of Corrections, *CDC Facts* (January 2003; http://www.cdc.state.ca.us/cdcfacts.htm).

26. United States General Accounting Office, *Report to the Attorney General: Improved Prison Work Programs Will Benefit Correctional Institutions and Inmates* (Washington, DC: Author, 1982), 2. Other commentators agreed. Noting that "less than 20 percent of the national prison population works," one expressed concern that most inmates just "sit around, becoming bored, restless and, sometimes, violent." He argued that the best way to keep the costs of incarceration low and the potential for rehabilitation high was to "give inmates a job." G. Mehler, "Prisoners Need Jobs, and We Can't Afford to Let Them Sit Idle," *Los Angeles Daily Journal*, July 23, 1984, p. 12. But there was little evidence that this advice was taken.

27. Michael King, "Male Rape in Institutional Settings," in *Male Victims of Sexual Assault*, ed. Gillian Mezey and Michael King (Oxford, England: Oxford University Press, 1992), 70.

28. P. Gunby, "Sexual Behavior in an Abnormal Situation," *Medical News* 245 (1981): 215.

29. See, e.g., H. Pontell and W. Welsh, "Incarceration as a Deviant Form of Social Control: Jail Overcrowding in California," *Crime & Delinquency* 40 (1994): 18.

30. Wayne Welsh, "The Dynamics of Jail Reform Litigation: A Comparative Analysis of Litigation in California Counties," *Law & Society Review* 26 (1992): 591, 604–605. *See, e.g.*, Paul Paulus and Garvin McCain, "Crowding in Jails," *Basic and Applied Social Psychology* 4 (1983): 89. In the era of overincarceration, jail crowding has become the norm. From 1984 to 2000 (the last year for which data were available), jails in the United States operated with inmate populations that were at 90% or above their overall rated capacity. Kathleen McGuire and Ann Pastore, *Sourcebook of Criminal Justice Statistics, 2000* [U.S. Department of Justice, Bureau of Justice Statistics] (Washington, DC: U.S. Government Printing Office, 2001), 501. Some facilities are much more crowded, and the problem does not appear to have subsided in recent years.

31. *See* John Wooldredge and L. Winfree, "An Aggregate-Level Study of Inmate Suicides and Deaths Due to Natural Causes in U.S. Jails," *Journal of Research in Crime & Delinquency* 29 (1992): 466. In addition, the same study found that natural deaths in jail can be reduced when overcrowding is alleviated and other humane standards of confinement are implemented.

32. S. Ekland-Olson, D. Barrick, and L. Cohen, "Prison Overcrowding and Disciplinary Problems: An Analysis of the Texas Prison System," *Journal of Applied Behavioral Science* 19 (1983): 163, 174; *See also* G. Gaes and W. McGuire, "Prison Violence: The Contribution of Crowding Versus Other Determinants of Prison Assault Rates," *Journal of Research in Crime and Delinquency* 22 (1985): 41.

33. P. Nacci, H. Teitelbaum, and J. Prather, "Population Density and Inmate Misconduct Rates in the Federal prison System," *Federal Probation* 41 (1977): 26, 29.

34. Here, too, there are "context effects" at work. Thus, Stephen Light found that the severity of inmate-on-officer assaults was a function of the age distribution of the prisoner population at the facility (and not the age of the prisoner who committed the assault per se). He concluded that the characteristics of the assaults he studied were "in large part determined by attributes of the prison environment rather than by prisoner characteristics. . . ." S. Light, "The Severity of Assaults on Prison Officers: A Contextual Study," *Social Science Quarterly* 71 (1990): 267, 281–282.

35. *See, e.g.*, S. Grassian, "Psychopathological Effects of Solitary Confinement," *American Journal of Psychiatry* 140 (1983): 1450; S. Grassian and N. Friedman, "Effects of Sensory Deprivation in Psychiatric Seclusion and Solitary Confinement," *International Journal of Law and Psychiatry* 8 (1986): 49; C. Haney, "Infamous Punishment: The Psychological Effects of Isolation," *National Prison Project Journal* 8 (1993): 3; C. Haney and M. Lynch, "Regulating Prisons of

the Future: A Psychological Analysis of Supermax and Solitary Confinement," *New York Review of Law & Social Change* 23 (1997): 477; and C. Haney, "Mental Health Issues in Long-Term Solitary and 'Supermax' Confinement," *Crime & Delinquency* 49 (2003): 124.

36. D. Farrington and C. Nuttall, "Prison Size, Overcrowding, Prison Violence, and Recidivism," *Journal of Criminal Justice* 8 (1980): 221, 230.

37. J. Bonta and L. Motiuk, "The Diversion of Incarcerated Offenders to Correctional Halfway Houses," *Journal of Research in Crime & Delinquency* 24 (1987): 302.

38. Ibid., 312.

39. Timothy Flanagan, "Correlates of Institutional Misconduct Among State Prisoners," *Criminology* 21 (1983): 29, 37.

40. Ibid., 161.

41. R. McCorkle, "Personal Precautions to Violence in Prison," *Criminal Justice and Behavior* 19 (1992): 160, 160–161.

42. There are other subtleties to the measurement of prison overcrowding effects that confound the basic input–output models often used in these studies. For one, not all prisoners adapt to even stable overcrowded conditions in the same ways. Yet, diverse reactions are not easily identified in aggregate data analyses. In addition to these individual differences in the ways prisoners react to overcrowding, there may be important situational differences within the separate institutions whose statistics are aggregated. That is, some kinds of prisons are better equipped to handle overcrowding than others, and some have staff members better trained to respond to the crises that overcrowded conditions provoke. Even variations in the so-called *microclimates* within the same prison (e.g., certain areas of a prison may be better able to absorb higher concentrations of prisoners than others) can complicate attempts to identify overall patterns or aggregate shifts in the frequency of measurable behaviors (e.g., disciplinary infractions) that may take place in response to overcrowding.

43. Ekland-Olson, "Crowding, Social Control, and Prison Violence: Evidence From the Post-*Ruiz* Years in Texas."

44. *See, e.g.,* Edwin Lemert, "Visions of Social Control: Probation Reconsidered," *Crime & Delinquency* 39 (1993): 447, and Jonathan Simon, *Poor Discipline: Parole and the Social Control of the Underclass, 1890–1990* (Chicago: University of Chicago Press, 1993). *See also* W. Kelly and S. Ekland-Olson, "The Response of the Criminal Justice System to Overcrowding: Recidivism Patterns Among 4 Successive Parolee Cohorts," *Law & Society Review* 25 (1991): 601.

45. Some commentators who de-emphasize the significance of prison overcrowding nonetheless are correct when they note that a particular rated capacity of any specific facility "may vary with a prison's physical configuration, staffing patterns, available services, and program design," and also that precise figures are "difficult to determine and easy to manipulate." Bleich, "The Politics of Prison Crowding," 1141 (footnotes omitted).

46. Bleich's contentions that no one really contests legal claims of prison overcrowding anyway and that courts regularly set unnecessarily low population limits

with which prison administrators are only too willing to comply bear no relationship to the prison conditions litigation with which I am familiar that occurred throughout the United States over the last several decades. *Cf.* Bleich, "The Politics of Prison Crowding."

47. L. Fry, "Continuities in the Determination of Prison Overcrowding Effects," *Journal of Criminal Justice* 16 (1988): 231, 239.

48. Ibid.

49. John Irwin, *The Warehouse Prison: Disposal of the New Dangerous Class* (Los Angles: Roxbury, 2005), 75.

50. Kathleen McGuire and Ann Pastore, *Sourcebook of Criminal Justice Statistics, 1996* [U.S. Department of Justice, Bureau of Justice Statistics] (Washington, DC: U.S. Government Printing Office, 1997), 561.

51. Ibid.

52. *See, e.g.*, Lee Bowker, *Prison Victimization* (New York: Elsevier, 1980); Daniel Lockwood, *Prison Sexual Violence* (New York: Elsevier, 1980); and A. I. Ibrahim, "Deviant Sexual Behavior in Men's Prisons," *Crime & Delinquency* 38 (1974): 20, for discussions of these issues.

53. D. Walcott, "Sexually Violent Predator Commitment Successfully Challenged on Basis of Conditions of Confinement and Treatment," *Journal of the American Academy of Psychiatry & the Law* 28 (2000): 244.

54. Juanita Diaz-Cotto, *Gender, Ethnicity, and the State: Latina and Latino Prison Politics* (Albany, NY: State University of New York Press, 1996), 114. In past times, the limited English proficiency of Latino prisoners was used in some prison systems as a basis to formally restrict their contact with the outside world. Thus, until 1970, in New York state prisons English was the only acceptable language for correspondence. For years thereafter, all outgoing mail had to be written in English.

55. Ibid. For an early and very brief acknowledgement that monolingual Spanish-speaking inmates may find incarceration "particularly stressful" and experience forms of psychological deterioration in prison as a result, *see* M. Bohn and G. Traub, "Alienation of Monolingual Hispanics in a Federal Correctional Institution," *Psychological Reports* 59 (1986): 560.

56. Diaz-Cotto, *Gender, Ethnicity, and the State*, 111.

57. M. M. Feeley and J. Simon, "The New Penology: Notes on the Emerging Strategy of Corrections and Its Implications," *Criminology* 30 (1992): 449.

58. As described in a federal lawsuit addressing conditions of confinement at the Marion Federal Penitentiary, "a 'black box' is a small box that fits over the chain connecting the two cuffs and that is designed to prevent an inmate from picking the lock on the handcuffs." Bruscino v. Carlson, 654 F. Supp. 609, 615, n. 4 (S.D. Ill, 1987). It is designed to immobilize a prisoner's wrists while he or she is handcuffed.

59. Here is how a federal judge summarized the use of lethal force inside California's Pelican Bay, a high-security supermax prison: "The firearms used at Pelican Bay are: (1) the Ruger Mini-14 .223 caliber rifle, (2) the Heckler & Koch Model 94 ('H & K 94') 9 millimeter carbine, using the Glaser Safety Slug, (3)

the Smith & Wesson . 38 caliber revolver, and (4) the Remington 12-gauge pump shotgun. Firearms were discharged 177 times in 129 incidents between the time the prison opened and September 9, 1993. Of the 177 shots fired, 23 were intended to be for effect (i.e., were fired with the intent to hit a person), 152 were intended to be warning shots, and 2 were accidental. 109 shots were fired outdoors and 68 indoors. Of the 152 warning shots, 13 caused or were alleged to have caused inmate injuries from ricochets or bullet fragments." Madrid v. Gomez, 889 F. Supp. 1146, 1179, n. 52 (1995).

60. C. Drew, "Behind Bars, an Iron Hand Drastically Lowers Violence," *New York Times*, 8 November 1999, A1–A27, p. A1.

61. Ibid., p. A27.

62. Ibid.

63. Ibid.

64. Abraham Kaplan is credited with enunciating this principle as the "law of the instrument"—when your only tool is a hammer, too many things look like nails. Abraham Kaplan, *The Conduct of Inquiry* (New York: Harper, 1964). *See* the discussion of this issue in Madrid v. Gomez, 889 F. Supp. 1146 (1995): "The Court is convinced that the instances of force being used excessively and for the purpose of causing harm are of sufficient scope, variety, and number to constitute a pattern. Plaintiffs have convincingly documented a staggering number of instances in which prison personnel applied unjustifiably high levels of force, both pursuant to, and in contravention of, official prison policies. Simply put, the evidence before the Court is proof of the most powerful, unambiguous kind that a pattern of excessive force has become an undeniable reality at Pelican Bay." *Id.* at 1181.

65. In addition to the articles cited at endnote 35, *see* M. Isikoff, "Hard Time: The Mission at Marion: Federal Prison Revives Debate on How to Handle Incorrigible Felons," *Washington Post*, May 28, 1991, p. A1, col. 1. *See also* R. Immarigeon, "The Marionization of American Prisons," *National Prison Project Journal* 7(4) (1992): 1; M. Isikoff, "Human Rights Group Faults Super Security Prisons," *Washington Post*, November 14, 1991, p. A36, col. 1; R. Perkinson, "Shackled Justice: Florence Federal Penitentiary and New Politics of Punishment," *Social Justice* 21 (1994): 117.

66. R. Slater, "Psychiatric Intervention in an Atmosphere of Terror," *American Journal of Forensic Psychiatry* 7 (1986): 5, 9.

67. *Cf.* M. Olivero and J. Roberts, "The United States Federal Penitentiary at Marion, Illinois: Alcatraz Revisited," *New England Journal of Criminal and Civil Confinement* 16 (1990): 21.

68. Madrid, 889 F. Supp., at 1229.

69. *Id.* at 1235. Indeed, the court's opinion acknowledged that "social science and clinical literature have consistently reported that when human beings are subjected to social isolation and reduced environmental stimulation, they may deteriorate mentally and in some cases develop psychiatric disturbances." *Id.* at 1230. The judge concluded that Pelican Bay inflicted treatment on prisoners that, in his words, "may well hover on the edge of what is humanly tolerable for those with normal resilience, particularly when endured for extended periods

of time." *Id.* at 1280. However, although the *Madrid* court also found that overall conditions in the supermax units were "harsher than necessary to accommodate the needs of the institution," for reasons I discuss in a later chapter, the judge concluded that he lacked any constitutional basis to close the prison or even to require significant modifications in many of its general conditions. *Id.* at 1263.

70. First articulated by sociologist Robert Merton, this concept has been extensively studied. *See, e.g.*, M. Harris, "Self-fulfilling Prophecies in the Clinical Context: Review and Implications for Clinical Practices," *Applied and Preventive Psychology* 3 (1994): 145; A. Kukla, "The Structure of Self-Fulfilling and Self-Negating Prophecies," *Theory & Psychology* 4 (1994): 5.

71. Labeling theory has deep intellectual roots in social psychology and sociology, extending from the early work of Charles Cooley and George Herbert Mead, to Edwin Lemert's more recent theorizing about the way deviant labels affect the persons to whom they are applied, to Howard Becker's analysis of how their use helps to produce social "outsiders." *See* Charles Cooley, *Human Nature and the Social Order* (New York: Scribners, 1902); George Herbert Mead, *Mind, Self, and Society: From the Standpoint of a Social Behaviorist* (Chicago: University of Chicago Press, 1934); Edwin Lemert, *Social Pathology* (New York: McGraw-Hill, 1951); and Howard Becker, *Outsiders: Studies in the Sociology of Deviance* (New York: Free Press, 1963). *See also* Francis Cullen and John Cullen, *Toward a Paradigm of Labeling Theory* (Lincoln, NE: University of Nebraska Press, 1978); and Edwin Schur, *Labeling Deviant Behavior: Its Sociological Implications* (New York: Harper & Row, 1971).

72. B. Strickland, "Surveillance and Trust," *Journal of Personality* 26 (1958): 200. Of course, there is much surveillance and little trust in many correctional facilities. Indeed, if we take one psychologist's operative definition of trust as a willingness to be vulnerable or to take interpersonal risks in relationships despite "uncertainty regarding the motives, intentions, and prospective actions of others on whom they depend," then it is clear that there is very little trust in most prison environments, and especially little in supermax facilities. R. Kramer, "Trust and Distrust in Organizations: Emerging Perspectives, Enduring Questions," *Annual Review of Psychology* 50 (1999): 569, 571.

73. Madrid, 889 F. Supp., at 1161.

74. Ibid., 1179–80.

75. H. Bidna, "Effects of Increased Security on Prison Violence," *Journal of Criminal Justice* 3 (1975): 33, 42. To be sure, conclusions reached on the basis of a single study of a single prison system must be interpreted with caution. Many of the same factors that make it difficult to isolate any simple relationship between overcrowding and prison disciplinary violations apply here as well. As in the case of overcrowding, confounding can occur when numerous variables over which researchers have no control often are part of the very dynamic that is under study. Thus, changes in violence levels in security housing or supermax units may have numerous influences that are difficult to specify or determine. Despite this qualification, there is no evidence that these severe and psychologically risky forms of extreme isolation achieve any of the long-term goals by

which their use has been justified. A recent study that has the advantage of looking at changes over time, during periods when extraneous variables could be taken into account, and in several systems rather than just one, challenged the notion that supermax prisons were uniformly effective in reducing violence. *See* C. Briggs, J. Sundt, and T. Castellano, "The Effect of Supermaximum Security Prisons on Aggregate Levels of Institutional Violence," *Criminology* 41 (2003): 1341.

76. Briggs et al., "The Effect of Supermaximum Security Prisons on Aggregate Levels of Institutional Violence," 1367.

77. *See, e.g.*, Inez Cardozo-Freeman, *The Joint: Language and Culture in a Maximum Security Prison* (Springfield, IL: Charles Thomas, 1984); T. Einat and H. Einat, "Inmate Argot as an Expression of Prison Subculture: The Israeli Case," *Prison Journal* 80 (2000): 309; Gilbert Encinas, *Prison Argot: A Sociolinguistic and Lexicographic Study* (Lanham, MD: University Press of America, 2001).

78. Pawel Moczydlowski, *The Hidden Life of Polish Prisons* (Bloomington, IN: University of Indiana Press, 1992).

79. Bessel van der Kolk, "The Role of the Group in the Origin and Resolution of the Trauma Response," in *Psychological Trauma*, ed. Bessel van der Kolk (Washington, DC: American Psychiatric Publishing, 1987), 155.

80. Kevin McDonald, "Marginal Youth, Personal Identity, and the Contemporary Gang: Reconstructing the Social World?" in *Gangs and Society: Alternative Perspectives*, ed. Louis Dontos, David Brotherton, and Luis Barrios (New York: Columbia University Press, 2003), 70.

81. Ibid., 66. McDonald sees these aspects as shifting in importance, arguing that, in the contemporary gang, a response to the "constant fragility of identity" has become the primary motive for membership. I see both the social and personal as still very much in operation in prison gangs especially.

82. Sociologist John Irwin and others have suggested that "in the absence of more effective social organization, the tip and clique (gang) networks established ties and bridged gaps between prisoners." John Irwin, *Prisons in Turmoil* (Boston: Little Brown, 1980), 60. However, as tensions and conflicts between prisoners increased, gangs "increasingly became organized for their own members' protection" (ibid., 74).

83. As one researcher described the motivation for and perceived advantages of gang membership for most prisoners, "the most pressing was protection from other inmates." Especially for someone arrested or incarcerated for the first time, "membership in an organization that applied blanket protection throughout the prison system was a blessing" that "bestowed status and prestige and allowed disputes with other members to be arbitrated peacefully." But gang membership also may offer psychological advantages when the members return to civilian life. That is, "Where many members' households were chaotic, the gang functioned as an alternative family that prescribed rules and justifications for behavior, thereby bringing order and structure into potentially unmanageable social and emotional situations." Ric Curtis, "The Negligible Role of Gangs in Drug Distribution in New York City in the 1990s," in Dontos, Brotherton, and Barrios, *Gangs and Society: Alternative Perspectives*, 50.

84. Craig Haney and Philip Zimbardo, "The Socialization into Criminality: On Becoming a Prisoner and a Guard," in *Law, Justice, and the Individual in Society: Psychological and Legal Issues*, ed. June Tapp and Felice Levine (New York: Holt, Rinehart & Winston, 1977), 217.

85. In some cases, prison systems have been implicated at several levels in the creation and proliferation of the prison gangs. For example, Robert Fong, a prison monitor who served in Texas during the implementation of court-ordered reforms in the early 1980s, noted that the most dominant gang in the Texas system "was originally formed for the purpose of self-protection against the 'building tenders'"—who, as I noted earlier, were prisoners who had been given supervisory responsibility over others by Texas prison authorities but whose brutality led a federal court to disband them. R. Fong, "The Organizational Structure of Prison Gangs: A Texas Case Study," *Federal Probation* 54 (1990, March): 36, 41. However, Fong argued that "as the building tender system faded away, it left behind a power vacuum" that the prison gang "wasted no time filling" (ibid). Of course, the gang's origins lay in the initial brutal treatment that had been created and condoned by the prison, and its increased success stemmed in part from the prison's inability to implement the court-ordered reforms quickly enough to fill the vacuum that had been created.

86. Phillip Kassel, "The Gang Crackdown in the Prisons of Massachusetts: Arbitrary and Harsh Treatment Can Only Make Matters Worse," in Dontos, Brotherton, and Barrios, *Gangs and Society: Alternative Perspectives*, 235.

87. National Institute of Corrections Information Center, *Management Strategies in Disturbances and with Gangs/Disruptive Groups* (Washington, DC: United States Department of Justice, 1991), 13.

88. Kassel, "The Gang Crackdown in the Prisons of Massachusetts," 235.

89. Bert Useem and Peter Kimball, *States of Siege: U.S. Prison Riots 1971–1986* (New York: Oxford, 1989).

90. *See, e.g.*, M. Colvin, "The 1980 New Mexico Prison Riot," *Social Problems* 29 (1982): 449; Mark Colvin, *The Penitentiary in Crisis: From Accommodation to Riot in New Mexico* (Albany, NY: State University of New York Press, 1992); Bert Useem, "Disorganization and the New Mexico Prison Riot of 1980," *American Sociological Review* 50 (1985): 677.

91. Colvin, "The 1980 New Mexico Prison Riot," 457.

92. Useem, "Disorganization and the New Mexico Prison Riot of 1980," 685.

93. Leslie Wilkins, "A Small Comparative Study of the Results of Probation," *British Journal of Delinquency* 8 (1958): 201, 207. *See also* United States General Accounting Office, *Intermediate Sanctions: Their Impacts on Prison Crowding, Costs, and Recidivism Are Still Unclear* (Washington, DC: Government Printing Office, 1990).

94. Gideon v. Wainwright, 83 S. Ct. 792 (1963).

95. For details of this study, *see* Charles Eichman, *The Impact of the Gideon Decision Upon Crime and Sentencing in Florida: A Study of Recidivism and Socio-Cultural Change*, Monograph No. 2. (Tallahassee: Florida Division of Corrections, 1966).

96. Ronald Beattie and Charles Bridges, *Superior Court Probation and/or Jail Sample* (Sacramento, CA: Bureau of Criminal Statistics, Department of Justice, 1970).

97. A. Hopkins, "Imprisonment and Recidivism: A Quasi-Experimental Study," *Journal of Research in Crime and Delinquency* (1976): 13, 27. See also L. Goodstein, "Inmate Adjustment to Prison and the Transition to Community Life," *Journal of Research on Crime and Delinquency* 10 (1980): 246.

98. Joan Petersilia, Susan Turner, and Joyce Peterson, *Prison Versus Probation in California: Implications for Crime and Offender Recidivism* (Santa Monica, CA: RAND Corporation, 1986),

99. T. Orsagh and J.-R. Chen, "The Effect of Time Served on Recidivism: An Interdisciplinary Theory," *Journal of Quantitative Criminology* 4 (1988): 155, 164 (emphasis added).

100. Ibid., 167. A more recent, comprehensive review of the relationship between the lengths of prison sentences and rates of recidivism indicated that longer prison sentences actually resulted in slightly higher rates of reoffending. See Paul Gendreau, Claire Goggin, and Francis Cullen, *The Effects of Prison Sentences on Recidivism. A Report to the Corrections Research and Development and Aboriginal Policy Brand.* (Ottawa: Solicitor General of Canada, 1999).

101. Patrick Langan and David Levin, *Recidivism of Prisoners Released in 1994* [Bureau of Justice Statistics Special Report NCJ 193427] (Washington, DC: U.S. Department of Justice, June 2002).

102. Alison Liebling, Linda Durie, Annick van den Beukel, Sarah Tait, and Joel Harvey, "Revisiting Prison Suicide: The Role of Fairness and Distress," in Alison Liebling and Shadd Maruna (Eds.), *The Effects of Imprisonment* (Cullompton, UK: Willan Publishing, 2005), 209, 216. Consistent with Liebling and her colleagues, other researchers have found that context-related factors help to account for emotional distress and even suicide in prison settings. For example, although Cooper and Berwick reported that there were individual factors and background characteristics that helped to predict suicide in different groups of incarcerated male prisoners, institutional factors—the severity of environmental stresses—also played a significant role in creating higher levels of anxiety, depression, and suicidality. C. Cooper and S. Berwick, "Factors Affecting Psychological Well-Being of Three Groups of Suicide Prone Prisoners," *Current Psychology* 20 (2001): 169.

103. As similar kind of predictability was reported by Claudia Kesterman in her analysis of the correlates of depressive symptoms among male prisoners in the correctional systems of several Baltic countries. Thus, poor relations with staff and other prisoners (i.e., perceived rejection), the presence of environmental stress factors, the experience of victimization, the lack of respect by staff, and the absence of home and/or work release at the facility were all significant predictors of whether prisoners manifested depression. Claudia Kesterman, "Prison Life: Factors Affecting Health and Rehabilitation." Paper presented at the European Conference on Psychology and Law, Vilnius, Lithuania, July, 2005. Building on the basic notion that unhealthy prisons can have unhealthy psychological effects on prisoners, Kesterman, Frieder Dunkel, and the others

involved in this project have concluded that there are a variety of specific conditions of confinement associated with certain adverse emotional reactions.

104. *See, e.g.*, C. Hemmens and J. Marquart, "Straight Time: Inmate's Perceptions of Violence and Victimization in the Prison Environment," *Journal of Offender Rehabilitation* 28 (1999): 1.

105. A. Hochstetler, D. Murphy, and R. Simons, "Damaged Goods: Exploring Predictors of Distress in Prison Inmates," *Crime & Delinquency* 50 (2004): 436. The researchers defined victimization broadly to include "theft, con games and scams, robbery, destruction of property, assault, and serious threats of bodily injury" (ibid., 444).

106. Ibid., 448. Guthrie also found a high prevalence of posttraumatic stress—30%—in the sample of federal prisoners he evaluated. He concluded that it was attributable in part to their prior histories of preprison trauma and in part to the prison experiences to which they were subjected. Robert Guthrie, *The Prevalence of Posttraumatic Stress Disorder Among Federal Prison Inmates*, Unpublished doctoral dissertation, West Virginia University, Morgantown, West Virginia (1998).

107. Adrian Grounds, "Understanding the Effects of Wrongful Imprisonment," in *Crime and Justice: A Review of Research*, Vol. 32, ed. Michael Tonry (Chicago: University of Chicago Press, 2005), 1, 15. Grounds found "evidence of personality change and adjustment difficulties in this group similar to those described in clinical studies of others who have experienced chronic psychological trauma," including "marked features of estrangement, loss of capacity for intimacy, moodiness, inability to settle, loss of a sense of purpose and direction, and a pervasive attitude of mistrust toward the world." He also identified many who were "withdrawn [and] unable to relate to the world," who manifested the diagnostic criteria for posttraumatic stress disorder, who suffered depressive disorders, and who encountered a whole range of serious problems with family contact, social adjustment, and employment. (ibid., 21–41)

108. Joan Petersilia, *When Prisoners Come Home: Parole and Prisoner Reentry* (New York: Oxford, 2003), 53. From a somewhat different perspective, John Irwin summarized the state of mind of many long-term prisoners preparing to leave a medium-security California prison: "For long-termers, the new situation of doing time, enduring years of suspension, being deprived of material conditions, living in crowded conditions without privacy, with reduced options, arbitrary control, disrespect, and economic exploitation is excruciatingly frustrating and aggravating. Anger, frustration, and a burning sense of injustice, coupled with the crippling processing inherent in imprisonment, significantly reduce the likelihood [that prisoners can] pursue a viable, relatively conventional, non-criminal life after release." John Irwin, *The Warehouse Prison*, 168.

109. Paula Smith, Claire Goggin, and Paul Gendreau, *The Effects of Prison Sentences and Intermediate Sanctions on Recidivism: General Effects and Individual Differences*, Unpublished Manuscript, Department of Psychology, University of New Brunswick (2004), 20. Other research suggests that, in addition to the length of imprisonment, the harshness of the conditions of confinement has an

adverse impact on the amount and nature of recidivism. Specifically, Chen and Shapiro found that "harsher prison conditions induce not only increased but systematically worse crimes." Keith Chen and Jesse Shapiro, "Does Prison Harden Inmates? A Discontinuity-based Approach," Unpublished manuscript, Yale University (2002), 1, 12. It may be that the negative effects of harsher forms of imprisonment result in part from the greater difficulties that prisoners in these facilities encounter in maintaining family ties and establishing connections to employers before they are released. That is, more punitive prisons may not only "harden" the persons confined in them but also harden the nature of the social world to which they return.

Indeed, the negative consequences that imprisonment has on recidivism are likely produced by a number of factors, only some of which are psychological in nature. For example, in addition to the direct negative effects of imprisonment on prisoners themselves, there is much evidence that prison adversely affects subsequent employment opportunities. Thus, not surprisingly, ex-convicts have higher rates of unemployment and earn lower wages when they do find jobs. For a review, see B. Western, J. Kling, and D. Weiman, "The Labor Market Consequences of Incarceration," *Crime and Delinquency* 47 (2001): 410. The long periods of time that prisoners are removed from the job market (during which time most obtain few, if any, marketable skills) and the stigma that employers attach to their having done prison time contribute to these employment effects. In fact, Pettit and Western characterized imprisonment as "an illegitimate timeout that confers enduring stigma." As they point out, this stigma deters many employers from offering even low-wage jobs. Moreover, a prison record also can create formal legal barriers for certain skilled and licensed occupations. B. Pettit and B. Western, "Mass Imprisonment and the Life Course: Race and Class Inequality in U.S. Incarceration," *American Sociological Review* 69 (2004): 151, 155.

110. Don Andrews, "The Psychology of Criminal Conduct and Effective Treatment," in *What Works: Reducing Reoffending*, ed. James McGuire (New York: John Wiley, 1995), 48.

111. See A. Liebling, "Suicide and the Safer Prisons Agenda," *Probation Journal* 49 (2002): 140; Alison Liebling, *Prisons and Their Moral Performance: A Study of Values, Quality and Prison Life* (Oxford, England: Clarendon Press, 2004); and Liebling et al., "Revisiting Prison Suicide: The Role of Fairness and Distress." Similarly, Gendreau and his colleagues concluded that, because serious disruptions in prison are often caused by "situational elements" inside the prison, prevention and control of these kinds of behaviors are possible through the monitoring and improvement of certain aspects of the "institutional climate." Further, they argued that in-prison behavior and postprison success can be improved through prison programming, especially programming that is "appropriate" to the prisoners in question—that is, directed to their particular needs. For summaries of, and citations to, the research that supports these propositions, see P. Gendreau and D. Keyes, "Making Prisons Safer and More Humane Environments," *Canadian Journal of Criminology* 43 (2001):

123. It is interesting to note that Gendreau had authored several widely cited literature reviews that—at the height of the movement toward more and harsher forms of imprisonment—seemed to defend these policies and, at least, provided support the prison status quo, including the use of solitary confinement. (I discussed one of these reviews at some length in chapter 5.) More recently, however, Gendreau expressed dismay that "[s]adly, there are repeated calls to make prison living conditions even tougher," and termed the current "growth industry [in] the use of various prison segregation environments" that came about over the last decade and a half "appalling." ibid., 124.

112. G. K. Chesterton, quoted in Jerome Frank and Barbara Frank, *Not Guilty* (London: Gollancz, 1957), 248–249.

113. *See* Harry Helson, *Adaptation-Level Theory: An Experimental and Systematic Approach to Behavior* (New York: Harper & Row, 1964).

114. Published accounts of the severity of life inside contemporary American prisons come from a variety of journalistic, autobiographical, and social scientific sources. *See, e.g.,* Sasha Abramsky, *Hard Times Blues: How Politics Build a Prison Nation* (New York: St. Martin's Press, 2002); Joel Dyer, *The Perpetual Prisoner Machine* (Boulder, CO: Westview Press, 2000); Alan Elsner, *Gates of Injustice: The Crisis in America's Prisons* (New York: Prentice Hall, 2004); Joseph Hallinan, *Going Up the River: Travels in a Prison Nation* (New York: Random House, 2001); Victor Hassine, *Life Without Parole: Living in Prison Today*, 3d ed. (Los Angeles: Roxbury Publishers, 2004); John Irwin, *The Warhouse Prison*; Paula Johnson, *Inner Lives: Voices of African American Women in Prison* (New York: New York University Press, 2003); Candace Kruttschnitt and Rosemary Gartner, *Marking Time in the Golden State: Women's Imprisonment in California* (Cambridge, UK: Cambridge University Press, 2005); and Christian Parenti, *Lockdown America: Police and Prisons in the Age of Crisis* (New York: Verso, 1999).

115. Garland, "Punishment and Culture," 203.

8

"SPECIAL NEEDS" PRISONERS
IN EXTREMIS

Prisons are filled with people in need of care and cure. Bad nerves, bad bodies, bad education—prisons are storing houses for deprived persons who stand in need of treatment and educational resources . . . .
—Nils Christie[1]

To run prisons humanely means to generate a climate of trust . . . [in which there is a] demonstrated concern for the reduction of inmate suffering, in the shape of provisions for prisoners whose survival may be at risk . . . .
—Hans Toch[2]

All prisoners are in some sense vulnerable to the harsh and sometimes cruel nature of the prison environment. But some are more vulnerable than others. A disproportionate number of them—namely, persons with mental illness and developmental disabilities—are incarcerated in the United States, and this fact raises special concerns.[3] Because the nature and magnitude of the added problems faced by "special needs" prisoners have too often been de-emphasized or ignored by criminal justice decision makers and prison authorities during the era of overincarceration, many of them have experienced prison as an especially painful, intolerant, and even intolerable place.

The overrepresentation of persons with mental disorders and developmental disabilities in the nation's prisons stems from a variety of social forces that are at work in the society at large. It has not come about because of any innate biological connection between mental illness or retardation and criminality, as was often asserted in past times. In fact, one important reason why there are high numbers of persons with mental illness in prison is that the same social forces and risk factors that are related to adult criminality—especially exposure to various forms of childhood trauma and mistreatment—also predispose people to subsequent emotional problems and mental illness later in life.[4]

In addition, a number of societal-level phenomena—including harsher life experiences, special social and economic challenges in the workplace and other settings, and differential treatment at the hands of the criminal justice system—help to account for the greater number of persons with mental disorders or developmental disabilities in prison. All of these factors may combine to make these individuals more likely to come to the attention of the criminal justice system and—once they have been taken into custody—often, to be treated more harshly than others.[5] This chapter examines only one aspect of the process by which these things occur: the nature and consequences of their special status in prison.

Ironically, the tradition of psychological individualism that has long dominated criminal justice thinking for so many years has never produced much corresponding sensitivity to individual differences in prison. Despite the rhetoric that emerged in the early years of the 20th century and that surrounded the individualization of punishment and the stated desire to make the punishment fit the offender rather than the offense, historically, most prisons have typically treated most prisoners as though they were more or less the same. That is, once the legal system established that persons were responsible enough to be punished, prison administrators tended to view them as psychologically fungible. That is, all prisoners at the same classification level are presumed to be equally able to withstand whatever treatment and conditions they are exposed to. In fairness, this approach has often been resource driven; even in the heyday of individualized sentencing, few prisons had the flexibility to precisely calibrate conditions of confinement and rehabilitative programming to the unique needs of prisoners.

Especially in recent years, as the criminal justice system gave up any pretense of tailoring prison treatment to the uniqueness of individual offenders, the vulnerabilities or special needs of prisoners became an even less pressing concern. Although certain special-needs prisoners do have a separate legal status with which to request protection from especially harsh conditions of confinement,[6] the prison systems in which they are housed often have been unwilling or unable to honor their claims. As prison law expert Fred Cohen has observed, "inmates who look to litigation to further their desire or need for various forms of help must somehow fit themselves into a variety of 'special needs' groups."[7] Yet, as I will suggest in this chapter, and as Cohen's own analysis shows, the fate of special-needs prisoners is still somewhat uncertain and unpredictable, dependent on the particular facility in which they are housed and the particular time they are placed there. However, the increased importance attached to the context of imprisonment should make prison administrators more aware of the way in which prisoners with special needs and vulnerabilities are adversely affected by their treatment and the conditions under which they are kept.

THE LEGAL STATUS OF "SPECIAL NEEDS" PRISONERS

Historically, the status of special-needs prisoners has undergone several significant transformations. In the early years of imprisonment in the United States, persons with mental illness or developmental disabilities were thought to constitute a very large percentage of the prison population. This was because of the widespread but erroneous belief that mental disorders, including mental retardation (or what was then indelicately referred to as *idiocy* or *feeblemindedness*) were among the most important causes of criminality. In fact, broadly defined mental deficiencies were once thought to be equivalent to "moral defects" that predisposed persons to criminal behavior.

Similarly, the term *moral insanity* was commonly used in 19th-century American society to describe the psychological affliction from which most (if not all) criminals were thought to suffer. Indeed, by the end of the 19th century, criminality was often equated with moral insanity.[8] In many sectors of American society, prisoners were viewed as mentally and morally sick or defective and, therefore, much in need of special treatment or therapy of some sort. For the most part, this treatment equated with the rehabilitative purpose of prison.[9]

By the 1920s, many writers still asserted what they called "the obvious facts in the matter"—that is, that a great many "offenders are mentally deficient in gross and palpable ways, that still more are of low intellectual power and that the great majority of convicts are from the stupid, unlettered and debased ranks. . . . Practically all inmates of prisons and all real criminals are either deficient or defective. . . ."[10] Indeed, well into the early 20th century, feeblemindedness was widely thought to be a major, if not the primary, cause of crime. One researcher reported that there were some 300 studies of the relationship between feeblemindedness and criminality published in the United States between 1910 and 1950.[11]

As I noted in chapter 2, in the early decades of the 20th century, prisons assumed primary responsibility for reducing crime by attempting to provide cures for the "affliction" of criminality.[12] The Progressive Era in the United States heralded the *age of rehabilitation*, in which prisons and other correctional institutions committed themselves—perhaps more in spirit than in fact—to addressing the range of psychological and other maladies from which prisoners were alleged to suffer.[13] Unfortunately, there was no professional consensus on which particular treatments were most useful in curing these ills. Certainly, the early 19th-century prison systems had lacked the means and expertise with which to provide truly effective remedies. And, even after some meaningful treatments and rehabilitative programs emerged during the 20th century, prisons still had no official mandate to treat prisoners with mental illness. Inmates continued to be very much at the mercy of correctional institutions to provide therapy, or not, whenever they chose. Meager therapeutic resources meant that effective treatment was sporadic at best.

Thus, as a practical matter, vulnerable prisoners had neither the power nor the skill to demand special treatment. Along with prisoners in general, they lacked the legal status to insist that prisons safeguard their physical and mental well-being. Until relatively recently, they could not make any legally cognizable claims to obtain prison services—no matter how badly needed—and they were without legal protections against potentially harmful or overly intrusive interventions performed in the name of treatment. Although the legal and constitutional rights of prisoners evolved and expanded over the last quarter of the 20th century, there was a puzzling irony associated with this development. That is, as the legal rights of prisoners were being expanded, the purpose of imprisonment was shifting abruptly from rehabilitation to punishment.[14] Eventually, the latter trend would put a stop to the former.

As I have noted in previous chapters, the progressive legal and political climates of the 1960s and early 1970s were replaced by a punitive atmosphere in which criminal offenders were targeted for especially harsh treatment. In part as a result, therapy, counseling, and other care-oriented prison programs were criticized as "coddling" dangerous and recalcitrant "offenders." The fundamental realignment of the U.S. Supreme Court that took place in the 1970s and 1980s helped to buttress these "get tough" views. Enthusiasm for upholding the rights of criminal defendants and prisoners correspondingly waned.[15] Like all inmates, vulnerable prisoners could still claim legal protection from the Constitution's ban on cruel and unusual punishment. Yet, those protections continued to be narrowly drawn and, by the late 1980s and 1990s—in part in response to U.S. Supreme Court decisions and in part because of federal legislation—were less effectively enforced by many courts.

RECENT TRENDS IN INCARCERATING VULNERABLE PERSONS

Most analysts agree that the recent increases in the numbers of vulnerable inmates in the nation's prisons can be explained by the decreased availability of therapeutic, social, and habilitative services for persons with mental illness or developmental disabilities in society at large. Because persons with special psychological needs now are less likely to be adequately protected by social welfare agencies and other institutions, or to be buffered from the social and economic hardships to which their disabilities make them vulnerable, their numbers in the criminal justice system have grown. Thus, the criminal justice system has filled the void left by drastic reductions in public mental health programs. Similarly, fewer programs for the accommodation and habilitation of persons with developmental disabilities has meant that they are less well cared for in the communities in which they live. Criminal justice system intervention has become the preferred response.

Among other things, a trend toward deinstitutionalization in general resulted in larger numbers of vulnerable persons living on the streets, residing in homeless shelters, or otherwise unsupported and unsupervised.[16] Commentators began to make the connection between the "major urban crisis" of homelessness and the lack of treatment services for those who were previously hospitalized with mental illness: "The streets, the train and bus stations, and the shelters of the city have become the state hospitals of yesterday."[17]

As one measure of the impact of deinstitutionalization on this group, for example, a 1994 study reported that the population of persons with mental retardation living in specialized institutions ostensibly designed to address their needs was only one third of its 1967 total. Specifically, there were 194,650 persons with developmental disabilities living in such institutions in the United States in 1967, compared with only 65,735 in 1994.[18]

In addition, many state governments have transferred the responsibility for the care of special-needs citizens to local counties and municipalities, which—because states simultaneously have reduced the funds provided to assist with such services—cannot adequately address them. Increasingly, persons with mental illness or developmental disabilities who would have been placed in treatment-oriented institutional settings outside the criminal justice system now are arrested and incarcerated instead. A self-fulfilling budgetary prophecy has resulted: Allocations for statewide prison systems have continued to rise to meet these increased demands, and fewer resources remain for community-based programs. This shift in resources and services— simply put, from communities to prisons—has meant that large numbers of persons with mental illness or developmental disabilties were diverted out of local service agencies that lacked the funding to respond to them and funneled instead into state correctional facilities that at least had the capacity to house them (despite often lacking the wherewithal to actually treat them).

Joan Petersilia and others have examined the ways that these social trends and political decisions have combined to produce "an increase in the prevalence of [persons with mental retardation] and other low-income persons within the California justice system."[19] The same kinds of increases have occurred in a number of states, and for prisoners with mental illness. As one commentator summarized the impact of these trends in a large Midwestern state,

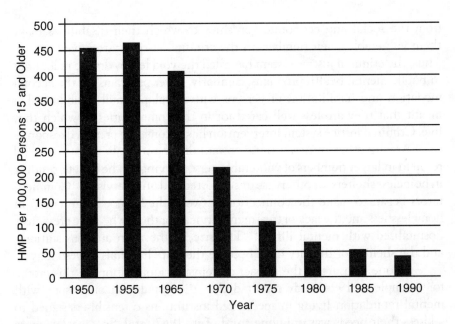

Figure 8.1. Decline in the number of hospitalized mental patients over time. HMP = hospitalized mental patients. From "Deinstitutionalization: An Appraisal of Reform," by D. Mechanic and D. Rochefort, 1990, *Annual Review of Sociology, 16,* p. 301. Copyright 1990 by Annual Reviews. Adapted with permission of publisher and D. Mechanic.

In Michigan, it is estimated that the number of prisoners who were former patients in state mental hospitals increased by 23 percent over the last four years. At one time the state of Michigan estimated that at least 30.7 percent of its prison population needed psychiatric intervention. Today, there are 952 mental health beds set aside for prisoners in the state system out of a total population of 43,712.[20]

Figure 8.1 illustrates the overall reduction in the number of beds available in state mental hospitals over the same period of time that—as I discussed at length in chapter 3—the nation's prison system was rapidly expanding. Of course, I do not mean to suggest that all or even most of the formerly hospitalized mental patients were absorbed directly into the criminal justice system. Among other things, the advent of psychotropic medications at the start of this period meant that many mental patients could be treated or managed in noninstitutional settings. But many of those persons whose problems were not handled effectively in this way likely made their way into prison.

Increases in the number of vulnerable prisoners were hastened by another development during this same period. New sentencing laws enacted to reduce the amount of discretion that judicial authorities could exercise in deciding on the fairness of the punishment they meted out has meant that judges have fewer options to take the special needs and vulnerabilities of offenders into account in the sentencing process. This has increased the chances that defendants with mental illness or developmental disabilities— who, in past times, might have been diverted out of the criminal justice system or sentenced more leniently because of their vulnerabilities—will be treated like all other convicted persons. That is, they are likely to be sentenced to the same terms of imprisonment, in the same facilities, and live under the same harsh conditions of confinement as other prisoners.[21] And, because the individual characteristics of criminal defendants now have less relevance to most of the legal decisions that pertain to them, less time is spent on pretrial evaluation and presentence reports in which potential special needs and vulnerabilities are assessed. Of course, if mental illness and developmental disability are overlooked, ignored, or minimized in these early stages of criminal justice processing, some form of proactive correctional screening and monitoring would be necessary to ensure that they do not go undetected and untreated in prison.

In addition, persons who have mental illness or developmental disabilities may be particularly disadvantaged once they do enter the criminal justice system, and their ability to get a fair trial or to assist in their own defense especially compromised. For example, research suggests that persons with developmental disabilities are more susceptible to social influence and more likely to acquiesce generally in social interaction, especially in encounters with perceived authority figures.[22] This susceptibility may translate into a greater willingness to confess in the course of police interrogation and to plead guilty once charges have been filed.[23] At the same time, the unexplained and unpredictable behavior of defendants with mental illness or developmental disabilities may lead decision makers to mistakenly perceive them as more dangerous than others. Thus, they may be less likely to be released from jail pending trial and more likely to be convicted by judges or juries who fear them or do not understand their unusual behavior.

Moreover, because of special difficulties they may have in adjusting to prison life, prisoners with mental illness or developmental disabilities may be more likely to be kept in custody (i.e., less likely to be released early on probation or parole). Similarly, because they may be less able to negotiate access to limited programming opportunities and more likely to experience adjustment-related problems, they may serve longer average sentences than others. Finally, in the punishment-oriented regimes that now dominate the criminal justice system, prisoners whose preexisting disorders are exacerbated by severe conditions of confinement and those who develop new prison-related symptoms and maladies are less likely to have their problems acknowledged and effectively addressed.

PREVALENCE ESTIMATES OF ESPECIALLY
VULNERABLE PRISONERS

Mental illness and developmental disability represent the two largest categories of vulnerabilities from which prisoners suffer. For example, in a 1996 national survey of prison inmates with disabilities, less than 1% of the prison population had visual, mobility, speech, or hearing deficits, 4.2% had a developmental disability, 7.2% had psychosis, and another 12% reported "other psychological disorders."[24] In part because prisoners with mental illness and developmental disabilities have received little careful, systematic attention from prison authorities over the last several decades, their true numbers in the prison population can only be estimated. Those estimates vary from study to study and state to state and are discussed in detail in this section of the chapter.[25]

Mental Illness Among Prisoners

Remarkably, many prison systems have never attempted to systematically determine exactly how many of their inmates have mental illness. Some systems use rough estimates obtained from mental health staff, but these estimates are necessarily limited to cases of which the staff is personally aware. Significant underestimates can occur—especially in poorly staffed facilities—which, in turn, may ensure that mental health services and programs will continue to be underfunded and prisoners underserved. California's experience over the last several decades illustrates the pitfalls of this approach. In the late 1980s, the state legislature funded a sophisticated and comprehensive study of the prevalence of mental illness in the state prison system. Its results were surprising and unsettling. By conducting a series of face-to-face diagnostic interviews with a carefully selected, representative sample of prisoners, the study determined that approximately 7.9% of all of the prisoners incarcerated in California had one of the four "severe mental disorders" (i.e., severe organic brain disorder, schizophrenia, major depressive disorder, and bipolar disorder) and had experienced current symptomatology within a month of being interviewed. Another 17% had less severe, but still serious, mental disorders.

However, the study also found that nearly 7% of the entire prisoner population had current symptoms and severe mental disorders that nonetheless were *undetected* by the prison authorities. In the large California prison system, this translated into more than 4,000 prisoners at the time of the study who were currently experiencing severe mental disorders but whose problems had not been identified by prison authorities.[26] Of course, prisoners with mental illness who were not classified as needing treatment were not likely to get any, especially in a system that—like many during this period—

de-emphasized treatment and therapy. In fact, in 1992, when the study was released, the outpatient clinical staff in the California prison system was less than 20% of what widely accepted professional guidelines indicated it should have been, given the actual prevalence of mental illness among the prisoners. Seven of the state's prisons, most of them large facilities with several thousand prisoners each, did not have a single psychiatrist on staff, 6 prisons had no mental health professionals of any kind, and 10 had less than one full-time mental health clinician (i.e., they had only part-time help).[27]

Thus, treatment resources and staffing levels were woefully inadequate in comparison to the actual magnitude of the need. As a result, many vulnerable prisoners had painful and potentially disabling psychiatric conditions that were overlooked or disregarded. Treatment resources were stretched so thin that even prisoners who were classified by the prison system as having serious mental disorders were being ignored. In fact, fully 64% of the previously diagnosed prisoners also reported that they had not received professional mental health services at any time during their present incarceration.

Other direct studies of the number of prisoners with mental illness in different jurisdictions in the United States have produced varying, but equally unsettling, estimates. Consistent with the notion that over time the prison system has become the default placement for persons with mental illness, studies suggest that as resources have been shifted away from the public mental health system, the prevalence rates for major psychiatric disorders in prison are not only high but appear to be increasing.[28] Whether the numbers of prisoners with mental illness are increasing or not, Table 8.1 suggests that there are a great many of them.

For example, Linda Teplin's review of some 18 studies of mental disorder among samples of jail inmates found rates of psychosis ranging from 5% to 16%.[29] Henry Steadman and his colleagues focused on mental illness among prison (as opposed to jail) inmates. They found that about 8% of New York prisoners had "severe" mental disabilities and another 16% had "significant" mental disabilities.[30] As Cohen and Dvoskin summarized, "The current reality . . . is that prisons have a large relatively predictable number of inmates with severe mental illnesses."[31] Although that number varies somewhat by jurisdiction and the methodology that is used to estimate it, somewhere between 10% and 25% of prisoners have some form of serious mental illness.

Even though the magnitude of the problem now has been well documented, the provision of adequate mental health services remains a low priority in many prison systems. For example, even after the elaborate California prevalence study that I described earlier was completed, prisoner mental health services did not improve until a successful statewide class

TABLE 8.1
Prevalence Estimates of Prisoners With Mental Illness

Study/review	Location	Database	Prevalence
Chiles, Von Cleve, Jemelka, and Trupin (1990)	Washington	109 prisoners	5% schizophrenic, 18% mood disorder, including depression
Herman, McGorry, Mills, and Singh (1991)	Australia	89 male and female prisoners	18% psychosis or mood disorder, including depression
Jordan, Schlenger, Fairbank, Fairbank, and Caddell (1996)	North Carolina	805 female prisoners	10.8% major depression, generalized anxiety, and/or panic disorder
Motiuk and Porporino (1991)	Canada	2,812 prisoners	3% psychosis, 8% depression, 18% generalized anxiety
Neighbors, Williams, Gunnings, Lipscomb, Broman, and Lepowski (1987)	Michigan	1,070 prisoners	9% psychosis, 33% mood disorder, including depression, 1% general anxiety
Norman and Cotton et al. (1989)	California	413 prisoners	27.5% current psychiatric symptomatology
Powell, Holt, and Fondacaro (1997)	a "rural Northeastern state"	118 prisoners	12.7% schizophrenic or schizoaffective, 25.5% mood disorder, including depression, 5.1% generalized anxiety, 27.1% posttraumatic stress
Steadman, Fabisiak, Dvoskin, and Holohean (1987)	New York	3332 prisoners	8% "very substantial," 16% "significant," psychiatric and functional disabilities
Veneziano and Veneziano (1996)	National	Unspecified	7.2% psychotic disorders, 12% "other psychological disorders"
Walters, Mann, Miller, Hemphill, and Chlumsky (1988)	Unspecified	51 prisoners	5% schizophrenic, Hemphill, and 7% affective disorders

Note. Chiles, J., Von Cleve, E., Jemelka, R., & Trupin, E. (1990). Substance abuse and psychiatric disorder in prison inmates. *Hospital and Community Psychiatry, 41,* 1132; Herman, H., McGorry, P., Mills, J., & Singh, B. (1991). Hidden severe psychiatric morbidity in sentenced prisoners: An Australian study. *American Journal of Psychiatry, 148,* 236; Jordan, B., Schlenger, W., Fairbank, J., & Caddell, J. (1996). Prevalence of psychiatric disorders among incarcerated women. *Archives of General Psychiatry, 53,* 513; Motiuk, L., & Porporino, F. (1991). *The prevalence, nature and severity of mental health problems among federal male inmates in Canadian penitentiaries.* Ottawa: Correctional Services of Canada; Neighbors, H., Williams, D., Gunnings, T., Lipscomb, W., Broman, C., & Lepowski, J. (1987). *The prevalence of mental disorder in Michigan prisons: Final report submitted to the Michigan Department of Corrections.* Lansing: Michigan Department of Corrections; Norman & Cotton, & Associates. (1989). *Current description, evaluation, and recommendations for treatment of mentally disordered criminal offenders: Vol. 1: Introduction and prevalence.* Sacramento: California Department of Corrections, Office of Health Care Services; Powell, T., Holt, J., & Fondacaro, K. (1997). The prevalence of mental illness among inmates in a rural state. *Law and Human Behavior, 21,* 427; Steadman, H., Fabisiak, S., Dvoskin, J., & Holohean, E. (1987). A survey of mental disability among state prison inmates. *Hospital and Community Psychiatry, 38,* 1086; Veneziano, L., & Veneziano, C. (1996). Disabled inmates. In M. McShane & F. Williams (Eds.), *Encyclopedia of American Prisons* (p. 157). New York: Garland; Walters, G., Mann, M., Miller, M., Hemphill, L., & Chlumsky, M. (1988). Emotional disorder among offenders: Inter- and intrasetting comparisons. *Criminal Justice and Behavior, 15,* 433.

action lawsuit forced the necessary changes to be made. A federal judge determined that the large number of prisoners with mental illness in the system were not receiving constitutionally adequate mental health services, and he ordered massive improvements.[32] Nonetheless, the Department of Corrections balked at providing the enhanced mental health services that the court had ordered.

Prison administrators in California continued to give the mental health needs of prisoners a far lower priority than basic custodial concerns. Thus, despite having a study that documented the large numbers of prisoners with mental illness whose needs were not being met, and a federal court order that required officials to give this problem their highest priority, department officials still designated all correctional officer positions as *essential* and labeled mental health positions as *nonessential*. This meant that whenever the number of prisoners assigned to an institution went up—something that occurred continuously in California throughout this period—the required allocation of mandated correctional officers, correctional supervisors, and support staff increased automatically. However, no such upward adjustments were mandated for medical and mental health staff. The problem of chronic understaffing and underfunding in these areas persisted until a series of contentious encounters between court-appointed experts and monitors eventually resulted in significant improvements.[33]

However, California officials were not alone in the low priority that they attached to addressing the needs of prisoners with mental illness. According to a U.S. Department of Justice study published in 2001 that surveyed over 1500 state public and private adult correctional facilities, nearly one quarter of prisons in the United States do not, as a matter of policy, even screen inmates at intake to determine their mental health needs; nearly 1 in 5 fails to conduct any psychiatric assessments of prisoners; nearly 1 prison in 6 fails to provide inmates with any therapy or counseling by trained mental health personnel; more than one third have no around-the-clock mental health care available for prisoners who may experience acute psychiatric crises; and more than one quarter of all prisons fail to assist inmates in obtaining community mental health services upon their release.[34] Because the study relied entirely on the estimates of the correctional administrators themselves, it likely provided a conservative statement of the magnitude of the problem. Moreover, the survey asked respondents only about the *availability of various services*; it did not address whether the services—in those cases in which they were provided—were adequate or sufficient overall.[35]

To be sure, the adequacy of treatment services and the provision of humane conditions of confinement for prisoners with mental illness cannot be assumed. Even prison systems that have been the target of protracted litigation and in which deficiencies supposedly were corrected can quickly return to shockingly substandard conditions. Thus, despite "years of litigation and multiple court orders," here is how one team of experts more recently characterized the "hapless condition" of prisoner mental health services in the Alabama system:

> Every aspect of what goes by the name treatment, or a treatment unit, is seriously deficient in some critical respect.... Seriously ill inmates are locked-down under primitive conditions.... Physical conditions, especially in some areas . . . are essentially unfit for human habitation; and the litany goes on.[36]

Developmental Disability Among Prisoners

As with mental illness, estimates of the prevalence of prisoners with developmental disabilities also vary by jurisdiction and depend in part on the quality of the screening that is used to identify them. Some of these variations are due to the use of different criteria to determine whether a prisoner has a developmental disability and the use of different test instruments to make these determinations.[37] Here, too, because not every correctional system bothers to screen incoming prisoners for developmental disability, it is impossible to know precisely how many prisoners with developmental disabilities there are in the United States. A simple extrapolation from the population at large, among which 2% to 3% of the population has a developmental disability, would lead to an estimate of between 40,000 and 60,000. However, for some of the reasons mentioned earlier in this chapter, most experts believe the percentages to be higher in the prisoner population than among citizens at large.

In a national survey of correctional systems, two researchers found that some 36 states routinely screened new prisoners for mental retardation. On the basis of data collected from almost 270,000 prisoners, they found that 1.5% to 19.1% (average = 6.2%) of prisoners in states using group IQ tests and .2% to 5.3% (average = 2%) of prisoners in states using individual IQ tests were identified as having developmental disabilities.[38] Given the fact that over 2 million persons are incarcerated in the United States,[39] the variations in the estimates are significant (placing the classification of 100,000 or more prisoners who may have a developmental disability at issue).

Setting aside the question of whether group or individual IQ tests are used, most empirical estimates of the number of prisoners with developmental disabilities put the figure at somewhere between 3% and 10% (a range of 64,000 to 210,000 prisoners). As Table 8.2 illustrates, those reported in individual studies and various literature reviews fall within this broad range. Estimates from other experts knowledgeable about prevalence rates in various prisons systems in the United States similarly suggest that the number of those with developmental disabilities is "about 4%–10%."[40] Taking an esti-

TABLE 8.2
Prevalence Estimates of Prisoners With Developmental Disabilities

Study/review	Location	Database	Prevalence (%)
Brown and Courtless (1971)	National	90,000	9.5
	California	5.4	
Browning (1976)	National	39,000	4.1
Denkowski and Denkowski (1985)	National	270,000	2–6.2
	California	32,065	2.3
Harbach (1976)	Georgia	Unspecified	28.6
Irion (1988)	Georgia	~300	3.9–5.4
Lampert (1987)	Texas	520	6.9
Spruill and May (1988)	Florida	~68	1–4
Sundram (1989)	New York	Unspecified	8
TDMHMR	Texas	500	6.9–23.4
Veneziano, Veneziano, and Tribolet (1987)	National	Unspecified	.05–35
Veneziano and Veneziano (1996)	National	Unspecified	4.2

Note. TDMHMR = Texas Department of Mental Health and Mental Retardation. Brown, B., & Courtless, T. (1971). *The mentally retarded offender.* DHEW Pub. No. (HSM) 72-90-39. Washington, DC: Government Printing Office; Browning, P. (1976). *Rehabilitation and the retarded offender.* Springfield, IL: Charles Thomas; Denkowski, G., & Denkowski, K. (1985). The mentally retarded offender in the state prison system: Identification, prevalence, adjustment, and rehabilitation. *Criminal Justice and Behavior, 12,* 53; Harbach, R. (1976). An overview of rehabilitation alternatives. In P. Browning (Ed.), *Rehabilitation and the retarded offender* (p. 122). Springfield, Il: Charles C. Thomas; Irion, J. (1988). *Mentally retarded inmates in Georgia's prison system.* Atlanta: Georgia Department of Corrections; Lampert, R. (1987). The mentally retarded offender in prison. *Justice Professional, 2,* 60; Spruill, J., & May, J. (1988). The mentally retarded offender: Prevalence rates based on individual versus group intelligence tests. *Criminal Justice and Behavior, 15,* 484; Sundram, C. (1990). *Inmates with developmental disabilities in New York correctional facilities.* Albany: New York State Commission of Quality Care for the Mentally Disabled; Texas Department of Mental Health and Mental Retardation. (1973). Project CAMIO [Correctional Administration and the Mentally Incompetent Offender] (Vols. 4 & 5). In *The mentally retarded in an adult correctional institution.* Austin, TX: Author; Veneziano, L., Veneziano, C., & Tribolet, C. (1987). The special needs of prison inmates with handicaps: An assessment. *Journal of Offender Counseling, Services & Rehabilitation, 12,* 61; Veneziano, L., & Veneziano, C. (1996). Disabled inmates. In M. McShane & F. Williams (Eds.), *Encyclopedia of American Prisons* (p. 157). New York: Garland.

mate from the lower end of the range, one national survey concluded that an average of approximately 4.2% of prisoners had a developmental disability,[41] a percentage that would translate into almost 90,000 persons.

Like prisoners with mental illness, many of those with developmental disabilities remain officially undetected in the prison systems in which they are housed. Moreover, even prisoners who have been identified as having developmental disabilities often do not have access to meaningful habilitation programs designed to prepare them for postprison life. Again, the situation in California is instructive. Until the very end of the 1990s, the California Department of Corrections did not conduct any systematic screening for cognitive disability among incoming or already incarcerated prisoners.[42] Solely on the basis of estimates from the various studies previously cited, there should have been somewhere between 3% and 10% of California prisoners who had developmental disabilities. Because there were approximately 160,000 persons imprisoned in the state at the time, this percentage translated into somewhere between 4,800 and 16,000 prisoners.[43]

Yet, California corrections officials claimed that there were no more than a handful of such prisoners in their entire system. Indeed, they argued that they did not need to use any special screening procedures to detect them because their developmental disabilities made them "readily identifiable."[44] A prison system that admitted to having only a handful of prisoners with developmental disabilities, when there was good reason to believe that there actually were thousands of them, obviously was ignoring the special needs of a great many of its inmates. Thus, instead of receiving special considerations in their housing assignments and being given opportunities to receive appropriate habilitation services, those prisoners were forced to fend for themselves in the complicated and harsh environment of prison. Moreover, the prison system could not be expected to provide special transitional services for a disorder or condition that had not been identified while those prisoners were incarcerated. That meant that whatever special problems they might face in attempting to reintegrate into the community upon release were ones they would be required to address on their own.

CONTEXT-BASED SPECIAL CHALLENGES: RULES, CONFLICT, AND DISCIPLINE

Previous chapters have underscored the power of the social context of prison to shape the behavior of nearly everyone who enters it. However, individuals—and even entire classes or categories of people—may experience the same or similar settings very differently. The plight of prisoners with mental illness and developmental disabilities underscores exactly this point. Many of them will experience prison as a more perplexing, dangerous, and painful environment as a result of their vulnerabilities. There are several obvious reasons why this is so.[45]

For one, there is little that is commonsensical about prison. The rules that permeate the social context of prison are not always obvious or easily intuited; many of them seem arbitrary. The institutional jargon, or *bureaucratese*, through which they are communicated compounds the problem. Yet, prison staff and administrators assume that all prisoners process the information with relative ease. Especially for persons with limited intellectual abilities or impaired contact with reality, the nature and logic of these invasive, complex, and arbitrary regulations may be difficult or impossible to grasp. Nonetheless, there is little margin for error, confusion, or misunderstanding. Deviations from prescribed courses of action are usually noticed in correctional settings and often punished harshly. A trial-and-error approach is not the best way to learn the rigors of prison life, and "slow learners" in prison may quickly amass a long disciplinary record. Many are regarded as troublemakers by prison officials, and treated accordingly.

Institutional reformer Jerome Miller once reflected that when he headed the Massachusetts juvenile system he came to depend on three groups of inmates for reliable information about institutional abuse—those who are emotionally disturbed, those with developmental disabilities, and "the occasional middle-class inmate." The reason, he said, was that these three groups of inmates had one thing in common: "They don't know, don't understand, or don't care about the codes which govern institutional life." Unlike most inmates, who "know the realities of their situation only too well" and do not want to "make matters worse for themselves by unnecessarily stirring things up," these three groups of inmates were more likely to be candid and less tactful in describing mistreatment.[46] But, for prisoners with mental illness or developmental disabilities, not knowing or not understanding how to negotiate the complicated psychological demands of an institutional regime creates additional problems and brings more pain.

Note also that prisoners must develop their own strategies to ensure that their most important needs are met in prison. They have to master whatever procedures must be followed to receive visits, attend classes, change their work assignment, obtain phone privileges, replace toilet paper, use the canteen, file a grievance, and on and on. Even though, over time, most prisoners do manage to navigate this maze of prison rules and regulations in a reasonably straightforward manner, the ones who cannot are at risk of going without these things. Moreover, rules and regulations can change without warning in prison. New administrative directives may be issued, and inmates can be transferred to institutions with different standard operating procedures. In addition, frequent changes in personnel bring new staff members on the scene who have their own ideas about which rules and procedures should be enforced and how. Rules can even be interpreted and applied differently each day, as shifts change and new correctional officers come on duty. Adjusting to these changes may require a level of awareness and adaptability that few inmates with mental illness or developmental disabilities have.

As previously noted, correctional institutions are particularly unforgiving places. The consequences of doing things incorrectly or inadvertently violating a rule may be severe. Similarly, the result of unintentionally relinquishing access to a privilege or activity because of a misunderstanding or failure to comprehend may be irreversible. In extreme cases, inmates who violate certain kinds of rules are subject to especially painful and potentially damaging disciplinary sanctions, such as placement in solitary confinement or punitive segregation units. Conditions there are even more stark and disorienting, and the deprivation, isolation, and enforced inactivity are not only more intense and complete but also can be very harmful.[47]

However, neither the context of the infraction nor the special vulnerabilities of the person who commits it are likely to be taken into consideration. Prisoners who attempt to provide their own mitigating accounts of the violations may find themselves punished more severely than otherwise. Indeed, Pamela Steinke found that such explanations, including those in which prisoners attempted to contextualize their actions by pointing to the situational factors that played a role in what they did, increased both the judgments of blame that were made by officials and the harshness of the punishment that was meted out.[48] A prisoner with mental illness or developmental disability who lacks effective communication skills may fare especially poorly in these encounters. Needless to say, prisoners who incur disciplinary sanctions and the loss of privileges and good-time credits at higher rates than others—in part because of vulnerabilities over which they have no control—will experience imprisonment as more frustrating, hurtful, and debilitating.

PATTERNS OF "MALADAPTATION" AMONG VULNERABLE PRISONERS AND THE IMPLICATIONS OF "PRISON MADNESS"[49]

As I noted earlier, correctional institutions are notoriously unsympathetic to repeat offenders—those inmates who continue to violate rules and appear not to learn from their mistakes. The presumption in such cases is that the repeat offending is a conscious and willful flaunting of institutional authority that must be forcefully addressed. Even minor rule violations can result in very severe punishment if they are committed frequently enough. These infractions can accumulate and, over time, become the basis for concluding that a prisoner is unreasonable, uncontrollable, and perhaps dangerous. Inmates who have (sometimes undiagnosed) disabilities that impair their contact with reality and make it difficult for them to monitor and control their feelings and behavior, or disabilities that limit their ability to comprehend instructions or learn from mistakes can easily develop reputations as troublemakers rather than as troubled or poorly functioning individuals.

For example, one commentator has described the "vicious cycle" into which prisoners with mental illness or developmental disability can fall. A lack of appropriate treatment and care may worsen their condition, "causing hostile and aggressive behavior to the point that they break prison rules and end up in segregation units as management problems." Because of highly stressful conditions in segregation and the fact that mental health care there may be sporadic and of uneven quality, "this regression can go undetected for considerable periods of time before they again receive more closely monitored mental health care." Unfortunately, this is a cycle that "can, and often does, repeat."[50]

There is another special set of challenges that prisoners with mental illness and developmental disabilities face in the social context of prison that may lead them disproportionately into punitive segregation and the vicious cycle of lockup. In addition to the formal rules, regulations, and procedural requirements imposed by the institution itself, and the negative consequences that are attached to violations, the surrounding prisoner culture makes its own demands on them. That is, it imposes an equally important set of norms to which inmates must conform. This elaborate set of shared understandings shapes the day-to-day institutional life of prisoners and establishes many of the informal rules and regulations that govern their social interactions.

One of the most important of those shared understandings is the value that is placed on masking vulnerability, covering weakness, and refusing to seek help. As I noted in chapter 6, outward signs of vulnerability may be interpreted as invitations to exploitation and victimization. People who appear weak and in need of help may be scorned by other prisoners, marginalized, and taken advantage of. For this reason, prisoners with a mental illness, developmental disability, or other vulnerability may be reluctant to admit that there are things that they do not understand or cannot do; they are reluctant to acknowledge their limitations or to seek assistance.

Prisoner culture also establishes expectations about how people who live in very close—sometimes intolerable—proximity to one another must behave in each other's presence. The nature of inmate interactions—tone of voice, level of eye contact, facial expressions, violations of personal space, the nature and extent of permissible cross-racial contact, and so on—are governed by such informal rules. Prisoner-established groups and hierarchies—gangs, cliques, and "tips"—create expectations about the level of interpersonal respect that one's position supposedly warrants. Many of these norms are subtle and unspoken, requiring prisoners to make quick, nuanced judgments. The inevitable influx of new prisoners means that inmates must be continuously socialized into such norms, and judgments regularly remade. Similarly, prisoners who are transferred to different facilities must analyze and understand the somewhat different set of norms to which they must readjust.

Because mentally ill and developmentally disabled prisoners cannot as easily grasp or comply with all of the subtleties of prisoner culture, they are at greater risk of committing unintended violations or inviting victimization. This, in turn, not only increases the painfulness of prison life but also may lead to short-term survival strategies that have problematic long-term consequences. For example, as one observer put it, "An inmate with mental retardation whose circumstances have placed him or her among brighter peers without support may well learn to survive through aggression."[51] Other studies confirm this. For example, "Research evidence has suggested that the mentally retarded are slower to adjust to the prison routine, have more difficulty learning rules and regulations, and as a result, accumulate more rule infractions than the average inmate."[52]

Persons with mental illness experience similar problems. For example, psychiatrist Terry Kupers has argued that an unusually high number of persons with mental illness in prison are funneled into long-term segregation (i.e., lockup or supermax), where they are kept confined to their cells for as many as 23 hours a day. Indeed, my own research and a number of other studies indicate that a high percentage of the prisoners who are confined in these special disciplinary units do have serious forms of mental illness.[53] In fact, one Canadian study estimated that approximately 29% of prisoners in special-handling and long-term segregation units had "severe mental disorders."[54] A more recent study conducted by a group of Washington state researchers found exactly the same thing: Twenty-nine percent of intensive management prisoners in the state's correctional system manifested at least one predefined indication of serious mental disorder (such as multiple admissions to an acute-care mental care facility or having been in one of the prison system's residential mental health units).[55]

In light of what I have said so far in this chapter, at least one reason for this disproportion is obvious: Many prisoners with mental illness lack the capacity to comply with the special demands of prison life, and they end up in trouble as a result. As two prison researchers have succinctly put it, "an unknown proportion of people who *are* problems (who prove troublesome to settings in which they function) also *have* problems (demonstrate psychological and social deficits when they are subjected to closer scrutiny."[56]

Moreover, too many mental health staff members keep a safe physical, intellectual, and emotional distance from the complex social realities of prison. This compromises their ability to recognize and treat acute psychiatric reactions that may have been exacerbated by adverse conditions of confinement, as well as those maladies that are caused by harsher segregation or supermax units themselves. As two knowledgeable commentators put it,

> The prison itself is a difficult environment, and mental health professionals are often poorly equipped, both in knowledge and skill, to deal with the unique dynamics of the prison culture. Treatment staff frequently do not have direct access to actual mainline experiences,

which limits their ability to prepare inmate–patients for the transition back into that environment.[57]

If troubled prisoners are not treated for their prison-related problems, their patterns of disruptive behavior are likely to be repeated. If mental health professionals do not fully understand the "unique dynamics" of the prison context or are prohibited by prison officials from taking them appropriately into account, troubled prisoners are likely to be blamed for their problems. In many cases, as a result, confinement in disciplinary segregation or supermax units follows. Thus, prison systems that ignore context end up blaming—and punishing—prisoners who manifest the very psychological symptoms for which they should have been treated. Especially in prison systems that do not have the resources or inclination to treat prisoners with mental illness, disciplinary isolation or supermax confinement offers a short-term (but shortsighted) solution to a difficult long-term problem. Disciplinary units become the default placements for disruptive, troublesome, or inconvenient prisoners with mental illness.

However, despite the individual level at which these problems are understood and addressed, the disproportionately high numbers of vulnerable prisoners in disciplinary segregation reflect context-related failures of system-wide proportions. By ignoring the painful nature of the contexts in which these prisoners initially are placed and the effects of the worse ones to which they typically are sent for in-prison punishment, these policies exacerbate the vulnerabilities of many inmates whose needs have been neglected.

Thus, many persons with preexisting psychiatric disorders who are entering prisons—and who, in past times, likely would have been treated elsewhere—will find that their problems are made worse by the stress of confinement. Indeed, symptoms that may have been muted, kept under control, or in remission can emerge in more diagnosable, flagrant, and disabling form during imprisonment.[58] As Kupers put it, "Mentally disturbed prisoners have a very difficult time remaining stable in the absence of safe, supervised social interactions and meaningful structured activities. Too many end up confined to their cells, where their condition deteriorates."[59]

Moreover, increasingly stressful, painful prison conditions have the capacity to create psychological problems in previously healthy prisoners. If these problems go untreated—which, as I have noted, may be the normative case in many chronically understaffed prisons—diagnosable clinical disorders and other more serious conditions may emerge. As the prevalence figures cited earlier indicated, the sheer number of prisoners who currently have these kinds of psychological vulnerabilities is extremely high. It is apparent that large numbers of persons with mental illness are entering the prison system, others are finding that their preexisting conditions are worsened by the stress of confinement, and still others develop forms of psychopathology as part of their ill-fated efforts to adjust to the pains of imprisonment. Whatever the cause of these prisoners' worsened condition, many prisons have done far too little to address their problems or alleviate their suffering.

CONCLUSION

Prisons are difficult places in which to live. Obviously, for prisoners who have serious personal vulnerabilities—such as mental illness or developmental disability—prison life will be even more challenging. The number of special-needs prisoners has increased in recent decades, and there are now hundreds of thousands of persons with mental illness or developmental disabilities housed in American prisons. Indeed, the various prevalence estimates for mental illness and developmental disability that I reviewed in this chapter suggest that somewhere between one sixth and as many as one third of the prisoners in the United States suffer from one of these two conditions. On the basis of 2004 prison and jail population figures,[60] this translates into somewhere between 350,000 and over 700,000 persons who are currently in prison or jail in the United States who are mentally ill or developmentally disabled.

Yet, many chronically overcrowded prison systems are still unable to properly identify, let alone adequately treat, them or to prepare them for their eventual release. As researchers in the mid-1990s concluded, "the prospect of screening inmates for mental disorder and treating those in need of mental health services has become a daunting and nearly impossible task in the present explosion of prison growth."[61] There is no evidence that the situation has improved significantly. Even by the estimation of the prison officials themselves, many of these prisoners are receiving less than appropriate or adequate care, and a great many have no access to care at all.[62]

The plight of those with mental illness and developmental disabilities provides a clear example of how the harsh prison policies of the last several decades have been hurtful and harmful to a large and growing number of vulnerable prisoners. Especially for these prisoners, the era of overcrowding, the abandonment of rehabilitation, and the drastic reductions in prisoner services have been painful and problematic. Obviously, ignoring the psychiatric problems of prisoners with mental illness and the habilitative needs of those with developmental disabilities decreases their chances of leading productive, law-abiding lives once they are released.

As I noted earlier, one of the ironies of the punitive correctional policies on which the nation has relied over the last several decades is that, having insisted on locating the source of criminal behavior exclusively inside its perpetrators, they neglect to address the needs of those same persons during their incarceration. And, as this chapter has indicated, this policy extends to even the most vulnerable prisoners whose special needs make them particularly susceptible to the pains of imprisonment.

NOTES

1. Nils Christie, *Limits to Pain* (Oxford, England: Martin Robertson, 1982), 49.
2. Hans Toch, *Corrections: A Humanistic Approach* (Guilderland, NY: Harrow & Heston, 1997), 65.
3. *Mental retardation* is defined by the American Association on Mental Retardation as "a disability characterized by significant limitations both in intellectual functioning and in adaptive behavior as expressed in conceptual, social and practical adaptive skills. The disability originates before age 18." American Association on Mental Retardation, *Mental Retardation: Definition, Classification, and Systems of Supports*, 10th ed. (Washington DC: Author, 2002), 8. *Developmental disability* is a broader category than mental retardation. It includes all types of severe disabilities attributable to physical or mental impairment that occur before adulthood and that are likely to continue indefinitely. Mental retardation is the most common developmental disability but not the only kind. However, the terms are often used interchangeably. *See* John Noble and Ronald Conley, "Toward an Epidemiology of Relevant Attributes," in *The Criminal Justice System and Mental Retardation*, ed. Ronald Conley, Ruth Luckasson, and George Bouthilet (Baltimore: Brooks, 1992), 22.
4. See chapter 5, this volume, for a discussion of these social–historical factors and the role that they play in increasing the likelihood of adult criminal behavior.
5. *See, e.g.,* T. Howard, "Therapeutic Implications of Incarceration for Persons with Severe Mental Disorders: Searching for Rational Health Policy," *American Journal of Criminal Law* 24 (1997): 283.
6. An excellent analysis of the legal issues that apply to prisoners who have mental disorders can be found in Fred Cohen, *The Mentally Disordered Inmate and the Law* (Kingston, NJ: Civic Research Institute, 1998).
7. Fred Cohen, "The Limits of the Judicial Reform of Prisons: What Works, What Does Not," *Criminal Law Bulletin* 40 (2004): 421, 453. Yet, as I suggest in this chapter, and as Cohen's own analysis shows, the fate of special-needs prisoners is uncertain, unpredictable, and dependent on the particular facility in which they are housed and the particular time they are placed there.
8. *See, e.g.,* C. Rosenberg, *The Trial of the Assassin Guiteau: Psychiatry and Law in the Gilded Age* (Chicago: University of Chicago Press, 1968).
9. I discuss this issue in greater detail both in chapter 2, this volume, and in C. Haney, "Criminal Justice and the Nineteenth-Century Paradigm: The Triumph of Psychological Individualism in the 'Formative Era,'" *Law and Human Behavior* 6 (1982): 191.
10. Max Schlapp and Edward Smith, *The New Criminology* (New York: Boni & Liveright, 1982), 149.

11. M. Woodward, "The Role of Low Intelligence in Delinquency," *British Journal of Delinquency* 5 (1955): 281. For a discussion of the changing views about persons with mental retardation, as well as the belief that criminality and retardation were causally connected, *see* J. Ellis and R. Luckasson, "Mentally Retarded Criminal Defendants," *George Washington Law Review* 53 (1985): 414, 416–421.

12. Haney, "Criminal Justice and the Nineteenth-Century Paradigm."

13. *See, e.g.,* David Rothman, *Conscience and Convenience: The Asylum and Its Alternatives in Progressive America* (Boston: Little, Brown, 1980).

14. *See* chapters 3 and 4, this volume.

15. *See, e.g.,* C. Haney, "Riding the Punishment Wave: On the Origins of Our Devolving Standards of Decency," *Hastings Women's Law Journal* 9 (1998): 27.

16. On deinstitutionalization (or *decarceration*, as it is sometimes called) and its negative consequences, see T. Arvanites, "A Comparison of Civil Patients and Incompetent Defendants: Pre and Post Deinstitutionalization," *Bulletin of the American Academy of Psychiatry & the Law* 18 (1990): 393; K. Hoehne, "Deinstitutionalization and the Criminalization of the Mentally Ill" [Special Issue: Deinstitutionalization], *American Journal of Social Psychiatry* 5 (1985): 39; H. Richard Lamb, "Deinstitutionalization in the Nineties," in *Treating the Homeless Mentally Ill: A Report of the Task Force on the Homeless Mentally Ill*, ed. H. Richard Lamb, Leona L. Bachrach, and Frederic I. Kass (Washington, DC, American Psychiatric Association, 1992); H. R. Lamb, "Lessons Learned from Deinstitutionalization in the US," *British Journal of Psychiatry* 162 (1993): 587; Andrew Scull, *Decarceration: Community Treatment and the Deviant* (Englewood Cliffs, NJ: Prentice-Hall, 1977); A. Scull, "Deinstitutionalization: Cycles of Despair" [Special Issue: Challenging the Therapeutic State: Critical Perspectives on Psychiatry and the Mental Health System], *Journal of Mind & Behavior* 11 (1990): 301; D. Smith and E. Polloway, "Patterns of Deinstitutionalization and Community Placement: A Dream Deferred or Lost?" *Education & Training in Mental Retardation & Developmental Disabilities* 30 (1993): 321; J. Talbott, "The Care of the Chronic Mentally Ill: Deinstitutionalization and Homelessness in the United States," *Psychiatria Hungarica* 7 (1992): 615.

17. S. Lipton, A. Sabatini, & S. Katz, "Down and Out in the City: Homeless Mentally Ill," *Hospital and Community Psychiatry* 34 (1983): 817, 819. For additional discussions of some of these trends and their broader causes and effects, *see* Y. Aderibigbe, "Deinstitutionalization and Criminalization: Tinkering in the Interstices," *Forensic Science International* 85 (1997, February 28): 127; J. Geller, "The Last Half-Century of Psychiatric Service as Reflected in *Psychiatric Services*," *Psychiatric Services* 51 (2000): 41; M. Severson, "The Impact of a State Hospital Closure on Local Jails: The Kansas Experience," *Community Mental Health Journal* 36 (2000): 571; and S. Sharfstein, "Whatever Happened to Community Mental Health?" *Psychiatric Services* 51 (2000): 616.

18. Charlie Lakin and Robert Prouty, *Trends in Institution Closure*, 9 IMPACT (Minneapolis, MN: Institute on Community Integration, University of Minnesota, 1994).

19. J. Petersilia, "Justice for All? Offenders with Mental Retardation and the California Corrections System," *Prison Journal* 77 (1997): 358, 365.

20. P. Streeter, "Incarceration of the Mentally Ill: Treatment or Warehousing?" *Michigan Bar Journal* 77 (1998): 166, 166 (footnotes omitted). In 1939, British psychiatrist Lionel Penrose proposed what he termed "Penrose's Law"—that the population of the prisons and mental hospitals in society were inversely related. L. Penrose, "Mental Disease and Crime: Outline of a Comparative Study of European Statisics," *British Journal of Medical Psychology* 18 (1939): 1. The relationship is a bit more complicated, of course, but it is certainly true that drastic cuts in services for persons with mental illness of the sort that have occurred over the last several decades are likely to be accompanied by increased demands on the criminal justice system.

21. *See, e.g.,* D. Freed, "Federal Sentencing in the Wake of Guidelines: Unacceptable Limits on the Discretion of Sentences," *Yale Law Journal* 101 (1992): 1681; C. Montgomery, "Social and Schematic Injustice: The Treatment of Offender Personal Characteristics under the Federal Sentencing Guidelines," *New England Journal on Criminal & Civil Confinement* 20 (1993): 27. In some jurisdictions, the limitations of this approach have been recognized and special "mental health courts" have been established to provide an explicit alternative sentencing process for persons with mental illness convicted of criminal offenses. I discuss these alternatives in greater detail in chapter 10 of this volume. However, despite the promise that they show, these approaches are the exception rather than the rule.

22. *See, e.g.,* C. Sigelman, E. Budd, C. Spanhel, and C. Schoenrock, "When in Doubt, Say Yes: Acquiescence in Interviews with Mentally Retarded Persons," *Mental Retardation* 19 (1981): 53; C. Sigelman, J. Winer, and C. Schoenrock, "The Responsiveness of Mentally Retarded Persons to Questions," *Education & Training of the Mentally Retarded* 17 (1982): 120.

23. *See, e.g.,* Bertram Brown and Thomas Courtless, *The Mentally Retarded Offender* [DHEW Pub. No. (HSM) 72-90-39] (Washington, DC: Government Printing Office, 1971).

24. Louis Veneziano and Carol Veneziano, "Disabled Inmates," in *Encyclopedia of American Prisons,* ed. Marilyn McShane and Frank Williams (New York: Garland, 1996). *See, e.g.,* L. Long and A. Sapp, "Programs and Facilities for Physically Disabled Inmates in State Prisons," *Journal of Offender Rehabilitation* 18 (1992): 191. More or less the same kind of disparities were identified a decade earlier in a similar study by the same authors. *See* L. Veneziano, C. Veneziano, and C. Tribolet, "The Special Needs of Prison Inmates With Handicaps: An Assessment," *Journal of Offender Counseling, Services & Rehabilitation* 12 (1987): 61.

25. Epidemiologists typically refer to two different kinds of rates in estimating the magnitude of a disorder, disability, or "special need": *Prevalence* refers to the number of cases that exist in a given population at a specific point in time. *Incidence* refers to the number of times an event occurs in a given population over a particular period of time (usually during a single year or over a lifetime).

Prevalences are more meaningful to calculate and report for lifelong conditions, whereas either term may be used to describe more transient or acute conditions.

26. Specifically, the study concluded, "A large number of *unidentified* individuals in the general population, were they to be screened, would be diagnosable with the same serious disorders and exhibit related symptoms. Given the size of the unidentified population (over 57,000 at the time of the survey), even the small base-rate of 7% for the four serious disorders amounts to over 4,000 *undetected* individuals [with serious mental disorders]." Norman & Cotton Associates, Arthur Young, and SCC Consortium, *Current Description, Evaluation, and Recommendations for Treatment of Mentally Disordered Criminal Offenders*, Vol. 1, *Introduction and Prevalence* (San Rafael, CA, June 1989), ii-9 (emphasis in original). Before the state took steps to begin to effectively remedy this problem, nearly a decade had passed in which there were significant increases in the prisoner population and no corresponding increases in mental health personnel or services. Thus, it seems very likely that the number of prisoners with serious mental disorders who were undetected by the Department of Corrections continued to rise.

27. *See, generally*, D. Specter, "Cruel and Unusual Punishment of the Mentally Ill in California's Prison System: A Case Study of a Class Action Suit," *Social Justice* 21 (1994): 109. At the time the litigation was filed to compel the state to provide adequate care for prisoners with mental illness, California prisons housed "almost 10,000 prisoners with a current major mental illness, another 20,000 with other serious mental disorders, [and] approximately 18,000 prisoners [who] need some form of treatment on any given day. The [Department of Corrections] currently has the capacity to house only 737 prisoners in a psychiatric hospital, and about 3,000 in residential treatment programs. In 1992, the outpatient clinical staff was less than 20% of that recommended by [the statewide prevalence study]. . . ." (ibid., 110–111).

28. *See, e.g.*, R. Jamelka, E. Trupin, and J. Chiles, "The Mentally Ill in Prison," *Hospital and Community Psychiatry* 40 (1989): 481.

29. L. Teplin, "Detecting Disorder: The Treatment of Mental Illness Among Jail Detainees," *Journal of Consulting & Clinical Psychology* 58 (1990): 233.

30. H. Steadman, S. Fabisiak, J. Dvoskin, and E. Holohean, "A Survey of Mental Disability Among State Prison Inmates," *Hospital and Community Psychiatry* 38 (1987): 1086.

31. F. Cohen and J. Dvoskin, "Inmates with Mental Disorders: A Guide to Law and Practice," *Mental and Physcial Disability Law Reporter* 16 (1992): 462, 463.

32. *See* Coleman v. Gomez (United States District Court, Northern District of California, 1991).

33. *Special Master's Compliance Report Re: Medical and Mental Health Remedial Plan*, November 11, 1997, p. 14.

34. Allen Beck and Laura Maruschak, *Mental Health Treatment in State Prisons, 2000* [Bureau of Justice Statistics Special Report NCJ 188215] (Washington, DC: U.S. Department of Justice, July 2001). The figures actually were less favorable when "community-based facilities" were taken into account, resulting

in the overall calculation that nearly one third of adult correctional facilities in the United States do not screen inmates at intake to determine their mental health needs, about one third fail to conduct any psychiatric assessments of prisoners, nearly 30% fail to provide inmates with any therapy or counseling by trained mental health counselors, nearly half have no around-the-clock mental health care available for prisoners who may suffer acute psychiatric crises, and one third fail to assist inmates in obtaining community mental health services upon their release.

35. I should note that my interpretation of these data differs from that of the authors of the study. The tone of the Department of Justice report seemed to suggest that mental health coverage in state prison systems was adequate, perhaps even impressive. Thus, at various points the authors noted that "nearly all" of the facilities accomplished one or another of the important mental health tasks that they identified. Yet, prisoners with mental illness are so numerous in the United States that even attending to nearly all of them still leaves tens of thousands whose needs are neglected. Moreover, prisoners with mental illness who are in need of therapeutic services, but who are housed in one of the many facilities—between 16% and 29% depending on the type of facility—in which no such services are available (let alone readily accessible or properly provided), represent a serious problem that must be addressed if the overall pains of imprisonment are to be appropriately and humanely reduced.

36. Expert report by Kathryn Burns, Fred Cohen, and Jane Haddad, dated March, 2000, quoted in Cohen, *The Mentally Disordered Inmate and the Law*, 437–438.

37. Studies of the prevalence of developmental disability among prisoners generally use several interrelated criteria to reach the diagnosis, including (a) a low measured intelligence quotient, or IQ, score of 70 or less; (b) additional deficits in adaptive behavior or adaptive functioning; and (c) the requirement that these disabilities began before the age of 18 or, under some definitions, 22. *See, e.g.*, Tom Fryers, "Epidemiological Thinking in Mental Retardation: Issues in Taxonomy and Population Frequency," in *International Review of Research in Mental Retardation*, ed. Norman W. Bray (Novato, CA: Academic Therapy, 1993).

38. G. Denkowski and K. Denkowski, "The Mentally Retarded Offender in the State Prison System: Identification, Prevalence, Adjustment, and Rehabilitation," *Criminal Justice and Behavior* 12 (1985): 53.

39. The most recent available estimates indicate that there are just over 2 million persons incarcerated in prisons and jails in the United States: 1,355,748 in state and federal prisons and 665,475 in local jails, for a total of 2,019,234. Paige Harrison and Jennifer Karberg, *Prison and Jail Inmates at Midyear 2002* [Bureau of Justice Statistics Bulletin NCJ 198877] (Washington, DC: U.S. Department of Justice, April 2003).

40. J. Petersilia, "Justice for All? Offenders with Mental Retardation and the California Corrections System," *Prison Journal* 77 (1997): 358, 358. *See also* Orville Endicott, *Persons With Intellectual Disability Who Are Incarcerated for Criminal Offences: A Literature Review*, Research Report No. 14 (Research Branch,

Communications and Corporate Development, Correctional Services of Canada, 1991), 2, who placed the estimate at "generally . . . between five and ten percent."

41. Veneziano and Veneziano, "Disabled Inmates."

42. A change in policy and sudden willingness to begin such screening occurred only after litigation had been filed on the issue. *See* Craig Haney and Donald Specter, "Vulnerable Offenders and the Law: Treatment Rights in Uncertain Legal Times," in *Treating Adult and Juvenile Offenders With Special Needs*, ed. José Ashford, Bruce Sales, and William Reid (Washington, DC: American Psychological Association, 2001).

43. Using the only California-specific empirical data to appear anywhere in the literature—Bertram Brown and Thomas Courtless, *The Mentally Retarded Offender* [DHEW Pub. No. (HSM) 72-90-39] (Washington, DC: Government Printing Office, 1971)—a dated figure of 5.4% of California prisoners would lead to a present-day estimate of more than 8,600 prisoners with mental retardation.

44. The statements were made by numerous prison officials in various depositions given in the course of a prison lawsuit that focused on the treatment of prisoners with developmental disabilities in the California prison system: Clark v. California, No. C-96-1486 FMS (N. D. Cal. 1998).

45. Some of the observations contained in following paragraphs are discussed more fully in C. Haney and T. Pettigrew, "Civil Rights and Institutional Law: The Role of Social Psychology in Judicial Implementation," *Journal of Community Psychology* 14 (1986): 267; Craig Haney and Phillip Zimbardo, "The Socialization into Criminality: On Becoming a Prisoner and a Guard," in *Law, Justice, and the Individual in Society: Psychological and Legal Issues*, ed. June Tapp and Felice Levine (New York: Holt, Rinehart & Winston, 1977); Zimbardo and Craig Haney, "Prison Behavior," in *International Encyclopedia of Psychiatry, Psychology, Psychoanalysis, and Neurology*, vol. 9, ed. Benjamin Wolman (New York: Van Nostrand Reinhold, 1977).

46. Jerome Miller, *The Last One Over the Wall: The Massachusetts Experiment in Closing Reform Schools* (Columbus, OH: Ohio State University Press, 1991), 111.

47. *See, e.g.*, Craig Haney, "Infamous Punishment: The Psychological Effects of Isolation," in *Correctional Contexts: Contemporary and Classical Readings*, ed. James Marquart and Jonathan Sorensen (Los Angeles: Roxbury Publishing, 1997); C. Haney and M. Lynch, "Regulating Prisons of the Future: The Psychological Consequences of Supermax and Solitary Confinement," *New York University Review of Law and Social Change* 23 (1997): 477; *See also* Langley v. Coughlin, 709 F. Supp. 482 (1989); Madrid v. Gomez, 912 F. Supp. 1282 (E.D. Cal. 1995).

48. P. Steinke, "The Effect of Inmates' Accounts on Disciplinary Penalties," *Journal of Social Psychology* 132 (1992): 474.

49. Here I borrow psychiatrist Terry Kupers's term, used in his fine book *Prison Madness: The Mental Health Crisis Behind Bars and What We Must Do About It* (San Francisco: Jossey-Bass, 1999).

50. Streeter, "Incarceration of the Mentally Ill: Treatment or Warehousing?" 167.

51. J. Nelson Hall, "Correctional Services for Inmates With Mental Retardation: Challenge or Catastrophe?" in *The Criminal Justice System and Mental Retardation*, ed. Ronald Conley, Ruth Luckasson, and George Bouthilet (Baltimore: Brooks, 1992), 172.

52. M. Finn, "Disciplinary 'Careers' of Mentally Retarded Inmates," *Journal of Offender Rehabilitation* (1993): 57, 60.

53. *See* C. Haney, "Mental Health Issues in Long-Term Solitary and Supermax Confinement," *Crime & Delinquency* 49 (2003): 24.

54. S. Hodgins and G. Cote, "The Mental Health of Penitentiary Inmates in Isolation," *Canadian Journal of Criminology* 33 (1991): 177.

55. D. Lovell, K. Cloyes, D. Allen, and L. Rhodes, "Who Lives in Super-Maximum Custody? A Washington State Study," *Federal Probation* 64 (2000): 33.

56. Hans Toch and Kenneth Adams, *Acting Out: Maladaptive Behavior in Confinement* (Washington, DC: American Psychological Association, 2002), 13.

57. S. MacKain and A. Streveler, "Social and Independent Living Skills for Psychiatric Patients in a Prison Setting," *Behavior Modification* 14 (1990): 490, 511.

58. The few studies that have attempted to address this issue directly suggest that although prior psychiatric history has some effect on symptomatology during incarceration, conditions of confinement independently contribute to levels of psychopathology. For example, John Gibbs concluded that "going to jail can substantially increase the severity of some symptoms of psychopathology, and the increase is not accounted for by dramatic changes in symptom levels among those with a history of psychological problems prior to confinement." J. Gibbs, "Symptoms of Psychopathology Among Jail Prisoners: The Effects of Exposure to the Jail Environment," *Criminal Justice and Behavior* 14 (1987): 288, 307. In fact, Gibbs found that "jail influences the symptoms of those with a history of psychiatric disorders less than it does for other prisoners" (ibid). However, for more recent data on this issue that pertain to prisons rather than jails, see endnotes 102–111 in chapter 7 and accompanying text.

59. Kupers, *Prison Madness*, 82–83.

60. *See* Harrison and Beck, *Prison and Jail Inmates at Midyear 2004*.

61. F. DiCataldo, A. Greer, and W. Profit, "Screening Prison Inmates for Mental Disorder: An Examination of the Relationship between Mental Disorder and Prison Adjustment," *Bulletin of the American Academy of Psychiatry and Law* 23 (1995): 573, 574.

62. Beck and Maruschak, *Mental Health Treatment in State Prisons, 2000*.

III

USING PSYCHOLOGY
TO LIMIT PRISON PAIN

9

PRISON LAW AND THE DISREGARD OF CONTEXT

> Training in law is training in simplification. It is a trained incapacity to look at all values in a situation, and instead to select only the legally relevant ones. . . . So few elements of the totality are considered that complete equality is guaranteed. But it is, through its simplifications, a primitive system.
>
> —Nils Christie[1]

> The Court's unduly narrow definition of punishment blinds it to the reality of prison life. . . . Where a legislature refuses to fund a prison adequately, the resulting barbaric conditions should not be immune from constitutional scrutiny simply because no prison official acted culpably.
>
> —Justice Harry Blackmun[2]

This chapter and the one that follows address an issue that has been implicit in many of the preceding pages: How can psychological theory and research on the causes of crime and the effects of institutions help reformulate contemporary prison policy? Many possible avenues of institutional reform are implied by the contextual model of behavior that has emerged over the last several decades. In the present chapter I want to examine the potential strengths and the practical limitations of what, at first, would seem like the most obvious source of much of that reform—the law. The chapter after this moves beyond purely legal remedies to discuss a broad range of badly needed reforms that are derived even more directly from psychological theory and research.

The relationship between law and prisons presents a paradox of sorts: Our legal system depends on prisons for much of its force and effect, yet prisons themselves must be constrained primarily through law. Because of the absence of "natural limits" to prison pain, and the potentially corrupting influence of the near absolute power that prison places in the hands of a few, the legal system itself must counterbalance the forces that it has set in motion and on which it depends. In recent years, as I suggested at the outset of this book, the legal restraining edge that is supposed to prevent prison policies and conditions from becoming too harsh or harmful has been blunted by an emerging, politically driven consensus that prison pain does not necessarily need to be mercifully held in check.

This chapter briefly discusses the evolution of the main legal mechanisms by which the power of prisons has been sporadically controlled. This is a vast and important topic, worthy of book-length analyses of its own.[3] However, my discussion of the relevant legal doctrine is intentionally brief. Instead of making a comprehensive review of prison-related legal doctrine, I focus on the much narrower topic of whether and how these doctrines meaningfully address the social contextual aspects of prison life. I conclude that potentially important constitutional standards have been significantly compromised over the last several decades because they have systematically ignored the lessons of modern psychological theory.

Indeed, the U.S. Supreme Court's unwillingness to examine or acknowledge many of the key social contextual aspects of imprisonment that I have spent much of this book discussing, along with a remarkable new law—literally, the attempt by Congress to "reform prison reformers" by limiting the nature and scope of their access to the courts—has constrained and constricted the legal options available for regulating prison pain. It is ironic that, as the critically important role of context and situation was being theoretically developed and empirically documented in modern psychology, the Supreme Court and the Congress were retreating from the social realities of prison life and returning instead to an increasingly outmoded, individualistic model of crime causation and institutional behavior.

To be sure, prisons have been changed in dramatic and positive ways over the last several decades by the advent of prison litigation. Todd Clear and George Cole certainly are correct in suggesting that, even as recently as the early 1960s, before the courts became involved in hearing claims of unconstitutional treatment from prisoners, "formal codes of institutional conduct either did not exist or were ignored; punishment was at the full discretion of the warden, and inmates had no opportunity to challenge the charges."[4] Prison litigation changed much of that. Thus, by 1984, when the unprecedented increases in rates of incarceration in the United States were fully underway, 33 states had at least one major prison operating under court order to improve conditions (including 8 states where the entire system was under such an order).

Moreover, despite the U.S. Supreme Court's increasingly narrow interpretation of the scope of prisoners' rights and the Justices' reluctance to confront the day-to-day realities of prison that I discuss in some detail later in this chapter, the effective monitoring and careful oversight of correctional facilities by many lower courts has continued for decades. Thus, it is important to keep the limitations that I discuss in this chapter in perspective. I certainly agree with distinguished prison law expert Fred Cohen that prison litigation has done much to correct the worst extremes and excesses of American prison life: Many of the "brutal, uncivilized conditions of penal confinement, the total absence of medical or mental health systems, naked physical brutality, and the absence of any procedural regularity in the disciplinary system" have been addressed in most places.[5] Prison litigation and court orders were instrumental in bringing those reforms about.

However, I also agree with Cohen's observation that, despite decades of litigation, many painful and potentially harmful aspects of prisoners' day-to-day existence remain, so that the average inmate "who wants or needs more than the minimal conditions of human survival" now will find little recourse in the courts.[6] Moreover, as Cohen also noted, the worst aspects of prison life can quickly return—and have returned—even in some places where litigation once appeared to have successfully corrected or eliminated them.[7]

Thus, I argue that some of the promise and potential of prison litigation to accomplish important institutional reform has waned over the last several decades, and important opportunities to significantly restructure prisons were lost. This chapter analyzes the nature and effect of this change in fortune in prison litigation, and does so from a largely psychological perspective that is consistent with the framework I have used throughout this book.

THE EVOLUTION OF THE EIGHTH AMENDMENT

The legal mechanism by which the pains of imprisonment have been most directly limited in the United States is the Constitution's Eighth Amendment prohibition against inflicting "cruel and unusual punishments." The Amendment is rooted in the English Bill of Rights and the principles of the Magna Carta, as well as colonial hostility toward barbarous punishment at the hands of tyranny.[8] Although the original intent of prohibiting cruel and unusual treatment was to preclude only certain extreme punishments that had been allowed under English law,[9] its scope was progressively broadened and eventually applied to prisoners—persons once regarded as "slaves of the state" who lacked rights or legal protection.

Early in the 20th century, the Supreme Court expressed the Eighth Amendment's underlying rationale: "With power in a legislature great, if not unlimited, to give criminal character to the actions of men, with power unlimited to fix terms of imprisonment with what accompaniments they might, what more potent instrument of cruelty could be put into the hands of power?"[10] Thus, the Eighth Amendment was to stand as a shield against a "potent instrument of potential cruelty"—the government's ability to set and impose the terms and accompaniments of imprisonment. Historically, however, this shield was raised infrequently and with arguably little significant effect on actual living conditions in the vast majority of the nation's prisons. As one legal commentator observed, "The eighth Amendment was invoked so rarely in its first 100 years of existence that the Supreme Court of Indiana speculated in 1893 that it had become obsolete."[11] It took the U.S. Supreme Court a century and a half to explicitly acknowledge that prisoners had the right of access to the courts and the legal status to complain about aspects of their confinement.[12]

First extending the reach of the Eighth Amendment to states and then extending constitutional protections to state prisoners prepared the way for courts to examine conditions of confinement. But judges still were left to resolve the substantive issue of what constituted cruel and unusual punishment. Landmark Eighth Amendment cases tended to place much more emphasis on the unusualness than the cruelty of the punishment under examination. Ushering in the modern era of Eighth Amendment law, Chief Justice Warren addressed the substantive limits of legal punishment in a way that seemed to give them contemporary meaning. Although he expressed the concept succinctly—"while the State has the power to punish, the Amendment stands to assure that this power be exercised within the limits of civilized standards"[13]—determining the precise nature of those civilized standards has proven exceedingly difficult in practice.[14]

In fact, over the last several decades—precisely the era in which the United States committed to its harsh policies of overincarceration—the Supreme Court has consistently ignored many of the realities of prison life. With few exceptions, the Justices simply have refused to engage in very in-depth, meaningful analyses of the extremely powerful institutional environments where the right to be free of unnecessary pain is exercised. As I discuss in the remainder of this chapter, the Court has shifted the focus of Eighth Amendment inquiries away from the prison context and onto the consciousness of prison officials. That is, the Justices have drastically narrowed the remedies that are available to limit prison harm by making them contingent on a showing of personal wrongdoing—literally, blameworthy states of mind by individual prison officials and staff members.

A brief recap of recent prison trends is in order to fully understand the atmosphere in which the Court's modern Eighth Amendment jurisprudence was fashioned. Recall that the unprecedented growth in the state prison population in the United States began in the mid- to late 1970s. The influx of prisoners continued essentially uninterrupted for the next several decades. As facilities became increasingly overcrowded, and day-to-day living conditions began to deteriorate, many prisoners turned to the courts for redress. By 1978, there were already some 82 court orders in effect that pertained to conditions of confinement at either federal or state correctional facilities, nearly one third of which involved the issue of overcrowding.[15] During approximately the same period, an estimated two thirds of all inmates in federal, state, and local correctional facilities were being housed under conditions that provided less than the amount of living space that correctional organizations had deemed minimally necessary.[16]

However, key Supreme Court decisions near the beginning of the trend toward overincarceration signaled the Justices' "hands off," minimalist approach to correctional oversight. The outcomes of the cases and deferential tenor of the decisions gave legislatures the latitude they needed to significantly increase sentence lengths and rates of incarceration, and eventually to fill the nation's prisons well beyond their capacities. If the Court had adopted a different approach—for example, if the Justices had taken the simple step of prohibiting the housing of two prisoners in cells that had been designed for one, or even had endorsed the American Correctional Association's standards on the amount of space that should be minimally afforded to prisoners,[17] recent prison history would have been written very differently. But by the end of 1970s, a majority on the Court seemed to respond to widespread fears of crime by embracing many of the punitive views that were beginning to become so popular in the larger society.

DEVELOPING MINIMAL STANDARDS FOR REGULATING HARSH CONDITIONS

One of the Court's very first discussions of conditions of confinement appeared to establish an appropriate psychological framework for the meaningful analysis of prison effects. *Hutto v. Finney*[18] was an important 1978 prison case in which the Court was called on to address only a narrow issue that was left unresolved in an otherwise sweeping lower federal court order. A majority of the Justices accepted the basic logic of the lower court's analysis concerning abysmal conditions of confinement in the entire Arkansas prison system and endorsed the federal judge's extensive involvement in fashioning a broad remedy. Justice Stevens's majority opinion not only acknowledged that "confinement in a prison or in an isolation cell is a form of punishment subject to scrutiny under Eighth Amendment standards,"[19] but also noted approvingly that the district judge had considered the whole range of conditions to which the prisoners were exposed. Thus, it was not just the windowless, barren cells into which prisoners were crowded, but also the substandard prison diet, continued overcrowding, rampant violence, vandalized cells, and lack of professional staff at the prison, that helped to frame the constitutional violation.

Indeed, Stevens ruled that the lower court's order was "supported by the *interdependence of the conditions* producing the violation."[20] This standard— that a prison environment needed to be "taken as a whole"[21] in order for courts to properly evaluate whether it inflicted cruel and unusual punishment—seemed to establish a *totality-of-conditions* approach to Eighth Amendment inquiries. Conceptually, of course, this was an important step if the courts were to have any continuing, meaningful role in examining conditions of confinement. Social scientists certainly understand that social contexts often derive their power from the way in which specific conditions combine and interact with one another. Properly evaluating the psychological effects of conditions of confinement requires taking into account all of the relevant conditions and also recognizing that the whole of any environment may be much more powerful and problematic than the simple sum of its individual parts.

Unfortunately, *Hutto* would be the last time that the Court took this sensible approach to the evaluation of prison conditions. Instead, a very problematic limiting principle that was proposed in Justice Rehnquist's lone dissent eventually swallowed the psychologically informed analysis in which the *Hutto* majority had engaged. Specifically, Rehnquist's view—that the Court should reject a totality-of-conditions approach and approve only remedies directed at specific practices or conditions (like punitive isolation) that were individually unconstitutional (rather than changing a whole set of conditions that collectively produced cruel and unusual prison punishment)—soon became the Court's majority view.[22]

As the 1970s drew to a close, the Supreme Court decided another case that foreshadowed several doctrines that would shape prison law over the next several decades. In *Bell v. Wolfish*,[23] lower courts had declared three practices in a New York City jail unconstitutional—double-bunking of inmates in cells built for one, severe restrictions on the receipt of outside mail and packages, and frequent and indiscriminate body cavity searches. Justice Rehnquist's majority opinion overturned the ruling. He characterized the austere and substandard living conditions to which pretrial jail inmates were subjected as not really punishment, describing them instead as mere "incident(s) of some other legitimate governmental purpose."[24] The defining quality of punishment, Rehnquist argued, was not the painfulness of the experience, but whether it reflected an "expressed intent to punish on the part of detention facility officials."[25]

This focus on the mind-set of officials—rather than the effect of the conditions on the inmates themselves—eventually came to dominate the Court's prison jurisprudence. So, too, did the view expressed in *Bell* that "prison administrators [are to be] accorded wide-ranging deference in the adoption and execution of policies and practices that in their judgment are needed to preserve internal order and discipline and to maintain institutional security."[26] It is important to note that the expertise of the corrections officials to which the Court mandated judicial deference in *Bell* and subsequent cases was essentially conferred by the Justices themselves. Moreover, they applied it categorically—all prison administrators presumably had it. Indeed, none of the Justices felt compelled to explain in detail why they thought it was so well deserved.[27] Such wide-ranging deference meant that the Court would rarely, if ever, look past the allegedly expert decisions of prison administrators to assess the psychological effects of their policies on prisoners.[28]

In addition, there was a decidedly unsympathetic tone to the Court's discussion of the harsh jail conditions at issue in *Bell*. As much as the substantive rulings in the case, this tone gave pause to prison litigators and others who had hoped that the Justices would play an important role in moderating the rapidly deteriorating conditions of confinement in prisons and jails around the country (especially in facilities that were experiencing unprecedented levels of overcrowding). The Court's view—that "maintaining institutional security and preserving internal order and discipline are essential goals that may require limitation or retraction of the retained constitutional rights" of jail and prison inmates—suggested that any policy, set of conditions, or form of treatment that could be justified in these terms would trump almost any assertion of prisoners' rights.[29]

Thus, it was not surprising when, 2 years later, the Justices were equally unsympathetic in their first direct evaluation of a broad range of prison conditions. In a landmark 1981 case, *Rhodes v. Chapman*,[30] the Court for the first time considered "a disputed contention that the conditions of confinement at a particular prison constituted cruel and unusual punishment."[31] The key issue was crowding—specifically, the constitutionality of *double celling* in a prison that had been designed to house one prisoner per cell. To be sure, at no point did any of the Justices suggest that the then-controversial practice of double celling was positive or beneficial; instead, Justice Powell's majority opinion acknowledged that the practice had been "made necessary by the unanticipated increase in prison population."[32] However, just as in *Bell*, the Supreme Court again reversed District Court and Court of Appeals findings that particular institutional conditions violated minimal constitutional standards.

Although the Southern Ohio Correctional Facility was a new, relatively modern prison, it housed two prisoners in cells 63 square feet in size that were built for one, kept some inmates confined inside these cells for all but a few hours a week, denied hundreds of inmates any meaningful activity because the facility was so overcrowded that there were not enough jobs to assign to all of them, and assigned others jobs that entailed no more than an hour or so of work each day. In evaluating these conditions, the Court began by stating the obvious: "The Constitution does not mandate comfortable prisons, and prisons . . . which house persons convicted of serious crimes cannot be free of discomfort."[33] However, when it came time to suggest exactly how much discomfort the Justices found acceptable, Powell's opinion actually borrowed several phrases from death penalty cases to establish a sense of the Court's cruel-and-unusual pain threshold. Thus, punishment that stopped just short of involving "the *unnecessary* and *wanton* infliction of pain"[34] and pains of imprisonment that were not "*grossly dispro-portionate to the severity of the crime*"[35] were acceptable. Similarly, harm that was not "totally without penological justification"[36] would be tolerated. As prison law expert Fred Cohen has suggested, the Court appeared to be "looking for a formula to patrol the outer limits of human decency" to give maximum deference to states' rights.[37] Such a formula already had been implemented in the Court's death penalty jurisprudence.

Justice Brennan wrote separately in *Chapman* in a seeming attempt to reassure lower courts that the "decision should in no way be construed as a retreat from careful judicial scrutiny of prison conditions,"[38] but that was exactly how it was construed (and what, in fact, it did signal). As one commentator noted, the Supreme Court's opinions in *Bell* and *Chapman* "appeared to call into question the preceding decade of federal intervention" in prisons.[39] In fact, the Burger Court (and the Rehnquist Court that fol-lowed) remained purposefully on the path staked out in these first few prison cases—overruling the judgments of lower courts that were much closer to the actual conditions of confinement at issue, giving much deference to what the Justices regarded as the expert judgments of prison officials, and largely ignoring the effects of adverse conditions on the psychological well-being of prisoners.[40]

THE INDIVIDUALIZING OF THE CONSTITUTIONAL LAW OF PRISONS

Over the last several decades, the Court has expressed a view of prison life that demonstrates an increasingly tenuous grasp of the harsh realities that exist inside many of our nation's prisons. The Justices simultaneously have extended greater discretion to correctional authorities to govern prisons—almost in whatever ways they see fit—and have chosen to intervene to correct only individual aberrations (rather than address systemic dysfunc-tion that produces broadly harmful conditions or widespread forms of mis-treatment).

For example, in *Whitley v. Albers*,[41] the Court reaffirmed the use of an extremely high threshold—the "wanton and unnecessary infliction of pain"—for finding an Eighth Amendment violation in a case in which excessive force was alleged. The case stemmed from a sequence of events in which an Oregon prisoner was shot in the leg during an attempt by prison guards to quell a disturbance. Justice O'Connor wrote for a narrow majority that, although an express intent to inflict unnecessary pain was not required in Eighth Amendment cases, the offending conduct "must involve more than *ordinary* lack of due care for the prisoner's interests or safety."[42] Indeed, the Court ruled that only "obduracy and wantonness" on the part of prison officials were prohibited; more commonplace instances of the inadvertent, mistaken, or simply unreasonable infliction of pain presumably would be acceptable. Unless the pain was inflicted "maliciously and sadistically for the very purpose of causing harm,"[43] the Court would regard it as unproblematic.[44]

In another line of cases, the Court used curious language to establish the scope of the prisoners' substantive due-process rights. That is, the majority asserted that the "extent of a prisoner's right under the [Due Process] Clause to avoid the unwanted administration of antipsychotic drugs must be defined in the context of the inmate's confinement."[45] But what apparently was meant by *context* reflected only an institutional perspective—the "legitimate needs" of the institution as understood by the staff.[46] Thus, the Court noted that

> There are few cases in which the State's interest in combating the danger posed by a person to both himself and others is greater than in a prison environment, which, "by definition" is made up of persons with "a demonstrated proclivity for anti-social criminal, and often violent, conduct."[47]

Of course, the Justices could have taken a different view of the context of the inmate's confinement, one that also acknowledged the relative powerlessness of the prisoner in retaining his autonomy, obtaining help, or gaining redress in the face of more powerful prison staff members with a range of institutional control mechanisms at their disposal, making the threat of coercive treatment ever present and problematic. Or they could have focused on the tendency for prison staff to sometimes deal with troublesome or disruptive behavior in this context by resorting to forceful techniques and approaches in placing what they perceive to be the immediate needs of the institution (or even their own convenience) ahead of the longer term interests of the prisoner. But to do so would have required a more in-depth and sensitive inquiry into, and balancing of, the realities of institutional life from the perspective of the targets of the treatment in question: the prisoners. This was a very different inquiry from the one in which the Court was prepared to engage.

Just a year later, in another totality-of-prison-conditions case, the Justices effected an additional, major change in approach. In *Wilson v. Seiter*,[48] a group of Ohio prisoners filed a claim that focused on overcrowding, noise, unsanitary conditions, and being housed with mentally and physically ill prisoners. Justice Scalia wrote for the majority that Eighth Amendment claims concerning conduct that did not purport to be punishment required an inquiry into prison officials' *state of mind*—in this case, their "deliberate indifference." Conditions alone would not violate the Constitution; there had to be a culpable state of mind on the part of the officials who created or maintained them.

Thus, Scalia applied the same standard to prison conditions cases as Justice Marshall earlier had used to evaluate claims of inadequate medical care in a Texas case, *Estelle v. Gamble*.[49] In *Gamble*, the Court had said that the threshold of unnecessary and wanton infliction of pain could be reached by proving deliberate indifference to serious medical needs; inadvertence or mere negligence on the part of prison officials was not a significantly culpable state of mind. The Court of Appeals in *Wilson* had applied a somewhat different and more stringent standard—"behavior marked by persistent malicious cruelty"—which the Supreme Court now said was set too high. However, Scalia found that a standard of "mere negligence" was set too low; if that was all the petitioners could make out, then the Court would find it "harmless."[50]

Four Justices disputed this interpretation in *Wilson* and concurred only in the judgment. They argued that conditions of confinement were themselves "part of the punishment" imposed by the sentencing authority, whether they were or were not specifically meted out by statutory law.[51] The concurring Justices noted—surely correctly from a social science standpoint—that "inhumane prison conditions often are the result of cumulative actions and inactions by numerous officials inside and outside a prison, sometimes over a long period of time." Not only was it difficult to know exactly whose intent should be examined but "in truth, intent simply is not very meaningful when considering a challenge to an institution, such as a prison system."[52]

NARROWING THE LEGAL SCOPE OF PRISON "HARM"

From the perspective of modern psychological theory, other aspects of the *Wilson* opinion were equally, if not more, troublesome. In addition to some fine-tuning of the definition of deliberate indifference that set the parameters for future totality-of-conditions cases, Justice Scalia limited the way the Court analyzed the nature of the prison context and its effects on prisoners. One limitation was the Court's rejection of the distinction between short-term deprivations and "continuing" or "systemic" problems. Lawyers representing the prisoners had made the argument that evidence of systemic problems should obviate the need to demonstrate state of mind on the part of officials, who, of necessity, must have long tolerated the problems as part of the correctional status quo. Scalia conceded that the long duration of a cruel condition might make it easier to establish knowledge and, hence, intent, but he defended and retained the intent requirement itself.

In addition, in a change that appeared to be designed to significantly narrow the range of cases in which prisoners could petition for relief, the Court explicitly adopted the psychologically unreasonable construction of prison effects to which I alluded earlier. Specifically, Justice Scalia rejected the notion that courts could consider the way in which prison conditions combined and interacted overall to become an Eighth Amendment violation. Instead, lower courts would be required to find that a particular problematic aspect or condition of confinement rose to the level of an unconstitutional deprivation before they could intervene.

From a psychological perspective, this forced judges to examine each complaint of violation in isolation, rather than in the larger context in which it was experienced. No respectable social scientist would approach the problem in this way. For example, the deprivation of contact visiting might have one psychological effect in a prison environment in which prisoners were afforded a range of other meaningful activities in which to engage, or had frequent occasions to interact with one another under conditions that permitted some semblance of normal social intercourse, or were housed in an otherwise well run facility with ample opportunity to maintain family contact by phone and some reasonable expectation of release after a reasonable period of time.[53] However, in an institution where none of those things were true, the absence of contact visiting might be experienced as acutely painful and psychologically damaging over the long run. Requiring courts to focus only on individual, isolated aspects of potentially unconstitutional confinement, and to tailor remedies that were designed to address only those specific violations, would also require them to ignore these kinds of basic psychological facts.[54]

In several other cases, the Supreme Court limited the scope of meaningful inquiry into the issue that has been the focus of much of this book: the nature of unnecessary prison pain and when and how it can be more effectively regulated and reduced. For example, in one case, *Hudson v. McMillian*,[55] the Court ruled that whenever prison officials are accused of using excessive physical force in violation of the clause on cruel and unusual punishment, the "core judicial inquiry" should focus on the state of mind of the perpetrator: "whether force was applied in a good-faith effort to maintain or restore discipline, or maliciously and sadistically to cause harm."[56]

In a partial concurring opinion, however, Justice Blackmun addressed an issue about which the Court had said very little, in this or any previous case: whether psychological, as opposed to purely physical, harm was permissible to inflict in a prison setting. Noting that the Eighth Amendment "prohibits the unnecessary and wanton infliction of 'pain,' rather than 'injury,'" he observed that the ordinary meaning of pain "surely includes a notion of psychological harm."[57] He then appropriately suggested that it was "not hard to imagine inflictions of psychological harm—without corresponding physical harm—that might prove to be cruel and unusual punishment."[58] *Pain*, in Blackmun's estimation, surely included psychological harm, and he noted that there was no existing precedent to indicate that "psychological pain is not cognizable for constitutional purposes."[59] Unfortunately, none of his colleagues wrote in support of this view.

Even more unfortunately, perhaps, Congress soon joined the Supreme Court in discouraging subsequent meaningful Eighth Amendment analyses of actual conditions of confinement and their psychological effects on prisoners. In April 1996, the U.S. Congress passed the Prison Litigation Reform Act (PLRA), which significantly limited the ability of the federal courts to monitor and remedy constitutional violations in detention facilities throughout the country. Among other things, it placed substantive and procedural limits on injunctions and consent decrees (by which both parties reach binding agreements to fix existing problems in advance of trial) designed to improve prison conditions. The legislation also constrained the appointment of *special masters* to oversee a prison system's compliance with court orders and to ensure that reforms actually were implemented.

From a psychological perspective, however, one of the act's most damaging provisions barred prisoners from filing a claim for mental or emotional harm without a prior showing of physical injury.[60] Some courts have interpreted this provision broadly, concluding that the term *mental or emotional injury* as used in the PLRA had "a well understood meaning as referring to such things as stress, fear, and oppression, and other psychological impacts."[61] Construed in this way, of course, many of the core psychological pains of imprisonment would seem to be exempted from judicial scrutiny unless they occurred in conjunction with some form of physical mistreatment or injury.

Many prison law experts pronounced the PLRA "a disaster for prisoner claims."[62] Although the true long-term impact of this remarkable legislation is impossible to determine just a decade after its passage, it does seem to effectively restrict judicial inquiries into—and judicially imposed solutions to—many harmful aspects of prison life. Combined with the Supreme Court's reluctance to look carefully at the social context of prison and address its negative psychological effects, the PLRA has limited legal efforts to improve the conditions under which many prisoners are confined. Moreover, the PLRA has compromised many lower federal court orders that already were in place, undoing some of the progress made over the last 3 decades of prison reform litigation.

THE WAGES OF DEFERENCE: RACE AND THE
CONTEXT OF IMPRISONMENT

One recent case illustrates the way in which ignoring the context of imprisonment allows problems to worsen beyond the point at which they can be easily solved. In *Johnson v. California*,[63] the U.S. Supreme Court addressed a crucial prison issue: the explicit use of racial segregation in the treatment of prisoners.[64] In chapter 4, I discussed both the race-related influences on and consequences of the policies of overincarceration that have characterized American corrections over the last several decades. But I said little about the way race functions inside prison—after persons have been incarcerated there.

Unfortunately, racism is pervasive and pernicious inside many prisons in the United States.[65] Although not everyone succumbs to—or is targeted by—the virulent racism in these facilities, few persons who live and work in them are untouched by it. Indeed, there is probably no other place in our society where racial tensions run so deep and racial conflicts erupt so often and with such drastic, potentially deadly, consequences than prison.

Many factors contribute to these high levels of racial tension in prison. To be sure, some prisoners and staff members bring racist beliefs with them to prison (which, in the case of the prisoners, may be the product of earlier experiences in racially charged juvenile justice institutions). But there are powerful, immediate contextual forces at work as well. Incarceration forces persons of different races and ethnicities into closer, more intimate daily contact than is typical in the freeworld; those who harbor dormant or suppressed racist feelings and beliefs may resist this closeness, and previously hidden racial animosities are likely to come to the fore.

In addition, racial characteristics act as convenient markers in the dangerous environment of prison, allowing people to quickly categorize one another. These overt characteristics substitute for real knowledge about others and—no matter how imperfectly—they allow prisoners to infer commonalities and shared values, whether they are present or not. Finally, the pervasive scarcities and the assaults on individual self-esteem that characterize prison life also provide fertile ground for group-based competition and hostilities to develop. Racial pride and solidarity are especially important in environments where there may be little else on which to rely for a sense of self and connectedness to others.

These racial dynamics are built into the very environment of prison. Prison administrators who do not acknowledge this fact and attempt to proactively control the racial conflict that inevitably results—by promoting racial tolerance at every turn—usually find that the tensions continue to escalate. Yet, arguably more than any other institution in our society, many prisons give official status to racist beliefs by implementing both formal and informal policies that appear to reify racial differences and legitimize racial animosities.

For example, nowhere else in our society do public officials regularly use racial classifications in their decision making (e.g., by overtly keeping close track of the racial makeup of housing units, or designating some exercise yards as accessible to prisoners of only certain racial groups). Nor do they introduce race explicitly into their record keeping (e.g., by routinely listing race on inmate rosters and, in some places, even color coding inmate identities according to their racial or ethnic group). And nowhere else do public officials openly use racialized language in their everyday workplace communications (e.g., by announcing over the prison intercom that "all Blacks are now permitted to use the yard," or routinely saying things like "I'm sending a group of five Mexicans over to B-section" or "There are six Whites coming out of the law library now.").[66]

This is the troubled and unusual racialized context into which the Court stepped in *Johnson* when it was called on to examine one of these race-based policies. Specifically, the Court ruled on the constitutionality of the California Department of Corrections's (CDC) practice of racially segregating double-celled prisoners for up to the first 60 days after they had entered a new facility—whether they were coming into the prison system initially or were being transferred between prisons. The Court condemned the practice and was certainly right to do so.[67] But several things about the opinion are revealing.

The first is the Court's seemingly superficial grasp of the realities of prison life. Thus, Justice O'Connor wrote for the majority that "with the exception of the double cells in reception areas, the rest of the state prison facilities—dining areas, yards, cells—are fully integrated."[68] Anyone who has ever been in a California prison knows that this is not remotely accurate. Numerous aspects of life in these institutions are bounded by racial considerations—ones that result in the segregation of racial and ethnic groups from each other and that are accomplished with the implicit or often active assistance of the prison officials and staff. Thus, noting that "all racial classifications [imposed by the government] . . . must be analyzed . . . under strict scrutiny,"[69] the Court ignored the fact that racial classifications are made constantly in California and other prisons with virtually no scrutiny at all.

Further, all of the Justices, including those who dissented, accepted essentially at face value the California prison system's justification for its policy of racial segregation in terms of a "prison-gang culture" that is "violent and murderous."[70] Thus, they failed to ask or consider whether and how adverse prison conditions (of the sort the Court itself had approved in the past), or ill-advised correctional management strategies (implemented by officials to whom the Court previously had mandated unquestioned deference, and a broad array of other problematic race-based policies (to which the Court seemed oblivious) may have contributed to the rise of the gangs and their sometimes "murderous" conflicts. Justice Stevens's dissent came closest, but even he accepted the "poignant evidence" that California prisons were "infested with violent race-based gangs" without really trying to determine why, or considering whether other correctional conditions, practices, and decisions were perhaps at the root of this problem. Although appropriately proclaiming the need to "scratch below the surface of this evidence," even he did not scratch very deeply, and certainly not deeply enough to see the potential interconnections between these various factors—at least some of which the Court had a hand in allowing to continue—and the existence of racial conflict in prisons.[71]

Finally, *Johnson* did surface a long overdue—but still very limited—debate about the merits of continued judicial deference to the decision making of correctional officials. The majority concluded that in this one instance—the use of explicit racial classifications without any compelling justification—the logic and legitimacy of prison officials' policies could be appropriately questioned. However, Justices Thomas and Scalia argued that even here the Court should defer. Indeed, Thomas seemed somewhat taken aback at "the majority's refusal—*for the first time ever*—to defer to the expert judgment of prison officials."[72] Neither he nor Scalia thought that this was the right time to begin. Although Thomas was correct that "there are no obvious, easy alternatives to the CDC's policy" of racial segregation,[73] none of the Justices seemed to appreciate the way that the very dilemma the CDC faced—no obvious, easy alternatives to a policy that nonetheless was not working very well—might be due in part to the Court's own inattention to the nature of the prison context and its effects on prisoners.

BEGINNING TO EVALUATE AND LIMIT PAINFUL CONDITIONS OF CONFINEMENT

The legal doctrines I have reviewed so far provide little basis for optimism about the use of law to further reduce the pains of imprisonment. Until the Supreme Court signals lower courts that it is once again appropriate to look carefully at the realities of prison life and to consider the broad effects of the totality of conditions to which prisoners are exposed, court-ordered solutions—except in the most egregious cases—are likely to be limited. I say this without intending to diminish the significance of the extraordinary efforts made by prison litigators, many effective court-ordered reforms brought about by numerous conscientious judges, and the very real progress made in some of the areas to which I referred earlier.

Indeed, to the extent to which these efforts may have fallen short, I believe that politics—rather than any lack of skill or dedication—is largely responsible. Supreme Court doctrines that individualized cognizable prison harm and narrowed the scope of Eighth Amendment review certainly were consistent with, if not driven by, the political spirit of the times. So, too, was the passage of the PLRA, which clearly came about as a result of explicitly political motives and forces at work. Of course—and here is the optimistic lining in this otherwise dark legal cloud—political interests and alignments are subject to modification and change, just as they were in the mid-1970s, when seemingly progressive policy trends abruptly reversed course and began to move in another direction.

Yet the problem is more than just politics. Perhaps because of the dampening effect that these powerful political forces have had on law-related prison reform, there have been few advances in the development of more useful conceptual tools to help revamp the legal doctrines used to address the cruel and unusual aspects of prison life. Thus, the legal categories that encompass the pains of imprisonment remain conceptually limited. Among other things, the doctrines used to assess cruel and unusual prison punishment have failed to incorporate key aspects of the contextual model of behavior that has emerged over the last several decades.

As I argued in previous chapters, modern psychological theory provides an analytical framework with which to develop a much more sophisticated and careful assessment of the real pains of imprisonment, one that includes a greater appreciation of the powerful situational forces that are at work in prison settings as well as of their long-term consequences. As one legal commentator reminded, echoing Justice Blackmun's observations in *Hudson*, "the cruel punishment clause is not bound by the infliction of physical pain. Psychological no less than physical pain can be diagnosed and quantified."[74] But some new conceptual tools are needed to stimulate better legal assessments of the psychological pains of imprisonment.

For example, one way to more accurately and openly acknowledge these pains—and to allow them to be taken into account in assessing the likely consequences of confinement in different institutional settings—would be to develop a "prison index" that classified correctional environments along a continuum of psychological pain and potential harmfulness.[75] The insight that not all prisons are created equal—and that, therefore, not all prison sentences of equal length impose the same level of punishment—has escaped the attention of most legal analysts and decision makers.

Justice Blackmun made a similar observation. He noted that the plight of someone sentenced to "a period of confinement in a relatively safe, well-managed prison" is hardly equivalent to that of another prisoner housed in "a prison characterized by rampant violence and terror." Despite the presumed intent of the two different sentencing judges to subject each prisoner to roughly the same amount of prison pain, radical differences in conditions of confinement would "resul[t] in differing punishment for the two convicts."[76]

A prison index would underscore the fact that prisons inflict varying amounts of psychological pain and carry different levels of risk for long-term damage. It also would permit more meaningful comparisons between prison systems of the sort that could be taken into account in judicial analyses of the proportionality of sentences. Finally, by stimulating attempts to calibrate levels of prison pain, the index might lead us to a deeper and more precise understanding of the relationship between harsh punishment and subsequent criminal behavior. Greater insight into the long-term impact of different kinds of incarceration could help to highlight the fact that "brutal prison conditions do not necessarily serve as a deterrent to criminal behavior."[77]

Indeed, a prison index also could assist in educating the public about the real psychological consequences of imprisonment. Knowledge about the different effects of separate prison environments—specific information about the way that context matters in the case of correctional settings—would provide a deeper and more informed basis for the evolving standards of decency that are supposed to be used to judge our systems of punishment. Public standards and values are of little use in limiting the pains of imprisonment if citizens "are unaware of the punishments actually inflicted."[78]

In addition to the construction of a prison index, a psychologically sophisticated perspective that acknowledges the devastating impact of inhumane conditions of confinement might influence sentencing policies in a number of ways. For example, greater awareness of the costs of harsh prison conditions might lead to a requirement that, before legislators could enact any new law meting out increased prison time, they be required to demonstrate that the statute would not compromise basic prison living conditions. That is, a kind of "prison-environmental impact report" could serve as a prerequisite to the passage of any bill that affected the number of people sent to prison or the length of time they would stay there.[79]

Many states have made their sentencing laws and related prison policies much harsher over the last several decades, without giving any consideration to the impact of these changes on the existing prison system. Among other things, they are now grappling with overcrowded and deteriorating facilities that are expensive to run, are at risk of violating even the generous legal standards that govern their operation, and are yielding very questionable benefits in terms of controlling crime. For example, some states have found that implementing tough sentencing guidelines, or so-called *truth-in-sentencing* laws (that require all prisoners to serve at least 85% of their prison terms before they can be paroled), unexpectedly increased overall incarceration rates beyond the prison system's ability to absorb additional prisoners. In some cases, in fact, analysts have concluded that the resulting poor conditions and lack of programming opportunities actually increased recidivism rates. Lawmakers and prison officials in these jurisdictions have begun to reconsider past policies and to look instead to less restrictive alternative sentencing models, such as house arrest for minor offenses, that appear to be both more economical and more effective.[80]

Another conceptual innovation, beyond the prison index and prison environmental impact report, pertains to the way we think about legal culpability for offenses that are committed in prison. For example, if the "general atmosphere of fear, apprehension and degrading conditions all have their effects on the minds of those confined in prison," then prisoners may be more likely to act under some form of institutionally created *diminished capacity* due to the adverse prison conditions to which they are exposed. Thus, these factors could be taken explicitly into account in assessing the culpability of persons who have committed crimes "while under the influence of these types of stress."[81]

The pressures of the prison environment and the powerful contingencies that are applied to prisoner behavior also constrain the choices prisoners make and the alternative courses of action they perceive are available to them. This parallels an observation that Philip Zimbardo and I made many years ago: "When people are fully aware and informed about their choices, *and when they live in circumstances that offer genuine opportunity to choose otherwise*, then—and only then—can they be said to make truly 'moral' decisions," and be held fully accountable for their actions.[82] Genuine opportunities to "choose otherwise" are often lacking in the harsh prison settings where powerful institutional contingencies and the strong pressures of a prison culture may combine to virtually compel certain behaviors. Thus, the nature and magnitude of the environmental pressures to which prisoners are subjected could play a more explicit role in assessing their levels of legal culpability in prison.

This perspective can be applied to postrelease behavior as well, especially for those prisoners who most acutely suffer the long-term debilitating effects of imprisonment. In any given case, a carefully evaluated history of past incarceration may serve to mitigate the punishment for criminal behavior committed after release. Prisoner Jack Abbott's observation about how at least some prisoners' lives have been profoundly shaped by their long-term incarceration adds another dimension to this issue: "Some of us prisoners—not many; there are only a few of us left who have *never* been free—are a *product* of prison conditions that are today recognized as 'unconstitutional,' indeed, *criminal*."[83] Thus, the extent to which harsh prison environments force prisoners to adapt in ways that prove deeply dysfunctional once they have returned to free society is a factor that can be carefully considered in calculations of blameworthiness. And, for prisoners who have been forced to endure especially extreme (even unconstitutional) prison conditions, the amount of punishment that is deserved for later crimes might be correspondingly mitigated. Although these are unsettling notions to contemplate—because they fit uncomfortably with the existing individualistic legal doctrines by which we typically hold people accountable despite their exposure to harmful contexts in the past—the implications are straightforward. The alternative solution, of course, would be to seriously address and effectively alleviate the most criminogenic aspects of prison itself.

A final set of contextually oriented proposals to better limit the pains of imprisonment would entail bringing social psychological principles to bear in court-ordered prison reform to increase the effectiveness of judicial implementation. Taking psychology seriously in the judicial restructuring of penal institutions would require a host of techniques and perspectives to be used that have been largely ignored or de-emphasized to date.[84] As one legal commentator observed, law-related institutional reform litigation "requires a greater understanding of the extent to which a particular institutional context presents special demands, limitations, and potential for judicial intervention than presently exists."[85] Paying close attention to the context of reform underscores "the dynamic relations between judicial intervention and organizational change."[86]

For example, modern psychological theory can contribute directly to the enforcement of complex, structurally based judicial remedies in prison-conditions cases.[87] As I have noted, recognizing the power of social contexts to shape, transform, and harm the persons within them represent one starting point from which to articulate and define fair and humane limits to pain. In addition, however, contemporary psychology's recognition of the importance of context, situation, and structure provides a principled social scientific basis for law professor Owen Fiss's decades-old argument that structural reforms rather than individualistic models of litigation are needed to remedy unconstitutional prison conditions and to redress other group-based claims concerning institutional mistreatment.[88]

Indeed, this perspective also can be applied self-reflexively by judges to the context in which they operate and function. Specifically, judges are required to simultaneously act as sentencing authorities and evaluators of the very prisons to which they have exiled convicts. As Hans Toch once observed, "Judges cannot intervene in a prison with a clear conscience after spending years routinely shipping inmates to substandard settings with callous disregard of their fate. Intervening when things fall apart (crisis intervention) is a poor excuse for not providing advice and consent."[89] Performing these roles with fairness and sensitivity would require judges to attain a keen understanding of both the social contextual determinants of crime and the psychological impact of imprisonment, as well as a greater awareness of the inherent tensions in the dual role that they are required to play here.

In structural terms, there may be a context-based argument for insulating judges even further from political pressures, perhaps by having them depend to an even greater degree on prison monitors or special masters. Otherwise, politically motivated misrepresentations of their actions and integrity are easily mounted by groups that lack knowledge of the kind of psychological harm that must be addressed in prison cases and who overlook the long-term criminogenic consequences of completely ignoring the needs of prisoners.[90] Alternatively, there may a context-based argument for creating a separate administrative corps of correctional ombudsmen who are trained to analyze the psychology of imprisonment and who are empowered to intervene and make changes in those dimensions of the prison environment that are most problematic and potentially harmful.[91]

CONCLUSION

The Eighth Amendment is thought to "draw its meaning from the evolving standards of decency that mark the progress of a maturing society."[92] Yet, developing a process to systematically determine whether and how any particular conditions of confinement might offend the evolving standards held by members of the public—measuring cruelty in the prison context— is a difficult task. I have suggested in this chapter that, in addition to providing a framework with which to better analyze the social realities of imprisonment, modern psychological theory provides a starting point from which to identify cruel contexts and alleviate their effects.

I agree wholeheartedly with the consensus view that judicial involvement in the American prison system over the last several decades is "responsible for virtually all modern changes in the prison environment beneficial to inmates."[93] Yet, the scope and magnitude of those changes (as well as, in some instances, their permanence) have been compromised by many of the issues discussed in this chapter, including the Supreme Court's reluctance to look carefully at actual conditions of confinement and take into account the impact of harsh realities to which prisoners are exposed.[94] In addition, the Court has constricted its own role in developing limits to prison pain in several important ways: by rejecting a totality-of-conditions framework, by regularly deferring to the presumed expertise of prison officials, and by focusing on the state of mind of correctional actors and decision makers to the exclusion of almost everything else in Eighth Amendment inquiries. Together, these doctrines have diverted much legal attention away from the nature of actual prison conditions and their real effects on prisoners.

In a certain sense, the fate of prisoners with special needs—those with mental illness and developmental disabilities that I discussed in the last chapter—underscores the law's limitations in reducing the pains of imprisonment. Successful claims by prisoners who "need or desire various forms of help" have been limited largely to those who have special vulnerabilities. Of course, even then these claims are granted only sporadically and with uncertain results.[95] But this has meant that the majority of prisoners who do not fall into one of these special-needs categories are hard pressed to have their plights addressed or find a legal forum in which they will even be considered.

Thus, law professor Margo Schlanger ended a comprehensive survey of prisoner litigation with the accurate observation that the "presence or absence of education, employment, and rehabilitative programming; general decisions about custody levels or security restrictions . . . all are beyond the narrow concerns of current constitutional law."[96] As I have tried to show, the law's ineffectiveness in adequately safeguarding the well-being of all prisoners stems in part from its insensitivity to the core focus of this book: the power of context. By decontextualizing prisoners' rights and individualizing applicable legal doctrines over the last several decades, judges and lawmakers have retreated, politically and intellectually, from the important challenge of limiting prison pain.

In this constrained legal context, it useful to consider South African psychologist D. H. Foster's admonition that "discourse about psychological hurt or ill effects is itself a political matter" and that any analysis that "merely labels effects in order to strengthen disciplinary legitimacy and collect more clients is likely to be neither enlightening nor useful."[97] This is a direct and valid challenge to psychologists (and practitioners in any prison-related discipline) that to merely label a problem like prison pain (and thereby enhance one's own apparent expertise) does not contribute much to its solution. Yet, the discourse about psychological hurt in prison can be put to better purposes, ones that, in certain ways, call disciplinary legitimacy itself into question and reduce the number of clients by addressing the adverse conditions that have helped to create their problems. Some of these issues—ways of going beyond "merely labeling" the pains of imprisonment to propose strategies of psychologically based reform—are developed in the next chapter.

NOTES

1. Nils Christie, *Limits to Pain* (Oxford, England: Martin Robertson, 1982), 57.
2. Justice Harry Blackmun, concurring in Farmer v. Brennan, 511 U.S. 825, 855 (1994).

3. There have been many comprehensive treatments of this important topic. *See, e.g.*, Lynn Branham and Sheldon Krantz, *Cases and Materials on the Law of Sentencing, Corrections, and Prisoners' Rights*, 5th ed. (St. Paul, MN: West, 1997); Nicholas Kittrie and Elyce Zenoff, *Sentencing, Sanctions and Corrections: Federal and State Law, Policy, and Practice* (New York: Foundation Press, 2002); Michael Mushlin, *The Rights of Prisoners*, 3d ed. (St. Paul, MN: Thomson/West, 2002); Richard Singer and William Statsky, *Rights of the Imprisoned: Cases, Materials, and Directions* (Indianapolis: Bobbs-Merrill, 1976); and Christopher Smith, *Law and Contemporary Corrections* (Belmont, CA: West/Wadsworth, 2000).

4. Todd Clear and George Cole, *American Corrections*, 4th ed. (Belmont, CA: Wadsworth, 1997), 339.

5. F. Cohen, "The Limits of the Judicial Reform of Prisons: What Works, What Does Not," *Criminal Law Bulletin* 40 (2004): 421, 421–422.

6. Ibid., 423.

7. Ibid., 436–441.

8. *See* R. Dunham, "The Cruel and Unusual Punishment and Excessive Fines Clauses," *American Criminal Law Review* 26 (1989): 1617, for a discussion of some of these issues.

9. *See* A. Granucci, "'Nor Cruel and Unusual Punishments Inflicted': The Original Meaning," *California Law Review* 57 (1969): 839.

10. Weems v. United States, 217 U.S. 349, 372 (1910) (examining the Philippine Islands penalty of 12 to 20 years "hard and painful labor" while chained at the ankle and wrist, plus "perpetual" disqualification of political rights and a lifetime of official surveillance for the crime of falsification of records). *Weems* also served as the foundation for what came to be known as *proportionality* in Eighth Amendment analysis—the notion that the severity of the penalty should roughly approximate the severity of the crime and the culpability of the person who committed it.

11. J. Philips, "Jailhouse Shock: *Hudson v. McMillan* and the Supreme Court's Flawed Interpretation of the Eighth Amendment," *Connecticut Law Review* 26 (1993): 355, 358 [citing to Hobbs v. State, 32 N.E. 1019, 1020 (Ind. 1893)]. *See also* M. Gutterman, "The Contours of Eighth Amendment Prison Jurisprudence: Conditions of Confinement," *Southern Methodist University Law Review* 48 (1995): 373, 378: "For almost two centuries the Supreme Court failed to address the actual conditions endured by citizens confined in prison."

12. Ex parte Hull, 312 U.S. 546 (1941).

13. Trop v. Dulles, 356 U.S. 86, 86 (1958). *Trop* was a case in which the Court examined the constitutionality of the punishment of expatriation for the crime of desertion.

14. Although the Warren Court did not do a great deal to *directly* address the plight of prisoners, the way the Court approached the rights of other powerless groups encouraged prisoners to seek redress from the judiciary. As one commentator put it, "Prisoners and their advocates, seeking to assert the rights of a politically powerless minority often ignored in American society, saw the courts

as their most accessible forum and began to take advantage of doors opened by the Warren Court." "Developments in the Law, The Law of Prisons," *Harvard Law Review* 115 (2002): 1838, 1849 (footnote omitted).

15. National Institute of Justice, *American Prisons and Jails*, vol. 3. (Washington, DC: U.S. Department of Justice, 1980), 32.

16. American Public Health Association Jails and Prisons Task Force, *Standards for Health Services in Correctional Institutions* (Washington, DC: American Public Health Association, 1976), 62; U.S. Department of Justice, *Federal Standards for Prisons and Jails* (Washington, DC: U.S. Department of Justice, 1980), Standard No. 2.04, p. 17. *See also* National Institute of Justice, *American Prisons and Jails*, vol. 3, 85, n. 6.

17. The American Correctional Association recommended that prisoners be afforded a minimum of 60 square feet and, for those confined in their cells for more than an average of 10 hours per day, 80 square feet. *See* Commission on Accreditation for Corrections, *Manual of Standards for Adult Correctional Institutions* (Rockville, MD: American Correctional Association, 1977), Standard No. 4142, p. 27. The National Sheriffs' Association recommended between 70 and 80 square feet. *See* National Sheriffs' Association, *A Handbook on Jail Architecture* (Washington, DC: Author, 1975). The National Council on Crime and Delinquency (NCCD) recommended at least 50 square feet of living space per inmate. *See* National Council on Crime and Delinquency, "Model Act for the Protection of Rights of Prisoners," *Crime & Delinquency* § 1, 18 (1972): 4, 10. Overcrowding meant that few prisons were able to adhere to even the NCCD's more modest recommendations.

18. 437 U.S. 678 (1978). For insight into the earlier Arkansas litigation, see Holt v. Sarver, 300 F. Supp. 825 (E.D. Ark. 1969); Holt v. Sarver, 309 F. Supp. 362 (E.D. Ark. 1970).

19. 437 U.S. at 684.

20. 437 U.S. at 688 (emphasis added).

21. *Id.*

22. Rehnquist had written, "The District Court's order limiting the maximum period of punitive isolation to 30 days in no way relates to any condition found offensive to the Constitution." *Id.* at 712.

23. 441 U.S. 520 (1979). *Bell* technically was not about the Eighth Amendment at all. The question was whether exposing pretrial detainees—who had not been convicted of a crime—to these severe conditions amounted to depriving them of liberty without due process of law.

24. *Id.* at 538. As pretrial inmates, the persons held in the jail were not supposed to be punished. Because their conditions were not intended as punishment, the Court ruled, they were beyond the reach of the Eighth Amendment. As legal analyst Donald Gottlieb correctly noted, courts that tried to apply this "punitive-intent" analysis "reached bizarre results," largely because its logic suggested that even the most horrendous set of conditions would be constitutional so long as the intent of the jailers was not to inflict punishment. Donald Gottlieb, "The Legacy of *Wolfish* and *Chapman*: Some Thoughts About 'Big Prison Case' Litigation in the 1980s," in *Prisoners and the Law*, ed. Ira Robbins

(New York: Clark Boardman, 1985), 11. Even though the Court in *Bell v. Wolfish* did say that conditions of confinement that created "genuine privations and hardship over an extended period of time" might be taken as the equivalent of punishment (441 U.S. at 542), Gottlieb pointed out that "The courts have been unable . . . to articulate any consistent measuring rod for privations and hardship. *Wolfish* itself provides scant help." Gottlieb, "The Legacy of *Wolfish* and *Chapman*," 12.

25. 441 U.S. at 538.

26. *Id.* at 547.

27. There are many prison administrators who undoubtedly deserve the confidence the Court has placed in them. Yet it seems doubtful that a nearly irrebuttable presumption of legitimate expertise—something the Court has instructed lower courts to reject in the case of, say, expert witnesses—should be categorically conferred in this way in this arena. Indeed, for the serious threshold inquiries the Court demands in the case of expert witnesses—despite the fact that their qualifications and expertise are routinely tested by the adversarial process—*see, e.g.*, Daubert v. Merrell Dow Pharmaceuticals, 509 U.S. 579 (1993), and Kumho Tire v. Carmichael, 526 U.S. 137 (1999).

28. Indeed, as I note later in this chapter, Justice Thomas has suggested that the Court has refused to defer to prison administrators only once, in 2005, when presented with a policy of explicit racial segregation. He and Justice Scalia disagreed with the refusal even in this case, implying that it should be absolute (or nearly so). *See, infra*, note 72 and accompanying text.

29. Bell, 441 U.S. at 546.

30. 452 U.S. 337 (1981).

31. *Id.* at 345.

32. *Id.* at 348. The majority opinion seemed especially mindful that population pressures were driving the use of double celling. Indeed, Justice Powell offered a theory about the causes of increased prison crowding, although he provided no data in support of it: "Since [1974], the problems of prison population and administration have been exacerbated by the increase of serious crime and the effect of inflation on the resources of States and communities." *Id.* at 351. Justice Marshall was more pointed in his dissent, in which he emphasized the fact that no one in the case had argued that double celling represented sound correctional policy:

> None of those conditions results from a considered policy judgment on the part of the State. Until the Court's opinion today, absolutely no one—certainly not the "state legislatures" or "prison officials" to whom the majority suggests . . . that we defer in analyzing constitutional questions—had suggested that forcing long-term inmates to share tiny cells designed to hold only one individual might be a good thing.

Id. at 370.

33. *Id.* at 349.

34. *Id.* at 345, citing Gregg v. Georgia, 428 U.S. 153, 173 (1976) (joint opinion) (emphasis added).

35. *Id.*, citing Coker v. Georgia, 433 U.S. 584, 592 (1977) (emphasis added).

36. *Id.*, citing *Gregg* at 183 (emphasis added).

37. Personal communication.

38. 452 U.S. at 353.

39. Gottlieb, "The Legacy of *Wolfish* and *Chapman,*" 3–4.

40. This formula was articulated clearly in *Bell*: "Prison administrators [are to be] accorded wide-ranging deference in the adoption and execution of policies and practices that in their judgment are needed to preserve internal order and discipline and to maintain institutional security." 441 U.S. at 547. Similarly, although Justice Powell's majority opinion in *Chapman* cautioned lower court judges not to "assume that state legislatures and prison officials are insensitive to the requirements of the Constitution or to the perplexing sociological problems of how best to achieve the goals of the penal function in the criminal justice system," the Court began to regularly commit the opposite kind of error. That is, they started assuming in seemingly every case, often when there was evidence to the contrary, that legislators and prison officials *were* sensitive to these requirements and problems. 452 U.S. at 352.

41. 475 U.S. 312 (1986).

42. *Id.* at 319 (emphasis added).

43. *Id.* at 320.

44. *Whitley* involved a so-called "riot situation." But the Court later applied the very same test when force was applied in a one-on-one situation. *See* Hudson v. McMillian, 503 U.S. 1 (1992).

45. *Id.* at 222.

46. *Id.*

47. *Id.* at 225 (citations omitted).

48. 501 U.S. 294 (1991).

49. Estelle v. Gamble, 429 U.S. 97 (1976). However, the result was just the opposite. As one commentator put it,

   Justice Thurgood Marshall enunciated the "deliberate indifference" test in 1976 to advance prisoners' rights by recognizing that the Eighth Amendment applies to protect incarcerated offenders and their limited right to medical care. Fifteen years later, Justice Scalia appropriated the test as a means to advance the contrary policy goal of limiting prisoners' abilities to challenge prison conditions as violations of the Eighth Amendment.

   C. Smith, "The Malleability of Constitutional Doctrine and Its Ironic Impact on Prisoners' Rights," *Boston University Public Interest Law Journal* 11 (2001): 73, 86.

50. 501 U.S. at 305.

51. *Id.* at 306.

52. *Id.* at 310.

53. The Supreme Court recently turned this approach on its head in a Michigan case. The majority opinion emphasized that "alternatives to visitation need

not be ideal," to nonetheless represent adequate substitutes in prisons where officials have chosen to punish prisoners by prohibiting contact with loved ones. The Justices did so without real analysis of the quality of those alternatives or the larger context of deprivation in which prisoners would experience them. *See* Overton v. Bazzetta, 539 U.S. 126, 136 (2003).

54. The doctrine limiting the scope of a lower court's remedial authority is not limited to prison cases, but has been applied more generally in institutional reform litigation. Chief Justice Rehnquist's majority opinion in Missouri v. Jenkins, 515 U.S. 70 (1995), a school desegregation case, stated the doctrine succinctly: "The remedial components must directly address and relate to the constitutional violation and be tailored to cure the condition that offends the Constitution." *Id.* at 145. Of course, much turns—indeed, everything turns in this kind of review—on how one defines—narrowly or broadly—"the condition that offends the Constitution."

55. Hudson v. McMillian, 503 U.S. 1 (1992). The Court shifted the focus of the inquiry from the magnitude of the harm (the issue on which the lower courts had concentrated) to the state of mind of the perpetrators. Although it was a victory of sorts for plaintiffs—the decision did allow the prisoner's Eighth Amendment claim to proceed—the case itself sheds a disturbing light on how the issue of prisoner mistreatment is viewed and handled by some other decision makers in the legal system. Trial testimony indicated that a corrections officer—McMillian—punched a prisoner—Hudson—"in the mouth, eyes, chest, and stomach" with blows whose force, among other things, bruised his body and face, "cracked [his] partial dental plate, split his lower lip and loosened his teeth." 929 F. 2d 1014 (1990), 1015. While this beating was underway, another "held [the prisoner] in place and kicked and punched him from behind," and a third officer—the shift supervisor—watched, telling his two charges "not to 'have too much fun.'" *Id.*

In an opinion deploring these actions and expressing the hope that "someday this blight on our criminal justice system will be forever removed," the Fifth Circuit nonetheless ruled that the injuries were not "significant" enough to make out a case of excessive force, largely because they "required no medical attention." *Id.* Notwithstanding what this suggests about the level of prisoner abuse that may be tolerated as "insignificant," the Fifth Circuit's focus on whether the injuries "required medical attention" sidesteps the important contextual factors that help shape the way judgments like these are made. The issue of whether a harm or injury "requires" medical attention in a prison setting is an complicated one, not unlike the question I discussed in the last chapter concerning whether and how prison systems themselves decide that the needs of prisoners with mental illness are being "adequately" addressed. That is, these are matters of opinion that reflect a complex interplay between care providers (who make judgments about what is needed in a particular case) and prisoners (whose decision to request medical, or any, "attention" is in part a function of whether they perceive that genuine help is likely to be forthcoming). In a prison culture where correctional supervisors cheer on officers who are beating prisoners, judgments about which injuries require medical attention (or, from the prisoner's perspective, whether to bother—or perhaps risk—seeking such attention) might be difficult to accurately interpret.

In addition, an amicus brief filed in *Hudson* on behalf of the attorneys general of Florida, Hawaii, Louisiana, Nevada, Texas, and Wyoming provided further insight into the mind-set with which some legal decision makers have come to view prisoner complaints. The top law enforcement officials in each of these states urged the Court to apply a "significant injury requirement" and reject the prisoner's beating claim *because* this higher threshold would help "to control . . . system-wide docket management problems" by significantly reducing the number of lawsuits prisoners could successfully file. 503 U.S. at 15. What is remarkable is not that some litigators might feel that the convenience of judges should outweigh a prisoner's interest in avoiding beatings at the hands of prison staff (or even that a rare judge might agree), but rather that they felt comfortable and confident enough about this trade-off to assert it in their brief.

56. *Id.* at 7. In a 7-to-2 ruling, the Supreme Court reversed the Fifth Circuit. But the Court shifted the inquiry to the state of mind of the correctional officers rather than the magnitude of the injury suffered by the prisoner.

57. *Id.* at 16.

58. *Id.*

59. *Id.* Justice Blackmun also correctly noted that "psychological pain often may be clinically diagnosed and quantified through well-established methods, as in the ordinary tort context where damages for pain and suffering are regularly awarded." *Id.* at 17.

60. James Robertson has written very thoughtfully this issue. *See* J. Robertson, "Psychological Injury and the Prison Litigation Reform Act: A 'Not Exactly,' Equal Protection Analysis," *Harvard Journal on Legislation* 37 (2000): 105. *See also* J. Robertson, "The Jurisprudence of the PLRA: Inmates as 'Outsiders' and the Countermajoritarian Difficulty," *Journal of Criminal Law & Criminology* 92 (2001): 187.

61. Amaker v. Haponik, 1999 WL 76798 (S.D. N.Y. February, 17, 1999), at 7.

62. Cohen, "The Limits of the Judicial Reform of Prisons," 453. Some commentators predicted that the PRLA would not have "large-scale systematic effects on the outcomes" in prison cases, primarily because prisoners already had such low success rates in them. Even before the PLRA was passed, only an estimated 3% of prisoners' civil rights claims reached pretrial hearings on evidence, and only 2% ultimately resulted in trial verdicts. M. Tushnet and L. Yackle, "Symbolic Statutes and Real Laws: The Pathologies of the Antiterroism and Effective Death Penalty Act and the Prison Litigation Reform Act," *Duke Law Journal* 47 (1997): 1, 85. Yet, nearly 10 years after its passage, many prisoner litigators agree with Margo Schlanger that the PLRA effectively "restricts the legal rights of some of the most disempowered and vulnerable people in this country," and that it places "real obstacles . . . in the way of even legitimate cases." *See* M. Schlanger, "The Politics of Inmate Litigation," *Harvard Law Review* 117 (2004): 2799, 2799, 2801.

63. Johnson v. California, 125 S. Ct. 1141 (2005). The case was decided by an unusual 5-to-3 vote in which the majority remanded the case to the courts below in light of its ruling that strict scrutiny should be used to evaluate the suspect racial classification at issue. Chief Justice Rehnquist took no part in the case, and the dissenters included Justice Stevens, who believed that the practice in question was clearly unconstitutional and could not possibly be justified by California prison officials (making remand to the lower courts unnecessary), and Justices Thomas and Scalia, who did not see any constitutional problems with the policy of segregation (and therefore would have approved it).

64. Many years earlier, in Lee v. Washington, 390 U.S. 333 (1968), the Court had outlawed Alabama's systematic racial segregation in its jails and prisons. Justices Black, Harlan, and Stewart wrote separately "to make explicit" something that they felt could only be inferred from the Court's per curiam opinion: that prison officials "acting in good faith and in particularized circumstances" had the right "to take into account racial tensions in maintaining security, discipline, and good order in prisons and jails." Id. at 334. This caveat—reasonable at the time—seemed over the years to serve as the basis for allowing prison officials to manage racial tensions in whatever way they saw fit, sometimes with disastrous consequences. The Lee Court cited Brown v. Board of Education for the proposition that no state-run institutions could be operated on a racially segregated basis. However, unlike its involvement in Brown and schools, the Court never again got involved in the details of whether and how well prison officials were managing the process of desegregation in penal institutions. As I suggest in this section of the chapter, many prison systems did little, if anything, to proactively promote racial harmony or explicitly reduce racial conflicts and tensions between groups of prisoners.

65. Prison expert John Irwin recently suggested that racial conflict may have subsided somewhat over the years, at least in certain prisons: "The racial prejudice and mostly informal racial segregation that characterized prison social organization in the 1960's, '70's, and '80's continues, though at a greatly reduced level." John Irwin, The Warehouse Prison: Disposal of the New Dangerous Class (Los Angeles: Roxbury, 2005), 93. If racial tensions have been greatly reduced in some facilities, in my experience they have been greatly intensified in others. In numerous prisons throughout the California system (in which the facility Irwin studied is located), racial and ethnic conflicts regularly erupt, leading to prison lockdowns that can last for long periods of time. These tensions and conflicts also have been used to justify a policy that assigns prisoners to supermax prisons exclusively on the basis of their alleged racial and ethnic gang affiliations. S. Tachiki, "Indeterminate Sentences in Supermax Prisons Based Upon Alleged Gang Affiliations: A Reexamination of Procedural Protection and a Proposal for Greater Procedural Requirements," California Law Review 83 (1995): 1117.

66. In many California prisons nowadays, prospective visitors who telephone the prison's visiting information line will hear recorded messages to the effect that, for example, "Black inmates will be permitted to visit on Tuesday afternoon,

Whites on Wednesday morning, and all Mexicans remain locked down until further notice"—referring to the special restrictions—lockdowns and cancelled or restricted visiting—that come about when certain groups of prisoners are suspected of being involved in prison conflicts. Imagine a school using similar tactics, for example, by telling parents that White parents could meet with their children's teachers on one night, Black parents on another, and Mexican parents on a third. Or try to imagine a school in which the principal and classroom teachers openly and scrupulously tallied and posted a classroom-by-classroom breakdown of the students' race and ethnicity. As I say, we regularly accept official race-based policies in prison that would not be tolerated in any other institutional setting in our society.

67. For a thoughtful discussion of the origins of the wrongheaded California segregation policy, an examination of the way that early mistakes in prison management—if they go uncorrected—can result in increasingly insoluble problems, and some useful suggestions about what might be done instead with prisoners who enter the state's racially charged prison system, see H. Toch and J. Acker, "Racial Segregation as a Prison Initiation Experience," *Criminal Law Bulletin* 40(5) (2004): 2.

68. Johnson v. California, 125 S. Ct. at 1145.

69. *Id.* at 1146, quoting Adarand Constructors, Inc. v. Pena, 515 U.S. 200, 227 (1995). The Court's statement that "virtually all other States and the Federal Government manage their prison systems without reliance on racial segregation" similarly reflects very little appreciation of how day-to-day prison operations unfold elsewhere. *Id.* at 1148. Although the precise form of the segregation varies greatly from place to place, and certainly not every prison system implements the kind of explicit segregated housing policies that California does in its reception centers, virtually all prison systems take race into account (i.e., use racial classifications of some sort), and most systems, at some point and in some way, use forms of racial segregation. Race and racial tension are facts of prison life that are most often dealt with through policies and practices based on separation and exclusion.

70. *Id.* at 1145.

71. *Id.* at 1155. In fairness, Stevens did acknowledge that the CDC's segregation policy could be "counterproductive" because it "may initiate new arrivals into a corrosive culture of prison racial segregation, lending credence to the view that members of other races are to be feared and that racial alliances are necessary." *Id.* at 1157, n. 4. Yet he did not seem to recognize that this was just the *start* of a process by which prison officials—aided and abetted by racial gangs, to be sure—would continue to immerse prisoners in a racially corrosive prison culture. Justice Thomas's dissent seemed even less well informed. He emphasized that "to understand this case, one must understand just how limited the policy at issue is." *Id.* at 1157. In fact, the policy is just one visible tip of a much larger set of policies and practices that are submerged throughout the prison system.

72. *Id.* at 1171 (emphasis added).

73. *Id.* at 1163.

74. M. Gutterman, "The Contours of Eighth Amendment Prison Jurisprudence: Conditions of Confinement," *Southern Methodist University Law Review* 48 (1995): 373, 405.

75. William Selke, *Prisons in Crisis* (Bloomington, IN: University of Indiana Press, 1993). Charles Logan used this term in a paper that, although written from a "retributive" perspective that is very different from the one I have advanced in this book, provided "a set of empirical indicators that can be used as performance measures for prisons and that concentrate on the competent, fair, and efficient administration of confinement. . . ." Charles Logan, "Criminal Justice Performance Measures for Prisons," in *Performance Measures for the Criminal Justice System*, Bureau of Justice Statistics Discussion Papers NCJ 143505 (Washington, DC: U.S. Department of Justice, October 1993), 20. Despite referring to prisoners variously as incorrigible, wretched, determined, dangerous, wicked, and generic "others" (e.g., emphasizing the importance of keeping "them" in line), he conceded that all prisoners were entitled to access to care (albeit not to services or degrees of personal welfare "that exceed what they are able to obtain with their own resources"). He also argued that prisoners should be kept under conditions of confinement "without undue suffering" (albeit conditions that were not "too good for them"). Toward those and other ends, he articulated a number of indices by which prisons could be evaluated and compared: the quality of security, safety, order, care, activity, justice, conditions, and management provided. (ibid.)

76. Farmer v. Brennan, 114 S. Ct. 1970 (1994) (concurring), 1988.

77. Selke, *Prisons in Crisis*, 93. *See also* Logan, "Criminal Justice Performance Measure for Prison," 19–69. G. Styve, D. MacKenzie, A. Gover, and O. Mitchell, "Perceived Conditions of Confinement: A National Evaluation of Boot Camps and Traditional Facilities," *Law and Human Behavior* 24 (2000): 297; K. Wright, "Developing the Prison Environment Inventory," *Journal of Research in Crime and Delinquency* 22 (1985): 257.

78. M. Wheeler, "Toward a Theory of Limited Punishment: An Examination of the Eighth Amendment," *Stanford Law Review* 24 (1972): 838, 855. Wheeler observed some time ago that "Eighth amendment jurisprudence remains undeveloped," (ibid., 838). This is still largely the case, in part because of the failure to systematically address what should be an important component of most inquiries into the nature of cruel and unusual punishment: the psychological pains of imprisonment. Constructing a prison index would help to remedy this problem.

79. A similar requirement has been implemented in Minnesota, where the state's sentencing commission can alter sentencing guidelines only so long as the prison population does not exceed the capacity of the prison system. *See* Sandra Shane-DuBow, Alice Brown, and Erik Olsen, *Sentencing Reform in the United States: History, Content, and Effect* (Washington, DC: U.S. Government Printing Office, 1985). However, one subsequent study indicated that linking determinate sentencing reforms to prison populations has had unexpected con-

sequences for jail overcrowding in Minnesota jails, leading to the reasonable proposal that jail populations also can and should be tied to sentencing policy. *See* S. D'Alessio and L. Stolzenberg, "The Impact of Sentencing on Jail Incarceration in Minnesota," *Criminology* 33 (1995): 283; and L. Stolzenberg and S. D'Alessio, "The Unintended Consequences of Linking Sentencing Guidelines to Prison Populations—A Reply to Moody and Marvell," *Criminology* 34 (1996): 269.

80. *See, e.g.,* S. Byrd, "Prison Chief: Long Sentences Cost State, Truth-in-Sentencing Law Keeps Incarceration Rate High," *Biloxi Sun Herald*, November 13, 2003, at www.sunherald.com/com/mid/sunherald/news/state/7248899.html.

81. M. Marx, "Prison Conditions and Diminished Capacity—A Proposed Defense," *Santa Clara Law Review* 17 (1977): 855, 856. Like most legal defenses, traditional diminished capacity doctrines focus on the individual characteristics of defendants rather than the context in which they act. Thus, they reduce levels of responsibility only when a mental disease or defect has precluded the formation of a mental state that is an element of a crime. The suggestion here is that a person's capacity may be diminished by the surrounding social circumstances in addition to an individual disease or defect.

82. Craig Haney and Philip Zimbardo, "The Socialization Into Criminality: On Becoming a Prisoner and a Guard," in *Law, Justice, and the Individual in Society,* ed. June Tapp and Felice Levine (New York: Holt, Rinehart & Winston, 1977), 243 (emphasis in original).

83. Jack Abbott, *In the Belly of the Beast: Letters From Prison* (New York: Random House, 1981), 24.

84. For a discussion of some of these techniques, see C. Haney and T. Pettigrew, "Civil Rights and Institutional Law: The Role of Social Psychology in Judicial Implementation," *Journal of Community Psychology* 14 (1986): 267. A very useful, practical discussion of the role of psychologists in past prison reform litigation can be found in Carl Clements, "Psychological Roles and Issues in Recent Prison Litigation," in *Abnormal Offenders, Delinquency, and the Criminal Justice System,* ed. John Gunn and David Farrington (New York: Wiley, 1982).

85. S. Sturm, "Resolving the Remedial Dilemma: Strategies of Judicial Intervention in Prisons," *University of Pennsylvania Law Review* 138 (1990): 805, 810.

86. Ibid.

87. *Cf.* Note, "Complex Enforcement: Unconstitutional Prison Conditions," *Harvard Law Review* 94 (1981): 626.

88. Owen Fiss, *The Civil Rights Injunction* (Bloomington, IN: Indiana University Press, 1978). There was much legal discussion of structural reform litigation several decades ago, when Fiss first articulated this proposal and a significant amount of institutional reform litigation was underway. However, very few of these discussions incorporated social science or psychological perspectives. *See* L.C. Anderson, "Implementation of Consent Decrees in Structural Reform Litigation," *University of Illinois Law Review* 1986 (1986): 725; A. Chayes, "The Role of the Judge in Public Law Litigation," *Harvard Law Review* 89 (1976): 1281; W. A. Fletcher, "The Discretionary Constitution: Institutional Remedies

and Judicial Legitimacy," *Yale Law Journal* 91 (1982): 635; D. L. Horowitz, "Decreeing Organizational Change: Judicial Supervision of Public Institutions," *Duke Law Journal* 1983 (1983): 1265.

89. H. Toch, "Revisionist View of Prison Reform," *Federal Probation* 12 (1981): 3, 9.

90. This is in part why broad-based public education is also important to long-term strategies of legal change. *See, e.g.,* F. Cullen, G. Clark, and J. Wozniak, "Explaining the Get Tough Movement: Can the Public be Blamed?" *Federal Probation* 16 (1985): 21.

91. The use of judicially appointed prison monitors or "special masters" who report directly to courts and oversee the day-to-day implementation of, and compliance with, court orders has been a mainstay in prison litigation for some time. *See, e.g.,* Note, "'Mastering' Intervention in Prisons," *Yale Law Journal* 88 (1979): 1062. For the insights and reflections of one of the nation's most experienced and highly regarded prison special masters—Vincent Nathan—see his early analysis of this approach to prison reform: V. Nathan, "The Use of Masters in Institutional Reform Litigation," *University of Toledo Law Review* 10 (1979): 419; and also his retrospective assessment some 25 years later: V. Nathan, "Have the Courts Made a Difference in the Quality of Prison Conditions? What Have We Accomplished to Date?" *Pace Law Review* 24 (2004): 419. However, see also C. Smith and C. Nelson, "Perceptions of the Consequences of the Prison Litigation Reform Act: A Comparison of State Attorneys General and Federal District Judges," *Justice System Journal* 23 (2002): 295, to the effect that the PRLA has led to the "virtual elimination of the use of special masters to oversee the implementation of remedial orders in prisons," 311.

92. Trop v. Dulles, 356 U.S. 86, 101 (1958).

93. Cohen, "The Limits of Judicial Reform of Prisons," 425. Like Cohen, I also believe that there are many corrections officials who have been inspired by court orders to "do the right thing" in their treatment of prisoners, and many others who no doubt would have done the right thing anyway. I also agree that, as a matter of historical fact, many of those right things simply were not being done in most places until courts became involved in prison oversight.

94. Of course, there is merit to the view that the courts are composed of judges, not psychologists or sociologists. Yet, there are many issues on which courts must render decisions and exercise oversight despite lacking any direct, specialized expertise of their own. Given judges' unique role both in meting out punishment and in restraining its excesses, it seems reasonable that prison-related issues should be numbered among them. Because judges cannot avoid inquiries into prison life altogether, I have suggested only that their assessments should be in depth and informed by the best available theory and research.

95. Cohen, "The Limits of Judicial Reform of Prisons," 453.

96. M. Schlanger, "Inmate Litigation," *Harvard Law Review* 116 (2003): 1555, 1668 (emphasis added).

97. D. Foster, "Political Detention in South Africa: A Sociopsychological Perspective," *International Journal of Mental Health* 18 (1989): 21, 35.

10

LIMITING PRISON PAIN: A PSYCHOLOGICALLY INFORMED CORRECTIONS AGENDA

If human beings are in prison to receive punishments, they ought to get a maximum of treatment to improve their general conditions and soften their pain.

—Nils Christie[1]

Prison reform is a daunting task, made more so by the sheer size to which the correctional system has grown in recent years and the many political and economic interest groups that now have a stake in maintaining it. In addition, as many commentators have lamented, there seems to be no "basic public policy vision from which penal reform may grow."[2] Other critics have noted that "following the collapse of the rehabilitation theory of the 1970s, prison reformers lacked a theoretical basis with which to justify their proposed alternatives."[3] Thus, we may have entered "an era when penal institutions will direct penal change" for themselves.[4] Indeed, the absence of a public policy vision or theoretical basis for reform—so that the impetus and the rationale for change have been relinquished primarily to correctional insiders—does seem to explain the impasse in prison policy-making, wherein high levels of prison pain are dispensed now as much by default as anything else.

With these sobering realities in mind, this chapter returns to the thesis with which I began: Acknowledging the powerful influence of past and present contexts and situations on behavior has important implications for correctional policy and practice. Instead of persisting with the prison status quo, modern psychological theory encourages a reconceptualization of the

303

causes of crime and a recalibration of the fairness of legal punishment. It represents an important framework from which to generate new and better crime control and prison policies.

In conceptual terms, I will suggest three basic categories of correctional reform that follow directly from a contextual model of behavior. The first is that exclusively individualistic approaches to crime control are too limited in scope to be effective over the long term. This implies that prison—as a people- rather than a context-changing institution—should be used more sparingly and supplanted instead by more context-based strategies of controlling crime.

Second, understanding the transformative power of contexts and situations forces us to acknowledge the pains and potential harms of imprisonment per se, and highlights the need to identify and reform potentially damaging conditions of confinement. Indeed, because this is a book primarily about the context of prison itself, the reforms I suggest in this chapter are focused mostly on that goal—changing the nature of imprisonment rather than developing genuine alternatives to incarceration (as essential as those reforms clearly are).

Finally, however, recognition of the important role of social context and circumstance in crime causation underscores the need to carefully assess and systematically address the criminogenic situations to which prisoners are returned following incarceration. Whatever gains prisoners may achieve in restructured prison contexts designed to minimize the damaging effects of incarceration and maximize programming opportunities are not likely to survive the harsh realities that most of them confront in their postprison lives. Those realities must become a major target of reform.

In fact, no amount of prison reform can substitute for the larger set of badly needed social and economic changes in the wider society. The overwhelming majority of persons in prison are poor and, disproportionately, of color. Thus, the social deviance for which they are being punished is rooted in large part in their social and economic circumstances. These circumstances and the marginalized status to which they give rise are assigned rather than chosen, and they cannot be meaningfully addressed by changes in prison policy alone, no matter how broad based or fundamental in nature those changes might be. Fair, effective, and humane approaches to crime control will require models of genuine social and economic justice to be implemented. Addressing structural inequality and unequal opportunity counts more than alleviating adverse conditions of confinement.

But prisons matter, too, especially because of the enormous numbers of persons who are now locked inside them. Modern psychological theory reminds us that prison contexts "possess unique and enduring characteristics that impinge upon and shape individual behavior,"[5] and they can serve as powerful and potentially criminogenic influences in their own right. Thus, this chapter concentrates on the various ways in which the powerful and important context of prison can and should be transformed. As Hans Toch put it, correctional institutions can be restructured and redirected in ways that "increase their humaneness and their sense of concern for inmates."[6]

Indeed, Toch's optimistic and idealistic vision—expressed before the worst excesses of the last several decades had surfaced—is worth renewing. He urged the corrections establishment to vigorously pursue "trends that variously include increasing social services to inmates, the 'opening up' of prisons to outside contacts, the humanizing of staff, the liberalizing of inmate self-expression, the upgrading of educational and vocational opportunities, and a general aligning of prisons with our conception of 'civilized' standards."[7] Recommitting prisons to programs like these would go a long way toward limiting the pains of imprisonment and reducing the harmful effects of confinement.

Referencing Toch's vision reminds me to situate my own. Books on institutional reform face an insoluble dilemma. They can attempt to deal at length with the numerous political forces and practical considerations that have helped to create and maintain the problems the authors seek to solve—and risk the inevitable criticism that they are too political. Or they can largely ignore these forces and contingencies to concentrate instead on the conceptual core of the problem and the intellectual framework needed for potential solutions—but incur the equally likely critique that they are unrealistic for having failed to anticipate and overcome all of the political and practical obstacles that impede change. I have chosen the latter course.

I noted early in this book that I had the luxury of writing as a psychologist, not as a politician or prison official. Nowhere is the extent of that luxury more apparent than in this chapter, in which I concentrate on a range of potential, psychologically inspired prison reforms. I acknowledge that I have not assumed the burden of answering many difficult questions about whether and how the large number of obstacles to these reforms can be overcome.[8] Instead, I hope that underscoring the need to transform certain aspects of the prison system and outlining the nature of the changes that should be made in order to better align it with modern psychological theory will itself help to create some of the political will and practical ingenuity that are needed to bring these changes about.

LIMITING PRISON PAIN BY ENDING THE OVERUSE OF IMPRISONMENT

In recent years, many social problems that were once addressed by social welfare programs and other institutions in our society have been folded into the prison system. Thus, not only have we increasingly criminalized various maladies like poverty, mental illness, and drug addiction over the last several decades, but we have "prisonized" their solutions as well. This is a trend that modern psychological theory argues to reverse. If prison is a painful and potentially harmful social context, then the risks associated with exposing people to it—especially people whose vulnerabilities and other special needs increase the probability that they will suffer psychological harm—must be weighed more heavily.

For these reasons, prison should be acknowledged as an inappropriate criminal justice placement for many persons who are mentally ill, have committed certain kinds of drug offenses, or have been convicted of only minor or trivial crimes. Indeed, the recent creation of mental health, drug, and other kinds of specialized courts that rely on more community-based, treatment-oriented approaches helps to address this concern. These innovative programs also reflect a growing recognition that, in many such cases, the nature of the underlying crime-related problem deserves a more benign (perhaps even therapeutic) and less punitive response—or no response at all.[9] Such "problem-solving" court reforms lead naturally to context-oriented solutions that address the real causes of criminality and allocate criminal justice resources accordingly. As a result, prison would be seen as one small component in a contextually oriented overall strategy of crime control.

At the same time, ways must be found not only to punish more serious wrongdoing but also to minimize the psychologically damaging aspects of the sanctions—for all defendants, not just for those with special vulnerabilities. More than 2 decades ago, sociologist David Ward observed, "When Americans think about punishing criminals, they do not think of probation or diversion to community corrections programs. Punishment in America means long-term confinement in state penitentiaries."[10] Although this is still the case, new perspectives on the causes of crime and an increased awareness of the severe psychological costs of imprisonment suggest a different, long-overdue approach. Intermediate sanctions—punishment short of prison—must be substituted in a much wider range of cases than at present. By allowing persons convicted of certain kinds of criminal offences to remain in or return earlier to community settings, these sanctions reduce the number of psychological and other transitions that they must undertake before reentering free society.[11]

Of course, intermediate sanctions—like any form of punishment—must be structured in context-sensitive ways that are designed not only to avoid the pitfalls of the prison environment they are supposed to replace but also to create the appropriate social conditions under which participants are likely to succeed. Intermediate sanctions certainly must function as genuine diversions from prison into the community (rather than widening the net of criminal justice system surveillance and control to include persons who otherwise would not be subjected to it).[12] In addition, however, these alternatives to prison—intensive community supervision and the like— must seek to reduce the number and magnitude of criminogenic forces in the communities where they operate.[13] Thus, intermediate sanctions programs should engage the participant's "family, employer, and neighborhood to create a support and supervision network," foster their direct involvement in the program, and facilitate prosocial activities and opportunities in the community.[14]

In addition to intermediate sanctions that keep participants in *community-based* facilities and maximize time in freeworld settings, *restorative justice* models that take the contexts of disputes, conflicts, and infractions explicitly into account should be used more often as alternatives to traditional, individual-centered criminal justice processing. Rather than focusing only on individual perpetrators and then applying typically individualistic, exclusively punitive solutions, restorative justice approaches to dispute resolution broaden the analysis of what happened and why, and are more likely to involve a larger segment of the community in deciding what should be done about it. Thus, these models include a consideration of contextual causes of conflict and crime, and attempt to implement context-based changes to resolve those problems at their source.[15]

Modern psychological theory also argues in favor of revamping the current decontextualized sentencing policies that I discussed in chapter 4, so that the defendant's social history and present circumstances can play a greater role in the decision-making process. At present, the lack of judicial discretion and the dramatically increased numbers of defendants who are being sent to prison have produced a system in which the overwhelming number of cases are resolved without any prison-related treatment or rehabilitation recommendations prepared, introduced, or considered by the courts. This has resulted in what one recent courtroom observer described this way: "The concept of studying an offender and devising a rehabilitation plan isn't frowned upon so much as not looked upon at all; the proper sentence is whatever both sides [in a plea bargain] can agree on to belch out one defendant and make space for the next."[16]

Finally, one of the most important ways to reduce the excessive pains of imprisonment is to reform the sentencing practices and related parole policies under which our society now incarcerates more prisoners for longer periods than at any other time in our history. In general terms, this broad set of reforms would significantly reduce the sheer number of people who are exposed to the potentially damaging social context of prison, as well as shorten the periods of time that prisoners are confined there. Prisons must return to being the criminal justice system's response of absolute last resort. Their current central role will be taken instead by a wide range of preventative programs that address the most important contextual causes of crime. If crime is caused in large part by past and present contexts and circumstances, then it follows logically that crime-control attention and resources should be allocated accordingly.

DO NO HARM: NORMALIZING PRISON CONTEXTS

Even in a more psychologically sophisticated overall system of crime control that used imprisonment as a last resort, conditions of confinement and the forms of correctional treatment to which prisoners are exposed would still matter greatly. Whether there are many prisons or few, there must be real limits to what prisons are permitted to do to the persons confined inside—nearly all of whom someday return to free society.[17] Indeed, each year well over half a million persons are released from prisons in the United States. As several previous chapters have underscored, what happens to them while they are incarcerated has a profound influence on what they will be like once they leave. Ensuring that the social contexts to which prisoners have been exposed during incarceration have done more good than harm serves the interests of the families and communities to which they return.[18]

Prisons punish by depriving prisoners of their liberty; anything more—unnecessary deprivations, indignities, and ill treatment—represents gratuitous pain. Especially when it is experienced over long periods of time, as I have tried to show, this kind of pain is not only cruel but can have debilitating psychological consequences for individual prisoners and lasting repercussions for society at large. A new appreciation of negative prison effects should sensitize prison policymakers and officials to the harmful consequences of adverse conditions and provide an impetus for reform.

Even very widespread problems, such as chronic idleness—confining prisoners for long periods in places where they lack meaningful activity of any sort—can be detrimental. As I noted earlier, the notion that large numbers of prisoners can be warehoused for years on end—placed in a kind of psychological suspended animation or "behavioral deep freeze"[19]—and then be unproblematically absorbed back into the communities from which they came is psychologically naive; it reflects an outmoded, asocial view of prison effects.

Recognizing the power of the prison context to so effectively shape behavior represents a strong argument in favor of making correctional environments as much like the freeworld as possible. Innovative prison administrator Dora Schriro has recommended creating a "parallel prison universe" in which "life inside prison should resemble life outside" and prisoners "can acquire values, habits, and skills that will help them become productive, law-abiding citizens."[20] The logic of the model is straightforward and psychologically sound—the more that the circumstances and situations that prisoners encounter during incarceration are like those they experience upon release, the more adjustment to prison will facilitate successful integration into the freeworld.

"Normalizing" the prison environment by removing some of its harshest edges might be accomplished by introducing some of the norms of therapeutic communities into correctional settings in general.[21] Housing prisoners in places where they "experience support, understanding, and affection from people who have had life experiences similar to their own," and "find a community with which they can identify [and] people toward whom they can express their best human emotions rather than their worst," should help to limit some of the pains of imprisonment and minimize the degree of prisonization that occurs.[22]

The fact that certain prison environments can cause stress-related and even traumatic reactions in prisoners is another reason to lessen the pains of imprisonment by modifying the context that creates them. For example, we know that, over time, prisoners who become involved in work and other activities and who maintain more extensive contact with the outside world make more positive adaptations to prison life. They also experience reductions in "dysphoric" emotional states and suffer lower levels of stress-related medical problems.[23] Thus, programs that involve prisoners in meaningful activity and reduce the psychological barriers between prison and the outside world—for example, ones that facilitate and encourage visitation and the maintenance of family ties—can actually change the prison environment in ways that reduce the harmful alienation that often occurs there.[24] As John Irwin put it, "the obvious recommendation here is that any situation of long-term confinement should maximize contacts between prisoners and the outside world."[25]

Addressing other aspects of the prison environment also can help to alleviate the unnecessary pains of imprisonment. When prisoners are disempowered and emasculated, subjected to forms of forceful institutional control, abuses of power, and even brutal mistreatment, they may experience forms of "retraumatization" that are psychologically reminiscent of abusive, traumatic childhood experiences. Highly problematic survival strategies may emerge in response. In some cases, prisoners seek to achieve and maintain a more defensible social status and personal identity in prison by exploiting whatever advantages they can gain over others. Exaggerated forms of masculine domination are still highly functional in many prisons, in part because of the role that they continue to play in the psychological survival under diminished and dehumanized circumstances. As Michael King noted, coercive sexual activity in prison "is primarily an expression of anger and frustration in men who may be unable to achieve masculine identification and pride in avenues other than sex."[26]

Yet, in a freeworld society where empathy, tenderness, and equity in intimate and interpersonal relations are valued, adapting to the sexually dysfunctional world of prison may guarantee a degree of social marginalization upon release that will compromise future relationships and long-term social adjustment in free society. Approaching the problem exclusively through punishment "is unlikely to change the root causes of assaults, which lie in the frustrations of a class of men who seldom have work, successful families, or opportunities for emotional expression." Often, the institutional structure of the prison makes these issues more problematic by further limiting access to work and family and narrowing (or eliminating) opportunities for emotional expression. Thus, "without humanitarian changes within institutions the problem is unlikely to be reduced." [27]

By examining the social contextual origins of this problematic prison dynamic, however, King was able to gain insights into those aspects of prison life that were most in need of monitoring and change. In the spirit of doing no harm, the kind of "humanitarian changes within institutions" needed to reduce sexual aggression would proceed from this kind of careful analysis of the dysfunctional dynamics of sexuality, in turn, to targeting those aspects of the prison context that are in need of change. Among other things, those changes would include providing prisoners with access to conjugal and family visits that help to preserve preexisting sexual and familial relationships and normalize the atmosphere that prevails inside prison itself.

Moreover, although this book has been focused on limiting the pains of imprisonment for prisoners—rather than the difficult and sometimes very compromised circumstances under which many correctional officers work— I am well aware that prison staff have an enormously important impact on conditions of confinement. They can significantly undermine or make vital contributions to the nature of prison life. Clearly, a comprehensive contextual approach to prison reform would focus on restructuring the environment in which they work as well. Thus, doing no harm in prison would also mean, in part, placing correctional officers in places where they would be encouraged to be helpful rather than hurtful, and where they would be institutionally supported and rewarded for having done so.

Consistent with the social psychological framework on which the reforms in this chapter are based, staff-related reforms would move from the traditional emphasis on the nature or characteristics of the people employed in prison (although certainly without suggesting that their traits and training are irrelevant) to a greater focus on the circumstances under which they work. Indeed, the Stanford Prison Experiment that Phillip Zimbardo, Curtis

Banks, and I conducted some 35 years ago is an instructive starting point for the proposition that context matters for guards as well as prisoners, and that even good people can do bad things if and when they are placed in an environment designed to elicit mistreatment.[28] The recent prison abuse scandals in Abu Ghraib, Iraq—as one important government report that drew on the insights of the Stanford Study reminded us—clearly underscore what can happen in real-world contexts in which this basic lesson is ignored.[29] But there are many domestic analogues to this lesson. Thus, the restructuring of prison environments to prevent mistreatment would include, among other things, introducing greater levels of accountability in those contexts where they have been lacking.[30]

Alison Liebling's work on the moral performance of prisons brings this point full circle. She and her colleagues have demonstrated the interconnectedness of the perspective that both prisoners and staff bring to bear on the quality of their lives in prison (including the shared importance of values such as respect, humanity, trust, fairness, order, and safety).[31] Because prison is a complex social environment in which the day-to-day life of the prisoners is very much influenced by the behavior and mind-set of the staff (and vice versa), it is not surprising that elevating the quality of prison life by improving the atmosphere and conditions under which the prison staff works can have beneficial effects for prisoners. In addition, there is evidence emerging from the study of other prison systems in Europe that increasing the professional orientation of prison officers and their commitment to helping rather than hurting prisoners not only appears to improve the overall quality of life in the prison and enhance the well-being of the prisoners but also may increase the job satisfaction of the officers themselves.[32]

MINIMIZING AND RESPONDING TO ADVERSE PRISON EFFECTS

Doing no harm also means being more sensitive to exactly where particular prisoners are placed in the correctional system once they have entered it. Recognizing the power of prison contexts to change persons—not just confine them—underscores the importance of careful screening and classification at the initial stages of incarceration. Assigning prisoners to those institutions that can assist them in obtaining the skills they will need to acquire before their release ought to be of utmost importance in a psychologically informed prison system.

Conversely, context-sensitive placements would ensure that prisoners are not sent to environments that are likely to worsen any preexisting problems from which they suffer, housed in places where their identified vulnerabilities are likely to be exploited, or assigned to prisons that put them otherwise clearly at risk. Thus, Kevin Wright, whose research on the causes of prison violence led him to conclude that "the environment (or at least the individual's perception of his or her environment) plays a significant role in who takes drastic and unacceptable action in response to the pressures of incarceration," also recommended that "attention to [prison] placements is important if inmates are to have the facilities to successfully adjust."[33]

As several earlier chapters emphasized, coping with the pains of imprisonment—the deprivations of prison life, its atypical patterns of living, and the skewed behavioral norms to which one is exposed—exacts a significant psychological price. Sociologist John Irwin noted more than 20 years ago that although the nature and amount of prisonization that prisoners undergo varies, "all prisoners acquire new definitions and special social responses that are different than those of outsiders. The longer the confinement, the greater the impact of prisonization."[34] I noted in chapter 6 that there are many dimensions to this process. Prisoners learn to be hypervigilant, to adopt a tough convict veneer, to suppress outward signs of emotion, to be generally distrustful of others, and to become more dependent on external structure to regulate their behavior. Some internalize the stigma of having been in prison and will reenter the freeworld with a diminished sense of self-worth. Those who have come to deeply embrace the convict code and regard it as second nature may find that it is difficult to relinquish upon their release. As Irwin noted, "prisoners can become ill-equipped for the experiences and interactions outside prison that we take for granted."[35]

Thus, prisoners need insight into prisonization to resist its worst effects. That is, they should be given the tools with which to identify the troublesome and dysfunctional habits of thinking, feeling, and acting that prison threatens to instill in them and that these changes may impede their successful reentry into the freeworld. They also need to be given assistance to reverse the process once it has taken place. Many of the psychological changes brought about by prisonization and related prison coping mechanisms can be addressed through transitional, or "step-down," programs in which prisoners learn to approach social interactions and relationships differently, in ways that are more consistent with the norms and expectations that they will encounter in social contexts outside of prison.[36]

Of course, some prisoners react in more extreme ways to their conditions of confinement, and some prison contexts have especially extreme effects on the persons exposed to them. I noted earlier that, although imprisonment does not appear to cause diagnosable clinical disorders in most prisoners—most prisons do not make most prisoners "crazy"—it does bring about extreme psychological changes that can prove debilitating for many ex-convicts.[37] Indeed, many prisoners—like many trauma victims in general—continue to manifest the effects of their exposure long after their traumatizing prison experiences have ended. As Judith Herman and others have suggested, long-term imprisonment represents a form of chronic and severe situational stress that, in extreme cases, may lead to the trauma-related syndrome termed *complex PTSD* in some prisoners.[38]

Thus, recognizing the way that context matters means weighing the risks of particularly extreme forms of confinement more heavily. It is an empirical and theoretical argument in favor of prohibiting the use of any prison sanction that is likely to have traumatic, damaging consequences. This means, for example, that no approach to the "management" of troublesome prisoners should be undertaken until very careful consideration has been given to the known risks and potential dangers involved. For example, a contextualist understanding of prison effects would lead to a better appreciation of the way in which the use of solitary confinement not only reflects a "very atomistic, unsocial" (and, therefore, outmoded) view of prisoners and prison behavior,[39] but also represents a potentially harmful practice that—depending on what it entails and how long it lasts—can inflict real pain on prisoners that may have enduring, damaging effects.[40]

In short, then, a psychologically informed approach to ameliorating the harmful aspects of prison life would involve broadly analyzing the context of prison itself to identify those features that produce the most adverse and problematic reactions and adaptations (staff and prisoners alike), and carefully but significantly restructuring harmful aspects of the prison environment to minimize potentially debilitating effects. It would also mean thoughtfully assessing and classifying prisoners' vulnerabilities and needs as they enter the prison system and assigning them to particular prisons accordingly, thereby providing prisoners with insight and assistance with which to resist the negative transformations brought about by prisonization and precluding the use of any harsh or punitive environment known to cause serious psychological harm.[41]

RESURRECTING THE REHABILITATIVE IDEAL

As critics often have noted, many past efforts at prison rehabilitation were inherently flawed and easily perverted.[42] Most rehabilitation programs and practices probably never worked as effectively as their enthusiasts claimed they did or could, and some were outright destructive to the psyches of prisoners. Indeed, it is difficult to dispute Edgardo Rotman's historical judgment that "the language of rehabilitation legitimated a prison system that was all too commonly abusive."[43] Although the reasons for these failures can be debated, few penal institutions ever devoted the kind of resources that were needed for the diverse prison programs and range of services from which most prisoners were likely to benefit. As one commentator put it,

"In retrospect it is clear that rehabilitation could not fail because it had never been tried."[44]

Moreover, even though the kind of rehabilitation programs that might have succeeded in the short-term—ones with adequate resources, qualified personnel, minimal custodial interference, and careful postprison follow-up—were rarely if ever implemented, they also were flawed by their inherent individualism. They could never have been the crime-control panaceas that many of their advocates promised. Much of this book has been devoted to examining the core limitations of an approach to reducing crime that ignores the context in which it occurs.

That said, rehabilitation—in a much revised, more realistic, and carefully monitored form—must be restored as the primary goal of imprisonment. Contexts are shaped in part by the purposes they serve, and prison environments that are mandated to provide prisoners with opportunities that will facilitate their reintegration into the freeworld function differently from ones whose only purpose is to punish. As Hans Toch once put it, "We can of course carelessly leave the environment's impact to chance by running warehouses where we unwittingly let negative influences predominate. Or, we can consciously try to maximize constructive and positive forces available to us even in last-resort prisons."[45] Maximizing the available positive forces helps to prevent inherently negative influences from accumulating in and dominating correctional environments. In this way, structuring prisons around the goal of rehabilitation can be seen as much as a program of institutional reform as one of individual change.

The restoration of the rehabilitative ideal, when conceived of in this way—prison "treatment" that is *not* premised on the notion that crime is sickness and prison programming that is *not* based on a trait-based deficit model in which prisoners are seen as needing to be "fixed" before they can be released—is entirely consistent with modern psychological theory.[46] A renewed emphasis on rehabilitation does not imply that all prisoners leave prison lacking the skills, talents, and strengths that can carry them through the transition to a productive freeworld life. But they too often obtain these things in spite of how they have been treated in prison, not because of it. Indeed, a context-based model of rehabilitation would reflect the fact that it is prisoners' past social histories and present circumstances that have often prevented them from leading more fulfilled and successful lives in the places to which they eventually will return. This means, of course, that prison rehabilitation is likely to succeed only when it is made part of a larger strategy of social contextual reform.

This is more than a mere shift in semantics. Thinking of rehabilitation in social contextual terms would require the creation of programs and services that were devoted to persons *and* situations as targets of potential change. These new rehabilitation programs would be focused primarily on specific context-related problems that prisoners were likely to encounter when released. Programs geared toward personal change also would be linked as realistically as possible to the freeworld settings in which they were likely to have the greatest effect. Thus, a social contextual model of rehabilitation would focus more on the kinds of circumstances and situations that prisoners were likely to be placed in later on and would assist them in acquiring the skills they would need to function and succeed in them.

This way of broadly conceptualizing rehabilitation would mean that individual-level prisoner change would be seen as only one small component in a larger program of crime control. It would be joined with an equally or more important mandate to *alter contexts*—by providing extensive community support designed to reinforce and buttress whatever positive gains may have been produced by rehabilitation programs inside prison. Because no amount of positive prison change can withstand or resist the powerful criminogenic forces at work in many of the communities where ex-convicts are concentrated, these places—rather than merely the prisoners themselves—must be targeted in the name of rehabilitation. Putting the implications of modern psychological theory in their simplest terms, what happens in prison to improve the outlooks, education, job skills, and psychological well-being of prisoners will not reduce crime in a significant way unless the freeworld contexts to which prisoners return are restructured to allow these positive changes to stabilize and be developed further.[47]

Correctional classification systems would need to be revamped with this broad range of new goals explicitly in mind. Prisoners would no longer be seen as decontextualized bundles of traits and deficits. Correspondingly, meaningful prison classification could not proceed without a real understanding of an individual's background and social history and the criminogenic contexts from which he or she came. Among other things, this means that the pro forma and often only marginally useful probation reports that are produced in many jurisdictions would be replaced by more comprehensive assessments of the broad array of social contextual as well as personal factors that contributed to the defendant's criminal behavior. These substantive and focused assessments would then serve as the basis for context-centered classification and programming decisions.

Because we now know that putting prisoners in the wrong environment can have long-term damaging consequences, classification officers would be required to justify their decisions on the basis of detailed knowledge about prisoner needs. Their recommendations also would include references to the nature and quality of available rehabilitative services and other features of the various institutions where prisoners were scheduled to be sent. Moreover, prison classification would proceed mindful of the freeworld context to which prisoners would return once their terms have ended.[48] Indeed, judges' sentencing orders and recommendations might be required to address these issues as well. That is, there is no reason why a context-sensitive approach to the reentry process cannot begin at the time of sentencing, with recommendations from probation officers and judges about the kinds of rehabilitative services prisoners will need to ensure their successful return to the communities from which they are being taken.

This modest recommendation implies several others, including requiring probation officers and judges to become more knowledgeable about the rehabilitative services and programs available in the institutions to which they sentence prisoners. It also suggests that they be required to do follow-up monitoring to ensure that prisoners receive the services and assistance that they need and to which they are entitled. Simultaneously, prison classification officers would need to become more responsive to the recommendations of the sentencing authorities themselves. Thus, prison staff would need to know and be able to justify their decisions on the appropriateness of the programming options available within the correctional system—those places where prisoners could maximize opportunities to receive the kind of education, vocational training, and counseling that was designed to increase their chances of successful community reentry.

Decision makers also would need to be explicitly responsible for avoiding placements of particular prisoners in environments likely to be harmful—for example, places where vulnerable and special-needs prisoners are likely to be victimized or to deteriorate psychologically or in other ways. This implies that some greater degree of accountability would be introduced into the classification process, so that officials would be responsible for harmful consequences that they knew or should have known would occur in certain kinds of prisons and, especially, for certain kinds of prisoners.

Indeed, there also is no reason why prison systems could not be required to answer to the communities to which prisoners eventually are returned, and to the judges whose programming recommendations should have guided at least some of the course of a prisoner's incarceration.[49] In the spirit of accountability that has become so important in other public service agencies and arenas—especially in our education system—prisons, too, can be evaluated, graded, and even funded on the basis of the results that they achieve. Indices of success might focus on a range of intermediate measures, such as the number of vocational and educational courses and other rehabilitative services the prisons offered and the amount of programming that prisoners completed at a facility. Of course, more long-term and definitive measures might include the number of ex-convicts who were successfully employed in the freeworld and the positive impact that the particular prison had in reducing the recidivism rate over a specified period of years.

Thus, a kind of "no prisoner left behind" system of correctional assessment and evaluation could be implemented that would result in a dramatic, but entirely appropriate, shift in the way we gauge the effectiveness of prison systems and those who run them.[50] For example, even though many prisoners suffer from poor educational backgrounds and lack job skills and significant work experience, *most* still do not participate in meaningful educational programs, vocational training, or prison industries while they are incarcerated.[51]

Indeed, the data on prisoner literacy and levels of educational attainment underscore this concern. Thus, among those entering state prisons in the United States in the mid-1990s, over 70% had not completed high school and 16% had no high school education whatsoever.[52] One national study reported that over two thirds of prisoners were functionally illiterate and one in five adult prisoners was completely illiterate.[53] For prisoners who are expected someday to reenter a labor force that requires increasingly higher levels of intellectual proficiency, the importance of providing remedial and even advanced educational opportunities should be obvious.[54]

Moreover, the value of prison educational programs has been well documented. For example, participation in college programs has proven to be an excellent predictor of institutional adjustment. It also is relatively inexpensive, and pays substantial dividends once prisoners are released. Numerous studies have found that participation in such programs produces positive effects and outcomes. Psychologist Michelle Fine and her colleagues found that among the women inmates at one correctional facility they studied, only 7.7% who participated in prison education courses recidivated, compared with 29.9% of those who did not participate.[55] In other research, college course work appears to have a substantial positive effect on postprison outcomes,[56] and actually completing a college bachelor's degree appears to have the greatest effect.[57]

Thus, one of the most important ways we can maximize the potential of prison to control crime is to greatly expand all levels of educational programming in prison—from basic literacy to college courses.[58] The great majority of prison wardens who have been surveyed on the issue acknowledge that these programs work.[59] However, recent estimates suggest that less than 10% of prisoners are enrolled in full-time job training or education programs.[60] A psychologically informed prison policy would acknowledge the educational demands that freeworld contexts will make on virtually all prisoners once they are released and, therefore, would make learning opportunities more widely available to them.

Other kinds of programs and services also are essential to improve prisoners' chances for postprison success. For example, we know that there is a significant relationship between drug and alcohol abuse and criminality. Nationwide data collected in the mid-1990s indicated that nearly two thirds (62%) of all persons under state correctional supervision and 42% admitted to federal prison suffered from "poly-substance" abuse problems before they were imprisoned. In addition, a very high percentage of persons had used drugs or alcohol before committing the crime for which they were arrested—indeed, data from some cities indicated that 70% to 80% tested positive for drug use at the time of their arrest.[61] Drug use brings users into contact with a criminal subculture in which illegal behavior may be condoned and rewarded. It thus influences the nature of the situations in which users find themselves and puts them in places where violence is more commonplace, including ones where weapons are more accessible.[62]

The Justice Department's own extensive data on this issue not only document the magnitude of the problem but also underscore the inadequacy of our current approach. According to a nationwide study published in the late 1990s, despite the high number of "alcohol- or drug-involved offenders" in state and federal prison, only 1 in 7 had been treated for drug abuse since the current admission to prison, and the same number—1 in 7—had received treatment for alcohol abuse while incarcerated.[63] Other studies have estimated that the percentage of prisoners in treatment is even lower—including one indicating that only about 1 prisoner in 10 received drug treatment while incarcerated.[64]

Ironically, lawmakers often embrace a causal analysis of crime that implicates drugs, but typically only to more intensely target—and then more severely punish—drug users. Yet modern psychological theory suggests that focusing exclusively on the punishment of individual users while ignoring the social contexts that precipitate and maintain their substance abuse is destined to fail. Punishing persons for drug offenses by imposing prison terms that do not include opportunities for extensive drug treatment is even more self-defeating. Thus, in addition to providing prisoners with meaningful educational and vocational training opportunities, prison rehabilitation services must include access to extensive and effective drug and alcohol programs and related counseling services.

Context sensitivity also means that these programs must be structured with the nature of the prison environment in mind. For example, because group therapy depends on the active and open participation of group members, "in a prison setting where trust and confidentiality are limited, the effectiveness of group counseling is also limited."[65] Instead, the creation of a different kind of prison atmosphere would need to be created, preferably one that separated drug treatment programs from the rest of the prison setting. Ideally, such an approach "isolates the program and the clients from the prison culture of manipulation, mistrust, violence and drug use, and creates an environment in which sensitive issues can be addressed."[66]

Indeed, the value of the therapeutic community model to which I earlier referred turns largely on the ability of such programs to change the prison context in which they are implemented—to create healthier, less destructive prison environments that support rather than undermine whatever positive changes are brought about. But, once again, context sensitivity means recognizing that no program of prison change can succeed without giving careful attention to the environment to which prisoners will return once they are released. Thus, successful therapeutic communities and other effective treatment models also develop extensive "aftercare" plans and provide assistance and follow-up services for prisoners once they have returned to free society.[67]

These contextually oriented models of rehabilitation can be implemented on a widespread basis to address the substance abuse problems and broader treatment needs of prisoners. Indeed, many newer forms of treatment focus explicitly on "dynamic interactions between multiple risk factors and situational determinants" of drug use, recognizing that "relapse prevention" often depends on the management and control of a variety of contextual factors.[68] Although they are no substitute for the creation of alternative treatment programs *outside* prison (into which many persons who have committed drug-related crimes can be diverted instead), in-prison drug treatment programs—because of the sheer numbers of people involved— are likely to remain an important part of prison rehabilitation.

In the long run, providing these kinds of rehabilitative services and other meaningful activities for prisoners should not add significantly to the overall expense of imprisonment. Indeed, commentators have suggested that prisons that strongly emphasize this kind of enriched programming are easier and less expensive to run; some have established track records that impress even conservative criminologists.[69] More generally, there is evidence that the implementation of a whole range of broad-based correctional standards intended to improve prison conditions actually may decrease rather than increase operating budgets.[70] In any event, the real cost-effectiveness of programs designed to enhance reentry and reduce recidivism comes from their ability to end cycles of crime, incarceration, and reoffending in the future.

PSYCHOLOGICAL TREATMENT IN A CONTEXT-ORIENTED PRISON SETTING

The use of more traditional forms of psychotherapy and psychological counseling in prison is a complicated and controversial topic. The many excesses that have been committed in the name of "prison therapy" in the past provides a basis for continued skepticism and legitimate concern. So, too, does the way that individual-level treatment models imply that criminality stems primarily from personal psychopathology. Thus, I have advocated psychologically informed programs of rehabilitation that focus broadly on preparing prisoners to reenter free society through educational and vocational training, rather than attempting to cure psychopathology that most of them do not have.

However, the psychological legacies of the past histories of trauma and mistreatment that many criminal defendants share should not be ignored. Recall, for example, that Donald Dutton and Stephen Hart found that over 40% of the prisoners they studied had been exposed to some form of serious childhood abuse, and those who had been victimized in this way were 3 times more likely to have engaged in violent offenses as adults. These and similar data argue strongly in favor of making some form of in-prison counseling available to those prisoners who seek to address these issues while incarcerated. In this regard, Dutton and Hart offered what they characterized as a "counterintuitive suggestion"—namely, that persons who have committed violent offenses should be treated in prison for their earlier experiences as victims. Such therapy would address whatever feelings of loss of control, emotional numbing, hyperactivity, and substance abuse have come about as longer term symptoms of severe early trauma.[71]

Moreover, the high rates of mental disorder among prisoners that were discussed in chapter 8 require a thoughtful and caring response. Although a contextual model of crime and punishment would explicitly reject an exclusive focus on individual-level causal factors in understanding and responding to criminal behavior, vulnerable prisoners nonetheless deserve opportunities to receive appropriate treatment in properly designed settings. For example, Kenneth Adams's study of maximum-security prisons in New York State found that prisoners who were referred for mental health treatment had "much in common with civil psychiatric patients by way of treatment experiences and little in common with stereotypic notions of the criminally insane as chronically violent offenders." He concluded that prisons obviously contained a significant number of persons "who can benefit from service delivery arrangements that merge mental health and criminal justice concerns."[72] More generally, the data that I cited earlier—indicating that as many as 20% or more of prisoners currently suffer from serious mental disorders or developmental disabilities—justify higher levels of mental health screening, monitoring, and treatment than are currently available in many correctional facilities.

Indeed, recall the nationwide data (cited in chap. 8, this volume) which showed that more than 1 in 5 prisons in the United States did not even screen incoming inmates to determine their mental health needs and that about the same number failed to conduct psychiatric assessments of prisoners or to make therapy or counseling available to them once they were incarcerated.[73] Obviously, one important way to address the needs of the hundreds of thousands of mentally ill and developmentally disabled prisoners would be to provide all of them with adequate intake screening and psychiatric assessments, access to well-trained mental health counselors,

24-hour mental health coverage, and community mental health referrals on a comprehensive and effective basis.

The increased presence and potential involvement of clinical personnel at the time of admission—when the pains of imprisonment are acute—also could improve the quality of correctional screening and classification decision making in general. It would allow prison staff to better address the needs of incoming prisoners and would help to avert irreversible psychiatric emergencies (such as suicide). Moreover, it would minimize the disruption that occurs when prisoners with mental illness or developmental disabilities have been assigned to institutions that are ill equipped to treat them.[74]

Beyond these commonsense recommendations—more and better screening and in-prison services—a social contextual approach to treatment in a correctional setting also would need to address the ways in which the prison setting itself compromises the nature and quality of the therapeutic response that is possible there. For example, the fact that "in institutions . . . the wearing of socially appropriate masks is frequently the condition of personal survival"[75] limits the amount of behavioral and attitudinal changes that are likely to occur in traditional prison environments. Thus, ways would need to be found to transform the prison contexts in which psychotherapy is conducted to overcome these barriers. This is another argument in favor of screening certain groups of prisoners with mental illness out of the traditional prison system entirely and placing them in facilities that are structured primarily for treatment rather than punishment.

Indeed, modern psychological theory underscores the numerous ways in which "the social organization of penal institutions is . . . antithetical to rehabilitative efforts"[76] and challenges reformers to address them. Among other things, the working relationship between treatment and custody personnel in correctional settings would need to be restructured so that recommendations like those previously mentioned—that prisoners with mental illness be carefully screened, given access to mental health treatment, and sometimes referred to more appropriate therapeutic settings—are more routinely implemented. When mental health workers are required to comply categorically with the judgments of custody personnel or are under pressure to defer to assignments made by classification or housing officers who may summarily override their clinical recommendations, of course, they cannot effectively address the needs of disturbed or vulnerable prisoners.[77]

In addition, both mental health and custodial staff members would need to be provided with specialized training that focused on the various context-related disorders that arise or are exacerbated in prison, as well as the range of additional psychological problems that come about in response to more severe prison conditions (such as solitary or supermax-type confinement). As I have suggested throughout much of this book, precisely because context matters, the individual-level consequences of even short-term exposure to deprived, degrading, and brutalizing prison conditions cannot be ignored. Prison staff need to be trained to recognize prison-related stressors, and to become sensitive to the ways in which the environment of prison can cause psychological distress in many prisoners. The tendency to automatically attribute psychiatric or mental health complaints to preexisting character disorders or to some form of malingering or "secondary gain" often reflects a naïve view of the pains of imprisonment and their psychological consequences. This dismissive approach is less defensible or justified in light of the more psychologically sophisticated context-sensitive perspective on institutional behavior that has emerged over the last several decades.

In broader terms, Hans Toch described an approach to "multiproblem" prisoners in which case managers serve to coordinate the delivery of a wide range of services to them.[78] Despite the limited role that mental illness per se plays in crime causation in general, there are some prisoners whose underlying psychological disorders not only should be taken into account in classification decisions and housing assignments but also must be addressed before they are likely to make a successful transition to the freeworld.[79] Indeed, effective programs of rehabilitation would include enhancing the capability of prison counselors to engage in needs assessments of prisoners and actually to deliver appropriate services accordingly—not just directly to prisoners in confinement but also as participators in the coordination of continuing care in the broader freeworld contexts to which those prisoners will return.[80]

One caveat is in order concerning the complex and sensitive topic of correctional mental health programs. As I acknowledged earlier in this chapter, in the days when "treatment" was the stated mission of many prisons, there were many abuses committed in its name. Distinguished forensic psychiatrist Bernard Diamond once criticized what he saw as a "prevailing attitude of hypocritical cynicism" in which, despite an "official posture" that the prison provide therapy, prisoners still experienced the prison as "deprivation and punishment." However, they also knew that some ostensible participation in the therapeutic process was crucial to their release. Thus, as he put it, "a complex confidence game results in which staff administers treatments which they know full well to be ineffective and inadequate to inmates who are quite aware that they are not being treated but are undergoing punishment."[81] No intelligent, psychologically informed set of reforms would ignore this history or risk re-creating such a cynical, hypocritical system.

To avoid doing so, a dramatic shift in correctional budgets must occur, so that the context of prison itself can be broadly reshaped. Prison staff and administrators would need to acknowledge that harsh punishment and severe deprivation are incompatible with treatment-oriented environments. At the same time, to be sure, strict oversight of treatment programs is needed to avoid delivering punishment in the name of therapy. Moreover, except in the most acute cases, treatment programs must be made available on a voluntary basis, and participation never made a precondition for release from prison. Involuntary, coercive therapy in an already overcontrolled environment like prison is unlikely to produce positive and lasting change. Instead, participation should be ensured by the quality of the programs themselves. This, in turn, would require adequate numbers of highly trained, properly funded, and institutionally empowered therapy and counseling personnel to be in place to effectively screen, monitor, and treat those prisoners who enter the system with preexisting psychiatric conditions, as well as those who may become the psychological casualties of incarceration.[82]

I should note that the tendency to see the negative effects of imprisonment in exclusively clinical terms has sometimes produced an anomalous pattern of treatment that has harmful long-term consequences for mentally ill prisoners who are subjected to it. Because their clinical disorders have been approached from a traditional perspective that discounts or ignores the nature of the social context in which they occur, acutely disturbed prisoners often are removed from especially harsh prison conditions (such as solitary confinement) only long enough to be treated and stabilized, after which they are returned to the same adverse conditions that helped to precipitate their mental health crisis. This kind of "revolving door" approach seems to be a remnant of the individualistic view of behavior in which patients are treated independent of context. A more psychologically sophisticated appreciation of the interaction between painful conditions of confinement, acute threats to the psychological well-being of prisoners, and acute forms of mental illness would result in a different approach—either to drastically change the harsh context that precipitated or exacerbated the psychological disorder or to permanently remove vulnerable prisoners from it.

Finally—and perhaps most importantly—in recognition of the fact that certain countertherapeutic aspects of the prison environment simply cannot be overcome, many more community-based alternatives need to be created to which prisoners who are mentally ill and psychologically vulnerable can be diverted. In the final analysis, the appropriate solution to high numbers of prisoners with mental illness is not to turn prisons into mental hospitals but rather to provide adequate treatment outside (and instead) of prison, so that their incarceration can be avoided altogether.

RACE-RELATED PRISON REFORMS

Chapter 4 was devoted largely to a discussion of the racialized nature of prison punishment in American society, a topic that also was acknowledged in passing in many other parts of this book. Many of the forces that have resulted in significant racial disparities in imprisonment are generated outside of the correctional system itself and, therefore, are beyond the scope of traditional prison reform. This is a clear example of the limitations of bringing change to only one sector of a highly interconnected set of socioeconomic, political, and legal institutions (especially because prison systems typically respond to, rather than produce changes in, these other institutional systems).

To underscore just one aspect of this dilemma, note that prison policy alone is hardly responsible for the larger social equation by which our nation sentences almost twice the percentage of young African American men to prison than it awards bachelor's degrees.[83] Although sentencing reform certainly could have some impact on that stark disproportion, it cannot directly address the broader lack of educational opportunity that obviously plays a more significant role.[84]

At the same time, however, this means that community-level reforms that helped to bring social and economic justice to minority neighborhoods would go a long way toward reducing racial disproportions in rates of imprisonment. Given the finite resources available to address these problems, the choice to approach drug-related and other kinds of crime by focusing so aggressively on individual perpetrators has precluded the simultaneous investment in preventive and other community-oriented programs. The construction of a very large and costly correctional system (that holds a disproportionate number of minority prisoners) has come at the expense of programs that address the structural roots of crime. As I have noted, our crime control policies continue to be based on a narrowly individualistic model of behavior, and certain groups in our society have paid an especially high price for the pursuit of these outmoded and ineffective approaches.[85]

In addition, other factors that contribute to the race-based disparities in incarceration—although they are located outside the prison system— nonetheless are subject to reform and could be addressed in a more psychologically informed system. These certainly include current drug law enforcement, prosecution, and sentencing policies that ignore social context to produce clear racially disparate consequences. Recall that the dramatic increase in incarceration rates over the last several decades was produced in part by the targeting of drug offenders that occurred in the course of the War on Drugs.

Notwithstanding their unfairness, these policies should be vulnerable on the basis of their sheer ineffectiveness. According to their proponents, imprisonment policies that concentrated so intensely on drug-related crime certainly should have produced massive decreases in drug use. They did not. As one political analyst of the use of imprisonment as a weapon in the war on drugs concluded, "The massive growth of prison cells to incarcerate a small percentage of the nation's addicts has done nothing meaningful to reduce the staggering number of civilian addicts. Neither the public safety nor the drug addiction problem has been satisfactorily addressed."[86] In fact, drug use continued to rise, leading the American Bar Association to recommend in 1998 that the nation rethink its exclusive reliance on arrest and incarceration for drug offenders.[87]

Race-related sentencing reforms also might address the relatively recent legal doctrines that have precluded any meaningful judicial consideration of background and circumstance in calculating culpability and meting out punishment. In addition to its general effects, the law's decontextualized view of the social behavior of crime has meant that race-based differences in exposure to criminogenic circumstances are ignored in the sentencing process. As I discussed at length in chapter 4, the failure to improve the life chances of persons exposed to these criminogenic conditions and instead to intensify their criminal prosecution and incarceration reflects an intrinsically dispositional view of crime control. It also has had discriminatory consequences and allowed the characteristics of the perpetrators (rather than their circumstances) to be used as the basis of causal inferences that are erroneous as well as racialized in nature. As one partial solution to some of these problems, legislation such as the proposed Racial Justice Act—which was designed to trigger inquiries into state death penalty sentencing practices whenever significant race-based disparities were identified—might be broadened to include those instances in which significant racial disparities in prison sentences occurred as well.[88]

Inside prisons, proposals to improve prison life in general should have some ameliorative effect on racial conflict—including the way in which creating program-rich environments may lessen racial and other kinds of tensions overall. In addition, however, practices that afford institutional legitimacy to racial divisions inside prisons or give credence to the notion that racial animosities cannot be overcome other than by segregating or separating different racial and ethnic groups must be prohibited. Consistent with the modern psychological view that individual-level attitudinal change alone will not be sustained unless it is supported by the appropriate situational contingencies, polices of racial tolerance will have to be implemented that both require and reinforce behavioral change on the part of inmates and officers.

This means, of course, that proactive strategies of racial integration would need to be pursued—frank acknowledgement of the potential for racial tension and conflict in prison must be followed with the implementation of diversity-related racial tolerance programs for staff and prisoners alike. To be sure, racial integration may need to be phased in in prison settings where equality between prisoners has been little more than an idle claim halfheartedly pursued. Yet, despite the need to strike a sensitive balance between prisoner safety and legitimate preferences, on the one hand, and genuine race-neutral official policies, on the other, prison systems must structure living arrangements and day-to-day procedures in ways that break down the institutionally sanctioned racial barriers that exist inside many correctional facilities.[89]

Of course, it is unrealistic and unfair to expect prisons to become engines for broader social reform, or to insist on a level of racial harmony and cooperation in correctional institutions that has proven difficult to attain elsewhere in society. Yet the intimate and intense nature of prison life virtually requires that an extraordinary level of interpersonal tolerance be achieved and maintained. Indeed, government policymakers with a stake in promoting improved race relations outside of prison should consider the long-term societal-level implications of widespread, deeply engrained prison-based racism. Specifically, each year hundreds of thousands of ex-convicts are released back into the freeworld, many having spent years housed in the racially toxic and sometimes hate-filled world of prison. Policies of overincarceration in environments like these may contribute to race-related gang violence and the persistence of racism in society at large. This, too, is a kind of negative "prison effect," but one with potential consequences for contexts outside of prison.

GANGS AND CONTEXT:
REDUCING PRISON PATHOLOGIES

Correctional officials typically have viewed the prison gang problem as a reflection of the individual pathology of gang members, and they have responded accordingly. That is, they have undertaken much the same approach that they use with other troublesome inmate behavior—punishing the people whom they believe are most involved. For the most part, as I pointed out in chapter 7, this strategy ignores the contextual factors that contribute to the formation of the gangs themselves. Not surprisingly, there is little evidence that it has been effective.

Moreover, this individualistic response has certain contextual consequences of its own that can worsen the very problem it is designed to solve. For one, the punitive isolation of gang leaders—done with the intent both of punishing them and preventing their communication with other members—creates vacuums within the power structure of the gangs themselves. It allows many younger prisoners to compete for leadership positions vacated by those sent to isolation. Because the conditions that gave rise to the gangs are not addressed, new leaders, new members, and even new gangs often emerge as a result to fill this vacuum. In addition, the policy of isolating gang members and housing them all in the same places—usually punitive segregation units that lack any programming opportunities or other meaningful activities—focuses their attention even more intensely on gang-related issues. In the absence of anything else to become involved in or care about, the gang assumes even greater significance in their lives. Moreover, those persons who are misclassified as gang members—ones with little or no actual gang affiliation before being placed in segregation—are surrounded with committed members and leaders. Many feel they have no choice but to become more actively involved.

Finally, punitive isolation may be counterproductive in another sense. If it is true that "alienation, anger, and conflict tend to feed and reinforce gang membership,"[90] then placement in these harsh units can exacerbate these feelings. Thus, the intense punishment that characterizes prison isolation—the deprivation, harsh conditions, and especially punitive forms of control to which they are subjected—may have the paradoxical effect of intensifying loyalties to the group for which the prisoners feel they are suffering.

A similar approach to "gang suppression" that punishes individual leaders and members has been unsuccessful outside of prison—when it has been tried in communities and neighborhoods plagued by chronic gang problems. It has fared no better in correctional settings. A context-oriented approach to prison gangs would look instead beyond exclusively person-centered policies that repress only individual members and simultaneously ignore the conditions that foster gang activity. It would recognize that, like other voluntary associations, gangs gain strength when recruits have little hope and are given few meaningful pathways through which to achieve desired goals—that is, when they perceive that important needs cannot be met any other way.

Thus, the lure of the gangs begins to fade in program-oriented prisons in which prisoners are provided with useful and productive activities in which to engage and are not deprived of basic amenities (that many gangs become skilled at providing). Gangs also lose power when prisoners can become invested in their own progress within the prison in ways that they anticipate will carry over to free society—so that there are some future-oriented goals that they are reluctant to jeopardize or lose. As prison analyst John Conrad once observed, "without full and genuine work and activity it is inconceivable that the gangs will attenuate in influence, numbers and violence."[91]

Sophisticated gang-reduction programs in local communities have succeeded by merging individual-level counseling with context-oriented programs designed to change the circumstances that have created and maintained gang allegiances. One such program provides participants with opportunities to explore the basis for the feelings of anger and rage that many of them share, and helps them find behavioral alternatives to violence that they formerly "displaced onto people and property in the community."[92] Mentoring-based programs like these are designed to enable gang members to understand and address past abuse issues, develop more positive identities, "differentiate between emotional states and behavioral actions," and explore the nature of the sociological stressors that have impacted their own family dynamics.

However, because these feelings and behaviors so often arise from structural and neighborhood-related forces and factors, their ultimate resolution must be accomplished within the community as well as with individual gang members. By embracing this perspective, other innovative programs have recognized that the twin goals of achieving community-level peace in neighborhoods torn by gang violence and attaining "inner peace" for gang members "needs a transitional bridge to institutions that will support and open the doors" to the current generation of at-risk youth. That is, the decision to relinquish gang life must be reinforced "most of all, [with] remedial education, training, and employment at decent wages."[93]

There is no reason why many of the same insights—such as the use of mentoring-based counseling and structural change that is designed to provide meaningful opportunity—cannot be applied to the gang problem that exists inside many prisons. Of course, here, too, the current rigid separation between in-prison programming and neighborhood-based transformations will have to be bridged. Community-based organizations will need to be given access to the prisons to facilitate these interconnections and to begin to create transitional pathways—opportunities for productive work and meaningful activity in community settings that will be in place at the time of a person's release from prison. When combined with the opportunity to move into neighborhoods that are not dominated by gang activity, or to work in programs that are designed to transform communities so that the grip of the gangs is loosened, this kind of contextual approach to prison "peacemaking" represents a more viable way of addressing this important problem.

THE CONTEXT OF REENTRY:
PRESERVING POSITIVE CHANGE

Even properly designed and well-funded prison programs often have failed to improve recidivism rates, largely because they have disregarded the contexts and circumstances to which prisoners are released. Here, too, the individualistic bias that characterizes traditional correctional thinking has limited the scope of reform. As people-changing institutions, prisons (at their best) have been charged with the task of producing only individual-level change. No matter how good or effective we make them, their beneficial effects are limited unless they are supported and maintained in the settings and circumstances that follow incarceration. A psychologically sophisticated, context-oriented approach would recognize this fact and implement a fundamentally different strategy.

For example, a deeper appreciation of the nature and consequences of the prisonization process that occurs as prisoners adapt over time to the pains of imprisonment highlights the importance of providing direct assistance to help reverse these changes as release dates approach. Indeed, because of the obvious challenges that arise whenever persons move into dramatically different social contexts—and few transitions in our society are more dramatic than the one from prison to the freeworld—intensive "decompression" programs are needed to prepare prisoners for the sudden and often wrenching changes they will undergo. Even though the value of these kinds of programs has been known for many years,[94] few prison systems have adopted them on a widespread and routine basis.[95]

In addition, however, recognizing the extent to which context matters also significantly broadens the perspective through which decompression and reintegration are approached. That is, here, too, it underscores the extent to which changing the context to which prisoners return is at least as important as changing the readiness with which prisoners themselves undertake the transition. Indeed, postprison environments exercise a major influence over whether and how prisoners make the transition back to the families, social networks, and communities from which they have been taken. As Dina Rose and Todd Clear observed, a contextualist approach like the one I am proposing would recognize "that reentry is not just about individuals coming home; it is also about the homes and communities to which ex-prisoners return."[96] Because community context is as important to reintegration as prison itself—and, for some prisoners and some communities, more important—altering this environment by providing resources and supportive services is critical.

Of course, ex-prisoners are children, spouses, parents, and loved ones, who must be welcomed back into their families and friendships as well as the neighborhoods and communities, where they once again will become residents and citizens. Psychologically sophisticated prison policies would make a concerted effort to assist families in preparing for the return of loved ones, help communities acclimate and absorb prisoners back into their neighborhoods, and create infrastructural supports (such as employment counseling, job placement services, counseling opportunities, and so on) to facilitate their reentry.[97] Basic issues—such as helping prisoners prepare for difficult reunions with family members, giving families access to longer term family counseling, and working with community and neighborhood employers to facilitate job placement and retention[98]—are essential components in a context-based approach.

Among other things, this approach suggests that probation and parole agencies should be restructured and revamped to provide services and meaningfully assist in reintegration (a drastic change from their present emphasis on surveillance and social control).[99] Unfortunately, as a recent Urban Institute analysis of parole underscored, the parole function itself has shifted from providing services to becoming a "surveillance-oriented, control-based strategy centered on monitoring behavior." Its authors also drew this context-based conclusion: "Parole officers are often located far from the neighborhoods where parolees reside, and therefore lack an understanding of the situational context that geographically oriented supervision could provide."[100] As the focus and mission of probation and parole shift to the provision of services and the maintenance of postprison success, agents' knowledge of and connection to the local communities in which ex-convicts are concentrated will have to be greatly improved.[101]

Moreover, truly contextual models of reintegration would focus on the core task of transforming the actual social and economic circumstances to which prisoners return—conceptualizing community and neighborhood-level change as part of the process by which successful postprison adjustment is made possible. That is, models of crime control that embody modern psychological theory must include structural change—the supportive networks, viable economic circumstances, and hospitable living conditions that would have to be created to replace the chronically "high risk" situations to which many prisoners return.[102]

Finally, the important task of interconnecting the entire set of these context-related reforms would need to be addressed in order to ensure their effectiveness. Just as proposals to change the way prison life is structured will have limited long-term effects in the absence of postprison programs that address the obstacles to reentry, elaborately structured reentry programs—in the absence of genuine prison reform—are unlikely to fare much better. Thus, so-called second-chance programs that focus on the needs of prisoners *after* they are released must be joined with efforts to reduce the numbers of persons who enter prisons in the first place and, for those who do go, to minimize the damage that overly harsh and punitive conditions of confinement can inflict.[103] For prisoners whose vulnerabilities should have precluded their incarceration in the first place, or for those persons who were deeply and perhaps irrevocably harmed by their exposure to painful and damaging prison settings, or for those who were the victims of psychologically or physically disabling forms of correctional mistreatment, second-chance programs realistically may offer no chance at all.

CONCLUSION

This chapter has set out an overarching, unifying vision that both establishes the logic with which prison policy changes can be guided and provides an intellectual framework from which specific reforms can be generated. As I have repeatedly noted, we now understand the important causal role played by traumatic social histories, criminogenic social conditions, and broad structural inequalities in the origins of criminal behavior. The growing recognition that context matters also means that there is greater appreciation of the way in which the process of prisonization and exposure to the situational pathologies of prison can create unwanted changes in prisoners that may have severe personal and community-level consequences.

Just as the contextual model of behavior developed in the preceding chapters would predict, "most studies support the idea that intervention is more likely to be effective if it focuses on certain areas that have been shown to be risk factors for criminal activity."[104] Yet, over the last several decades, many politicians and prison policymakers have been less than completely candid about these issues. Indeed, they often have refused to address crime control and prison-related problems in meaningful ways, leaving citizens largely ignorant of the real long-term implications of the "get tough" movement in which they have been encouraged to participate.[105]

The transformative nature of the prison experience, the kind of adaptations it requires prisoners to undergo, and its potential to inflict long-term harm all must become the focus of context-based prison change. From a modern social contextual perspective, "doing no harm" in corrections means minimizing or prohibiting exposure to painful and damaging prison contexts and environments, where the risk of psychological harm is great (no matter the short-term practical convenience they seem to afford). Because many current legal approaches to these prison-related challenges are limited and do not encompass the behavioral aspects of crime and punishment that I have presented in the preceding chapters,[106] a psychologically inspired set of prison reforms seems to be in order.

Among other things, limiting the pains of imprisonment—and doing so in the name of a psychologically sophisticated model of crime control—would mean increasing the number of alternatives to prison, creating places where otherwise dysfunctional adaptations to prison are far less necessary, housing prisoners in environments where they are not constantly challenged to survive the dangerous extremes of confinement, and making a significant investment in ensuring their postprison adjustment by properly preparing them for this dramatic transition. Finally, it would mean restructuring the nature of the environments to which they eventually return, and providing them with a wide range of context-sensitive support services once they do.

NOTES

1. Nils Christie, *Limits to Pain* (Oxford, England: Martin Robertson, 1982), 49. Christie also cautioned that presumably well meaning reforms often have unintended consequences. For example, "Recent experiences with 'alternatives to prison' indicate that they easily turn into 'additions to prison,' and that conditional sentences in reality turn into more time spent in prison. The lesson from periods of 'treatment for crime' ought also to be kept vividly in mind. If pain delivery is limited, will we then get a rehearsal of the old story? . . . Skeptics will be greatly needed" (ibid., 110). All proposals to make prison systems "better"—including my own—should be judged with these lessons in mind.

2. S. Pillsbury, "Understanding Penal Reform: The Dynamic of Change," *Journal of Criminal Law & Criminology* 80 (1989): 726, 779.

3. J. Bleich, "The Politics of Prison Crowding," *California Law Review* 77 (1989): 1125, 1166.

4. Pillsbury, "Understanding Penal Reform," 779.

5. Kevin Wright and Lynne Goodstein, "Correctional Environments," in *The American Prison: Issues in Research and Policy*, ed. Lynne Goodstein and Doris MacKenzie (New York: Plenum Press, 1989), 266.

6. H. Toch, "A Revisionist View of Prison Reform," *Federal Probation* 45 (1981): 3, 9.

7. Ibid., 4 (footnote omitted).

8. Not surprisingly, given what I have said up to this point about the causes of the current corrections crisis, I believe that many of the most important obstacles to prison reform are political in nature. Thus, I agree with the late Norval Morris on this point. He wrote, "The major impediment to reducing the use of imprisonment in the United States, and to bringing its imposition into accord with that of other developed countries, lies in its having become, over the past two decades, the plaything of politics. Being 'tough on crime' has become a necessary precondition of election to political office and of the retention of incumbency." Norval Morris, "The Contemporary Prison, 1965–Present," in *The Oxford History of the Prison: The Practice of Punishment in Western Society*, ed. Norval Morris and David Rothman (New York: Oxford University Press, 1995), 230. Numerous accounts have been published recently that examine how and why these political forces were applied to criminal justice issues and with what effect. Among the best ones are Sasha Abramsky, *Hard Time Blues: How Politics Built a Prison Nation* (New York: St. Martins Press, 2002); Joe Domanick, *Cruel Justice: Three Strikes and the Politics of Crime in America's Golden State* (Berkeley, CA: University of California Press, 2004); Joel Dyer, *The Perpetual Prisoner Machine: How America Profits From Crime* (Boulder, CO: Westview Press, 2000); Alan Elsner, *Gates of Injustice: The Crisis in America's Prisons* (Upper Saddle River, NJ: Prentice Hall, 2004); and Christian Parenti, *Lockdown America: Police and Prisons in the Age of Crisis* (New York: Verso, 1999). For other perspectives, *see also* P. Chevigny, "The Populism of Fear: Politics of Crime in the Americas," *Punishment & Society* 5 (2003): 77; and C. Haney, "Riding the

Punishment Wave: On the Origins of Our Devolving Standards of Decency," *Hastings Women's Law Journal* 9 (1998): 27.

9. On the use of drugs courts, *see, e.g.,* P. Hora, W. Schma, and J. Rosenthal, "Therapeutic Jurisprudence and the Drug Treatment Court Movement: Revolutionizing the Criminal Justice System's Response to Drug Abuse and Crime in America," *Notre Dame Law Review* 74 (1999): 439. For a discussion of the use of mental health courts, *see* E. Stratton, "Solutions for the Mentally Ill in the Criminal Justice System: A Symposium Introduction," *Capital University Law Review* 32 (2004): 901, and the other articles in the symposium special issue. The emergence of these problem-solving courts that are designed to address specialized crime-related problems and implement specialized—typically non-prison—solutions is a good example of the contextual perspective at work. *See, e.g.,* D. Rottman and P. Casey, "Therapeutic Jurisprudence and the Emergence of Problem-Solving Courts," *National Institute of Justice Journal* 240 (July, 1999): 12. It is true that these new specialty courts "focus on large scale social problems that are difficult to resolve," but this is in part because other social agencies no longer address them (because the agencies now lack either the resources or, in some instances, the legal mandate to attempt to do so). T. Case, "When Good Intentions Are Not Enough: Problem-Solving Courts and the Impending Crisis of Legitimacy," *Southern Methodist University Law Review* 57 (2004): 1459, 1516. The concern raised by Case and others—that courts may not have the expertise to solve such large-scale social problems—overlooks the fact that the problems are not likely to solve themselves. Eventually, courts will be called on to address many of them (albeit in a different, perhaps less solvable, form). Indeed, the movement toward greater numbers of problem-solving courts also seems to be a reflection of the increasing awareness that solutions to these difficult problems must be implemented earlier in the process and can be better fashioned by judges who are working closer to the context in which the problems first arise.

10. D. Ward, "Punishment by Imprisonment: Placing Ideology Into Concrete [Reviewing Michael Sherman and Gordon Hawkins, Imprisonment in America: Choosing the Future. Chicago, IL: University of Chicago Press (1983)]," *Michigan Law Review* 81 (1983): 1202, 1202.

11. *See, e.g.,* John Smykla and William Selke, ed., *Intermediate Sanctions: Sentencing in the 1990s* (Highland Heights, KY: Anderson Publishing, 1995); Michael Tonry and Kate Hamilton, ed., *Intermediate Sanctions for Overcrowded Times* (Boston: Northeastern University Press, 1995); and Norval Morris and Michael Tonry, *Between Prison and Probation: Intermediate Punishments in a Rational Sentencing System* (New York: Oxford, 1990). For a discussion of the framing of these proposals in ways that are likely to achieve public support, *see* Michael Castle, *Alternative Sentencing: Selling it to the Public* (Washington, DC: National Institute of Justice, 1991).

12. Early versions of intermediate sanction programs—adopted during the "tough on crime" era—proved more punitive than rehabilitative and did little to actually steer persons who were headed for prison into the community instead. Appropriately designed intermediate sanction programs should "divert low-

risk prisoners to the community or place higher-risk probationers on smaller caseloads with more restrictions," or both. J. Petersilia, "A Decade of Experimenting With Intermediate Sanctions: What Have We Learned?" *Federal Probation* 62 (1998): 3, 5.

13. Thus, as Joan Petersilia reported, intermediate sanction participants who were involved "in treatment, community service, and employment programs—prosocial activities—had recidivism rates 10% to 20% below that of those who did not participate in such additional activities." Petersilia, "A Decade of Experimenting With Intermediate Sanctions," 6. Similar conclusions were reached by Paul Gendreau and his colleagues. *See* P. Gendreau, T. Little, and C. Goggin, "A Meta-Analysis of the Predictors of Offender Recidivism: What Works!" *Criminology* 34 (1996): 401.

14. Petersilia, "A Decade of Experimenting With Intermediate Sanctions," 7, describing aspects of Wisconsin's "community confinement and control" program.

15. The Europeans have made a much more serious commitment to restorative justice alternatives in their criminal justice and prison systems. For example, one innovative restorative justice program implemented inside selected Belgian prisons—a "restorative detention" project—includes the creation of a "culture of respect" for staff and inmates alike (to counteract the negative aspects of imprisonment); the introduction of a genuine restorative process that includes a victims' perspective in different justice-related activities (that allows prisoners to shift their focus from prison survival to understanding the causes and consequences of their actions); and, finally, programs that address "the financial problems of prisoners (insolvency, impoverishment, debts, fines, legal costs, civil action remedies and the lack of possible remedies)" and are designed not only to help them meet their restorative justice obligations but also to "provide prisoners with sufficient means to manage their budget as independently as possible." Luc Robert and Tony Peters, "How Restorative Justice Is Able to Transcend the Prison Walls: A Discussion of the 'Restorative Detention' Project," in *Restorative Justice in Context: International Practice and Directions*, ed. Elmar Weitekamp and Hans-Jurgen Kerner (Devon, England: Willan Publishing, 2003), 95, 103, 115. *See also* D. Miers, "Situating and Researching Restorative Justice in Great Britain," *Punishment & Society* 6 (2004): 23, and the references cited therein.

16. Steve Bogira, *Courtroom 302: A Year Behind the Scenes in an American Criminal Courthouse.* (New York: Knopf, 2005), 41.

17. *See, e.g.,* Timothy Hughes and Doris Wilson, *Reentry Trends in the United States: Inmates Returning to the Community After Serving Time in Prison* (Washington, DC: Bureau of Justice Statistics, 2002).

18. As Human Rights Watch noted, the collective social good is advanced whenever "individuals who walk out of prison each year . . . do not leave more dangerous than when they entered." Human Rights Watch, *Prison Conditions in the United States* (New York: Author, 1991): 11.

19. *See* E. Zamble, "Behavior and Adaptation in Long-Term Prison Inmates: Descriptive Longitudinal Results," *Criminal Justice and Behavior* 19 (1992): 409.

20. Dora Schriro, "Correcting Corrections: Missouri's Parallel Universe," in *Sentencing and Corrections: Issues for the 21st Century* (U.S. Department of Justice, Papers from the Executive Sessions on Sentencing and Corrections, May 2000). Available at http://www.ncjrs.org/pdffiles1/nij/181414.pdf.

21. For a review of this model, *see* George De Leon, *Community as Method: Therapeutic Communities for Special Populations and Special Settings* (Westport, CN: Praeger, 1997). Here is how several European experts described the advantages of this approach: "The main theoretical assumption is that healthy and participatory environments in custodial institutions will bring about greater psychological balance in prisoners and will reduce their anti-social behavior, both during the individual's stay in the custodial institution and afterwards." Santiago Redondo, Julio Sanchez-Meca, and Vincente Garrido, "Crime Treatment in Europe: A Review of Outcome Studies," in *Offender Rehabilitation and Treatment: Effective Programmes and Policies to Reduce Re-offending*, ed. James McGuire (Chichester, England: John Wiley, 2002), 113, 118.

22. B. Peat and L. Winfree, "Reducing the Intra-Institutional Effects of 'Prisonization': A Study of a Therapeutic Community for Drug-Using Inmates," *Criminal Justice and Behavior* 19 (1992): 206, 207. Although therapeutic community models can improve some of the worst aspects of prison life, they have some limitations of their own. Among other things, many of them place the causal locus of psychological problems exclusively inside the patient. Thus, although the ameliorative aspects of the therapeutic community are worth adopting, its psychological assumptions need to be critically analyzed from the same social contextual perspective I have applied to other forms of prison treatment.

23. Zamble, "Behavior and Adaptation in Long-Term Prison Inmates." *See also* J. Gibbs, "Environmental Congruence and Symptoms of Psychopathology: A Further Exploration of the Effects of Exposure to the Jail Environment," *Criminal Justice & Behavior* 18 (1991): 351, for a discussion of the ways in which conditions of confinement interact with prisoner characteristics to increase or decrease symptoms of psychological distress.

24. Creasie Hairston and others have addressed the importance of maintaining family ties for both in-prison and postprison adjustment. *See* C. Hairston, "Family Ties During Imprisonment: Do They Influence Future Criminal Activity?" *Federal Probation* 52 (1988): 48; C. Hairston. "Family Ties During Imprisonment: Important to Whom and for What?" *Journal of Sociology and Social Welfare* 18 (1991): 87. *Cf. also* W. Collins, "The Effect of Social Isolation on Inmate Self Concept," *Dissertation Abstracts International* 45 (1984): 643, who found that the more isolated prisoners—those who had less contact with persons outside the prison—tended to experience greater reductions in measured self-concept during their incarceration.

25. John Irwin, "Sociological Studies of the Impact of Long-Term Confinement," in *Confinement in Maximum Custody: New Last-Resort Prisons in the United States and Western Europe*, ed. David Ward and Ken Schoen (Lexington, MA: DC Heath, 1981), 49, 51.

26. Michael King, "Male Rape in Institutional Settings," in *Male Victims of Sexual Assault*, ed. Gillian Mezey and Michael King (Oxford, England: Oxford University Press, 1992), 67, 73.

27. Ibid.

28. Discussions of this study can be found in C. Haney, C. Banks, and P. Zimbardo, "Interpersonal Dynamics in a Simulated Prison," *International Journal of Criminology and Penology* 1 (1973): 69; Craig Haney and Philip Zimbardo, "The Socialization into Criminality: On Becoming a Prisoner and a Guard," in *Law, Justice, and the Individual in Society: Psychological and Legal Issues*, ed. June Tapp and Felice Levine (New York: Holt, Rinehart & Winston, 1977); and C. Haney and P. Zimbardo, "The Past and Future of U.S. Prison Policy: Twenty-five Years After the Stanford Prison Experiment," *American Psychologist* 53 (1998): 709.

29. One of the most widely cited official analyses of the prison abuse scandals at Abu Ghraib came from a governmental review panel that produced a document known as the "Schlesinger Report," after the panel's chair, James Schlesinger. Appendix G ("Psychological Stresses") of the Schlesinger Report noted that "In 1973, Haney, Banks and Zimbardo published their landmark Stanford study.... Their study provides a cautionary tale for all military detention operations. . . ." In detailing that cautionary tale, the Schlesinger Report quoted both our 1973 article to the effect that the abnormality in the behavior of the student guards in the Stanford study "resided in the psychological nature of the situation and not in those who passed through it," and our retrospective discussion in 1998: "Haney and Zimbardo noted their initial study 'underscored the degree to which institutional settings can develop a life of their own, independent of the wishes, intentions, and purposes of those who run them.'" The Schlesinger panel acknowledged one of the overarching implications of our study—"the need for those outside the culture [of the institution] to offer external perspectives on process and procedures [inside]." The report also listed a series of social psychological forces inherent in prison contexts that help to explain "why humans sometimes mistreat fellow humans." The list included *deindividuation* (the way that anonymity allows persons to suspend "customary rules and inhibition[s]"); *groupthink* (illusions of moral superiority and unanimous group support ensures that "pressure is brought to bear on those who might dissent"); *dehumanization* (which depicts others "as somehow less than fully human"); *enemy image* (whereby one's own group is seen as good in comparison to an enemy that is "seen as evil and aggressive"); and *moral exclusion* (in which viewing others as "fundamentally different" from one's own group obviates the need to treat them in accord with "prevailing moral rules"). *See* James Schlesinger et al., *Final Report of the Independent Panel to Review Department of Defense Detention Operations* (Arlington, VA: Independent Panel to Review Department of Defense Detention Operations, August 2004). Of course, these social psychological forces inhere in domestic prison contexts as well as military detention facilities.

30. Legal commentators have begun to address the need for greater accountability in corrections—including accountability in the day-to-day operations of the prison and especially those cases in which prisoners complain of use of excessive

force by staff. *See, e.g.,* A. Jacobs, "Prison Power Corrupts Absolutely: Prison Guard Brutality and the Need to Develop a System of Accountability," *Case Western Law Review* 41 (2004): 277.

31. *See* Alison Liebling and David Price, *The Prison Officer* (Leyhill, England: Prison Service and Waterside Press, 2001); and Alison Liebling, *Prisons and Their Moral Performance: A Study of Values, Quality and Prison Life* (Oxford, England: Clarendon Press, 2004).

32. *See* Claudia Kesterman, "A Comparative Analysis of Cognitive Concepts of Prison Officers in the Baltic Sea States," in *Psychology and Law: Facing the Challenges of a Changing World,* ed. A. Czerederecka et al. (Krakow, Poland: Institute of Forensic Research Publishers, 2004); and Claudia Kesterman, *Prison Life: Factors Affecting Health and Rehabilitation.* Paper presented at the European Conference on Psychology and Law, Vilnius, Lithuania, July 2005.

33. K. Wright, "The Violent and Victimized in the Male Prison," *Journal of Offender Rehabilitation* 16 (1991): 1, 23, 24.

34. Irwin, "Sociological Studies of the Impact of Long-Term Confinement," 51.

35. Ibid.

36. Nowadays very little of this kind of basic preparation is provided. For example, in California in 1997, approximately 142,000 persons were released from prison, but no more than 5% of them had completed a reentry program beforehand. *See* J. Petersilia, "Challenges of Prisoner Reentry and Parole in California," *CPRC Brief* 12 (June, 2000): 1. The nationwide statistics were only slightly better—on the basis of 1997 figures, only about 8% of state prisoners participated in prerelease, reentry programs. Joan Petersilia, *When Prisoners Come Home: Parole and Prisoner Reentry* (New York: Oxford University Press, 2003), 95.

37. Without in any way intending to diminish the significance of the added pains of imprisonment for prisoners with mental illness or developmental disabilities— which were the focus of chapter 8 and are discussed later in this chapter— concentrating on this group of especially sympathetic and vulnerable inmates has sometimes diverted attention from the conditions of confinement and treatment to which the great majority of other prisoners are subjected. In a related way, because of the exclusively clinical framework that often has been used to understand and respond to prison-related maladies and adverse psychological reactions, pains of imprisonment that stop short of creating diagnosable psychiatric disorders often have been ignored or discounted. This narrow and now outmoded view of context-related trauma has impeded the systematic assessment of, and legal sensitivity to, a broader range of negative prison effects.

38. *See, e.g.,* Judith Herman, "A New Diagnosis," in *Trauma and Recovery,* ed. Judith Herman (New York: Basic Books, 1992); J. Herman, "Complex PTSD: A Syndrome in Survivors of Prolonged and Repeated Trauma," *Journal of Traumatic Stress* 5 (1992): 377; and Judith Herman, "Complex PTSD: A Syndrome in Survivors of Prolonged and Repeated Trauma," in *Psychotraumatology: Key Papers and Core Concepts in Post-Traumatic Stress,* ed. George Everly and Jeffrey Lating (New York: Plenum, 1995), 87.

39. H. Franke, "The Rise and Decline of Solitary Confinement: Socio-Historical Explanations of Long-Term Penal Changes," *British Journal of Criminology* 32 (1992): 125, 139. This view is discussed at some length in chapter 7, this volume.

40. These ideas are developed more fully in C. Haney and M. Lynch, "Regulating Prisons of the Future: The Psychological Consequences of Supermax and Solitary Confinement," *New York University Review of Law and Social Change* 23 (1997): 477.

41. As one researcher has observed, "Those who take an exclusively person-centered or importation view of the prevalence of psychological disorder in jail should broaden their perspective to include situational or environmental factors." Gibbs, Environmental Congruence and Symptoms of Psychopathology, 351. *See also* James Gibbs, "The First Cut Is the Deepest: Psychological Breakdown and Survival in the Detention Setting," in *The Pains of Imprisonment*, ed. Robert Johnson and Hans Toch (Beverly Hills, CA: Sage, 1982), 302. *Cf.* Anthony Bottoms, William Hay, and J. Sparks, "Situational and Social Approaches to the Prevention of Disorder in Long-Term Prisons," in *Long-Term Imprisonment: Policy, Science, and Correctional Practice*, ed. Timothy Flanagan (Thousand Oaks, CA: Sage Publications, 1995), 186.

42. Jessica Mitford was perhaps the most trenchant of these critics. *See* Jessica Mitford, *Kind and Usual Punishment* (New York: Knopf, 1973).

43. Edgardo Rotman, "The Failure of Prison Reform: United States, 1865–1965," in *The Oxford History of the Prison: The Practice of Punishment in Western Society*, ed. Noral Morris and David Rothman (New York: Oxford University Press, 1998), 152.

44. J. Willens, "Structure, Content and the Exigencies of War: American Prison Law After Twenty-Five Years, 1962–1987," *American University Law Review* 37 (1987): 41, 94, n. 308.

45. Hans Toch, "Classification for Programming and Survival," in *Confinement in Maximum Custody: Last Resort Prisons in the United States and Western Europe*, ed. David Ward and Ken Schoen (Lexington, MA: DC Heath, 1981), 39, 40.

46. Fred Cohen's distinction between traditional forms of "treatment" (premised on a limited disease model) and "rehabilitation" (as a social construct "that seeks to restore the individual to socially acceptable behavior") is useful here. *See* F. Cohen, "The Limits of the Judicial Reform of Prisons: What Works, What Does Not," *Criminal Law Bulletin* 40 (2004): 421, 454. A definition that many European prison experts endorse—"at present, the 'ideal of rehabilitation,' in the context of the penal system, is achieved by applying educational strategies and giving social support"—also seems applicable. Redondo, Sanchez-Meca, and Garrido, "Crime Treatment in Europe," 114. I would add only that socially acceptable behavior must be understood in the context in which it occurs and can be realistically achieved and reliably maintained only in those settings that are structured to support it.

47. This is why juvenile justice system reformers and others have learned that the most effective approaches are ones that offer a "diversity of programs" to address the various needs of different inmates and that maintain "strong community

linkages." Jerome Miller, *Last One Over the Wall: The Massachusetts Experiment in Closing Reform Schools* (Columbus: Ohio State University Press, 1991), 222. It is also why, although prison treatment programs sometimes do work, contrary to the view that emerged in the mid-1970s, it is also true that "on balance, community-based interventions have larger effect sizes than those delivered in institutions." James McGuire, "Integrating Findings From Research Reviews," in *Offender Rehabilitation and Treatment: Effective Programmes and Policies to Reduce Re-offending*, ed. James McGuire (Chichester, England: John Wiley, 2002), 3, 21.

48. It is not surprising that research shows that the most effective prison treatment and rehabilitation programs are ones that address prisoners' needs and include some form of postprison follow-up. For a variety of perspectives, *see, e.g.,* Gerald Gaes, Timothy Flanagan, Laurence Motiuk, and Lynn Stewart, "Adult Correctional Treatment," in *Prisons*, ed. Michael Tonry and Joan Petersilia (Chicago: University of Chicago Press, 1998); McGuire, *Offender Rehabilitation and Treatment*; J. Shine and M. Morris, "Addressing Criminogenic Needs in a Prison Therapeutic Community," *Therapeutic Communities: International Journal for Therapeutic & Supportive Organizations* 21 (2000): 197; Tony Ward and Lynne Eccleston, ed., "Special Issue: Offender Rehabilitation," *Psychology, Crime & Law* 10 (2004): 223, and the articles contained therein; T. Ward and C. Stewart, "Criminogenic Needs and Human Needs: A Theoretical Model," *Psychology Crime & Law* 9 (2003): 125. Obviously, carefully coordinating both the in-prison and outside components of these context-based forms of rehabilitation— conducted with prisoners' needs and circumstances in mind—should increase the overall effectiveness of these programs.

49. I know that talking about the programming recommendations of judges assumes facts that are not in evidence in most jurisdictions where judges sentence to terms of years and nothing else. But this, too, would need to be changed in a context-based system.

50. On January 8, 2002, President George Bush signed into effect Public Law 107-110, the "No Child Left Behind Act of 2001." Among other things, the act attempted to ensure successful learning by providing a series of benchmarks or performance standards that schools were required to meet in order to retain their federal funding. According to the rhetoric that surrounded the bill's passage, under the rubric of "increasing accountability" and "focusing on what works," the federal government sought to improve teacher training, fund schools where the greatest needs appeared to be concentrated, and promote educational excellence. It also was intended to reduce the achievement gap between rich and poor, and White and minority, students. All of these worthy goals can be applied to the context of prison—accountability, focusing on what works, putting resources where needs are greatest, and the like. The poor level of postprison success that is achieved by the graduates of many correctional systems—just as with many school systems—should be improved by implementing these kinds of reforms.

51. For the record, it is worth noting that prison systems in the United States have been doing a progressively worse job in providing educational and other

programming opportunities to prisoners. This was true even over the decade of the 1990s—when crime was decreasing at a modest, but consistent, rate—as Lynch and Sabol found when they compared program participation for two cohorts of prisoners: In 1991, 31% of prisoners who were released that year had participated in vocational training and 43% had participated in educational training; by 1997, only 27% of prisoners released that year had participated in vocational training and only 35% had participated in educational training. See James Lynch and William Sabol, *Prisoner Reentry in Perspective* (Washington, DC: Urban Institute, 2001), 11. Persistent overcrowding and the rejection of the rehabilitative ideal appeared to have taken a continuing toll on programming opportunities.

52. Kathleen Maguire and Ann Pastore, ed., *Sourcebook of Criminal Justice Statistics, 1995* (Washington, DC: U.S. Department of Justice, 1995), 567.

53. Karl Haigler et al., *Literacy Behind Prison Walls: Profiles of the Prison Population from the National Adult Literacy Survey* (NCES Publication No. 94-102) (Washington, DC: U.S. Department of Education, 1994), 124. A California study reached similar conclusions. It found that some 20.8% of California prisoners read at below the third-grade level, and another 30% were only "marginally literate" by accepted educational standards. Gary Sutherland, *Reading Proficiency of Inmates in California Correctional Institutions* (Sacramento: California State University, 1997).

54. *See, e.g.,* R. Tewksbury and G. Vito, "Improving the Educational Skills of Jail Inmates: Preliminary Program Findings," *Federal Probation* 58 (1994): 55; Tootoonchi, A., "College Education in Prisons: The Inmates' Perspectives," *Federal Probation* 57 (1993): 34. *See also* the American Bar Association Report, Task Force on Youth in the Criminal Justice System, ABA Criminal Justice System Section, *Youth in the Criminal Justice System: Guidelines for Policymakers and Practitioners* (2001) (available at http://www.abanet.org/crimjust/pubs/reports/index.html), which found a positive correlation between high school education and employment and also found that high school dropouts are at risk for arrest as well as unemployment. One scholar found that young White men who lacked a high school diploma were more than 5 times as likely to be incarcerated as their peers who graduated. She concluded, "More schooling is associated with lower probabilities of committing illegal activities. . . . There is potential for affecting crime rates through education programs, either broad-based efforts or targeted to a criminally active population." Ann Piehl, *Economic Issues in Criminology*, unpublished doctoral dissertation, Princeton University (1994), 70, 96. In a related vein, Becky Pettit and Bruce Western found that the risks of being incarcerated in the United States are highly stratified by education level. That is, "high school dropouts are 3 to 4 times more likely to be in prison than those with 12 years of schooling. . . ." B. Pettit and B. Western, "Mass Imprisonment and the Life Course: Race and Class Inequality in U.S. Incarceration," *American Sociological Review* 69 (2004): 151, 160. In addition, they found that the risk of incarceration created by low levels of education was especially great for Black men: "Incredibly, a black male dropout, born

1965–1969, had nearly a 60 percent chance of serving time by the end of the 1990s" (ibid., 161).

55. *See* Michelle Fine et al., *Changing Minds: The Impact of College in a Maximum Security Prison* (New York: Ronald Ridgeway, 2001).

56. For example, "Simply attending school behind bars reduces the likelihood of re-incarceration by twenty-three percent. Translated into savings, every dollar spent on education returns more than two dollars to the citizens in reduced prison costs." Stephen Steurer, Linda Smith, and Alice Tracy, *The Three State Recidivism Study* (2001) (available at http://www.research.umbc.edu/~ira/ Recid_Study.doc). *See also* Florida Department of Corrections, *Return on Investment for Correctional Education in Florida* (1999) (available at http://www.dc. state.fl.us/pub/taxwatch/index.html).

57. *See, e.g.*, J. Chase and R. Dickover, "University Education at Folsom Prison: An Evaluation," *Journal of Correctional Education* 34 (1983): 3, who found that recidivism rates 3 years following release from prison were 55% for California prisoners in general and 0% for those who obtained their B.A. degrees. *See also* D. Stevens and C. Ward, "College Education and Recidivism: Educating Criminals Is Meritorious," *Journal of Correctional Education* 48 (1997): 106, which reported dramatic differences between prisoners in several states who completed college degrees in prison versus prisoners in general. States included were Alabama (1% vs. 35%), Maryland (0% vs. 46%), New York (26% vs. 45%), and Texas (10% vs. 36%). Finally, *see* J. Gilligan, "Reflections from a Life Behind Bars: Build Colleges, Not Prisons," *Chronicle of Higher Education*, October 16, 1998, p. B7, who wrote that, among several hundred Massachusetts prisoners who had completed bachelor's degrees over a 25-year period, not one had been returned to prison on a new conviction.

58. In 1994, Congress eliminated the primary mechanism by which indigent state and federal prisoners were able to pay for college courses. The Violent Crime Control and Law Enforcement Act of 1994 S 20411, 200 U.S.C. §1070 a (b) 8 (2000) excluded prisoners from Pell Grant eligibility, as part of the general rejection of rehabilitation in vogue during those years. College programs in prison dwindled as a result. *See* E. Blumrosen and E. Nilson, "How to Construct an Underclass, or How the War on Drugs Became a War on Education," *Journal of Gender, Race, and Justice* 6 (2002): 61. *See also* R. Tewksbury and J. Taylor, "The Consequences of Eliminating Pell Grant Eligibility for Students in Post Secondary College Educational Programs," *Federal Probation* 60 (1996): 60. For an especially thoughtful and informed analysis of the political uses to which the debate over prisoner education was put, *see* J. Page, "Eliminating the Enemy: The Import of Denying Prisoners Access to Higher Education in Clinton's America," *Punishment & Society* 6 (2004): 357. Setting the antirehabilitation and politically expedient prisoner-hating rhetoric aside, however, prisoners' Pell grant eligibility needs to be restored. As I have tried to show, it can and should be done in the name of genuine and effective crime control.

59. Peter Elikann, *The Tough-On-Crime Myth: Real Solutions to Cut Crime* (New York: Insight Books, 1996), 151.

60. F. Butterfield, "Getting Out: A Special Report," *New York Times*, November 29, 2000, p. A1.

61. Bureau of Justice Statistics, *Sourcebook of Criminal Justice Statistics 1989* (Washington, DC: Department of Justice, 1990), 591. Kevin Early, "Introduction," in Kevin Early, ed., *Drug Treatment Behind Bars: Prison-Based Strategies for Change* (Westport, CN: Praeger, 1996), 3. Data collected 5 years earlier indicated much the same thing—that over half of those incarcerated were under the influence at the time they committed the crime for which they were locked up. George Camp and Camille Camp, *The Corrections Yearbook 1991 (Adult Corrections)* (Washington, DC: Criminal Justice Institute, 1991), 54–55. Nearer to the end of the 1990s, the percentage was essentially unchanged: Over half the state prisoners and one third of federal prisoners in 1997 reported being under the influence of alcohol or drugs at the time of their commitment offense. Kathleen McGuire and Ann Pastore, *Sourcebook of Criminal Justice Statistics, 1999* (Washington, DC: U.S. Department of Justice, 2000), 525. Other studies have shown that over three quarters of all jail inmates and state and federal prisoners had some or all of these things in common: They were regular users of illegal drugs (at least weekly for 1 month), were under the influence of alcohol or other drugs at the time of the offense, had committed the crime for which they were incarcerated in order to obtain money for drugs, and/or had a history of alcohol abuse or had been incarcerated for alcohol abuse violations. *See* H. Wald, M. Flaherty, and J. Pringle, "Prevention in Prisons," in *Prevention and Societal Impact of Drug and Alcohol Abuse*, ed. Robert Ammerman, Ralph Tarter, and Peggy Ott (Mahwah, NJ: Lawrence Erlbaum, 1999): 369. The general relationship between drug and alcohol use and criminal behavior, of course, is not unique to the United States. For example, one Canadian study found that among a large sample of jail detainees, 77% had alcohol use or dependency disorders and 63% suffered from drug use disorders. Cited in J. Ogloff, R. Roesch, and S. Hart, "Mental Health Services in Jails and Prisons: Legal, Clinical, and Policy Issues," *Law & Psychology Review* 18 (1994): 109, 115. In addition, certain kinds of drug use has been implicated in a wide range of crimes, including serious violent offenses. *See, e.g.,* Ogloff, Roesch, and Hart, "Mental Health Services," 133–134. *See also* B. Spunt et al., "Drug Use by Homicide Offenders," *Journal of Psychoactive Drugs* 27 (1995): 125; and A. Friedman, "Substance Use/Abuse as a Predictor to Illegal and Violent Behavior: A Review of the Relevant Literature," *Aggression and Violent Behavior* 3 (1998): 339.

62. *See, e.g.,* Paul Goldstein, "Drugs and Violent Crime," in *Pathways to Criminal Violence*, ed. Neil Wiener and Marvin Wolfgang (Newbury Park, CA: Sage, 1989), 16. And, as I noted in chapter 4, even in cases where drug use does not initiate a criminal career, the nature and extent of drug use appears to significantly influence the pattern of subsequent criminal behavior. *See, e.g.,* D. McBride and C. McCoy, "The Drugs–Crime Relationship: An Analytical Framework," *Prison Journal* 73 (1994): 257. *See also* W. Holcomb and W. Anderson, "Alcohol and Multiple Drug Abuse in Accused Murderers," *Psychological Reports* 52 (1983): 159.

63. Christopher Mumola, *Substance Abuse and Treatment, State and Federal Prisoners, 1997* [Bureau of Justice Statistics Special Report NCJ 172871] (Washington, DC: U.S. Department of Justice, January 1999).

64. Marcia Chaiken, "Prison Programs for Drug-Involved Offenders," *National Institute of Justice Research in Action* (Washington, DC: National Institute of Justice, 1989), 1. *See also* Harry Wexler, Ronald Williams, Kevin Early, and Carlton Trotman, "Prison Treatment for Substance Abusers: Stay 'N Out Revisited," in *Drug Treatment Behind Bars: Prison-Based Strategies for Change*, ed. Kevin Early (Westport, CN: Praeger, 1996), 101: "An overwhelming proportion of all offenders in our nation's prisons lead lives associated with substance abuse prior to their incarceration. . . . [Yet] the vast majority of these offenders still remain without treatment while in prison" (ibid., 101).

65. J. Inciardi, D. Lockwood, and J. Quinlan, "Drug Use in Prison: Patterns, Processes, and Implications for Treatment," *Journal of Drug Issues* 23 (1993): 119, 126.

66. Ibid.

67. Many experts recognize this. *See, e.g.,* D. Hartmann, J. Wolk, J. Johnston, and C. Colyer, "Recidivism and Substance Abuse Outcomes in a Prison-Based Therapeutic Community," *Federal Probation* 61 (1997): 18; H. Wexler, "Progress in Prison Substance Abuse Treatment: A Five Year Report," *Journal of Drug Issues* 24 (1994): 349.

68. K. Witkiewitz and G. Marlatt, "Relapse Prevention for Alcohol and Drug Problem: That Was Zen, This is Tao," *American Psychologist* 59 (2004): 224, 224. For a description of an effective therapeutic community model that emphasized the importance of a transitional component that included work release as well as effective aftercare following incarceration, *see* J. Inciardi, S. Martin, C. Butzin, R. Hooper, and L. Harrison, "An Effective Model of Prison-Based Treatment for Drug-Involved Offenders," *Journal of Drug Issues* 27 (1997): 261.

69. *See, e.g.,* R. Worth, "A Model Prison," *Atlantic Monthly* 276 (November, 1995): 38.

70. *See* W. Trumbull and A. Witte, "Determinants of the Costs of Operating Large-Scale Prisons with Implications for the Cost of Correctional Standards," *Law & Society Review* 16 (1981): 115.

71. *See* D. Dutton and S. Hart, "Evidence for Long-Term, Specific Effects of Childhood Abuse and Neglect on Criminal Behavior in Men," *International Journal of Offender Therapy and Comparative Criminology* 36 (1992): 129.

72. K. Adams, "Who Are the Clients? Characteristics of Inmates Referred for Mental Health Treatment," *Prison Journal* 72 (1993): 120, 135.

73. Allen Beck and Laura Maruschak, *Mental Health Treatment in State Prisons, 2000* [Bureau of Justice Statistics Special Report NCJ 188215] (Washington, DC: U.S. Department of Justice, July 2001).

74. F. DiCataldo, A. Greer, and W. Profit, "Screening Prison Inmates for Mental Disorder: An Examination of the Relationship Between Mental Disorder and Prison Adjustment," *Bulletin of the American Academy of Psychiatry and Law* 23 (1995): 573. *See also* K. Adams, "Former Mental Patients in a Prison and Parole

System: A Study of Socially Disruptive Behavior," *Criminal Justice and Behavior* 10 (1983): 358.

75. *See, e.g.*, L. McCorkle, "Guided Group Interaction in a Correctional Setting," *International Journal of Group Psychotherapy* 4 (1954): 199. *See also* R. Craddick, "Group Therapy With Inmates in a Canadian Prison," *Group Psychotherapy* 15 (1962): 312.

76. Elaine Genders and Elaine Player, *Grendon: A Study of a Therapeutic Prison* (Oxford, England: Clarendon Press, 1995), 187. This observation applies not only to institutions that are intended to function as therapeutic prisons (such as the Grendon facility in England), but also even more pointedly to therapeutic programs that are administered in otherwise more typical correctional settings.

77. There is simply no reason why mental health professionals should be required to categorically abide by or defer to the judgments of correctional officers on how a prisoner who is experiencing emotional distress should be treated, where he should be housed, or which procedures he should be subjected to. The notion that security concerns *always* supersede mental health concerns has provided a blanket justification for some questionable and even—from a psychological perspective—indefensible practices in prison. What we now know about adverse prison effects and their psychological consequences for prisoners suggests that qualified mental health staff should be consulted on—and sometimes given decision-making authority over—placement, treatment, and retention decisions in housing units. This is especially true *whenever* there is any doubt about an inmate's stability or emotional state. In addition, however, there is no reason why they cannot be consulted even earlier—on the design of the units into which prisoners are placed, the arrangements that are set up, and the routines and procedures that are followed once prisoners have been placed there.

78. H. Toch, "Case Managing Multiproblem Offenders," *Federal Probation* 59 (1995): 41.

79. Thus, effective programs of rehabilitation must include access to psychotherapeutic services for at least some prisoners. As Adams observed, the group of prisoners referred for mental health treatment often is made up of persons who are less sophisticated and have committed more minor offenses (which likely increases their amenability to treatment). Moreover, for those prisoners with mental health problems, "it appears that criminality is a problem that is secondary to their legitimate psychological difficulties," which increases the importance of providing therapeutic services to help reduce their likelihood of reoffending. Kenneth Adams, "Who Are the Clients?" 134.

80. So-called multisystemic therapies that are conducted with families, schools, and communities are consistent with the contextual model of behavior I have advanced here. *See* Scott Henggeler et al., *Multisystemic Treatment of Antisocial Behavior in Children and Adolescents* (New York: Guilford, 1988).

81. B. Diamond, "From *Durham* to *Brawner*, a Futile Journey," *Washington University Law Quarterly* (1973): 109, 121.

82. Here, too, oversight should translate into accountability. Thus, programs and personnel can and should be subjected to regular and meaningful forms of evaluation, so that only the most valid and effective approaches are retained.

My earlier suggestion that prisons in general be held to the same kind of standards that we are beginning to apply to educational environments is especially important to adhere to in the context of correctional treatment.

83. Becky Pettit and Bruce Western have calculated the percentage of Black men and White men who have experienced certain life events by various ages. For the cohort of men born between 1965–1969, they estimate that 22.4% of Black men had been to prison by age 35, as opposed to 12.5% who earned bachelor's degrees. These figures compares with 31.6% of White men from the same cohort who earned a bachelor's degree and 3.2% who had been to prison. *See* B. Pettit and B. Western, "Mass Imprisonment and the Life Course: Race and Class Inequality in U.S. Incarceration," *American Sociological Review* 69 (2004): 151, 164, Table 6.

84. On the racial implications of policy choices between education and corrections, the Justice Policy Institute has calculated that in 1995 the United States spent more on building prisons than on constructing colleges and universities; between 1985 and 2000, state expenditures for corrections increased at a rate that was 6 times greater than the rate at which spending for higher education increased; at the turn of the present century, there were more African American men in prison than in colleges or universities; and between 1980 and 2000, approximately 3 times as many African American men were added to the prisoner population as were added to colleges and universities. *See* Justice Policy Institute, *Cellblocks or Classrooms? The Funding of Higher Education and Corrections and Its Impact on African American Men* (Washington, DC: Author, 2002). Available at http://www.justicepolicy.org/.

85. Vivid illustrations of this fact can be seen by mapping the concentrations of incarcerated citizens in certain communities and estimating the amount of government resources being devoted to their imprisonment instead of other social programs. Using a technique termed "justice mapping" that employs Geographical Information Systems (GIS) technology to depict the economic and other consequences and correlates of incarceration in certain neighborhoods and communities, Eric Cadora and Charles Swartz were able to identify many "million-dollar blocks"—ones where at least a million dollars was being spent incarcerating the residents. These blocks were located in the poorest areas of each community and also tended to be the ones with the highest concentrations of minority citizens. The sheer expense involved, on neighborhood blocks that had so many other needs, suggested that alternative and more preventative strategies of crime control might be far more cost effective. As Cadora and Swartz put it, "When considered as a pool of resources, more strategic options to affect positive changes in the neighborhood as a whole may become apparent." *See* Eric Cadora and Charles Swartz, *An Explanation of Justice Mapping: Three Examples* (Appendix 17 of the Report of the Re-Entry Policy Council). Available at http://www.reentrypolicy.org/documents/appendix_justicemapping.pdf, 595. *See also* J. Gonnerman, "Million-Dollar Blocks: The Neighborhood Costs of America's Prison Boom," *Village Voice* (November 16, 2004): 1.

86. D. Feldman, "20 Years of Prison Expansion: A Failing National Strategy," *Public Administration Review* 53 (1993): 561, 563.

87. American Bar Association, *The State of Criminal Justice* (Chicago: American Bar Association, December, 1998). As William Chambliss has argued, if these draconian policies are truly a war on drugs rather than a proxy for racial oppression, then it is a war we have lost. W. Chambliss, "Another Lost War: The Costs and Consequences of Drug Prohibition," *Social Justice* 22 (1995): 101.

88. *See, e.g.*, the discussion in E. Chemerinsky, "Eliminating Discrimination in the Death Penalty: The Need for the Racial Justice Act," *Santa Clara Law Review* 35 (1995): 519. Despite the fairness-based logic on which it is founded, the Act was never passed by Congress and has not been implemented on a widespread basis anywhere in the country.

89. For a study of prison desegregation that illustrates both the difficult transition that occurs when prison systems that have resisted integration attempt to rapidly undertake it and also the long-term benefits that may come about once meaningful, proactive polices of integration actually are implemented, *see* C. Trulson and J. Marquart, "The Caged Melting Pot: Towards an Understanding of the Consequences of Desegregation in Prisons," *Law & Society Review* 36 (2002): 743. For some thoughtful approaches to reducing and reforming harmful prison policies that permit or tacitly encourage segregation, *see* H. Toch and J. Acker, "Racial Segregation as a Prison Initiation Experience," *Criminal Law Bulletin* 40 (2004): 2.

90. George Knox, *An Introduction to Gangs* (Peotone: New Chicago School Press, 2000), 282.

91. Quoted in Phillip Kassel, "The Gang Crackdown in the Prisons of Massachusetts: Arbitrary and Harsh Treatment Can Only Make Matters Worse," in *Gangs and Society: Alternative Perspectives*, ed. Louis Dontos, David Brotherton, and Luis Barrios (New York: Columbia University Press, 2003), 241.

92. J. Belitz and D. Valdez, "Clinical Issues in the Treatment of Chicano Male Gang Youth," *Hispanic Journal of Behavioral Sciences* 16 (1994): 57.

93. Tom Hayden, *Street Wars: Gangs and the Future of Violence* (New York: The New Press, 2004), 50. Hayden describes the role of "peacemakers"—persons who are "former gang members or inmates with street knowledge, respect, and the capacity to be role models"—as critical to the success of these programs. Peacemakers facilitate community-level peace by helping to reduce conflict before it escalates into violence; they help to facilitate inner peace for former gang members by teaching them alternatives to gang life. (ibid., 50).

94. *See, e.g.*, D. LeClair, "Home Furlough Program Effects on Rates of Recidivism," *Criminal Justice and Behavior* 5 (1978): 249; Daniel LeClair, *Recidivism Trend Analysis* (Boston: Department of Corrections, 1985); L. Lowenstein, "Are There and Should There Be Alternatives to Present Forms of Sentencing and Imprisonment?" *Journal of Criminal Law* 1979 (1979): 165.

95. Psychologist Shadd Maruna has brought several important insights to bear on these issues. The first is that prisoners who are most successful at making the transition from prison to the freeworld often are those who have made sense

of their past lives in ways that include "redemption scripts"—an acknowledgment of their troubled past that does not preclude their own goodness or prevent them from envisioning and implementing ways of turning their lives around. Maruna also noted that this process of transformation is enhanced by social contexts that encourage or facilitate opportunities to "give back" to the community and also ones that involve community leaders, family members, and friends participating in and acknowledging a "psychological turning point" in which the ex-prisoner's contributions and reconnection with the community are formalized in some way. Shadd Maruna, *Making Good: How Ex-Convicts Reform and Rebuild Their Lives* (Washington, DC: American Psychological Association, 2001), 163. *See also* S. Maruna and T. LeBel, "Welcome Home? Examining the 'Reentry Court' Concept from a Strength-based Perspective," *Western Criminological Review* 4 (2003): 91, for a discussion of both the potential and the limitations of "reentry courts" that use the judicial process to manage the prisoner's return to the community.

96. Dina Rose and Todd Clear, "Incarceration, Reentry, and Social Capital: Social Networks in the Balance," in *Prisoners Once Removed: The Impact of Incarceration and Reentry on Children, Families, and Communities*, ed. Jeremy Travis and Michelle Waul (Washington, DC: Urban Institute Press, 2003), 337.

97. Although the issue of prisoner reintegration recently has gotten much needed public attention—including setting up a new governmental organization to facilitate the creation of useful programs—few states actually have implemented them. *See* the report of the Prisoner Re-Entry Policy Council, an entity created by the Departments of Justice, Labor, and Health and Human Services: Prisoner Re-Entry Policy Council, *Charting the Safe and Successful Return of Prisoners to the Community* (2004). As recent editorials have correctly observed, as yet "the social services necessary for successful re-entry are virtually nonexistent in most communities." Editorial, "New Strategies for Curbing Recidivism," *New York Times* (January 21, 2005), p. A28.

98. *See, e.g.*, the recommendations made in M. Fleisher and S. Decker, "Going Home, Staying Home: Integrating Prison Gang Members Into the Community," *Corrections Management Quarterly* 5 (2001): 65; and Dina Rose, Todd Clear, and Judith Ryder, *Drugs, Incarceration and Neighborhood Life: The Impact of Reintegrating Offenders Into the Community*, Final Report to the National Institute of Justice (New York: John Jay College of Criminal Justice, 2000).

99. The Urban Institute analyzed the results of a large-scale U.S. Department of Justice study that compared recidivism rates in the 1990s. The original Department of Justice study was discussed in chapter 3 of this volume and was published as Patrick Langan and D. Levin, *Recidivism of Prisoners Released in 1994* [Bureau of Justice Statistics Special Report NCJ 193427] (Washington, DC: U.S. Department of Justice, June 2002.) The Urban Institute analysts looked more carefully at three groups released from prison in 1994: those who were released on mandatory parole (i.e., persons paroled after having served the legally required portion of their sentence), those on discretionary parole (i.e., persons screened for fitness for early release), and those discharged from prison after serving their entire prison sentence (i.e., persons without parole). Two years after their

release, 61% of those released on mandatory parole had been rearrested compared with 54% of the discretionary parolees and 62% of those who had been unconditionally released. *See* Amy Solomon, Vera Kachnowski, and Avinash Bhati, *Does Parole Work? Analyzing the Impact of Postprison Supervision on Rearrest Outcomes* (Washington, DC: Urban Institute, March 2005). Obviously, there was a significant difference between prisoners selected for discretionary parole compared with the others. However, the relatively modest effect of parole supervision on recidivism rates for both mandatory and discretionary parolees underscores the compromised nature of the role that parole agents now play. They manage large caseloads that preclude much meaningful contact with parolees and are required to perform largely law enforcement functions. Obviously, the nature of parole supervision would need to be significantly modified to advance the kind of reforms I have advocated here. Among other things, parole agents and probation officers would return to their original goal of improving parolees' postprison success by enhancing their access to services in the neighborhoods and communities to which they were released.

100. Solomon, Kachnowski, and Bhati, *Does Parole Work?*, 16. *See also* Jonathan Simon's trenchant historical analysis of these issues: Jonathan Simon, *Poor Discipline: Parole and the Social Control of the Underclass, 1890–1990* (Chicago: University of Chicago Press, 1993).

101. I agree wholeheartedly with Joan Petersilia that the "nearly unfettered discretion" of parole officers to revoke the parole of persons under their supervision needs to reexamined and effectively limited. This is an important reform because, among other things, under the current system "the public can pass (or rescind) new laws but prison populations will not decrease dramatically as a result, since decisions made by parole officials can continue to feed the prison intake pipeline." Joan Petersilia, *When Prisoners Come Home*, 239, 241.

102. For an excellent model of how this might work, applied to the difficult case of chronic gang members returning from prison to the community, *see* Fleisher and Decker, "Going Home, Staying Home." Among other things, Fleisher and Decker note that "a community-wide solution must strengthen the social and economic link between gang neighborhoods and the dominant community. Doing that would require that the dominant community pour job training and employment opportunities into poor neighborhoods with the direct participation of residents of those poor areas" (ibid., 74).

103. For a thoughtful analysis of many of these issues written by an effective advocate of "second chance" programs, *see* Jeremy Travis, *But They All Come Back: Facing the Challenges of Prisoner Re-Entry* (Washington, DC: Urban Institute Press, 2005). *See also* information on these and related issues disseminated by the Re-Entry Policy Council. This information can be accessed at http://www.reentrypolicy.org. A "Second Chance Act" was introduced in the House of Representatives on April 19, 2005, as HR 1704 (108th Congress, 1st Session), and a companion bill was drafted for the Senate by Senator Sam Brownback (R-Kansas). Both bills are designed to provide federal funding to states to assist in "recidivism prevention." Among other things, "mentoring"

grants would be given to community and "faith-based" organizations as part of this effort. The text of the act quoted President George W. Bush's 2004 State of the Union Address to the effect that "America is the land of the second chance, and when the gates of the prison open, the path ahead should lead to a better life" [at Section 2 (4)]. It remains to be seen exactly how this vision—which has been lacking to date in the present administration (and previous ones for that matter)—will be implemented.

104. James McGuire, "Integrating Findings From Research Reviews," 22.

105. Many of the reforms I have suggested in this chapter are at odds with the politically expedient policies that have been followed over the last several decades, and some go well beyond the mainstream of current correctional thinking and practice (although many certainly do not). However, most of them are entirely consistent with alternatives now supported by many citizens who, despite the systematic miseducation they have received about these issues, are beginning to intuitively understand that our current approach to crime and punishment can and should be made much fairer and more effective. Thus, one broad-based study of public attitudes about crime revealed that, without rejecting punishment entirely (and certainly not for persons convicted of violent crime), "there is more support for rehabilitation and less for retribution than political rhetoric and media coverage would indicate." Most respondents thought that criminals should be punished by being sent to prison, but once there, they should receive programming designed to help them reintegrate back into free society. In addition, the researchers found that most citizens thought "more money should be spent on social and economic problems in an attempt to lower the crime rate." These views were not restricted to a few demographic categories but rather showed what the researchers termed "a remarkable robustness." *See* Jurg Gerber and Simone Engelhardt-Greer, "Just and Painful: Attitudes Toward Sentencing Criminals," *Americans View Crime and Justice: A National Public Opinion Survey*, ed. Timothy Flanagan et al. (Thousand Oaks, CA: Sage Publications, 1996), 62, 72–73. *See also* B. Applegate, F. Cullen, and B. Fisher, "Public Support for Correctional Treatment: The Continuing Appeal of the Rehabilitative Ideal," *Prison Journal* 77 (1997): 237.

106. In this regard, it is interesting and instructive to note that a number of Supreme Court justices who were unable to find sufficient constitutional grounds to limit the pains of imprisonment nonetheless have been troubled by them. Several even made recommendations not unlike many of my own. For example, former Chief Justice Warren Burger—whose court decided several key cases that were instrumental in legitimizing prison practices and policies that enabled much unprecedented prison growth over the last several decades—lamented the state of the prisons just a few years after some of those key decisions were rendered. *See* W. Burger, "The Need for Change in Prisons and the Correctional System," *Arkansas Law Review* 38 (1985): 711. Burger was troubled by the "prison building boom" that his court arguably contributed to, and asked whether the nation was "going to continue to build what some people call 'warehouses,' or are we going to convert them into, I hope, schools and production plants with fences around them?" (ibid., 720). He expressed

further concerns about prison conditions in most states, which he believed were "not good," in part because of the imposing "walls and guns in sight in most of them all of the time" and worried that even prisoners who stayed for only a few years left with "the imprint of that institution on them and no marketable skill" (ibid., 721). Nearly 20 years later—during which time the prison population was 3 to 4 times greater than when Chief Justice Burger spoke, and after a number of additional Supreme Court opinions in which the Justices declined to intervene in helpful ways to significantly improve conditions—Justice Anthony Kennedy told the American Bar Association (ABA) that no one who has "professional responsibilities for the criminal justice system can be neglectful when it comes to the subject of corrections." He described the state of the nation's prisons this way: "Our resources are misspent, our punishments too severe, our sentences too long." He urged the ABA to study these matters and to begin "a new public discussion about the prison system." Address by Associate Justice Anthony M. Kennedy, at the Annual Meeting of the American Bar Association (August 9, 2003), available at www.supremecourtus.gov/publicinfo/speeches/sp_08-09-03.html. (In response, the ABA formed the "Justice Kennedy Commission," whose report can be found at www.abanews.org/kencomm/reportintro.pdf.) Whatever else can be read into these statements, it would seem that, unless the Court changes its mind about the value and importance of intervening to correct the wide range of interrelated prison problems, ones that the Justices themselves acknowledge exist, the impetus for solving them will have to be found elsewhere.

11

TOWARD A RATIONAL
PRISON POLICY

Worse than the importance given to crime and individual blame is the legitimacy given to pain. Pain, intended to be pain, is elevated to being the legitimate answer to crime.

—Nils Christie[1]

This book has been about both limiting the pains of imprisonment and the value of using psychological insights to assist in the task of doing so. Of course, everyone understands that prison is painful. That is, in some sense, its purpose. As Hans Toch put it, simply, custodial power is power that "hurts and restricts."[2] But there must be meaningful limits, ones that come from the practical reality that too much pain is counterproductive, to be sure, and also from the recognition that humane societies limit what they do to their least fortunate members because of the noble values to which their citizens subscribe.

The distinction between applying just punishment and inflicting real harm is a basic one, with roots in antiquity. The roots are both moral philosophical and utilitarian in nature. Thus, Plato understood that any punishment that actually harmed or damaged its recipient was wrong, in part because it merely answered one unjust act with another. Much later, James Mill wrote eloquently against any form of punishment whose lasting effect was to degrade or diminish the person to whom it was applied: "If a criminal in a prison is ever to be let out again, and to mix in society . . . nothing should be done . . . to make him a worse member of society than when he went in. There cannot be a worse quality of punishment, than that it has a tendency to corrupt and deteriorate the individual on whom it is inflicted. . . ."[3] In the recent history of imprisonment, unfortunately,

351

we seem to have lost sight of this age-old distinction between punishing and harming. As a result, some of the essential limits to which this important distinction gives rise have been put aside.

However, the arguments I have made in favor of imposing stronger limits on the pains of imprisonment have not been framed in strictly utilitarian or moral philosophical terms. I am neither a social engineer nor a moral philosopher. Instead, I have suggested that there are compelling psychological reasons to reconsider and redirect the path our prison policies have followed over the last several decades. My decision to employ a psychological framework as the basis for reshaping these policies was more than professional convenience. The discipline of psychology has had a unique role in helping to legitimize the original prison form. As penal institutions were established and proliferated in our society more than a century ago, psychological justifications were offered for their widespread use. Since then, psychology has continued to provide the intellectual underpinnings for many prison policies, and psychologists themselves have participated in devising and implementing procedures and programs inside various correctional facilities.

And yet, in recent decades—as the prison system expanded at unprecedented rates, became especially harsh and unforgiving, and spread pain to larger numbers of people than ever before—the discipline of psychology was relegated largely to the margins of correctional debates. In fact, this marginalization occurred at precisely the time when psychological insights were being developed that raised profound questions about the wisdom and logic of the policies that were being pursued. Thus, advances in psychological science increased awareness of the importance of past and present social contexts in shaping behavior; they represented arguments in favor of reducing the role of imprisonment in an overall strategy of crime control and of configuring our prisons in ways that would limit the excessive pains of imprisonment.

Yet, prison policymakers moved forcefully in exactly the opposite direction. They have continued to do so. Problematic patterns of misunderstanding, mistreatment, and misallocation persist. Thus, there are too many people in prison who do not need to be there, and too many prisoners who are exposed to painful and potentially damaging conditions of confinement for too long a time. Moreover, there are too many resources that could be directed to programs of primary and proactive crime prevention, and to assist in the successful reintegration of persons back into the communities from which they came, but are not. Instead, these resources have been used to create and maintain a vast custodial system whose sheer size seems to dwarf all other concerns and to preclude any real commitment to more effective alternatives.

Few members of the public are privy to the realities of prison life. Indeed, one of the hallmarks of modern prisons is that they are effectively hidden from public view. Citizens rarely peer inside an actual correctional facility, they are not encouraged to dwell on the subjective experience of confinement, and very few have an informed perspective with which to judge the harmful effects of incarceration. Instead, their view of how much prison pain is too much is often shaped by misleading messages from political figures with separate agendas of their own and by sensationalized media images and storylines that are created more for their entertainment value than the accuracy of their analysis. Here, too, the discipline of psychology is uniquely positioned to play an important educational role, one that has not been effectively filled over the last several decades.

Because the number of people who are affected by the potentially destructive experience of imprisonment has risen to unprecedented levels, and because they tend to be concentrated among certain groups and in certain places in our society, there is real urgency to the task of developing crime control strategies that mitigate the most harmful social and psychological aspects of our current prison policies. Otherwise we risk permanently damaging entire generations of already at-risk citizens, dooming them not just to lives on the margins of this society but—in light of what we know about cycles of crime and the application of newly enacted three-strikes laws, which count juvenile as well as adult offenses—to lives that will be spent largely, if not exclusively, behind bars.

Michel Foucault understood the dangers of a penal form that sought to "improve" the psyche of the criminal by remaking it in the image of the captor. He and others wrote eloquently about the expansion of the state apparatus that resulted.[4] However, very few scholars ever seriously contemplated or anticipated that an already vast system of coercive institutions would be dramatically increased in size and then turned primarily to the task of imposing punishment for the purpose of causing pain. Yet, that is precisely what has happened in the era we have entered, one in which we seem to confront the worst of both worlds: Prisons justified and maintained in the name of benevolent intervention—however well or poorly this goal was realized—have multiplied and then been directed to inflict penal harm.

The excessive levels of prison pain now generated by this system must be candidly addressed, carefully analyzed, and effectively limited—in psychological terms as well as others. It is important to begin a thoughtful dialogue about humane alternatives to these painful policies before the damage becomes irreversible and the social, political, and economic accommodations to such widespread practices become so extreme and entrenched that we can no longer turn away from them. This book is offered as one small step in that direction.

NOTES

1. Nils Christie, *Limits to Pain* (Oxford, England: Martin Robertson, 1982), 46.

2. Hans Toch, *Corrections: A Humanistic Approach* (Guilderland, NY: Harrow & Heston, 1997), 65.

3. James Mill, "Prisons and Prison Discipline." In *Essays on Government, Jurisprudence, Liberty of the Press, and Law of Nations*, ed. James Mill (London: J. Innes, 1825): 1, 8. I have relied heavily on Terence Ball's discussion of the connections between Plato and Mill, and the central role that Mill's ideas played in the origins of both psychology and penology. *See* T. Ball, "Platonism and Penology: James Mill's Attempted Synthesis," *Journal of the History of the Behavioral Sciences* 18 (1982): 222.

4. Michel Foucault, *Discipline and Punish: The Birth of the Prison* (New York: Random House, 1977).

AUTHOR INDEX

Franke, H., 51n17, 338n39
Freed, D., 84n36, 263n21
Freedman, Richard, 90n106
Frese, Pamela, 194n87
Friedman, A., 342n61
Friedman, Lawrence, 53n45, 53n59,
    54n68, 83n16, 114n4, 226n3
Friedman, N., 229n35
Friedman, S., 191n59
Fry, L., 231n47
Fryer, G., 197n111
Fryers, T., 265n37
Fuchs, A., 51n28
Furnham, Adrian, 20n17

Gabrielli, W., 150n3
Gaddis, Thomas, 188n18
Gaes, G., 194n83, 227n10, 229n32,
    339n48
Garabedian, P., 192n66
Garbarino, James, 154n48, 155n62
Garber, Judy, 23n42
Garfinkel, H., 56n93
Garland, D., 226n2, 239n115
Garmezy, Norman, 153n33
Garrido, Vincente, 335n21, 338n46
Gartner, Rosemary, 239n114
Garza, C., 195n92
Gee, H., 85n58
Geller, J., 262n17
Genders, Elaine, 344n76
Gendreau, P., 187n11, 187n12, 188n17,
    189n21, 236n100, 237n109,
    238n111, 334n13
Georgiades, S., 196n102
Georgoudi, M., 21n29
Gerber, Jurg, 349n105
Giallombardo, Rose, 188n18
Gibbs, J., 192n66, 267n58, 335n23,
    338n41
Gibbs, R., 151n15
Gil, D., 154n49
Gilligan, J., 341n57
Giovannoni, J., 153n39
Glaser, D., 56n95, 81n3, 88n71
Glover-Blackwell, Angela, 118n39,
    119n53, 119n55, 120n57, 124n98
Glueck, Sheldon, 54n73, 54n74, 55n80
Goddard, Henry, 52n34, 52n35, 53n52
Goffman, Erving, 56n93, 188n16, 192n65

Goggin, Claire, 236n100, 237n109,
    334n13
Goldson, B., 156n65
Goldstein, Paul, 342n62
Gonnerman, J., 345n85
Goodstein, L., 190n43, 192n65, 236n97,
    332n5
Gordon, Diana, 83n26, 89n96
Gordon, R., 21n25
Gordon, T., 228n19
Gottfredson, Don, 88n71
Gottfredson, M. A., 87n70
Gottfredson, S., 83n21
Gottlieb, Donald, 293n24, 295n39
Gould, Stephen Jay, 52n37
Gover, A., 300n77
Goyer, P., 196n101
Granucci, A., 292n9
Grassian, S., 229n35
Greeman, Richard, 188n18, 189n19
Greenberg, D., 50n8
Greer, A., 228n20, 267n61, 343n74
Gregory, D., 197n111
Grogger, Jeff, 122n77
Grounds, Adrian, 237n107
Gubrium, Jaber, 152n27
Guggemos, J., 195n92
Gunby, P., 195n90, 229n28
Gunderson, E., 196n105
Gunn, John, 55n89, 196n103, 301n84
Gurr, Ted Robert, 89n95
Guthrie, Robert, 237n106
Guttentag, Marcia, 55n92
Gutterman, M., 83n17, 292n11, 300n74

Haan, Norma, 152n27
Hacker, Andrew, 118n34
Haddad, Jane, 265n36
Hagan, J., 157n83
Haigler, Karl, 340n53
Hairston, C., 191n60
Hall, J. Nelson, 267n51
Haller, M., 50n8
Haller, Mark, 52n38
Hallinan, Joseph, 239n114
Hamburg, D., 153n32
Hamilton, Anne, 188n18
Hamilton, K., 52n29, 333n11
Hamm, Mark, 239n114
Hammen, Constance, 20n18

Hampton, Robert, 154n44

Haney, C., xiv n3, xvii n8, 20n13,
    20n15, 51n18, 81n2, 82n12,
    82n13, 82n14, 86n65, 87n67,
    89n94, 116n20, 116n23, 150n3,
    151n5, 151n10, 159n97, 229n35,
    235n84, 261n9, 262n12, 262n15,
    266n42, 266n45, 266n47,
    267n53, 301n82, 301n84, 332n8,
    336n28, 338n40

Harding, T., 196n103

Harris, Fred, 118n31, 118n37

Harris, M., 233n70

Harrison, L., 343n68

Harrison, Paige, 83n32, 265n39, 267n60

Hart, S., 342n61, 343n71

Hartmann, D., 343n67

Harvey, Joel, 236n102

Hasian, Marouf, 52n38

Hassine, Victor, 188n18, 239n114

Hawkins, G., 89n99, 333n10

Hay, Douglas, 51n9

Hay, William, 21n28, 194n81, 338n41

Hayden, Tom, 346n93

Hayes, Lindsay, 198n112

Haynes, Milton, 82n8

Heaney, G., 114n3

Hebert, C., 114n3

Helfer, Ray, 154n49

Helson, Harry, 239n113

Helzer, J. E., 196n107

Hemmens, C., 237n104

Henderson, L., 23n45

Henggeler, Scott, 344n80

Hepburn, J., 21n30

Herman, J., 197n108, 197n109, 337n38

Hilliard, T., 82n12

Hirsch, A., 50n5, 50n7

Hirschman, C., 118n34

Hochstetler, A., 237n105

Hocking, F., 190n45

Hodgins, S., 267n54

Hoehne, K., 262n16

Hoffman, David, 51n27

Holahan, C., 20n19

Holcomb, W., 342n62

Holland, A., 196n102

Holoagan, E., 198n111

Holohean, E., 264n30

Holstein, James, 152n27

Homant, R., 192n65, 193n74

Honzik, Marjorie, 152n27

Hooper, R., 343n68

Hopkins, A., 88n71, 236n97

Hora, P., 333n9

Horan, P., 116n19

Horn, R., 90n106

Horowitz, D. L., 301n88

Housing Inventory and Population
    Impact Task Force, 84n44

Howard, T., 261n5

Hoze, Frances, 239n114

Huckabee, R., 226n6

Huesmann, L. Rowell, 23n42, 155n61

Huff-Corzine, L., 154n46

Hughes, Robert, 51n10

Hughes, Timothy, 334n17

Huizinga, D., 158n84

Human Rights Watch, 195n93, 334n18

Hume, David, 51n16

Hutchings, B., 150n3

Hyman, Ira, 151n11

Ibrahim, A. I., 231n52

Ignatieff, Michael, 50n4, 50n6, 51n13,
    51n22, 51n25

Immarigeon, R., 232n65

Inciardi, J., 120n59, 121n75, 343n65,
    343n68

Ingram, Rick E., 20n18

Irvin, J., 152n22

Irwin, John, 19n10, 190n50, 192n65,
    193n74, 231n49, 234n82,
    237n108, 239n114, 298n65,
    335n25, 337n34

Isber, H., 89n99

Isikoff, M., 86n65, 232n65

Jackson, B., 158n93

Jackson, George, 81n2, 81n6, 188n18

Jackson, Michael, 187n10

Jacobs, A., 336n30

Jacobson, J., 152n21

Jamelka, R., 264n28

James, Franklin, 118n49

James, J., 197n111

Jansson, D., 192n65

Jencks, Christopher, 118n40

Joffee, Justin M., 19n11

John, R., 155n59

Johnson, P., 121n71
Johnson, Robert, 20n12, 189n41,
    192n66, 338n41
Johnson, William, 118n43
Johnston, J., 343n67
Jones, D., 89n94
Jones, Michael, 123n86, 159n95
Jones, R., 190n42, 197n111
Jordan, Hallye, 84n46
Jose-Kampfner, C., 191n56, 192n63
Josselson, Ruthellen, 152n27
Justice Policy Institute, 345n84

Kachnowski, Vera, 347n99, 348n100
Kaiser, A., 153n37
Kane, T., 195n91
Kaplan, Abraham, 232n64
Karberg, Jennifer, 115n10, 187n8,
    192n70, 192n71, 265n39
Kass, Frederic I., 262n16
Kassel, Phillip, 235n86, 235n88, 346n91
Kassenbaum, Gene, 88n72
Katz, Michael, 116n25, 117n30
Katz, S., 262n17
Katzenbach, Nicholas, 56n94
Kauffman, Kelsey, 190n50
Kauffman, M., 21n24, 152n26
Kazdin, Alan, 153n33
Kelly, William, 231n44
Kempe, C., 155n54
Kempe, Ruth, 154n49
Kennedy, Anthony M., 349n106
Kennedy, Randall, 114n6
Kenyon, Gary, 153n28
Kerner, Hans-Jurgen, 334n15
Kerner, Otto, 85n57, 117n29
Kerner Commission, 56n96
Kesterman, Claudia, 236n103, 337n32
Keve, Paul, 191n54
Keyes, D., 238n111
Kilmann, P., 187n4
Kimball, Peter, 235n89
Kind, Ryan, 194n80
King, A., 84n38, 115n12, 122n78
King, Michael, 195n88, 195n94, 195n99,
    195n100, 229n27, 336n26
Kittrie, Nicholas, 292n3
Kleber, R. J., 196n106
Kling, J., 237n109
Klonoff, E., 158n93

Knapp, Daniel, 116n25
Knowles, C., 21n30
Knox, George, 346n90
Kopernik, L., 154n51
Koren, E., 84n37
Korn, R., 193n74
Kotlowitz, Alex, 155n63
Krahe, B., 21n23
Kramer, R., 86n59, 233n72
Krantz, Sheldon, 292n3
Kreutzer, T., 153n30
Krisberg, Barry, 156n67
Kruttschnitt, C., 153n40, 239n114
Kukla, A., 233n70
Kupers, T., 197n111, 266n49, 267n59
Kwoh, Stewart, 118n39

La Free, G., 89n98
Lahey, Benjamin, 153n33
Lakin, Charlie, 262n18
Lamb, Charles, 118n33
Lamb, H. Richard, 262n16
Lamott, Kenneth, 53n53
Lanagan, Patrick, 115n15
Landrine, H., 158n93
Langan, Patrick, 88n75, 122n82, 194n79,
    236n101, 347n99
Langley, T., 157n81
Laqueur, Thomas, 50n9
Larson, D., 52n31
Larson, Edward, 52n38
Lassiter, Ruby, 154n44
Lating, Jeffrey, 197n108, 337n38
Laufer, William, 116n23
Lauritsen, Janet, 21n30
Lazear, E., 118n44
Leary, Timothy, 188n18
LeBel, T., 346n95
LeClair, D., 346n94
Lefkowitz, M., 154n51
Legislative Analyst's Office (California),
    88n83, 88n87, 89n91
Lemert, Edwin, 230n44, 233n71
Leming, J., 20n21
Leopold, Nathan, 188n18
Lerner, Jacqueline, 152n26
Lerner, R., 21n24, 152n26
Lerner, Steve, 156n67
Levenson, H., 191n62

Tushnet, M., 297n62
Tweney, R., 53n49

United States Bureau of the Census,
    54n67
United States Department of Justice,
    293n16
United States General Accounting
    Office, 228n26, 235n93
Useem, Bert, 235n89, 235n90, 235n92
Usery, D., 197n111
US News & World Report, 83n19

Valdez, D., 346n92
van Alstyne, D. J., 87n70
van den Beukel, Annick, 236n102
van der Kolk, Bessel, 234n79
Vasta, Ross, 152n26
Vaughan, Victor, 155n54
Veneziano, Carol, 263n24, 266n41
Veneziano, Louis, 263n24, 266n41
Veroff, Joseph, 21n29
Villarruel, Francisco, 84n43, 122n79,
    123n85
Vito, G., 340n54
von Hirsch, Andrew, 83n15

Wagner, P., 123n93
Walcott, D., 231n53
Wald, H., 342n61
Walder, L., 154n51
Walker, B., 228n19
Walker, Nancy, 84n43, 122n79, 123n85
Wallman, Joel, 89n93, 89n101, 122n77
Wang, M., 152n22
Ward, C., 341n57
Ward, D., 88n72, 191n53, 192n65,
    333n10, 335n25
Ward, G., 123n93
Ward, Tony, 339n48
Waring, E., 22n38
Wasek, P., 196n106
Waters, Mary-Alice, 81n6
Waul, Michelle, 22n37, 347n96
Weary, G., 152n21
Weiman, D., 237n109
Weiner, Neil, 89n95, 89n96
Weinstein, Corey, 239n114

Weitekamp, Elmar, 334n14
Welsh, W., 229n29, 229n30
Wenk, E. A., 21n30
Western, B., 237n109, 340n54, 345n83
Wexler, H., 343n64, 343n67
Wheeler, M., 300n78
Wheeler, Stanton, 192n66
White, Robert, 153n28
Wicker, Tom, 82n8
Widom, C., 155n55, 155n57
Wiener, Neil, 342n62
Wikberg, Ron, 190n50, 194n87, 195n96
Wilkins, Leslie, 235n93
Wilkins, Roger, 118n31, 118n37
Willens, J., 189n38, 338n44
Williams, D., 153n38, 158n90
Williams, Frank, 263n24
Williams, K., 154n46
Williams, Ronald, 343n64
Wilner, Daniel, 88n72
Wilson, Doris, 334n17
Wilson, John P., 196n107
Wilson, W., 119n56, 158n84, 158n86
Winer, J., 263n22
Winfree, L., 229n31, 335n22
Winfree, T., 192n65
Witkiewitz, K., 152n22, 152n23, 343n68
Witte, A., 343n70
Witztum, E., 196n106
Wolfe, David, 154n47
Wolfgang, Marvin, 89n95, 89n96,
    342n62
Wolk, J., 343n67
Wolman, Benjamin, 20n13
Wong, M., 118n34
Woodward, M., 262n11
Wooldredge, John, 229n31
Worden, R., 20n22
Wordes, M., 159n96
Wormith, J. Steven, 187n7
Worth, R., 343n69
Wozniak, J., 302n90
Wright, Erik, xix n9
Wright, K., 21n30, 194n85, 300n77,
    332n5, 337n33
Wulbert, R., 193n74
Wyer, Robert, 152n19

Yackle, L., 82n10, 86n63, 297n62
Yee, Min, 81n2

Yochelson, Samuel, 150n3
Young, Malcolm, 194n80

Zalman, M., 83n25
Zamble, E., 187n7, 189n41, 192n67,
    334n19, 335n23
Zarefsky, David, 116n25
Zawitz, Marianne, 90n104

Zenoff, Elyce, 292n3
Ziedenberg, Jason, 117n26
Zimbardo, P., xvii n8, 20n13, 81n2,
    82n12, 82n13, 151n10, 157n81,
    235n84, 266n45, 301n82, 336n28
Zimmer, Lynne, 122n76
Zimmerman, E., 196n103
Zimring, F., 90n99
Zucker, Robert, 153n28

SUBJECT INDEX

Abbott, Jack, 288
Abu Ghraib prison abuse scandal, 311, 336n29
Accountability, 316, 344n82
Adams, Kenneth, 170, 173, 320, 344n79
Adaptation level theory, 225
Adaptive reactions, counterproductive, 146
Adoption of "tough" image, 179–180
African Americans, 78, 92–96, 98–103, 109, 340n54
    disproportionate rates of incarceration, 64–65, 80, 85n58
Aftercare plans, 319
Alabama, disenfranchisement of ex-convicts, 111
Alabama prison system, 59, 70, 86n64, 252, 298n64
Alcoholism, 132, 317–319, 342n61
Alienation, 13–14, 309, 327
Altruism, and social context, 6
American Association on Mental Retardation, 261n3
American Bar Association, 141, 172, 325
    Justice Kennedy Commission, 350n106
American Civil Liberties Union, National Prison Project, 201
American colonies, 29–30
American Correctional Association, 293n17
Amsterdam, Anthony, 131
Angry aggression, 137
Anti-Drug Abuse Act (1988), 112, 123n95
Arizona, 86n60, 86n64
Arkansas prison system, 275
Arpaio, Joe, 86n60
Arrest, 67
Arrest rates, 93, 104–105
Asylum movement, 33
Atlantic Monthly, 41–42
Attica Prison, 81n7

Autobiographical accounts of imprisonment, 166–167
Autonomy, loss of, 176, 191n62

Balance, psychological, 170
Ball, Terence, 354n3
Bandura, Albert, 129
Banishment, 29
Banks, Curtis, 130, 311
Barnes, Elmer, 45
Becker, Howard, 233n71
Behavior. *See* Contextual model of behavior
"Behavioral deep freeze," 175, 308
Behavior modification programs, 55n91
Belgium, prison system, 334n15
Bender, John, 33
Berkowitz, Leonard, 143
Bidna, Howard, 217
Bilingual programs, 213
Binet, Alfred, 52n37
Biologism, 35–36
Black, Justice Hugo, 298n64
Black Agency Executives, 119n45
Blackmun, Justice Harry, 281–282, 286–287, 291n2, 297n59
Bonta, James, 165–166, 168–169, 188n12
Bourne, R., 154n49
Brennan, Justice William, 278
Brockway, Zebulon, 38–40, 49, 53n58
Brodsky, Stanley, 5, 59
Brownback, Sen. Sam, 348n103
Bruner, Jerome, 131
Brutality, in prisons, 40, 46–47, 53n58, 58, 171, 273
"Building tenders," inmates as, 209, 235n85
Bureau of Justice Statistics, 61, 71, 93, 120n60, 193n73
Burger, Chief Justice Warren, 349n106
Bush, President George W., 348n103
"Bus housing," 210

371

Prison Litigation Reform Act
(PLRA) (1996), 282, 286,
302n91
Racial Justice Act (proposed), 325
Second Chance Act (proposed),
348n103
Sentencing Reform Act of 1984,
193n77
Violent Crime Control and Law
Enforcement Act (1994), 341n58
Feeble-mindedness, 35, 243
Feeley, Malcolm, 73, 82n9, 213–214
Fieldwork, author's, xvii–xviii
Fine, Michelle, 317
First Nations, 114n8
Fiss, Owen, 289
Flanagan, Timothy, 65, 208
Fleisher, M., 348n102
Florida, 86n64, 88n76, 111, 221
Follow-up, postrelease, 339n48
Fong, Robert, 235n85
Foster, D. H., 291
Foster care, 139–140
Foucault, Michel, 27, 162, 353
Fowler, Raymond, 5, 59
Franke, Herman, 31
Free will, 34–36
Freeworld, transition to. *See* Reentry
Fregier, M. A., 50n5
Friedman, Lawrence, 40, 42, 60
Frustration, 136–137, 147, 202–204
Fundamental attribution error, 95–98,
113–114

Gang abatement programs, 327–328,
346n93
Gang membership, 218–219, 234n83,
326–328
Garfinkel, Harold, 48, 56n93
Garland, David, 226
Garmezy, Norman, 134
Gendreau, Paul, 165–166, 168–169,
187n12, 224, 238n111, 334n13
"Get tough" movement, 75
Gibbs, John, 267n58
Gibbs, Raymond, 131
Glueck, Sheldon, 43
Goddard, Henry, 35, 37
Goffman, Erving, 48, 56n93
Good-time laws, 41

Gottlieb, Donald, 293n24
Grading, of convicts, 34, 45
Great Depression, 63
Grounds, Adrian, 223, 237n107
Group therapy, 318
Groupthink, 336n29
Gun cover, 214
Gurr, Ted, 89n95

Hairston, Creasie, 335n24
Halfway houses, 206
Harlan, Justice John Marshall, 298n64
Hart, Stephen, 319–320
Hawaii, 191n57
Hayden, Tom, 346n93
Helson, Harry, 225
Henderson, Lynne, 16
Herman, Judith, 185
High-risk situation, 152n23
Hirsch, Adam, 29, 33
Hocking, Frederick, 171
Hoffman, David, 34
Homelessness, 245
Homicide, 77–78, 89n101, 194n86
Homosexuality, 182–184
House arrest, 288
Housing, 102, 113
racially segregated, 101
for sex offenders, 212
Howard, John, 31
Humane concerns, xiv, 4, 57–59
Hume, David, 31
Hypermasculinity, 14, 179, 309–310

Identity attack, 144
Identity shifts, 170
Idiocy, 243
Idleness, 66, 72, 174, 178–179, 199–200,
204, 308
Ignatieff, Michael, 27, 29, 31
Immediate situations, 141–146, 149
Imprisonment, xvii–xviii, 29, 32–33,
37–38
alternatives to, 305–308
cost of, 66–68, 78–79, 319, 345n85
criminogenic effects of, xvi, 114,
221–224
initial period of, 184
long-term, 13–15, 288–289, 312–313

London Metropolitan Police Act, 50n8
Lynch, James, 339n51

Maladaptation, among special-needs
    prisoners, 256–260
Managerial parole, 73
"Manhood," issues of, 179–180. *See also*
    Hypermasculinity
Maori people, 114n8
Marshall, Justice Thurgood, 280, 294n32
Maruna, Shadd, 346n95
Massachusetts
    juvenile system, 255
    prison system, 341n57
Mass imprisonment, 74–80
Masten, Ann, 134
Mathiesen, Thomas, xvi n6
Mauer, Marc, 118n38
McCleery, Richard, 191n57
McCord, Joan, 138
McCorkle, Richard, 172–173, 208
McDonald, Kevin, 234n81
Mead, George Herbert, 174, 233n71
Measurement
    of crowding effects, 207–209,
        230n42
    of individual differences, 35
    of prison pain, 163–167
Media, role of, xiii, 94, 150n3
Medical historians, 22n36
Mednick, Sarnoff, 150n3
Mental health programs, 14–15, 211–213,
    249–251, 265n35, 319–323,
    344n79
Mental health staff, 45–49, 55n86, 249,
    258–259, 321–323, 344n77
Mental hygiene movement, 44
Mental illness, 241–243, 248–252,
    264n26, 319–323
Mental or emotional injury (PLRA), 282
Mental retardation, 243, 245, 261n3
Mentoring, 328
Merton, Robert, 233n70
Messinger, Sheldon, 74
Michigan prison system, 246, 295n53
Microaggressions, 147
Microevents, 142
Milgram, Stanley, 130
Mill, James, 351
Miller, Jerome, 255

Minnesota prison system, 300n79
Minority defendants, and offense-based
    sentencing, 95–98
Mischel, Walter, 131–132
Moczydlowski, Pawel, 218
Model prison, 39
Monitoring
    of prisoner behavior, 204–205,
        208–209
    of prison operations, 208, 272–273
    of vulnerable/problematic prisoners,
        203, 247, 320
Monotony, 70
Moore, Joan, 102
Moral charges (public-order offenses),
    120n61
Moral exclusion, 336n29
Moral insanity, 243
Moral instructor, 39
Moral philosophy, 34–35
Moral treatment, 40–42
Morris, Norval, 332n8
Multinational Monitor, xiiin1
Multisystemic therapies, 344n80
Myth of Black progress, 99–103

Nathan, Vincent, 302n91
National Advisory Commission on
    Criminal Justice Standards and
    Goals (1973), 58, 140
National Commission on the Causes and
    Prevention of Violence (1969),
    85n57
National Council on Crime and
    Delinquency, 293n17
National crime bill (1994), 69
National Institute of Corrections, 220
National Law Journal, 61
National Sheriffs' Association, 293n17
Needs assessment, of vulnerable/
    problematic prisoners, 203, 211
Neighborhood disadvantage, 145
Neisser, Ulric, 131
Netherlands, 50n6
Newberger, E., 154n49
New Mexico, 220–221
"New penology," 73
New York City, Rikers Island jail, 214
New York state prison system, 53n54, 65,
    73, 201, 231n54, 320

Sampson, Edward, 35
Sampson, Marmaduke, 39
Scalia, Justice Antonin, 280–281, 285,
    298n63
Scarry, Elaine, 9, 12, 15, 22n39
Schlanger, Margo, 291, 297n62
Schriro, Dora, 308–309
Screening, of vulnerable/problematic
    prisoners, 203, 247, 251–252,
    260, 320
Scull, Andrew, 58
Second-chance programs, 330, 348n103
Secure accommodation, 156n74
Segregation, racial, 283–285, 299n69,
    299n71, 325
Segregation units, 206, 208, 215,
    326–327
    and special-needs prisoners, 256,
    258–259
Self-control, 177
Self-isolation, 174
Self-medication, 108, 135
Self-monitoring, 173
Self-protection, 218–219
Self-worth, 178
Seligman, Martin, 23n42
Sellin, Thorsten, 44, 55n80
Sentence, 193n77, 236n100. See also
    Prison time
    indeterminate, 41–42, 54n66
    life, 181, 194n80
    life without parole, 194n80
Sentencing, 95–96, 105, 107, 247, 287–
    288, 307–308, 315–316, 324–325
Sentencing Project, 194n80
Sentencing reforms, 97, 193n76, 300n79
Serge, Victor, 167, 174, 189n19
Sex offender treatment programs, 212
Sexual assault, in prison, 182–184,
    195n93, 205, 309–310
Sexual relations, 179–180
Silent system, 37
Simon, Jonathan, 73–74, 213–214,
    348n100
Situational pathologies, 200, 218, 225
Slavery, legacy of, 92–95
Social context, xv–xvi, 6–8, 12, 32, 47–
    48, 131, 220, 225. See also
    Contextual model of behavior;
    Decontextualizing, of crime and
    punishment

past, 133–138
present, 141–146
prison as, 161–163
Social control, 4, 43–44
Social historical factors, 133–138, 142
Social Problems (journal), 102
Social service agencies, 15
Social setting, 6–7
Social workers, 44
Sociology, 166–167
Solitary confinement, 32–34, 70, 87n67,
    164, 191n62, 206, 215, 238n111,
    256, 313
South, the, 82n9, 86n64, 92, 114n5,
    190n47
South Africa, 63, 93
Special masters, 282, 290, 302n91
Special-needs prisoners, 11, 241–248,
    254–256, 260, 291, 296n55,
    319–323, 337n37. See also
    Developmental disability;
    Mental illness
Spelman, William, 77–79, 89n93, 90n102
Spivey, Michael, 131
Standards of decency, 290
Stanford Prison Study, xvii, 310–311,
    336n29
State laws
    career criminals, 69
    compulsory sterilization, 41
    good-time, 41
    habitual criminals, 69
    indeterminate prison sentences, 41–42
    parole, 42
    sexual predator laws, 212–213
    three-strikes, 68–69, 85n58, 98,
        117n26
    truth in sentencing, 193n78,
        287–288
    and victims' rights, 16
State mental hospitals, 246
States
    required to improve prison
        conditions, 64
    and responsbility for care of special-
        needs citizens, 245
Steadman, Henry, 143–144, 249
Steinke, Pamela, 256
Step-down programs, 312
Stevens, Justice John Paul, 275–276, 285,
    298n63, 299n71

ABOUT THE AUTHOR

Craig Haney, PhD, JD, is one of the nation's most widely respected experts on the psychology of imprisonment. He is professor of psychology at the University of California, Santa Cruz, where he began teaching after having received his PhD in psychology from Stanford University and his JD degree from Stanford Law School in 1978. Dr. Haney has won numerous academic honors and awards for distinguished teaching, research, and contributions to constitutional rights. He was one of the principal researchers on the landmark "Stanford Prison Experiment." Since then, he has been studying the psychological effects of living and working in actual prison environments. Professor Haney's work has taken him to dozens of maximum security prisons across the United States and abroad, where he has evaluated conditions of confinement, assessed the psychological consequences of incarceration, and interviewed staff and prisoners alike about their adaptations to prison life.

Professor Haney's scholarly writing and empirical research address a wide range of important crime- and punishment-related topics, including the causes of violent crime, the quality of fairness and justice that characterizes our system of criminal justice (especially the death penalty), psychological mechanisms by which prisoners adjust to incarceration, and the adverse effects of prolonged imprisonment, especially under severe conditions of confinement. His articles on these topics have appeared in a variety of scholarly journals, including the *American Psychologist*; *Psychology, Public Policy, and Law*; and the *Stanford Law Review*. Professor Haney also has served as a consultant to various governmental agencies and organizations, including the White House, the U.S. Department of Justice, the U.S. House of Representatives, the International Committee of the Red Cross, and the

California Legislature. He has served as an expert witness on many prison-related issues around the country and has testified before Congress and to the National Commission on Safety and Abuse in America's Prisons; his work has been cited by many state and federal courts.